Warrior in Gray

Major General Robert Emmett Rodes

Library of Congress

WARRIOR IN GRAY

General Robert Rodes of Lee's Army

James K. Swisher

WHITE MANE BOOKS

All maps were prepared by the author.

This White Mane Books publication
was printed by
Beidel Printing House, Inc.
63 West Burd Street
Shippensburg, PA 17257-0152 USA

In respect for the scholarship contained herein, the acid-free paper used in this book meets the guidelines for permanence and durability of the Committee on Production Guidelines for Book Longevity of the Council on Library Resources.

For a complete list of available publications
please write
White Mane Books
Division of White Mane Publishing Company, Inc.
P.O. Box 152
Shippensburg, PA 17257-0152 USA

Library of Congress Cataloging-in-Publication Data

Swisher, James K., 1939-
Warrior in gray : General Robert Rodes of Lee's Army / James K. Swisher.
p. cm.
Includes bibliographical references and index.
ISBN 1-57249-168-X (acid-free paper)
1. Rodes, Robert Emmett, 1829-1864. 2. Generals--Confederate States of America--Biography. 3. Confederate States of America. Army of Northern Virginia.--Biography. 4. United States--History--Civil War, 1861-1865--Campaigns. I. Title.

E467.1.R67 S95 2000
973.7'455'092--dc21

99-052477

PRINTED IN THE UNITED STATES OF AMERICA

CONTENTS

List of Illustrations ... vii
List of Maps ... viii
Preface ... ix
Introduction ... xiii
Chapter 1 A Product of the Institute ... 1
Chapter 2 A New Career ... 16
Chapter 3 Defending the Capital ... 28
Chapter 4 Across the Potomac ... 49
Chapter 5 A Winter of Renewed Hope ... 74
Chapter 6 Charge to Glory ... 84
Chapter 7 The Great Invasion ... 108
Chapter 8 High Tide at the Crossroads ... 119
Chapter 9 Keep to the Ranks ... 144
Chapter 10 A New Opponent ... 155
Chapter 11 An Angle to Remember ... 166
Chapter 12 Check and Checkmate ... 185
Chapter 13 Chasing Black Jack ... 193
Chapter 14 Shaking the Gates of Washington ... 201
Chapter 15 In the Footsteps of Jackson ... 215
Epilogue ... 229
Notes ... 235
Bibliography ... 271
Index ... 287

ILLUSTRATIONS

Major General Robert Emmett Rodes .... frontispiece
Rodes Residence 4
Barracks, Virginia Military Institute, Lexington 6
White's Ford on the Potomac, Leesburg 51
Turner's Gap, South Mountain 57
The Sunken Road, Antietam Battlefield 68
Catharine's Furnace, Chancellorsville 91
Hazel Grove, Chancellorsville 101
Oak Hill, Gettysburg 126
Gettysburg 126
Gettysburg, July 1, 1863 127
Wilderness, May 5, 1864 159
Wilderness 159
Spotsylvania Court House, May 10, 1864 174
Spotsylvania Court House, May 12, 1864 176
Quaker Meeting House, Lynchburg 196
Cool Springs, July 18, 1864 212
Cool Springs Battlefield 212
Third Battle of Winchester 223
Presbyterian Cemetery, Lynchburg 227
General Robert E. Rodes 234

MAPS

Seven Pines Attack Plan, May 31, 1862 31
Seven Pines, May 31, 1862 34
Battle of South Mountain, Fox's Gap, September 14, 1862 55
Battle of South Mountain, Turner's Gap, September 14, 1862 58
Battle of Antietam, Sunken Road, September 17, 1862 69
Battle of Chancellorsville, May 1, 1863 85
Chancellorsville, May 2, 1863 89
Chancellorsville, May 3, 1863 104
Route of Rodes' March North, June 10–25 114
Gettysburg, July 1, 1863 129
Gettysburg, July 1, 1863 130
Gettysburg, July 1, 1863 132
Gettysburg, July 2, 1863 137
Wilderness, May 5, 1864 161
Wilderness, May 6, 1864 164
Spotsylvania, May 8, 1864 169
The Spotsylvania Salient, May 10, 1864 173
Spotsylvania, May 12, 1864 177
Spotsylvania, May 12, 1864 180
Battle of Monocacy, July 9, 1864 205
Battle of Cool Springs, July 18, 1864 209
Battle of Cool Springs, July 18, 1864 210
Area of Valley Combat, Summer 1864 218
Third Battle of Winchester, September 19, 1864 225

PREFACE

So much exhaustive research and so many extensive writings on the American Civil War have occurred in recent years that few topics of note remain unexplored. Most significant participants in the tragic war have been subjected to meticulously detailed studies by well-known, masterful biographers. Only a scant few Southern general officers, usually of divisional or brigade level, have continued to be unrecognized by historians. In most instances these unacknowledged officers fall into one of two categories: those whose efforts are not worthy of study, or those who left so few traces that reconstructing their career is exceedingly difficult.

The subject of this endeavor, Maj. Gen. Robert Emmett Rodes, is certainly worthy of our attention. He played a significant role in the saga of that great body of men, the Army of Northern Virginia. His countenance can be seen in almost every action of that famed army. Like most mortals, he had his good days and bad, but never suffered either fate from lack of effort. He appears in the writings of those who knew him as a flesh and blood person, a leader akin to those he led. The absence of letters, particularly those to his wife are surely a handicap, but the absolute worthiness of this brilliant officer simply demands that his story be told. Whether successfully or not, the reader must judge.

It's virtually impossible to recall and express appreciation to all individuals who assisted or loaned their support to this project. The archivists, librarians, and staff members of various repositories, museums, and libraries about this country merit the utmost respect and admiration, for no task is too large, or historical trivia too small, nor request too trite, to deter their complete attention. The process of research, tedious and tiresome, becomes pleasant as well as exciting when one deals with such courteous, polite, and professional individuals. They offer complete attention to each researcher regardless of repute.

Sources of primary usage in this study included the Alabama Department of Archives and History, the University of Alabama Library, Alderman Library at the University of Virginia, the State Library of Virginia, the Library of Congress, the National Archives, and the Archives of Virginia Military Institute. In addition the Handley Library of Winchester, Virginia, the Jones Memorial Library of Lynchburg, and the Virginia Room of the City Library of Roanoke, Virginia provided extensive material and assistance.

All those connected with these institutions exerted every assistance, including Ms. Diane Jacobs, archivist at Virginia Military Institute, and Wayne Rhodes, Ed Gibson, and Lewis Averett of Jones Memorial Library. In addition, the staffs of the many National Park Service Battlefields were a wealth of information, recommendation, and resource. Despite a paucity of funding, these prideful custodians of our historical past continue to provide meritorious service to a public increasing in numbers and interest daily.

Many additional individuals provided critiques, offered notes, pictures, and unpublished papers. Thanks is due to T.G. Hobbs, Jr., who generously provided his notes on the North River Navigation Company; Ken Long of Atlanta who brings a unique perspective to Civil War history despite his New Jersey upbringing; Ron Lareau of Lynchburg who reviewed chapters in his uniquely critical style, and many others.

Robert Carter of Lynchburg, a high school band director and Civil War aficionado of impeccable quality, read every section, usually several times, providing comments, probing questions, and provoking arguments which caused the manuscript to be in a constant stage of revision. Robert accompanied the author on the trail of Rodes' Division from Gettysburg to South Mountain to Antietam and from Winchester and Cool Springs, through Chancellorsville, the Wilderness, and Spotsylvania, all the while providing details from his expertise and knowledge. This constant discussion helped develop a much wider perspective of these actions. Robert's selfless energy and boundless enthusiasm were a source of much inspiration throughout. In addition, much of the battlefield photography is his handiwork.

I must acknowledge my wife, Penny, for her constant encouragement and unlimited patience. She read each page of the text, took a number of the photographs, and served as a sounding board to steady the ship when frustration levels became high or the excitement of newly found material threatened euphoria. Without her constant support and encouragement, very little of importance is possible.

I also appreciate the willingness of those other members of my family to condone the time stolen to live with Robert Rodes these past months.

Perhaps unknowingly, Todd, Terri, Karen, and Jim have assisted by their understanding. In addition the source of unlimited inspiration and real perspective are the three "lights" of my daily routine, Sara, Chris, and Nick. Their eyes see only a grandfather, never a stuffy proponent of some long-passed historical endeavor.

Lastly, I'd like to dedicate this manuscript to the memory of

PRIVATE DANIEL TAYLOR SWISHER

3RD VIRGINIA LIGHT ARTILLERY

And to his children and their children's children.

INTRODUCTION

If history is indeed truth, not necessarily "the" truth as in a great moral precept, but truth in that it presents an honest account of events from the past, presented in a documented manner, then historical biography should depict men or women as they actually were, insofar as the biographer can ascertain. By altering facts to effect political correctness, or simply to tell a better tale, we lend a lie to and actually deny our real history. Those who honor our heritage would refuse to sacrifice our past to untruths, and face history as it really was; sometimes glorious and sometimes detestable, often admirable and too often dishonorable. So too are those individuals who create our history, for on occasion imminent historians have tended to whitewash our nation's important political figures in a form of hero worship that presents them as one-dimensional idols, free of controversy. Conversely "Revisionist" historians would eliminate from our past those who wrote, spoke, or acted in a manner that would be adjudged politically incorrect by modern standards. Both approaches are in error, for our history is neither the study of godlike olympians nor a review of past criminals. It is possibly the study of humans who rose to the accomplishment of significant deeds, despite their human frailties and weaknesses, and persevered to achieve desired ideals.

Douglas Southall Freeman, the South's greatest biographer, in his introduction to the writings of Confederate history, "The South To Posterity," stated that

> A man's place in history depends in large part on care and good fortune—care in preserving essential records, and good fortune in having a biographer who uses these records sympathetically.[1]

Many Civil War figures have been admirably portrayed in sterling biographical style by scribes of outstanding abilities. Others, some deservedly, have been less well served. But in an organization of note such as the Army of Northern Virginia, which contained so many outstanding individuals, perhaps none stands out as more worthy of our study than Maj. Gen. Robert Emmett Rodes. His elongated face, that of a serious, handsome, yet melancholy man stares down at us from the walls of his beloved Virginia Military Institute and the display cases of museums, archives, and libraries. Like many officers of his era Rodes was a young man attempting to appear older, wiser, more venerable in his portraits. A tall, lank figure with blond hair, piercing blue eyes, clean shaven, he seems to conceal the trace of a smile beneath his long, tawny mustache.

But Freeman's blond Norseman left few traces. Prior to her death on August 21, 1907, Virginia Woodruff Rodes burned all papers and letters from her husband.[2] While these keepsakes were surely hers to destroy, one can but wonder what hopes, dreams, aspirations, and opinions of this vigorous young officer were lost to history. Rodes' letters to others, mostly of a military nature, are revealing and well written. His correspondence with his father, while a student and then a struggling engineer, portrays his serious compulsion to succeed. During pre-war years he conducted an extensive correspondence with VMI Superintendent Francis Smith which furnishes considerable insight into his career in railway construction. Rodes' battle reports, published in the *Official Records*, are extremely informative concerning actions in which his brigade or division participated, as are several unpublished battle reports which Mrs. Rodes furnished to the *Southern Historical Society Papers*.

Like many noteworthy Confederate officers who gave their lives to the cause, there were no memoirs, no reminiscences, no Veterans Day speeches, and no published articles for Robert Rodes. Likewise there was no defense from the pointed finger of the military critic or escape from the encroachment of survivors seeking to purloin accomplishments for addition to their own laurels.

Rodes possessed no real family to protect and guard his fame. From a proud, middle-class Virginia family, his parents both deceased, he was survived primarily by stepsisters and stepbrothers of a younger generation. An adopted son of Alabama, his memory in that state was honored by a devoted wife, but who with meager funds was responsible for a boy of one and a girl-child yet unborn. Rodes lies buried, alongside his brother, in a largely forgotten grave in Lynchburg's Presbyterian Cemetery. Strangely, little attempt was undertaken to move his remains. Hampden Osborne, who followed the starry cross of Rodes' Division for four years, wrote years after the war:

> Each time I pass through Lynchburg, I go stand at the grave in Presbyterian Cemetery of Robert Rodes and wonder why the state of Alabama has not removed that sacred dust to her soil.[3]

Rodes' recognition in Alabama was probably curtailed by his serious dispute with the state's two-time post war governor and Democratic party boss, Edward O'Neal. This officer's military career with the Army of Northern Virginia was abruptly terminated following Gettysburg when Rodes adjudged his unit's poor performance due primarily to O'Neal's nefarious leadership. Subsequent lack of promotion, transfer, and Rodes' written preference for John Tyler Morgan, John Gordon, or Cullen Battle to command the Alabama Brigade provoked an unforgiving enemy in O'Neal.

Despite these handicaps, some traits of Rodes' persona are readily obtainable. Excellent passages of description can be found in the writings of Robert Stiles, Porter Alexander, Moxley Sorrell, and other first-hand witnesses. Additionally, the battle reports of officers such as Daniel H. Hill, Thomas J. Jackson, Richard Ewell, and John Gordon provide comprehensive insight on Rodes' performance in action. Col. Thomas Carter, Rodes' favorite gunner, and Maj. Green Peyton, his aide, wrote stirring articles for preservation at his Alma Mater, and Rodes is a prominent participant in a dozen or so diaries such as those authored by John Tucker of the 5th Alabama and Lt. Robert Park of the 12th Alabama.

Of even greater significance are the hundreds of references to Rodes found in the written recollections of the soldiers who marched in the gray-clad columns which followed him. Many of these articles were preserved in *The Confederate Veteran* or *Southern Historical Society Papers.* Men such as John Craddock of New Orleans, John Purifoy of the Jeff Davis Artillery, I.G. Braswell of the 31st Georgia, J.L. Schaub of Lagrange, Georgia, and Marcus Herring of Byholia, Mississippi eagerly recalled and vividly described their personal contact with their respected leader. Their memories, and those of scores of others, appropriately screened for similar narrative, provide a more intimate portrait of the stern-appearing general officer.

A consensus of these references presents history with quite a different Robert Rodes than the romantic figure portrayed by Douglas S. Freeman as "The Son of a Nordic God," "A Blond Viking," or "Appearing as if He Just Stepped from the Pages of Beowulf."[4] While Rodes may have physically appeared as Freeman described, his soldiers saw him quite differently.

He was first and foremost, by consentaneous accounts, a direct and truthful man. One who dealt with problems, individuals, and occurrences in a straightforward, honest, and just manner; completely without guile. Robert Rodes was not a particularly religious man, but he was a moral man with strong convictions and values and when convinced his purposes were true he could be stern, firm, and very demanding of others as well as self. Most soldiers considered Rodes a just, fair, but hard-nosed commander, while a few considered him a martinet in military matters.

Rodes was also a meticulous, watchful, and persistent officer who carefully planned his actions and worked best in harness with superiors such as Jackson or Hill who were similarly inclined. He was loyal, almost to a fault, to each superior, but in those few instances when he seemed to struggle as a unit commander it was invariably with a superior who could not, or would not, clearly articulate his expectations. While not dogmatic, his mathematical bend encouraged attention to detail and careful consideration of options when possible.

In addition, Robert Rodes was, by nature, a modest, quiet, unprepossessing man. His kind, considerate nature extended to every man in his command but should never be mistaken for weakness. He detested the petty politics of army life and refused to participate, in most instances, only becoming involved when officers of his division were wrongly accused. But he was ambitious, possessed of strong self-directed desires to achieve recognition for his achievements, although far too modest to espouse his own cause. His strong inner drive possibly developed from early reliance on his own resources for status in the world. Rodes was personally brave, undaunted by setbacks, and most individuals around him thought him the most optimistic of men.

Robert Rodes also possessed certain traits which might be defined as weaknesses or liabilities. While never recorded as guilty of overindulgence, it's also not remembered that Rodes ever refused a good drink of whiskey when offered. While not of a negative personal consequence, Rodes may have experienced some difficulties in correcting subordinates with whom he had, on occasion, enjoyed a comradely glass. Rodes was the possessor of a raging temper when provoked. This trait, combined with his propensity to use profane language, produced some classic and memorable tirades of splendid oaths. His reputation as a swearer seems to rival that of his contemporary, Jubal Early, although unlike "Old Jube" his kind nature returned rapidly once the object of his wrath was severely castigated.

In an army rich in good division commanders, and poor in outstanding corps leaders, many questioned why Rodes never received the distinction due him.[5] But Rodes never seemed to address that point or unduly concern himself therein. His ambition and pride were largely screened, and on several occasions he spoke of the disgusting scheming, posturing, and politicking of other officers, and even their wives, to attain higher rank.

Rodes advanced rapidly to command a division in an army marked for fame, abundantly served by officers of conspicuous ability. Quite honestly, he struggled for some months in divisional command until he became comfortable and began to grow in his own ability. He held the highest position in the army for a non-West Point-trained officer, for the Army of Northern Virginia never had a major general of infantry without professional military training until attrition rates demanded.[6] Perhaps he never realized his full potential, for in the fall of 1864, as Confederate general officers rushed more often into the thin front lines of wavering troops and attrition rates soared, he like others, fell prey to enemy shot and shell.

CHAPTER 1

A PRODUCT OF THE INSTITUTE
From Boyhood to Manhood

On a spring afternoon in May 1863, a young Confederate officer, with the three stars and wreath of a general officer showing on his collar, carefully aligned his division in the tangled thickets and shady alcoves of an area near Chancellor's, Virginia, known locally as simply "The Wilderness." Soon a second and then a third line appeared behind his meticulously drawn formation and shortly prior to five P.M. preparations were complete. Three gray-clad divisions, fifteen brigades, or 28,000 Confederate soldiers, were poised in thick wasteland, squarely on the right flank of a largely unaware and unprepared Union army. One of the most dramatic actions in the American Civil War was about to unfold.

Capt. James Power Smith, assistant adjutant general of Lt. Gen. Thomas J. Jackson's 2nd Corps, witnessed the dialogue which then occurred between Jackson and the tall, thin brigadier, Robert Emmett Rodes, who commanded the leading division. Smith's firsthand account of the moment of attack is perhaps the most memorable recorded. He wrote:

> It must have been after 5 o'clock in the evening when dispositions were complete. Upon his stout, long-paced, little sorrel, General Jackson sat with visor low over his eyes and lips compressed, with his watch in his hand. Upon his right sat General Robert E. Rodes, the very picture of a soldier and every inch all that he appeared. On Rodes' right sat his adjutant, Major Blackford.
>
> "Are you ready, General Rodes?," asked Jackson.
>
> "Yes, Sir" replied Rodes, eager for the advance.
>
> "You can go forward then," stated Jackson.
>
> A nod from Rodes was order enough for Blackford and suddenly the woods rang with the bugle calls, sweeping right and left from regiment to regiment along the divisions in line of battle. Then the

long lines of skirmishers through the wild thicket of undergrowth sprang eagerly to their work, followed quickly by the measured steps of the line of battle.[1]

The butternut and gray line, sweeping irresistibly through briars and tangles, preceded by startled deer, rabbits, and squirrels, burst suddenly into the clearing and before them lay the camps of the Federal XI Corps. This attacking flank force represented, at least to this author, the high tide of Confederate arms; the very pinnacle of Southern military power, actually the Confederacy itself, for that young nation was always only the space that her armies could hold.

This daring flank movement was orchestrated by the most famed of the pantheon of Confederate military heroes: "Old Jack," "Old Blue Light," or "Tom Fool Jackson," that idiosyncratic, reserved, sometimes cold, but brutally aggressive and relentless ex-instructor of artillery at the Virginia Military Institute. The list of capable assistants following Jackson that afternoon was long. Many of them would achieve their own fame in the coming months, and an equally large number would find their fate on the field of future battles.

The soldiers they led were, on the average, middle-class, rural, non-slave holding farmers, merchants, students, and tradesmen. They possessed little polish and less education but were considered respectable, reliable, and independent men. The typical gray-back soldier swore often, gambled a bit, but also was highly religious. His independent nature made him difficult to control in camp, but stubborn and terrible to face in battle. While not immune to sheer panic or cowardice, he possessed an unusual spirit and courage, and if properly led would stand a lot of killing. By this late date in 1863 those remaining were no longer the naive amateurs of 1st Manassas or Seven Pines. They were hardened professional soldiers, having witnessed the death of friends, having killed, and having endured long marches, cold camps, and short rations. The weak were long gone; only the true hard cases remained. Good friends and fearsome enemies.

These wild-eyed, screaming men who came out of the forests in the fading rays of the afternoon sun were at their zenith. Never again would they be so numerous or charge with such absolute and unquenchable spirit; never again would that leader they so worshiped show them the way. A hundred battles were yet to be fought, thousands were yet to die, but the apex of the Confederate army, the high point of a revered lost cause, rode on the gun muzzles and bayonet tips of the gray-backs who followed Robert Rodes and dashed headlong and recklessly forward that spring afternoon.

Just who was this tall, mustachioed brigadier, Robert Rodes? He was then and still remains one of the most mysterious of those officers who achieved rank, fame, and glory in the exalted levels of the Army of Northern Virginia. Robert Rodes, more than possibly any fellow officer, looked the part of just what he was to become. Douglas Southall Freeman described Rodes as a "Blond Viking in uniform,"[2] and other accounts depict him as the virtual manifestation of a Confederate hero. He simply looked, in uniform and astride his big, black horse, precisely as a great warrior was supposed to look. In his brief military career this martial appearance was both a blessing and a curse. While his extraordinary command presence demanded respect and obedience by those he led, his bearing brought expectations which a man without experience should not have faced.

It's far too simplistic to describe Rodes as a descendent of the Nordic gods, for he was a very complex and mortal man. Not a disciple of Jackson's Cromwellian god, not a product of plantations, cotton, and magnolias; not even a politician of secessionist fire, Rodes made his own way in the world using more modern tools. A product of the middle class, akin to few others except possibly Nathan Bedford Forrest, he earned a living with his hands and his mechanical aptitude as a civil engineer. An unusual background for a general officer in a Confederate army noted for wealthy, socially prestigious, West Point-trained leadership.

Robert Emmett Rodes was born on March 30, 1829, in the sleepy, central Virginia town of Lynchburg. His father, David Rodes, a native of Albemarle County, was the son of Matthew and Ann Blackwell Rodes.[3] Robert's mother was Martha Ann Yancey, daughter of a prominent Bedford County couple, Major Joel and Peggy Burton Yancey.[4] He was the third offspring of David and Martha's union, being preceded by a brother, Virginius Hudson Rodes, five years his senior, and a sister, Ann Maria Rodes, two years older. Another sister, Sallie Harrison Rodes, would be born just prior to Martha's premature death in 1843 at age forty.[5]

David Rodes once had served as deputy clerk of the Albemarle County Court, relocating in Lynchburg when he was appointed clerk of that city's court. He enjoyed prestige and respect in the community despite the handicap of rearing a family on the financial enumeration of a civil servant's salary. While he attempted to supplement family finances with various business partnerships and the rental of accumulated housing, the results were not always satisfactory.[6] David was an avid participant in the state militia, having been commissioned an ensign in 1814 when only nineteen years of age. He steadily advanced in rank until 1834 when he was commissioned a major general by Virginia Governor John Floyd.[7] He was active in a myriad of cultural and civic activities in the community, serving as marshal of the parade in July of 1826 which honored Thomas Jefferson of Albemarle.[8] Eight years later General Rodes presided over a similar ceremony on July 15, 1834, remembering the Frenchman Marquis de Lafayette, for whom he would later name a son.

David stretched his earning to purchase a modestly impressive house at 1008 Harrison Street in Lynchburg in October 1833 for the grand sum of $900.00, believing the prestigious location would be suitable for his growing family.[9] The large, five-bay facade mansion had originally been constructed by Mr. William B. Roane in 1816. Roane had purchased two lots,

Rodes Residence, 1008 Harrison Street, Lynchburg

This three-story, five-bay facade house was purchased by David Rodes and served as the family residence during Robert Rodes' youth. In September 1864 Robert E. Rodes' remains were borne back to lie in the parlor.

Penny Swisher

almost a full city block from the city's founder, John Lynch, for $1000 as a building site.[10] When David Rodes purchased the house he added an L-shaped addition of three floors, increasing the size of the structure to nine rooms. A double porch or piazza also was added which overlooked delightful gardens and provided an outstanding view of the hillside city. The building remained in the hands of the Rodes family from 1833 to 1879.

As a boy, Robert Rodes was stout, healthy, and robust. He favored his uncle and namesake, Robert Rodes of Charlottesville, in that both had tawny blond hair and blue eyes, in contrast to the dark-eyed Rodes family.[11] At age six, Bob underwent an operation to correct a slight foot impairment. A physician in Richmond severed a tendon and placed his foot in a restraining shoe or brace so that it might straighten and he could walk without limping. The operation was not painful, but his mother recalled that the youngster suffered much agony while wearing the brace, night and day. Within a year the brace was discarded and the foot "so much improved that a stranger could notice no difference in his feet."[12]

The small town, located on the wide, sluggish James River, provided an idyllic setting for youngsters to roam, dream, and grow. The land on which the town was erected ascended from the water's edge, gradually at first, then more abruptly until the rise terminated on an elevated table-land or plain. From that lofty sight the view was truly impressive. Lynchburg enjoyed an unprecedented economic "boom" in the decade following 1830 as did much of the South. The hill city's prosperity was, however, not based on cotton but rather on the obnoxious weed. Tobacco was king with warehouses rising all over the town and more than thirty-five concerns involved in selling or processing the golden leaf. Seven major tobacco warehouses averaged checking 15,000 to 18,000 hogsheads of 1,500 pounds each year.[13] With Lynchburg as the center of a burgeoning tobacco trade, transportation improvement was naturally essential to the smooth movement of the product to markets. In 1832 the General Assembly empowered the James River and Kanawha Company to construct a canal from Lynchburg to Richmond. Work finally began in 1835, the canal and its fifty-two locks taking five years to complete. In 1840 the first canal boat completed the 147-mile journey.[14] The rhythmic chants of the tobacco auctioneer, the songs of the Negro boat captains, and the ethnic brogues of the Irish and Italian stone masons surely conjured an exciting and worldly atmosphere for young boys, and Robert Rodes' early interest in construction and mathematics was probably fueled by his observations of these endeavors.

Lynchburg contained almost eight thousand citizens, more than one-half white, with only a handful of slave owners.[15] Most of this large free-black population was employed in the tobacco processing industry. Three newspapers, six churches, and a private lending library enhanced cultural awareness. Abundant fields and farms provided young boys with opportunities to learn to ride, shoot, and hunt. Streams and ponds were available for swimming and fishing, and in cold winter months for ice skating. Virginius, the family scholar, felt young Bob enjoyed the outdoor life too much and ignored his studies. Writing from his lofty perch as a Virginia Military Institute cadet, the older brother complained that Robert treated him shamefully when last at home, running out to play with Kirk Otey and ignoring his brother.[16] Virginius then threatened to force Bob's reading of a large tome and to pull his nose for his ignorance.[17]

At a young age Robert was enrolled in the local private schools for instruction in reading, writing, and arithmetic. Church Street in Lynchburg was called School Street by 1830 for the number of educational institutions operating at that locale. Five-month sessions traditionally cost each scholar $15.00. For a time Robert studied at a prestigious institution operated by Mr. Cary, a prominent teacher and University graduate.[18] The year 1843 was stressful for fourteen-year-old Robert. His mother died suddenly of illness in June, and in October, Ann Maria, his older sister, married. Her life was truly tragic. When she was just sixteen, she married Maurice Langhorne, a fine gentleman from a prominent Lynchburg family, and delivered one child, Maurice, Jr.[19] The couple was blessed with a second child, Allen Rodes, who died before his second birthday. Then Ann herself succumbed to fever at age twenty.[20] Virginius was not then at home and David surely found single parent child-rearing difficult, for he was then deeply involved in his rental of substantial properties as well as his clerk's assignment.[21] In 1845, at age sixteen, Robert was taken over the mountains and enrolled as a pay cadet at the Virginia Military Institute.

Some six years earlier, Virginia lawmakers had established the small military school in the beautiful and isolated Shenandoah Valley. As early as 1816, three arsenals had been authorized for the western areas of the state, each to hold 20,000 stand of arms and to be guarded by an officer and twenty men of the state militia.[22] A seven-acre plot near Lexington, overlooking the north fork of the James, was purchased for $278.62 and an arsenal built on the site. The original building resembled a medieval fortress with two-foot thick walls and narrow apertures for windows. The three-story structure was of brick as was the ten-foot surrounding wall.[23]

Colonel Claudius Crozet, a retired West Point teacher and veteran of Napoleon's winter campaign to Moscow, was empowered in 1837 to develop the military academy at Lexington, and the school was named the Virginia Military Institute.[24] Initially, the school's avowed purposes were threefold. First, the cadets would assume guardianship of state arms stored on site, thereby relieving the commonwealth of employing guards. Secondly, using those funds, a system of state cadetships was established whereby a number of deserving young men without sufficient resources could receive a gratis education. The final function was to train a cadre of well-prepared young officers for the state militia.[25]

Professor Francis H. Smith of Hampden-Sydney College was employed as the first superintendent,[26] and the stark, drab arsenal building was modified to house classrooms and dormitories for the students. The

Barracks, Virginia Military Institute, Lexington

Fifteen-year-old Robert Rodes entered as a cadet in the fall of 1845, graduating with honors in 1848.

Robert Carter

board adopted a light gray uniform with single breasted coatee with a standing collar, four-inch cuffs, and a single row of eight gilded state buttons. The faculty was to wear blue uniforms indicative of their membership in the state militia.[27] A severe conduct code was installed with regulations forbidding cadets having waiters or slaves, horses, or dogs; nor to use tobacco, play cards, or duel.[28]

The Institute was not a completely alien environment to young Robert since his older brother had attended and he had a fair idea of expectations of cadets. His academic background was surely adequate, for enrollment in the Institute's three-year program was considered demanding with its heavy emphasis on mathematics. The school's curriculum included Mathematics, Languages, Sciences, Military Studies and Drill.[29] Cadets rose early, marched to meals and classes, and were expected to maintain rooms and persons in a neat and orderly fashion. Each afternoon the corps paraded behind the fife and drum band of Reuben Howard and Mike Lyle, two free Negro musicians who achieved legendary status on the post. On full dress occasions the two musicians donned scarlet coats, white pants, and powdered wigs and were widely imitated by the young boys of Lexington.[30]

Robert, seemingly, had little trouble adjusting and performed well academically from the onset. At the conclusion of his initial year his rank was 20th in a class of 39. His ranking, however, was limited by his poor record in conduct. His individual course ranks for 1845–46 were:

MATHEMATICS (Algebra and Geometry)	#13
FRENCH	# 8
DRAWING	# 1
CONDUCT	#24[31]

Robert's later military rank in the cadet corps would indicate his demerits were not of a serious nature. One source of constant offense can be ascertained from Colonel Smith's remarks to David Rodes that

> He, your son, is harder on clothes than Virginius, not as careful of them and hence, consumes more.[32]

Smith continued to comment that Robert's studies were progressing well and that he would make a fine cadet in the end.

After a summer including the traditional military camp-out thoroughly enjoyed by Robert, he returned to the classroom for a second year. His grades improved and his class rank was 16th in a diminishing class of 25 cadets. He was promoted to sergeant in the corps of cadets and his individual ranks were as follows:

MATHEMATICS (Geometry and Calculus)	# 4
FRENCH	# 6
LATIN	#14
DRAWING	# 3
CONDUCT	#22[33]

Again his poorest rank was in conduct, and comments from his classmates indicate that cadet Rodes was, off duty, fond of high-jinx and late hours. David was still pleased that the Institute indicated he should be proud of his son.[34] Robert entered his 1st class year as first lieutenant in the cadet corps, an exalted rank when one considers the highest cadet rank was captain and the corps had only one company. Robert graduated 10th in a class of 24 and again earned excellent rankings.

MATHEMATICS	# 4
FRENCH	# 6
LATIN	#13
DRAWING	# 3
NATURAL PHILOSOPHY	# 3
CHEMISTRY	# 3
ENGINEERING (Civil and Military)	# 4
TACTICS	# 2[35]

Fellow cadets found Lieutenant Rodes a good companion, social and fun loving, always ready for a prank or escapade, yet responsible and serious in both military duties and studies.[36]

When David remarried in 1846, Robert realized that he was now to be responsible for himself and his immediate future. Attempting to seek a livelihood in a profession he admired, Robert applied for a commission in the regular Army of the United States. His application was supported by letters from Mr. William Yancy of New Orleans and Col. Francis Smith, superintendent of Virginia Military Institute.[37] Smith's letter complimented Robert's academic achievement and described the young man's military record as a cadet officer as without equal and the best he had ever observed. He concluded:

> So well do I value and esteem him, that we shall attempt to gain him as an assistant upon graduation.[38]

The minuscule officer requirements of a small peacetime army, however, were met by the national academy and Robert's application was denied.

David Rodes, while paying Robert's final accounts, made an attempt to pave the future for his son. He asked a favor of Colonel Smith when he wrote:

> I would request consideration of Robert for an office in the institute when he graduates, according to capacity and talents.[39]

He continued on to explain his concern for Robert's future considering his son's youth and inexperience. David further commented that he had planned to send Robert to the university for several years, but financial reverses made that impossible. Robert would need to immediately become self-supporting. General Rodes' desires were answered when Colonel Smith issued the following orders on July 4, 1848:

Order #42

Mr. R. E. Rodes, a recent graduate of the Institute having been appointed assistant professor with the rank of Lieutenant will be obeyed and respected accordingly.

He is assigned to duty in the departments of Philosophy, Mathematics, and Tactics.

By Order: Colonel Smith[40]

The following day Smith issued Order #43 appointing Rodes adjutant of the Institute.

Robert thoroughly enjoyed his initial assignments, assisting Smith in mathematics instruction and gradually assuming responsibility for tactics instruction. His first duty as adjutant was to coordinate the corps' summer field exercises. Traditionally, the corps marched from their summer encampment to one or more of the renowned Virginia spas for a brief stay; combining the military aspects of the march with an opportunity for the sharp, young cadets to mingle with the state's social elite who gathered each summer to "take the waters." That summer the cadets marched early on August 28, filing down from the heights to exit via Lexington's main street, taking the road to Rockbridge Alum Springs. The weather was hot and humid and soon the cadets were straggling badly. When they finally reached the spa in late afternoon they found Lieutenant Rodes waiting. He had ridden up the day before and laid out the camps in company order.[41] Wagons were waiting with tents and rations, so with a groan the young men began setting up their tents and building cooking fires to the satisfaction of their erstwhile companion. After remaining several days to the amusement of numbers of socially elite and eligible young lasses, the corps marched back to barracks under Rodes' direction, but as the moon was full, Robert decided to return by night march, thus avoiding the excessive heat.

During the fall Rodes served on court-martial boards. Charges were filed against several cadets and the board met to determine guilt and assign appropriate punishment. Neither the charges nor the findings were usually of a serious nature. The faculty valued the "courts" as teaching tools more than disciplinary vehicles.[42] Rodes' instruction, particularly in tactics to 1st classmen, was gaining widespread acclaim.

After one year's experience, Rodes was promoted to captain, his duties expanded, and his salary increased. He was made assistant professor in the important courses of Tactics and Chemistry.[43] He responded to this challenge by extensively modifying the practical exercises or laboratory portions of the Chemistry course. During the winter of 1850 Robert was assigned an unusual duty when his politically astute superintendent decided to send the corps on a tour of Richmond, Petersburg, and Norfolk. Legislative action was pending concerning appropriation of funds to erect a new barracks at the Institute, and public display of the finely drilled cadets could only be beneficial. The cadets were commanded by Major William Gilham assisted by Captain Rodes and Lieutenant James W. Massie.[44] The entourage departed Lexington on four river boats with boat #2 under Rodes' supervision. After a harrowing trip through Balcony Falls to Lynchburg, the cadets transferred to packet boats and leisurely followed the canal to Richmond. Once in the state capital they became quite active, attending the state legislature, meeting the governor, parading down Broad Street, and conducting close order drill exhibitions. Expectations were high and Rodes and Massie conducted uniform inspections each morning as well as bedchecks every night. After a few days they proceeded to Norfolk by steamer, being cheered and applauded by large crowds gathered along the banks. In the port city a drill display was conducted, the corps attended an Episcopal Church, and lunch was served in the local armory.[45] This lavish reception was heady stuff for impressionable cadets and swelled heads were numerous.

Their return trip was not so triumphant or near as comfortable. After the steamer trip to Richmond they again boarded the horse-drawn canal boats for the thirty-three-hour upstream ride to Lynchburg. Once in that city, cadets were permitted passes for the weekend and many stayed in private homes. On Monday, however, each cadet had to find his own return passage to the Institute. Most lacked funds for the stage and hiked back along the canal trace. Captain Rodes rounded up a large group and camped overnight with them en route.[46]

Robert had matured and grown in his two additional years at Virginia Military, but his pay was little more than the cost of room, meals, and uniforms and there seemed no prospects of a full professorship soon. Robert worried a great deal over his poor prospects for a financially successful career, once expressing to his father that "I am hardly fit for anything but teaching."[47] He very much enjoyed teaching young men and preferred to remain at the Institute but needed sufficient pay to elevate his status from poverty. In the spring of 1850 he made necessary arrangements to enroll at the University of Virginia to work toward a Master of Arts, which would greatly increase his marketability as a college instructor. He wrote, however, guardedly to his father:

> Unless you can send me to the University with perfect convenience to the rest of the family, I will not go one step....even if it is the best plan for me.[48]

His father's precarious financial position, coupled with some business setbacks and his growing second family dictated that Robert begin searching for other means to establish his status in the community. His skills seemed to be in engineering and construction, and when a company entitled the North River Navigation Company was organized to extend the James River and Kanawha Canal up the North River to Lexington, Rodes applied for employment. Maj. Thomas H. Williamson of the Institute was chief engineer in charge of surveying the route and he was authorized to hire two assistant engineers. Robert E. Rodes was hired at a salary of $70 dollars a month.[49]

By September Williamson was gone and Robert became senior engineer until January 1, 1851. He was compelled to resurvey some areas of the route and employed an assistant.[50] In late summer, 1850, a sudden event altered Robert's plans. In 1848 the Board of Visitors voted to increase the faculty by one position but was forced to delay hiring an individual while awaiting financial appropriation by the legislature. Major Gilham was teaching all courses in the growing science field, and Colonel Smith wished to divide that area into two chairs or professorships. Gilham preferred to retain the courses in the chair of Natural and Experimental Philosophy. Chemistry would be grouped with two new courses, Mineralogy and Geology, to form another teaching chair. By 1850 money was available and Smith's planning complete, thus he was authorized to accept applications for the new chair with a stipulation that a West Point graduate was preferred since the two new courses had been taught there for some years.

Rodes, after considerable deliberation, decided his love of teaching was more important than pay since a full professorship paid considerably more than his previous Institute assignment. Thus on September 23, the very day the board was to meet, Robert submitted an application by requesting Superintendent Smith to place his name before that body.[51] Smith replied at once, affirming that he would place Robert's name before the board, but he also informed Robert that although he admired him personally he did not feel Rodes was the right applicant for the position.[52] Smith went on to explain that he did not feel Institute graduates were qualified as they had never taken courses in the two new fields which the appointee would be expected to teach. Smith concluded by informing Rodes that he regretted that he must recommend another individual.

The board met on the afternoon of September 23 and reviewed all applicants including that of Captain Rodes. Colonel Smith recommended Major Peck, an active army officer, whose academic qualifications were impeccable. However, a major split occurred during the board's deliberations. Major Peck was a Northerner and held in some suspicion by board members due to his political leanings. Suddenly, in a surprise vote Rodes was nominated and approved by a 4-1 vote.[53] A frantic Superintendent Smith convinced the board to delay its decision until the following morning.

Smith worked long into the night and when the board reconvened on the twenty-fourth, Major Gilham shocked the members by standing and requesting a change in his preferred assignment. He now wished to be appointed to the chair of Chemistry, Mineralogy, and Geology, and since he was well prepared, the board acquiesced. This strategy eliminated Robert Rodes, for he was not prepared for nor did he apply for the Chair of Natural and Experimental Philosophy. Colonel Smith then presented the name of Professor Alexander Steward of Tennessee for that position and he was duly appointed. Steward was then instructing at Cumberland College and when contacted felt he must finish the year at that school. Eventually, Steward decided to stay at Cumberland, and in the spring, Maj. Daniel H. Hill of nearby Washington College recommended Maj. Thomas J. Jackson, United States Army, for that now vacant chair. On February 29, 1852, Jackson became professor of Natural and Experimental Philosophy.

Rodes was never aware of the manipulations which effectively sidelined his application or of others which had almost seen him employed. Colonel Smith had, after all, squarely informed Robert that he was too young and inexperienced and that he intended to recommend another. Years later, Jennings Wise, in his "Military History of the Virginia Military Institute," alleged that friends of the Rodes family on the Board of Visitors attempted to place young Rodes on the faculty despite Smith's objections.[54] While this fact is unsubstantiated, it is probable since the board usually contained several high ranking militia officers, all of which certainly knew Gen. David Rodes. Certainly, Rodes and Jackson never competed for the same position as was claimed by many after the war. Neither were they fellow teachers nor did they both attend the Institute together. Their future relationship was based on their mutual regard for the Institute, nothing more.

Robert was extremely busy on the canal as numerous alternative routes must be surveyed for the twenty-mile-long passage, ten miles of which were inclosed in a canal.[55] In November he accepted bids and employed a Buena Vista firm to provide cement at 25¢ a bushel.[56] But in January 1851 Robert suddenly left the canal company's employ to accept a position of engineer with the Southside Railroad. When Robert wrote his father to explain his decision to leave the North River Navigation Company and accept the post offered him by Mr. Sanford on the Southside Railroad, he was already packing his gear to move to Farmville. He dispatched his man-servant, George, to bring certain items including his fencing gear to Lynchburg and hired a nine-year-old Negro boy to ride his horse home so that David could sell horse, saddle, and bridle.[57]

In addition to the reasonable salary offered, Rodes felt that

> Railroads are the great improvement of the day and that canals were becoming unpopular, due to the slowness of travel upon them.[58]

This company was constructing a railway line from Petersburg to Lynchburg and offered attractive compensation and promise of rapid advancement.[59] Rodes continued in their employment until the line was completed on November 2, 1854.[60] But Robert continued to struggle financially. He was forced to borrow money from his father to replace a broken watch although only purchasing a second-hand timepiece from a friend, and he also pleaded that David Rodes send him some decent chewing tobacco as he could find none.[61]

The young engineer seemed to enjoy his work, the harried pace of construction, and the drive to complete sections on schedule. He suffered somewhat from the necessity of moving up the line with his division every few weeks and finding a new boarding place, remarking that he usually ended his quest in a garret or attic room with two portholes and a door.[62] While the rugged life was pleasant to the young outdoorsman most of the year, he missed the absence of social life found in this occupation which caused him to live in such an isolated environment. Writing to his sister Sallie, on occasions, Robert made inquiries about certain Lynchburg misses and requested that Sallie be certain to make their acquaintance before he arrived on Holiday.[63] This isolation from family, friends, and social peers seemed very difficult for the ambitious young man.

Inspired by the large salaries paid in railway construction and offered a job with powerful financial incentives, Robert took a position with the Texas Pacific Railroad; however, that company went broke within months. For several months he frequented New Orleans, staying with his mother's kin while searching for employment, even considering the cotton factor's vocation in which Virginius was employed. While living in the boisterous yet charming Southern city, Robert experienced what may have been his first serious affair of the heart.

The United States charge d'affaires to Vera Cruz, Mexico, a certain Mr. Dimond, was enjoying a vacation in New Orleans, accompanied by a number of family members. Among the entourage was Mr. Dimond's eighteen-year-old granddaughter, the beautiful and wealthy heiress, Miss Rose Dimond. Mr. Winthrop de Wolfe, a friend of the Dimonds inquired as to whether Miss Dimond would wish to meet a friend of his, Mr. Rodes from Virginia. When the young lady replied in the affirmative she asked for more information concerning Mr. Rodes. De Wolf replied that Rodes was "poor as a rat, proud as Lucifer, and most charming."[64] Miss Dimond and Mr. Rodes were duly introduced and she was immediately impressed with his fine face, figure, and military bearing. He obviously was equally impressed by the young lady and the two saw each other daily for almost three weeks. Suddenly he disappeared. No messages arrived and her queries were unanswered. When she inquired of de Wolf as to his friend he abruptly replied: "Leave him alone for he is a strange fellow."[65]

Several days hence while the family was packing to depart for Mexico, Mr. Rodes appeared. He had come to say goodbye and wish her well. After some preliminary conversation the perky young lady confronted Mr. Rodes as to why he had dropped her so rudely. He replied that when he looked into her beautiful brown eyes he realized he must leave, for he was losing his heart and he was penniless and, further, he had no opportunities.

Miss Dimond later heard from Rodes through de Wolf but never saw him again. Years later, while happily married, she heard that her penniless New Orleans beau had been killed in action, a Confederate general.[66]

Robert was, seemingly, mired in a streak of bad fortune. In 1855 he took a position in what seemed a well-planned enterprise. A railroad, the

Northeast and Southwest Alabama, was to be constructed diagonally across that state. Robert jumped wholeheartedly into this enterprise, but within a few months its operations were suspended for lack of funds.[67] Soon Rodes was off again, this time to employment with the Western North Carolina Railroad. This line was successfully completed and Rodes' extraordinary performance earned him considerable reputation in the railroad business.[68] Rodes then joined an exciting new endeavor: the North Missouri Railway Company.[69] But within three months he was back in Alabama; the company had gone default. He was distraught when he wrote Colonel Smith that the fates were against him.[70] Abruptly his fortune changed. The Northeast and Southwest Alabama resumed operations and requested his services. Soon his stellar work earned Robert promotion to chief engineer, and his life took on a less somber tone.[71] In late 1856, Colonel Smith wrote to Rodes and chided him severely over his marital status, asking, "Why are you not married? Too poor to support a wife? Marry one to support you or at least to know where you are docked."[72] The superintendent was critical of Robert's nomadic lifestyle, for a number of letters to Rodes had been returned as undeliverable. Little did Smith realize how painfully true were some of his jibes. He also expressed satisfaction that Rodes was at last happily employed and doing well.[73] Several of Smith's V.M.I. "boys" had settled in Alabama as teachers, ministers, and businessmen alongside this one engineer, and Smith used Robert as a contact for the whole group. A late December letter reminded Robert again that most of his friends were marrying while he remained a staid, old bachelor.[74]

As if to answer his critics, in August 1857, Robert Rodes announced his engagement to "the noblest and prettiest girl in Alabama," Miss Virginia Hortense Woodruff, daughter of David Woodruff, originally of Milford, Connecticut and his second wife Eliza Antoinette Bell of Tuscaloosa. Mr. Woodruff was a well-known bookdealer in the small college town.[75] On September 10, 1857, Robert and Virginia were married in the Presbyterian Church in Tuscaloosa.[76] Robert's fortunes seemed to rise with his marriage. A promotion soon made his employment quite profitable and he and Virginia purchased a modest home in Tuscaloosa.

Robert maintained an interest in education, and when Smith requested his impressions of the university located in Tuscaloosa, Robert was glad to assist. He found, upon investigation, that the University of Alabama was in deplorable condition. The faculty he "Considered to be terrible,"[77] and the physical plant little better. Smith was involved with a group of educators who contemplated a military academy in Alabama, but Robert's advice was to look elsewhere in the state and avoid trying to salvage the state university.

When Smith later told Rodes about a new military school being planned in Louisiana, Robert also indicated interest. Smith sent him quite a dossier. The school, to be called Louisiana Military Academy, would be very similar to V.M.I. and would pay $2,000 to $2,500 to professors and furthermore Smith would guarantee Robert the professorship of his choice.[78] But Robert expressed concerns over such a move. He was very interested as who would be superintendent in Louisiana, the curriculum, buildings, and the salary.

Robert finally reached a decision regarding his professional struggle of engineering versus education. He would surrender the lucrative security of engineering and return to the classroom as an instructor, but not in Louisiana.[79] There were too many variables involved to embark on a career in a newly opened institution. Since his services as an engineer were still valued, Robert would continue in that position until he located a teaching chair which he thought worthwhile. It seemed apparent that Rodes would not leave Alabama and engineering for any educational endeavor other than an assignment at his alma mater.

Soon, Smith was in contact with him again. Virginia Military was adding a Chair of Applied Science, was he interested? Rodes applied at once and on July 2, 1860, was appointed to the position by the board.[80] But due to the usual delay in funding, Robert was informed that his services would not be needed until September 1, 1861. Colonel Smith recommended Robert spend the interval by journeying to France and studying for a month at the School of Bridges and Roads, a suggestion not well received by the new husband.[81]

But the political climate would soon alter Rodes' plans. His long awaited goal of a professor's position at his alma mater was within his reach, but the revolution sweeping the South would prevent his ever serving in that position. Robert had enlisted in a Tuscaloosa militia company, the "Warrior Guards," and was elected captain. In January of 1861 his company received orders to report to Fort Morgan within two days. Alabama Governor Albert B. Moore intended to take possession of Fort Morgan, Fort Gaines, and the arsenal at Mount Vernon as soon as secession seemed certain.[82] Robert stated that "all Alabama is ablaze, the state is out of the union and we are expecting a brush with federal troops at Fort Morgan or Mobile."[83]

Reluctantly, Rodes wrote to Smith, thanking him for his assistance in obtaining the teaching chair but stated that "I cannot give you a promise of my move to Virginia....A week ago I would have accepted any place you offered. In time I would wish to accept service at the Institute someday, but at present I shall remain here as I am now."[84] Robert Rodes' professional struggle was now solved by a third vocational choice. He would now become a soldier.

CHAPTER 2

A NEW CAREER
Manassas–Williamsburg–Richmond

While in his seventies, Thomas Jefferson expressed his deepest fears in private conversation with friends when he remarked:

> This momentous question (slavery), like a fire bell in the night, awakens me and fills me with terror, I consider it the death knell of the union.[1]

In the summer prior to the presidential election of 1860, Jefferson's warning seemed a broodingly accurate prophecy, and the very foundations of American Democracy seemed to tremor and quake upon this issue. Never before had interest in politics absorbed so much time and energy of so many Americans, and never had the outcome appeared so critical. Not since the heated nullification doctrine proposed by John C. Calhoun had been militantly rejected by President Andrew Jackson, had actual separation of the states appeared so near.[2] The nation was poised on a teeter-totter of proslavery versus antislavery votes, as hordes of immigrants flooded into new territories, creating prospective states, each clamoring for admission to the golden club of unionism. It was obvious to even the inexperienced that the fragile "balance of power" on the slavery issue could not be maintained much longer in the face of growing militancy by both factions.

These differences, reaching into every home, church, business, and school, north or south, had first been exhibited during the 1856 election. A new political party had been born, the Republicans,[3] which adopted a firm antislavery position and adamantly stated that never would they condone expansion of this vile practice into new territories or states. While James Buchanan and the Democrats achieved an easy victory on election day their vacillating methods soon alienated both groups. Every issue, every vote, was maliciously contested in a Congress on the verge of sectional malevolence. As Buchanan's efforts angered the secessionists, states in the deep South began preparation for a split of the Federal Union. The Alabama state legislature appropriated $200,000 for organization and equipment of a state militia force,[4] and almost every state in the South followed with similar action.

Volunteer military units sprang up overnight in every Southern town and village. These company-size units were quite poorly equipped with arms of every possible description, including shotguns. Uniforms were often flamboyantly styled as each locality attempted to best another. Some companies in cities such as Richmond, Virginia or Montgomery, Alabama became social elite clubs into which only the wealthy needed apply. Units were named to reflect the particular locality while being as warlike as possible. In Tuscaloosa, Alabama the militia company was called the "Warrior Guards,"[5] so entitled for the Indian name Tuscaloosa which means "Black Warrior." The site had once been home to a huge Indian village on the Black Warrior River.

Robert E. Rodes, 1848 graduate of Virginia Military Institute, was selected as the Warrior Guards' first commanding officer and immediately his reputation as a stern taskmaster was forged. His military background, coupled with a serious approach to all tasks, shocked and surprised some Alabamians who had enlisted for comradeship and social prestige. But Rodes never wavered or compromised and soon the "Warrior Guards" were considered among the best drilled companies in the western area of the state. They consistently won prizes and cups at the drill and marksmanship competitions instituted at state fairs and other gatherings.[6]

Political campaigning reached a fever pitch in August. The compromisers in the Democratic party quickly lost power to the radicals. At a rescheduled convention in Baltimore on June 23 the Northern Democrats nominated the respected Stephen A. Douglas for president. Somewhat later, Southern Democrats, meeting in Richmond, selected the present vice-president, handsome John C. Breckinridge.[7] An additional party calling itself the Constitutional Union Party was formed from fragments of the old Whigs and a fringe group called the Know-Nothing Party and supported John Bell for president. On May 18, the infant Republican Party convened in Chicago and while not compromising their strong antislavery platform, ran a moderate, rough, backwoods lawyer, Abraham Lincoln, as their candidate.[8] Lincoln was neither radical nor conservative on the slavery question, and the ex-whig campaigned stoutly as a candidate for the common man. Southern newspapers favored Breckinridge, could tolerate Bell and Douglas, but advocated secession if Lincoln were elected. Robert Rodes, true to his father's party and his wife's strong Alabama Whig family, supported Bell in his deep-South campaign.

After a series of exciting debates and much glib oratory, on November 6 the nation's ballots were cast and an astonishing and unexpected verdict resulted. Abraham Lincoln was elected rather easily, carrying seventeen states to eleven for Breckinridge, his nearest competitor.

Within two brief months of Lincoln's election, South Carolina enacted an ordinance of secession. The firebrand gamecocks on December 20, 1860, repealed the state's previous 1778 approval of the United States Constitution, thereby dissolving the union existing between the two entities. Alabama scheduled a convention in Montgomery for January 7. However, Governor Moore, being concerned that Federal property within the state of Alabama should be immediately occupied by state troops, called out the militia. Specifically, Moore wished to possess Forts Morgan and Gaines in Mobile Bay and the United States Arsenal at Mount Vernon, Alabama.

On New Year's Day, 1861, Capt. Robert Rodes and his "Warrior Guards" received orders to proceed by rail to Mobile and assist in the capture of Fort Morgan. Rodes complied, he and his troops spoiling for a fight. But upon arrival on January 5, the minuscule Federal force withdrew and Fort Morgan was peacefully occupied. A member of the "Guards" recalled his tour of duty at Fort Morgan as principally camping in the sand dunes with seven other companies of Alabama soldiers, fighting sand fleas.[9] After several days the "Guards" returned to Tuscaloosa, now seasoned veterans. Rodes reinstated drill and privately began preparing his own job responsibilities for a prolonged absence. On April 13 he recorded his Will in the Tuscaloosa Courts, leaving most of his property to his wife, Virginia.[10] He realized, early on, the seriousness of the approaching endeavor which many were anticipating with high spirits and predictions of easy success for Southern armies. Rodes never wavered in his commitment, but he also never believed the task of disunion would be peaceful and easy.

Rapidly, a number of the cotton states joined South Carolina in disunion. Mississippi seceded on January 9, Florida on the tenth, and Alabama on January 11. Soon a convention of the seceding states was scheduled in Montgomery for February 4, and Mississippi, Florida, Alabama, South Carolina, Georgia, and Louisiana attended.[11] Texas joined the aforementioned six. The seven attending states organized a provincial government and elected Jefferson Davis of Mississippi as president. On March 11 a constitution was adopted, closely akin to the United States document but with certain pointed alterations.

Rodes received another directive in early May. He was ordered to report with his company to Montgomery for twelve months service. Governor Moore was organizing companies into state regiments and appointing appropriate field officers. The Warrior Guards became Company I, 5th Alabama Volunteer Infantry, and Robert Rodes was elected colonel of that unit.[12] The regiment's initial assignment was to report to Pensacola, Florida in response to a request for assistance from Governor Madison S. Perry.[13] When Rodes arrived in Florida he found chaos and confusion everywhere as large numbers of Florida, Georgia, Alabama, and Mississippi troops were gathered under various commanders but with little inclination to cooperate.

Originally there were five Federal installations about Pensacola, but Federal troops had withdrawn to Fort Pickens on Santa Rosa Island, strategically located in the harbor.[14] An impasse developed, not unlike that at Fort Sumter in Charleston. State forces did not wish to precipitate a war by initiating action, and the Federal forces were reluctant to reinforce Fort Pickens for similar reasons. Both governments were ready to fight but neither wished to be labeled the aggressor.

Colonel Tennett Lomax, in command of all Alabama troops, was pressured heavily by Alabama Governor Moore to storm the post, but he wisely deferred to Florida troops.[15] By May the militia troops, in overwhelming numbers, were simply manning a line opposite Pickens with no intent of attacking.[16] This was distasteful duty to Rodes since it was difficult to maintain good order in an atmosphere of idleness and abundant alcohol, so he requested a transfer of his regiment to Virginia where action seemed imminent. In early June he was surprised by orders to proceed at once to the new Confederate capital.[17] By June 12, 1861, the 5th Alabama, composed of Alabamians from Tuscaloosa, Green, Pickens, Sumter, and Dallas Counties, were encamped and drawing rations from a Confederate commissariat near Richmond, Virginia.[18]

The 5th Alabama, already inducted into Confederate service, did not travel to Richmond en masse. Rodes and a large part of the regiment moved directly from Pensacola to Richmond through Chattanooga.[19] But railways were of varying sizes and gauges and serviced by their own depots. Thus in any major city the troops were forced to detrain, march across town, and board another railway line. Eugene Blackford, captain of a 5th Alabama company, weeks later arrived in Virginia due to delays and breakdowns. Blackford, like Rodes, was a native Virginian, born also in Lynchburg and educated at the University of Virginia. He later became the extremely capable commander of sharpshooters for Rodes' Brigade.[20]

Gradually the regiment reassembled in its Richmond camps. The long train trip was an adventure to men who had never ventured far from their Alabama birthplace. One officer in the 6th Alabama wrote his mother that the handsome ladies of Chattanooga had been so kind providing food, flowers, and kisses that he thought he would return there some day and seek a wife.[21] He also recalled leaving Montgomery in first class coaches and being later shuttled into box cars. Such was travel in the Southern army. The many varied units from all over the South gave a cosmopolitan air to the capital, and the rapid swell in population resulted in inflated prices for clothing and food. Richmond was soon transformed from a sedate Southern city to an army depot with bawdy houses and bars on every street corner.

Soon the Confederate units were being shuttled from Richmond to Manassas Junction where General Pierre G.T. Beauregard, the hero of Fort Sumter, was assembling an army. Federal advances from Washington were rumored and Confederates were gathering in opposition. Beauregard hastily formed these regiments into brigades, led by brigadier generals, and dispatched them to outposts in northern Virginia. When the 5th Alabama arrived they were united with the 6th Alabama and 6th Louisiana to form the second brigade under command of Brig. Gen. Richard E. Ewell. Ewell was a West Point-trained career army officer who served years of hard duty on the frontier, primarily as a captain of dragoons. The somewhat odd looking forty-five-year-old spoke with a slight lisp and used profanity profusely. But he was considered reliable, honest, and was usually well liked by his men.

A few Confederate units advanced into northern Virginia where they formed a loose semi-circle about the Federal capital. In June Rodes' regiment was at Farris Crossroads, and in July and August he camped at Sangster's Crossroads.[22] William Blackford of Stuart's Cavalry commented in July that he visited Rodes' camp to call on his brother, Eugene, an officer in the 5th Alabama, and that he met Eugene's good friend and commanding officer, Colonel Rodes. He mentioned that the 5th was on picket duty and was the closest unit to the enemy.[23]

As Ewell's three regiments settled into a routine, it was quickly apparent that his brigade, like most others, was sadly deficient in brigade formation drill, which seemed to be the likely battle formation. Confederate militia had been organized in company unit size, and even well-trained companies performed regimental drill with a lack of cohesion and sometimes downright chaos. Few officers possessed experience or skill to instruct this formation as even General Ewell's largest United States Army command was fifty troopers. Robert Rodes, with his V.M.I. tactical background, soon assumed leadership for drill in the second brigade. So well did Rodes perform this task that Ewell was overjoyed and even General Beauregard noted and remarked on the outstanding leadership qualities of Colonel Rodes of the 5th Alabama.[24]

The Confederate army, assembled near Manassas Junction, was basically a brigade-oriented force, but the overall army commander, lacking intermediate command levels, was required to communicate his orders directly to each brigade commander. This wide span of control required excellent communication in order to function efficiently and was exasperated by the fact that capable, experienced staff officers in Confederate gray were non existent. When action began at Manassas, communication disappeared and the fight was decided solely by the ability and instincts of the army's brigade commanders.[25] Union organization was equally poor and the eastern theater's initial battle was truly a clash between two armed mobs.

Terrain along Bull Run presented difficulties for the Confederates. Its principal feature, the small stream which ran east to west, possessed steep, rocky banks and was crossed by numerous fords, easily accessible to large troop formations.[26] Small hills on the northern banks of Bull Run dominated many of the fords. Beauregard scattered his brigades for seven or eight miles, up and down the stream, attempting to defend each ford. Richard Ewell's second brigade was positioned on the far Confederate right holding Union Mills Ford.

Federal commander Maj. Gen. Irvin McDowell determined to swiftly end this rebellion by moving forward down the Warrenton Pike through Centreville to disperse this Confederate mob.[27] He planned to stage probing actions at the fords on the Confederate left, concealing his primary assault, which would fall near the Stone Bridge leading to Henry House Hill. Thus he would jab with his left and throw a strong right hook, gaining Beauregard's rear.

The Confederate commander, after expected reinforcements from Gen. Joseph E. Johnston's Valley Army arrived, planned to contain the Union army on his left front and attack toward Centreville on the right, led by the brigades of Brig. Gens. Ewell, D.R. Jones, and James Longstreet. Beauregard was planning a strong right hook of his own to gain McDowell's rear, and if both had succeeded they may have actually exchanged positions. McDowell really executed his plan much better than Beauregard, but the battle would be won or lost by the actions of individual brigade commanders, and decidedly more talented ones wore gray.

The Union army advanced through Centreville, probing the fords on their right until rudely repulsed at Blackburn's Ford by Longstreet's Brigade.[28] Federal units then settled on the banks above the fords and lazily shelled the Confederate positions. Rodes, with sixty pickets, was surprised on the north bank on June 16 by several thousand Federal soldiers. But he and his skirmishers fell back stubbornly and defiantly.[29] Soon strong Federal forces stormed across Bull Run near the Stone Bridge and advanced toward Henry House Hill. They were arrested by the brigade of Brig. Gen. Thomas J. Jackson, assisted by those of Jubal Early, Wade Hampton, and Nathan Evans. Far out on the Confederate right where the offensive was to be launched, chaos and confusion reigned.

Beauregard's complicated plan was to be kicked off with an advance from Union Mills Ford by Ewell's Brigade and he would be joined as he moved forward first by D.R. Jones from McClean's Ford, then by Longstreet at Blackburn's Ford.[30] Beauregard stated that he instructed Ewell to begin the action at dawn but Ewell stoutly disagreed, reporting that he was to be prepared to attack at dawn, but only to move when so instructed by his commander. Captain, later major general, and assistant adjutant general to Ewell, Fitzhugh Lee, supported Ewell's understanding when he wrote:

> The troops were ready at daylight....As hour after hour passed, General Ewell grew impatient at not receiving any orders beyond those to be ready to advance, and sent me between 9 and 10 o'clock to check with General D.R. Jones....I found Jones preparing to cross

> Bull Run stating he had orders to advance and Ewell had been send the same. Upon my return, General Ewell immediately started his command across Bull Run and toward Centreville.[31]

Robert Rodes, blue eyes flashing excitement, waved his skirmishers forward, splashing through the knee deep water. His regiment marched over the stream and as they reached the far side, he shook out the unit into line of battle and, unfurling their Alabama flag, began to advance with measured tread. Suddenly, Captain Lee was at Rodes' elbow with new orders; Beauregard had canceled the advance. The Confederate commander was being pushed hard on his left and with little reserves feared to commit these few brigades still uninvolved. A disappointed Rodes spurred forward, halting his advance, and fell back across Bull Run.[32] Within an hour a rider arrived with a dispatch for Ewell. Beauregard needed a demonstration on the right, so he again requested an advance until contact with the enemy was established, occupying the Federals whenever possible. Hurriedly, Rodes moved across the stream. Soon enemy skirmishers were contacted, and Rodes, listening to the sound of Col. Micah Jenkins' advance at McLean's Ford, continued to drive the enemy rapidly rearward.[33] But then a third messenger arrived. Beauregard needed help. Halt all advancements and send assistance to Henry House Hill at once.

The 5th Alabama sweated and gasped as they double-timed in searing afternoon heat toward the growling guns. But by 5 A.M. when Ewell's troops arrived, the battle was over and the ground covered with bodies.[34] Ewell, Rodes, and Colonel Taylor of the 6th Louisiana urged pursuit of the fleeing enemy but to no avail. The brigade was ordered back to Union Mills. They had marched and countermarched all day but seen no real action. As they plodded in a fine rain, back toward the ford, tired and hungry, the soldiers grumbled about inept leadership. Even some officers questioned the day's contradictory orders.

The following morning Rodes' 5th Alabama returned to Henry House Hill to assist in the collection of Federal arms and equipment. Captain Blackford recalled the wagons loaded with Confederate dead and wounded which rolled endlessly rearward.[35] At mid-morning a snappy new outfit, the 12th Alabama, marched smartly onto the field at Manassas accompanied by its band. By their arrival Confederate dead and wounded had been evacuated, but lines of blue-clad bodies lay about, and the rookie Alabamians were put to work digging trenches and burying the enemy. A member recalled:

> My detail spent the day burying Brooklyn Zouaves, who wore blue jackets and red pantaloons. These Zouaves had been lying on the ground several hours and their faces and hands had become black. The sight was a horrible one, and the removal of them to the long trenches which we dug, was anything but a grateful task, but it was a humane duty which we did not shrink from....this furious battle,

and these horrible sights as a result, made an indelible impression upon us all.[36]

Several companies of the 12th Alabama were undergraduates from Auburn College, eager for action and despairing of their late arrival. This sudden exposure to the sordid aftermath of a battle was a strong dose of reality which tempered their exhilaration. Soon the 12th, and the Alabama Brigade, would experience struggles which would make Manassas seem a skirmish, but many of these young men undoubtedly thought the war was over and they had been too late to test their manhood.

Within days the Confederate army forged across Bull Run and established lines further north across the Occoquon River running through Fairfax Court House. From nearby Munson's Hill, pickets could see the unfinished dome of the United States Capitol.[37] Rodes established his regimental camp near Langston's Crossroads, within supporting distance of pickets atop Munson's Hill.[38]

In October, recognizing the dire need of a more flexible command structure, the Confederate military command began grouping of brigades into divisions of three to five brigades, each to be led by a major general. Surprisingly, on October 4, Maj. Gen. Earl Van Dorn of Mississippi was transferred to the Virginia army and assigned the initial division, that of the brigades of Brig. Gen. Richard Ewell and Col. Jubal Early.[39]

While Van Dorn's Division was one of the first so organized, soon all Confederate brigades were placed in divisions and then subsequently united into corps. The potential of this progressive organizational move was apparent and while enthusiastically accepted, there were also early difficulties. The army already suffered from a lack of staff officers, and the creation of these new levels simply demanded more unavailable staff personnel. In addition, the competitiveness of those lobbying for promotion was not helpful. Political appointees were still plentiful and each used staff positions to reward their supporters. President Davis further increased organizational stress when he requested that General Johnston group state regiments into state brigades and reshuffle general officers to have state brigades led by an officer from that state. This well-meaning action was inspired by Davis' desire to equalize opportunities among states and to increase each state's pride in its soldiers. But in many instances it simply increased the uncooperative spirit existing among vain, petty officers.[40]

Johnston withdrew Confederate units from their exposed Virginia camps in mid-October to winter lines near the Manassas battlefield. Ewell's Brigade moved back to Union Mills and began extensively fortifying the hills along Bull Run.[41] South of the stream, soldiers began constructing their camps for winter although men from the deep South still remained naively unprepared for the ferocity of winter in Virginia. Eventually defensive works stretched for twenty-five miles as soldiers complained and grumbled that they were expected to work "harder than splitting rails."[42]

Colonel Rodes was pleasantly surprised on October 22 when a courier from the Confederate adjutant general's office arrived with a commission promoting him to brigadier general and appointing him to command the brigade in which he was now serving.[43] General Ewell, who heartily congratulated the shocked Rodes, was temporarily assigned to a brigade in Longstreet's Division, but subsequently was promoted to major general and transferred to Kirby Smith's small Tennessee command. Brigadier General Rodes assumed command of a brigade consisting of the 5th, 6th, and newly arrived 12th Alabama Regiments, joined by the 12th Mississippi.[44] Rodes surely benefitted by the efforts to create state brigades, for even though he was Virginian by birth he was considered a native Alabamian. His appointment was not, however, without its detractors. Senators William L. Yancey and Clement C. Clay of Alabama claimed that Rodes was a Virginian and they wished an Alabama native appointed to lead the Alabama unit.[45]

The army remained in winter quarters below Bull Run and the soldiers suffered intensely for lack of winter clothing, shoes, and adequate rations. Most had expected a brief summer war, then victory and a return home. Disease and illnesses were rampant and long casualty lists ensued from inept hospitals.[46] In December, the Confederate Congress evoked the "Furlough and Bounty Act" in a frantic attempt to keep the army intact.[47] Each soldier who reenlisted for the war's duration was promised fifty dollars bounty and sixty days furlough. Furthermore, after his furlough he could seek assignment to the unit of his choice, and once that was completed, the men could hold new elections for company and regimental officers.

Despite its intent, this act of democracy shook the infant organization to its foundations. The most serious problem was the election of new officers. Many very capable men who were demanding in their duties were unseated and more popular fellows substituted. Rodes' fellow officer and friend, Lt. Col. John Tyler Morgan of the 5th Alabama, had taken over the regiment upon Rodes' promotion but was deposed in the elective process and resigned, returning to Alabama to raise the 51st Alabama Cavalry and fight resolutely in the columns of Nathan Bedford Forrest.[48] Rodes was particularly annoyed by the loss of this fine officer to the brigade. Confusion and discontent caused by the Act triggered a general conscription act, passed by Congress in the spring, whereby all white males were declared liable for three years service.[49] Manpower needs of the Confederate army were partially met by the Conscription Act, but deferments, hiring of substitutes, and other loopholes continued to bedevil the nation.

On January 10 Van Dorn departed the Virginia Army. His division was temporarily assigned to Brig. Gen. Milledge L. Bonham, the senior brigadier. Soldiers continued their daily tasks of repairing bridges, resetting railway lines, and perfecting their winter quarters. On clear days drill could always be expected in the brigade of General Rodes. Bonham resigned in February when elected to Congress from South Carolina, relinquishing command to Brig. Gen. Jubal A. Early.[50]

It became apparent to President Davis and Gen. Robert E. Lee, his military advisor, that Federal General McClellan's massive army was moving by water transports toward Old Point Comfort, landing near Fortress Monroe. A Federal advance up the peninsula formed by the York and James Rivers seemed likely. General John Magruder's small force at Yorktown was surely not strong enough to resist McClellan, so in early March, Johnston's army at Manassas was ordered to move toward Richmond, preparatory to reinforcing Magruder.

By March 8 the division, now led by Early, marched east on roads parallel to the railway, and on the tenth crossed the Rappahannock River. Rodes' Brigade remained at the crossing for several days, awaiting Federal reaction. Longstreet's Division was already in the capital and paraded down Broad Street to loud ovations on a beautiful spring afternoon.[51]

On April 4 Early's Division boarded the railway cars for Richmond, Rodes' Brigade in the lead. As the trains proceeded east, a wreck occurred when one train loaded with troops crashed into the rear of the preceding one.[52] Thankfully injuries were minimal. By April 8 Rodes and Kershaw were in Williamsburg and Early well on the way.[53] Soon Rodes' men were posted in weak earthworks on the Yorktown line near the Warwick River. The next day Early's Brigade moved in alongside although both officers were concerned over their advanced and exposed positions in light of growing Federal numbers. The soldiers present at Williamsburg were re-organized into two new divisions. Maj. Gen. James Longstreet led one division, while the other division was commanded by Gen. Daniel H. Hill. Hill's command consisted of the brigades of Brig. Gens. Jubal Early, Robert Rodes, Gabriel J. Rains, and William S. Featherstone. Assorted artillery and cavalry was attached to each division.

Daniel H. Hill was a forty-year-old West Point-trained North Carolinian. He also had proven himself an outstanding educator, teaching at Washington College, Davidson College, and North Carolina Military Institute. Hill was, like his brother-in-law, Thomas Jackson, a distinguished Presbyterian layman. He was a serious soldier with an outspoken manner to all, subordinates and superiors. His caustic and sarcastic tongue prevented real popularity despite his military success as for a time he seemed the armies' best divisional commander. Hill was as personally brave as he was demanding of others, and it is regrettable that his personality and sensitivity prevented his achieving fame in the front rank of Confederate general officers.

Hill's initial move was to withdraw Rodes and Early, to their relief. He solidified his lines and assigned Rodes defense of Redoubt #5, a fortification on the Williamsburg Road. But sometime after midnight on May 1, Hill called his brigade commanders together and told them Johnston had decided to abandon the Yorktown Line and the army would withdraw the following night, spiking all guns too large to move.[54] Rodes' Brigade followed

Early's, slowly moving through the mire toward Williamsburg. After a brief halt, they assembled to continue, but Federal pursuit suddenly increased, and Hill was forced to countermarch these two brigades through a driving rainstorm to bolster Johnston's rear guard. After some initial maneuvering Early, with Hill's approval, launched an assault against what he perceived as an unsuspecting Union force under Federal Brig. Gen. John Hancock. But Early was abruptly repulsed with heavy casualties, including taking two minie balls himself. Rodes' men stood in formation as bullets clipped the trees overhead but Federals failed to follow Jubal's retreat. The Confederates continued to fall back up the peninsula toward the capital.

Campaigning around Yorktown and Williamsburg was extremely difficult for the men in the ranks. The Confederate Commissary Department, never very efficient, fell completely apart, and soldiers described themselves as "hungry as wolves."[55] The heavy rains and constant traffic turned the dirt roads to the thickness of glue. Tents were not available, and the constant rain caused everything and everyone to mold. It was a hungry, tired, and dispirited army which toiled west toward Richmond. Discipline broke down in many units as soldiers left the ranks to seek food and then moved on in a continual gray stream. Provost marshals sallied from Richmond, sweeping up thousands of stragglers and returning them to their units.

Rodes worked hard to keep his regiments under control and in good order. His soldiers were cheered somewhat when they passed through Williamsburg. A trooper recalled:

> As we passed through the Old Capital of Virginia....the sidewalks were crowded with beautiful women and children....waving handkerchiefs and flags and handing us sandwiches and water.[56]

As this generosity allayed their hunger the soldiers struggled in the knee deep mud, most losing whatever footgear they possessed. A Louisiana sergeant, J.W. Minnich, recalled much later a chance meeting with Rodes on the road west. He and a companion named Kelly were walking the sixty odd miles to Richmond in a terrible downpour. As they passed Rodes' Brigade, sheltering in a grove of trees alongside the road, Minnich recognized Rodes standing by the roadside with his arms folded under the cape of his great coat. Minnich knew Robert Rodes, for the two had met on the long train trip from Pensacola to Richmond, and additionally, he had talked with Rodes in Williamsburg. Minnich commented that "Rodes was always the same genial and courtly gentleman."[57] The two soldiers stopped, saluted, and Minnich inquired after his battalion and how long ago they had passed. Rodes replied, "A good while ago—they, should be about four miles ahead of you—why are you so far behind?"[58] Minnich related to the general that they had been transferring a wagon load of pikes when their wagon broke and they were forced to store the pikes in a barn. General Rodes, with a slow smile and a twinkle in his blue eyes, asked, "What did you expect to do with the pikes?"[59] Minnich reported that he and Kelly saluted and moved on, never to see the general again.

My May 13, Rodes and his soldiers were across the Chickahominy River and encamped, living on parched corn. But soon rations appeared, the sun reappeared, and Rodes began daily drill. General Hill, straight to the point as usual, blamed the poor discipline on the recently conducted elections and their repercussions. He complimented Rodes on keeping his brigade in order during the strenuous retreat, a marked distinction over Hill's other brigades. Rodes was, however, sadly disappointed. He had been with the army almost a year, been present at two battles, and been promoted to brigadier general but had seen no real action beyond some meaningless skirmishing. The thin, tall, young brigadier need not have worried. His time to fight would come, soon and often.

CHAPTER 3

DEFENDING THE CAPITAL
Seven Pines and Seven Days

A mud-caked, rain-soaked Confederate army finally straggled across the Chickahominy, a stream marking the final natural barrier between George McClellan's ponderous Union army and the capital of the Confederate States.[1] The Chickahominy runs northeast to southwest in front of Richmond and is actually part river, part swamp. During dry periods it's a mere trickle of shallow scum-covered water, but when the rains fall it spreads rapidly over its shallow banks, creating lakes, marshes, and mud flats. Its banks are densely vegetated with scrub trees, vines, reeds, and moss; its water undrinkable, and its bottom often quicksand. The Chickahominy is populated by snakes of every description, often poisonous, virulent, malaria-bearing mosquitos, ticks, and large black flies. A formidable and treacherous environment over which to walk, and a most deplorable terrain for large-scale military operations.

As McClellan moved closer he unloaded a train of heavy-caliber siege guns from transport ships at White House Landing, rapidly entraining these on the York Railroad. "Little Mac's" strategy was to pen the Confederate army inside its own capital and, stationing those huge guns close, pound the army as well as the city into submission. As the Federal troops advanced, President Davis and General Lee, his military advisor, increased pressure on the uncommunicative Johnston, insisting that he retreat no further. To surrender Richmond was unthinkable and if McClellan would not initiate action, Johnston must.

When Johnston began evacuation of his Yorktown lines, Confederate Maj. Gen. Benjamin Huger, commanding the garrison at Norfolk, also was forced to retreat.[2] Huger's evacuation created further dilemma for Johnston. His right flank on the James River was now open.

The sluggish, muddy James River was easily navigable for large vessels right up to the fall line at Richmond, mere blocks from the Virginia

State House where the Confederate Congress now met, consumed peanuts, and argued. The ironclad CSS *Virginia*, based at Norfolk, had maintained Confederate superiority on the James. But when Huger abandoned the port she was forced to attempt a retreat up the James, ran aground, and was blown apart by her crew.[3]

The United States Navy took immediate advantage of this opening on the James. A squadron of gunboats consisting of three ironclad vessels—the flagship USS *Galena*, the USS *Monitor*, and the USS *Naugatuck*—assisted by two wooden gunboats—the USS *Aroostook* and the USS *Port Royal*—all under command of Commodore John Rogers, began ascending the river. As the flotilla approached Drewry's Bluff tensions grew, for if the vessels were not halted at that point, they would soon anchor at Rockett's Landing and toss their potent, high-explosive shells onto the green lawn of the statehouse.

At Drewry's Bluff the river veers sharply eastward then turns back south, creating an elbow with a narrow channel. Alongside this elbow a ninety-foot bluff rose abruptly from the water, commanding a mile-long stretch of the twisting river. Confederate Engineers Corps hastily constructed an earthen fort atop that bluff. The Confederate navy gathered a number of wooden, masted vessels, filled them with stone ballast, and sunk these obstacles in the channel directly opposite the fort.[4] The vessels were then linked together with chains, precluding passage up river. Artillery was manhandled up the bluff and installed in well-built casements of earth, logs, and sandbags. At least two of the guns were eight-inch Columbiads which fired 64-pound projectiles. The remainder were 32-pound rifles removed from Confederate navy ships.

Early on the morning of May 15, the Federal squadron appeared in view, and prepared to bombard the fort into submission.[5] The gray-clad gunners atop the bluff concentrated all their fire on the flagship *Galena*. This Federal warship was protected by a new, experimental, light-weight armor which didn't successfully reduce the penetration of Confederate shot.[6] The ironclad was struck forty-four times, resulting in thirteen dead and eleven wounded sailors.[7] Federal naval officers concluded that reduction of the defenses of Drewry's Bluff was not possible unless a strong land force was utilized in conjuncture with the fleet.[8]

Thus one of Johnston's many worries, both real and imagined, was dispelled. His right flank was secure and he could now plan his army's actions to repel the enemy. Although the dapper general resented President Davis' constant pressure to fight, in truth, he had no other recourse. McClellan was already too close to the city's environs and must be forced to give ground.

Three separate roads issued eastward from Richmond, and Johnston decided to use all three to surprise the Federal IV Corps under Brig. Gen. Erasmus D. Keyes and the III Corps led by Brig. Gen. Samuel P. Heintzelman, both positioned near Seven Pines. Johnston would utilize four columns of infantry on the three roadways. Maj. Gen. Daniel H. Hill would proceed directly out the middle route, the Williamsburg Stage Road, and attack at Seven Pines. Benjamin Huger and his Norfolk garrison troops would use the southern route called the Charles City Road to advance, turn left and fall on the enemy's left flank. The northern or Nine Mile Road would be used by two columns. First, Maj. Gen. James Longstreet's men would assault the enemy's right flank while Brig. Gen. Chase Whiting's Division would follow Longstreet and screen the Confederate attackers from the possible interference of any Federal force which might attempt to cross the Chickahominy.[9]

It was an exceptional plan, worthy of use in many of Napoleon's European campaigns, but much too complicated for the inexperienced gray divisions to execute. Mistakes in communication coupled with weak, even inept, divisional leadership created another scenario, another action, which bore little resemblance to that which Johnston had planned.

However, as Johnston put the finishing touches on his scheme, nature intervened directly in the operations of all military units in the area. About mid-day on May 30, clouds began to gather, boiling ominously, and the heavens turned pitch-black. Then a violent windstorm swept through the camps, uprooting trees, scattering tents, and stampeding horses and mules. In late afternoon, a fearful storm broke with vivid displays of lightning. Tents were struck by lightning bolts in the 44th New York, killing a quartermaster, and four soldiers of the 4th Alabama were slain by one bolt from the heavens.[10] When darkness fell, instead of abating, the storm increased its intensity and power. Bolts of electricity shattered the gun carriages of Federal artillery, and soldiers watched, open mouthed, as fire leapt from muzzle to muzzle of artillery pieces in a gun park.[11] One Union officer described the rains "as if the very sluice gates of heaven were opened and water dropped for hours."[12] A British captain, traveling with McClellan's entourage, vowed it the worst storm he had ever witnessed in his travels throughout the empire, stating that the very earth seemed flooded.[13]

The sluggish Chickahominy was suddenly a torrent, with bridges destroyed or awash, and river bottoms converted to lakes. Johnston's confidence grew as he viewed the storm's aftermath, declaring it a God-sent act, isolating the Federals in their trenches.[14]

As day dawned bright and clear on May 31, Robert Rodes' Brigade was oddly posted astride the Charles City Road, three to four miles from its designated attackpoint on the Williamsburg Road. On the previous day, under direction of Major General Hill, armed reconnaissances of brigade strength were conducted by Rodes on the Charles City Road and Brig. Gen. Samuel Garland on the Williamsburg Road.[15] Rodes uncovered no opposition; nevertheless his brigade was ordered to remain in blocking position until Huger's column relieved him next day.[16] His soldiers had traveled light,

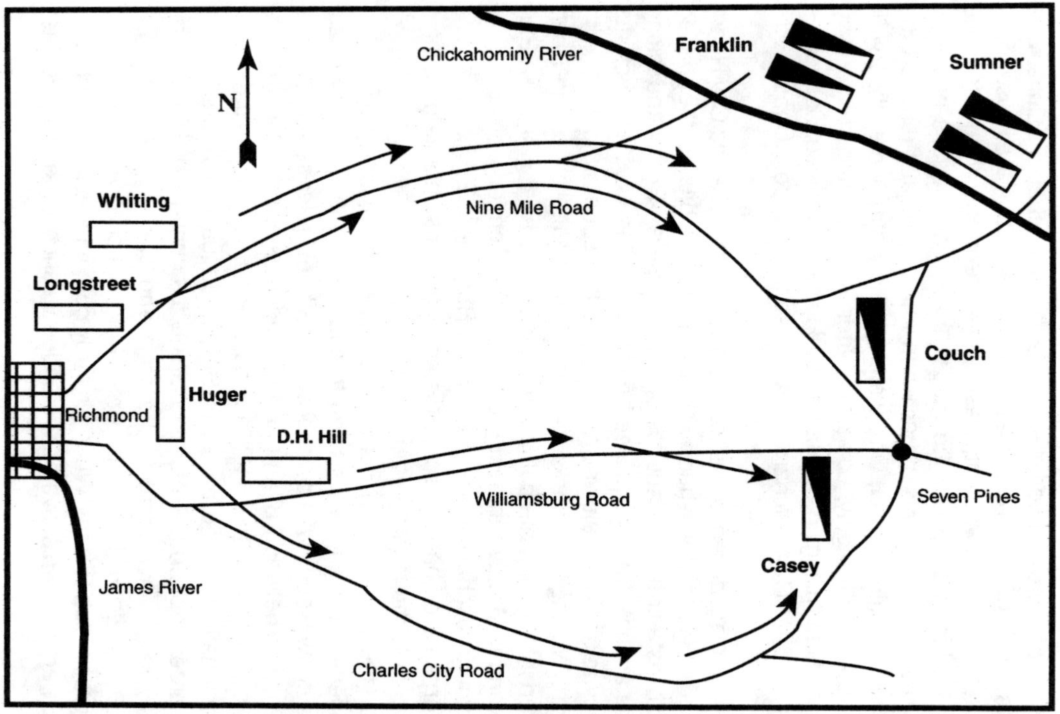

Seven Pines Attack Plan, May 31, 1862

General Johnston's attack plan would employ four Confederate divisions. While Whiting shielded Franklin's VI Corps and Sumner's II Corps from action, three columns under Longstreet, Huger, and Hill would converge on Casey's and Couch's isolated divisions near Seven Pines.

without shelters, and experienced a wet, uncomfortable night. General Hill's three additional brigades were camped at their proper attack jump-off points, awaiting Rodes' arrival.

Johnston's three-pronged assault was scheduled for sunrise, but the storm and lethargic leadership completely disrupted that idea. Huger's and Longstreet's troops were camped in such a fashion that their divisions were forced to cross each other's line of march in order to reach their respective advance routes.[17] Huger overslept, was delayed, and marched late while Longstreet held his brigades by the roadside awaiting Huger's passage. Thus Longstreet was so delayed that when his units finally reached the Nine Mile Road, Whiting's men, who were to follow him, were already in front marching east. Strangely, Longstreet then split his division, sending three brigades after Whiting and countermarching the brigades of Col. James L. Kemper and Brig. Gen. Richard H. Anderson to support Daniel Hill's attack.

Huger's men advanced for a short distance on the Charles City Road, which was badly pitted and washed by storm damage. Confused, they halted and stood idle, listening to the sounds of battle at Seven Pines, and taking no part in the action. Huger displayed herein one of his worst characteristics, hesitancy in battle, a trait which would see him soon out of favor with Lee. Up north, Whiting's column slowly marched out the Nine Mile Road and blundered into a separate battle with a Union line near Fair Oaks Station. Col. Evander M. Law and Brig. Gen. Dorsey Pender were soon involved in a tough exchange with the van of Brig. Gen. Edwin Sumner's Federal II Corps which had heroically disregarded considerable hardships and raced south to aid their comrades in blue.

Back on the Williamsburg Road, an exasperated and angry D.H. Hill paced impatiently, awaiting permission to attack and fuming over Rodes' absence. He knew Rodes was compelled to wait until released by Huger's arrival.[18] Sometime between 10 and 11 A.M. Rodes received orders to move his brigades cross-country to the Williamsburg Road.[19] He began the movement but personally galloped ahead to Hill's headquarters where he discovered the order erroneous. Returning rapidly to countermand the orders, Rodes surely must have recalled the start and stop nature of his 1st Manassas orders. Soon a follow-up order from Hill confirmed movement and Rodes proceeded to obey. When his tardy column reached the head of White Oak Swamp they discovered the bridge washed out and as he later reported:

> ...the men had to wade in water waist-deep and a number were entirely submerged. At this point it was absolutely necessary to proceed with great caution to prevent loss of both ammunition and life.[20]

Once across, Rodes double-timed his column for some distance, attempting to make up the delay.

Hill's assignment was the only part of Johnston's plan that almost worked. Marching out the Williamsburg Road two brigades abreast, Brig. Gen. Samuel Garland, leading the brigade of the wounded Jubal Early, deployed on the left or north side of the road, with file guides aligned on the roadway. Rodes' Brigade aligned identically on the right side and the two units swept forward toward Seven Pines. Featherston's Brigade, under Col. George B. Anderson, would follow Garland, and Brig. Gen. Gabriel Rains' Brigade was to support Rodes. General Hill was so impatient that the moment he saw Rodes' leading regiment arrive, he fired a signal gun to initiate the attack.[21] Frustrated, Rodes was forced to feed his regiments into the advance, en echelon, upon their arrival, to avoid impeding the attack. The 6th Alabama, his leading unit, was deployed as double skirmishers under Col. John Gordon and dashed smartly forward. Soon Col. Walter H. Taylor's 12th Mississippi followed, then the 4th Virginia Heavy Artillery under Capt. C.C. Otey (fighting as infantry). The 5th Alabama was next following Col. C.C. Peques, and the 12th Alabama brought up the rear. Col. Robert T. Jones of the 12th was quite ill, but insisted on accompanying his regiment on horseback. The King William Artillery followed along the roadway to provide support.[22] Capt. Thomas H. Carter, the battery commander of this fine Virginia unit, was an ex-Virginia Military Institute confidant of the brigade commander.

The soldiers stumbled and struggled through briars, vines, and underbrush, wading two-foot-deep pools, as they attempted to hold their regiment-wide front in the dense underbrush. Emerging from the brush, somewhat scattered and disorganized, they found themselves under heavy musket and artillery fire from a forbidding-appearing earthworks in their immediate front. The Federal IV Corps divisions of Brig. Gens. Silas Casey and Darius Couch had constructed strong defense works anchored by a pentagonal, open, earthen redoubt they called "Casey's Redoubt."[23] Abatis of sharpened tree limbs and brush were piled in front of the works, and to the rear extensive Federal camps could be observed.[24] Within the redoubt were located six guns of the 1st New York Artillery, well protected by three regiments of Federal infantry. The defenders were nervous but prepared for Rodes' emergence, as scouts had sighted the advancing gray-backs and tracked them easily in the underbrush. As Rodes' units cleared the woods, several groups of Confederates quickly ran forward into the abatis, took shelter and began a return fire. One Federal private in the defenses marveled at the willingness of the Southern infantry to take casualties and keep coming "as our fire was mowing them down like grass before a scythe."[25] Rodes and Capt. Green Peyton, his aide, raced to pull the emerging regiments together, forming a semi-circular line about the redoubt, the soldiers covering behind the abatis. Realizing that an all-out attack would be costly, Rodes sent a message to Rains to move up quickly on his right to flank the redoubt. While this was occurring, Carter's King William Artillery arrived, unlimbered, and opened an accurate and scalding fire into the

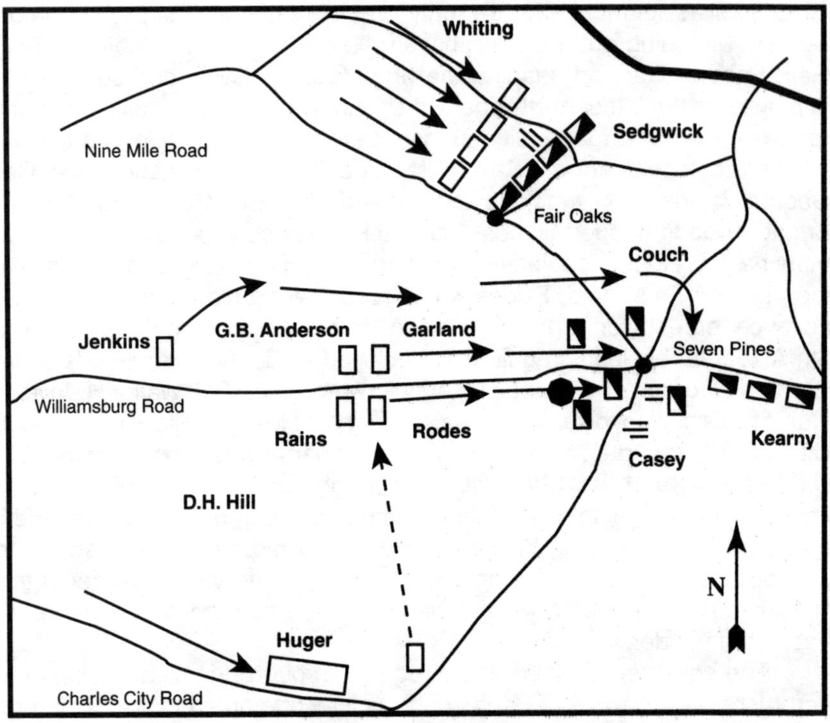

Seven Pines, May 31, 1862

The actual battle at Seven Pines developed quite differently from Johnston's plan. Only Whiting's and Hill's divisions saw action. At Seven Pines Rodes and Garland cracked Casey's Line as Jenkins penetrated into the Federal rear. Whiting's Brigades assailed the Union line further north at Fair Oaks.

redoubt, silencing the Union guns.[26] As Rodes watched he noted the Union infantry seemed to waver, and he brazenly ordered all his regiments to immediately assail the earthen walls. As battle flags were unfurled and the gray-clad infantry arose and began to yell, the enemy fled his works, abandoning guns and racing for a second line in the edge of some woods about one hundred fifty yards away. Rodes' men swarmed over the works and opened fire into the backs of the fleeing enemy. One unit, the 55th New York, the last unit to exit, was heavily punished by Confederate fire. A brave Union artillery officer, Col. Guilford Bailey, spurred his horse back into the little fort to spike his guns but took numerous minie balls and was slain.[27] Considerable amounts of Federal equipment were captured including seven cannon and a large supply of ammunition. But within minutes, from immediately to the rear and right of the redoubt, Federal soldiers began a brisk fire. Rodes surmised correctly that Rains had declined to advance on his right flank.

As Rodes dispatched riders in search of Rains, a second threat developed. From the woods on his left flank, where Garland's men were fiercely engaged, a full brigade of blue-clad reinforcements emerged marching in battle order. Brig. Gen. Phillip Kearny, one of McClellan's best officers, was leading a III Corps Division, and he deployed Brig. Gen. Hiram Berry's Brigade led by the tough 3rd Michigan, and instructed they retake the redoubt.[28] The 5th Alabama and 12th Mississippi redressed their lines, refusing the right, and occupied the vacant rifle pits on the right flank. A growing volume of rifle fire indicated the serious purpose of the new arrivals. As the blue line grew nearer, Captain Carter spurred up the Williamsburg Road with two guns, cleared for action, and opened a damaging fire into Berry's line. Meanwhile, Rodes and Capt. John Bagby who had assumed command of the 4th Virginia when Otey was slain, reversed several of the captured Federal guns, and when they also opened, this cross-fire was too much for Berry's men who fell back into the woods.[29] As the Federal troops retreated they uncovered a line of fire, and two masked Federal batteries opened on Carter's gunners who were exposed in the roadway. On one gun every man was killed or wounded in the first salvo. Confederate infantrymen leaped for cover as the gunners exchanged fire. At last, Rains' men approached the center of action. The cautious brigadier moved up on the right as Rodes made contact with Garland on his left and these two young brigadiers decided to continue the advance since the Union batteries seemed to have lost their bark. The brigades moved on line and advanced briskly forward through heavily flooded fields. So much water was standing in the fields that when soldiers were wounded, friends would stop and prop them against trees to prevent their drowning in the knee-deep morass.[30] Smartly and gallantly the regiments advanced through more abatis and into another trench line. An amusing incident occurred when Rodes halted his brigade to redress his lines. Colonel Gordon and the 6th Alabama, not hearing the order, pressed on. When Gordon realized he was exposed out front he halted the advance, about-faced his troops, and marched back to the brigade line. Rodes ordered the brigade to resume its advance, and when Gordon looked behind him his regiment was disappearing into the trees. He had forgotten to order another about-face and his soldiers had continued to march rearward. A red-faced, shouting Gordon spurred doggedly after the 6th Alabama.[31] The further Rodes' men moved forward the more effective the Federal enfilading fire from the right became. Gordon's regiment was the right hand unit and he remarked that the fire was so intense that half his line officers were shot dead or wounded including his own brother.[32] Rains had again declined to advance so Rodes was compelled to cease his forward movement and fall back to protect his right. The 6th and 12th Alabama on that flank were absorbing fearsome casualties, and when Colonel Jones of the 12th fell, Rodes was forced to temporarily exercise command of that unit as the regiment was wavering and almost all its officers were down. He moved them back into some cover, had them dig in and began exchanging fire with the enemy. The advance was stalled and Rodes angrily stated:

> I feel decidedly confident that if we had been properly supported in the last charge the brigade would have marched on with uninterrupted progress, because the enemy invariably yielded to a direct advance, and the men and officers of this brigade everywhere exhibited great courage and an earnest desire to close....[33]

The brigade remained in this static position for more than an hour awaiting reinforcements, repelling all Federal advances. Kemper's Brigade arrived too late to initiate further action. Rodes was wounded by a minie ball which struck his right arm below the elbow. Although he turned active command over to Gordon, Rodes would not leave the field for another ninety minutes or until nightfall when action ceased.[34] It is interesting that Rodes turned over the brigade to John Gordon, who was actually the most junior of his colonels in age and time in grade.[35] But possibly Rodes recognized at this early date the energy and natural zeal for leadership possessed by the cocky, young officer. He undoubtedly felt Gordon could best lead the unit in combat should such occur.

Pressure on Rodes' Brigade started to ease about thirty minutes prior to nightfall as Federal opponents became agitated and some even retreated. As return fire slackened, experienced foragers among the Confederates began rummaging through the captured Federal camps, searching each tent for food or valuables. Robert Miller wrote that "he had the pleasure of drinking Maj. Gen. Silas Casey's coffee, eating his ham, drinking his claret, and sleeping in his tents....all within the entrenched camp."[36] On the left, Garland's troops attempted one last attack bolstered by assistance from Anderson's Brigade, but soon lost their momentum. Hill's attack on the Williamsburg Road had burst open the Federal line, but the blue-clad soldiers resisted so strongly that the attackers were fought out, too exhausted to continue. Despite Hill's efforts he could get little action out of Rains or the idle brigades of Longstreet and Huger, which could have turned his local success into a major Confederate victory.

Hill was not one to give up, however. He had appropriated one excellent brigade from Longstreet and he used that unit well.[37] He split Anderson's Brigade into two half-brigades, deploying two regiments with Anderson into the small gap between Rodes and Garland. The other two regiments, the Palmetto Sharpshooters and the 6th South Carolina, he dispatched under twenty-six-year-old Col. Micah Jenkins around the Union right flank.[38] Somehow Jenkins discovered a gap in the Union front and penetrated cleanly, falling on and destroying the surprised 61st Pennsylvania Infantry. Jenkins then cleared the road, marching and countermarching in the Federal rear, aggressively assaulting any blue line he encountered.[39] The sheer audacity of his actions undoubtedly saved his force from extinction amid hordes of the enemy, but soon Union troops grew uneasy with his force in their rear, and they began to look for avenues of escape. Jenkins defeated five Federal lines by darkness and he convinced unnumbered others that they were in peril. The combined pressures of the line-breaking attack of Rodes and Garland, coupled with Jenkins' skillful and dramatically exploited breakthrough, erased Federal resistance at Seven Pines, and at dusk the battlefield belonged to Hill's tired gray soldiers.

Some few miles north, an entirely separate battle raged briefly around Fair Oaks. Chase Whiting's Confederates had advanced out the Nine Mile Road, Col. Evander Law's Brigade in the lead, and discovered a Federal line of battle of troops from Brigadier General Couch's 2nd Division of the IV Corps. Recklessly, the 6th North Carolina charged and Law had to commit two additional regiments in support. They hit a stone wall in Couch's make-shift line and could observe numbers of fresh Federal soldiers arriving. These Federals were accompanied by a superb six-gun battery of the 1st United States Artillery, which had a critical impact on the action that would follow. The Confederates regrouped, poured in more troops and advanced again without reconnaissance. The magnificently served 1st Artillery blasted the Confederate infantry in rows. Lt. Edmund Kirby, battery commander, reported that his red-hot barrels fired 343 rounds at the gray enemy.[40] Strangely, Confederate batteries were plentifully scattered in the marching column but were never summoned forward to challenge the Union guns.[41]

Gen. Joseph Johnston rode out about dark to reconnoiter near Fair Oaks and wandered too closely to the enemy as he was struck with a bullet in his right shoulder and simultaneously received a shell fragment in the chest. He fell heavily from his horse and at first was feared to be mortally wounded. Placed in an ambulance he was slowly conveyed back to Richmond to the Crenshaw House on Church Hill.[42] When Johnston fell, army command passed to an uninformed and unprepared second-in-command, Maj. Gen. Gustavus Smith, who immediately struggled to grasp the military situation.

In an oft-quoted statement, Joel Cook, a correspondent for the *Philadelphia Press*, described the shell that struck General Johnston as the saddest shot fired during the war by Union soldiers in that it completely changed the Federal army's opponent. "It took away incompetence, indecision and dissatisfaction and gave generalship, excellent plans, and good discipline."[43]

In two days of confused, misdirected action, casualties were high in both armies. Union reports indicated a loss of 5,031 men, 790 slain, while Confederate losses were assessed at 6,134 soldiers, 980 killed in action.[44] Robert Rodes' Alabama Brigade suffered as severely as any Southern unit. At least two-thirds of his unit's casualties were believed to have occurred after Casey's Redoubt was captured, inflicted by those Federal troops who retreated into the woods on his right flank and poured such a stiff fire into his exposed regiments. General Hill in his report was quite outspoken in explaining the high casualties in Rodes' Brigade. He stated:

> I now resolved to drive the Yankees out of the woods on the right of the road, where they were still strong in force. General Rains was near them, and a written order was carried to him by my adjutant to move further to the right. I regret that this gallant and meritorious officer did not advance....he would have taken the Yankees in flank, and the direct attack of Rodes would have been less bloody. The magnificent brigade of Rodes moved over the open ground to assault the Yankees, strongly posted in the woods. He met a most galling fire and his advance was checked....If Rains had pressed vigorously on the right, 500 casualties could have been saved in Rodes' Brigade.[45]

Rodes' Report contained a casualty table for his unit. His brigade entered the action with a total of 2,200 officers and men. Casualties were as follows:

Unit	K	W	Total
5th Alabama	29	181	210
6th Alabama	91	277	368
12th Alabama	59	149	208
12th Mississippi	41	152	193
4th Virginia Art.	16	67	83
King William Art.	5	25	30
Brigade Staff	0	2	2
TOTALS	241	853	1094[46]

These figures reflect a near 50 percent casualty rate for the entire brigade, a ghastly total in a unit which nonetheless continued to fight well until after dark. The 5th Alabama, which suffered so badly from enfilade fire, lost 60 percent. One company of the 6th Alabama lost twenty-one killed and twenty-three wounded from a fifty-five man roster, an 80 percent casualty figure.[47]

Neither army was in any way prepared to handle casualty rates from actions of this scope and ferocity. Union casualties were first evacuated to field hospitals, but they were too few and understaffed, so thousands of suffering blue coats were loaded into boxcars and transported by the York Railroad to the supply base at White House Landing. One official recalled that they came "dead and alive together, packed in the same boxcar."[48]

Wounded Confederates were shuttled back into Richmond by use of every possible type of conveyance. Maj. Heros Von Borcke, conspicuous volunteer on General Stuart's staff, recalled his attempts to proceed out the Williamsburg Stage Road late that night when he encountered hundreds of wagons, carriages, and omnibuses moving toward the city with loads of wounded men whose groans mixed with the curses of their drivers; or other vehicles lying broken on the impassable roadway.[49] The few hospitals were overrun, for the huge complex on Chimborazo Hill was not yet a reality. Almost every house in the city, whether stately mansion or modest cottage, was packed with Confederate wounded.[50] Most native Richmonders were dazed and shocked by the river of gray-clad wounded and dead, stacked in wagons like cord-wood, which flowed endlessly down Grace Street. Colonel Gordon detailed large work parties to assist in evacuation of severely wounded men. For the first time, soldiers of both armies experienced camping on the battlefield and observed the eerie glow of lanterns as search parties responded to the cries and groans which echoed hauntingly through the dark woods.

The Confederate foragers "liberated" all the booty that remained in the Union camps, finding books, letters, and large supplies of stationery materials in addition to rapidly consumed food and drink. Pvt. John Tucker of the 5th Alabama recalled the most popular prize was the new United States Army Enfield Rifle. Many of these fine weapons were "exchanged" by the still poorly armed Confederate infantrymen.[51]

This dual battle to establish initiative in the Richmond area was concluded and none too soon by Confederate standards. Johnston's fairly sound plans disintegrated within minutes, prompting the Confederate commander to comment that "he wished all his soldiers were back in camp," almost as soon as they marched out to fight.[52] Once fighting began he simply allowed the course of events to run to completion. His personal performance is only rivaled by the inept efforts of most of his division commanders.

Huger, the later most heavily criticized of these divisional commanders, earned most of the criticism he received, but he was not the lone culprit. He overslept, was late marching, was easily confused, and hesitantly allowed a single wrecked bridge to stop his column and keep him from the battle.[53] Instead he allowed 7,000 soldiers to stand idle, humiliated and ashamed, while their comrades fought and bled a short distance away. Huger's sins were those of omission.

Longstreet's performance did not receive the criticism of the public or his fellow officers. But he, oddly, took little part in the fight, seemingly becoming frustrated early and turning over the decisions to others. He and Johnston, from the beginning, were not working off the same page: their misunderstanding was colossal and total, good reason for a military leader to abandon use of verbal instructions.[54] Longstreet escaped public censure when he wrote an excellent report of the action and was able to point an accusing finger at others, mainly Huger.

Chase Whiting, who was supposed to screen the Confederate attack, actually conducted the fighting at Fair Oaks. He clearly demonstrated his aggressive nature and his willingness to commit troops to battle. But he did ignore a needed reconnaissance before letting his brigades charge into

Federal artillery fire, and once he discovered the Union guns, made no attempt to use his own.

Daniel Harvey Hill, alone of the four, demonstrated his ability to command and fight a division. Impatiently, he began his offense before Rodes was in position, but he clearly pointed out his objectives, kept his brigades within his control, attempted to adjust when necessary, and used wisely those reserves he obtained from Longstreet. The battle at Seven Pines, or the successful part of it, was indeed his fight.[55]

Confederate brigade commanders, on the other hand, often turned in very positive achievements. When properly directed they led men well, better than could be expected in light of their experience levels. Many of these young men would rise to important combat positions in the forming and soon to be feared Army of Northern Virginia.

Brig. Gen. Samuel Garland, newly promoted, displayed the energy and disregard for personal safety that would characterize his army career until the sad day at South Mountain when he would fall in combat. Garland's young wife and son had recently succumbed to disease and many thought the young brigadier purposely reckless. Col. George Burgwyn Anderson, commander of the 4th North Carolina and soon to be brigadier, led Featherston's Brigade and showed promise of his future brilliant and brief career.[56]

Richard H. Anderson, leading Longstreet's dispatched brigade, displayed the cool, steady personage that would see him a corps commander at war's end. This modest, patient, gentle man was not a seeker of fame or rank but would become a vital cog in the machinery of the Army of Northern Virginia.[57] Anderson's subordinate, Col. Micah Jenkins, was to develop into one of the armies' young geniuses. When given an opportunity by Hill he did not disappoint. Destined for early promotion, the future of the twenty-six-year-old Citadel graduate seemed bright indeed.[58]

Robert Rodes, seeing his first combat role, had equally excelled. He demonstrated mature coolness in decision making, yet, the fiery animation needed to inspire troops. His personal behavior demonstrated his complete lack of fear. General Hill observed and recorded Rodes' contributions as:

> Gen. Rodes took skillful advantage of commotion in the Union redoubt, caused by Carter's cannon fire, and moving up his brigade in beautiful order took possession of the redoubt and rifle pits. So rapid was his advance that six pieces of artillery were abandoned by the Yankees. These Rodes turned upon the retreating column with effect....Generals Garland, Anderson, and Rodes of my division, who led the attack in front, did all that brave and skillful officers could possibly do.[59]

Nor was Hill alone in noting and expressing admiration of Rodes' actions. In his report Longstreet added:

> I will mention Brig. Gen. Rodes of that division, as distinguished for coolness, ability, and determination. He made one of the most

important and decisive movements on the field and held his command for several hours after receiving a severe wound.[60]

Robert Rodes was fast earning recognition for his leadership qualities. That he was intelligent, intense, highly motivated, and meticulous in attention to detail was apparent to all observers. The fire that burned inside his calm demeanor could be stirred to the surface by the excitement of combat. The stellar performance of this green, untried brigade of soldiers from deep Alabama—charging an enemy line despite musket and cannon fire, advancing on a second line under heavy flanking fire due to lack of support, and holding on to their advanced position until relieved in the face of fierce resistance—was a tribute to the dogged persistence of Robert Rodes and the stubborn, prideful character of these fine young soldiers from the state of Alabama.

Several months after the battle, a Richmond newspaper carried a poem by an unknown author, a tribute to Rodes' Brigade at Seven Pines.[61] The prose has been published many times and is perhaps significant as the first piece of real "battlefield" poetry written during the war. It memorializes the sacrifice and effort of a fine fighting unit. Its author was probably either A.H. Whiting of Rodes' staff or W.P. Carter of Virginia, brother of Capt. Thomas Carter. This writing is included in the epilogue of this volume. Samuel Garland, Robert Rodes, and Micah Jenkins were not products of West Point. The first two were Virginia Military graduates and Jenkins a product of the Citadel, both state military academies. Neither were the three in any way political generals. They had no great influence in the courts of the Confederacy, rather they had advanced by selection of their regiments and whatever fame they would earn would be by the sweat of their own brows, courage of their own convictions, and results of their own efforts. They would soon typify many others of quality and promise, men whom Lee would develop and promote as he strove to built a truly fearsome army in Virginia.

LEE TAKES COMMAND

Robert Edward Lee was assuredly not the revered, awe-inspiring figure that he was later to become when he first took command of the Confederacy's principal field army. In fact, Lee's sudden elevation was considered with misgivings by many from both inside and outside the army. The soldiers were truly fond of Joe Johnston, feeling secure with his leadership and never suspecting his serious lack of ability to work cooperatively with his superiors.[62] Lee's pre-war reputation was sparkling, including a series of old army assignments that were the envy of his peers; an unsurpassed record of bravery and military skill extending to the engagement with Mexico, a successful tour as superintendent of the United States Military Academy, and a number of important, well-completed engineering assignments.[63]

Lee, however, had no record of success with Southern arms.[64] He had commanded in the western Virginia mountains in a forlorn and hopeless campaign, developed defensive schemes for the Carolina costal islands, and then was appointed military advisor to the president. Many considered Lee a staff officer, and even the *Richmond Examiner* engineered its own future ridicule when it proclaimed that it hoped Lee would "prove himself a competent successor to General Johnston and complete his great undertakings."[65] His calm, dignified, polite manner prevented many individuals from viewing him as a warrior. Many officers, including Col. Porter Alexander, wondered if he would prove aggressive enough to lead such an army. Alexander was surprised when Col. Joseph Ives rapidly and aptly predicted:

> His name might be audacity. He will take more desperate chances and take them quicker than any General, North or South.[66]

His future opponent, General McClellan, when he found Lee was to lead the Southern army, revealed his prowess in assessing ability when he expressed his preference to fight Lee over Johnston, as he believed Lee too cautious and weak.[67]

Lee brought immediate purpose and organization to the army.[68] Most initial changes in operation were easy to observe. Supplies, equipment, and rations began to flow to the proper locations. Discipline became a priority as Lee charged all officers with that responsibility, stating that they would be held accountable for the performances and actions of their units at all times. Gradually, many older, politically appointed officers began to disappear as competent, aggressive, and decisive men were promoted to replace them. Lee seldom brought officers up on charges or dismissed them precipitously; those he judged unworthy he transferred to other less critical duties. His eyes were everywhere and once an officer was found incapable there was no appeal.[69] Nepotism and political pressure were largely replaced by ability and zeal as traits of selection.

While Lee worked to reorganize his army, he also recognized that his immediate military situation was precarious. Johnston's battle at Seven Pines had not relieved the pressure which Union forces exerted on the city. Lee must secure the capital and he ordered his troops to begin digging, for earthworks would permit small numbers to resist larger Federal masses.[70] He then began to increase his force by pulling additional units from various points of the eastern Confederacy and within weeks his army numbered 67,000 soldiers. When Maj. Gen. Thomas J. Jackson's Valley Army was added, Lee's total would top 85,000. But Jackson was first needed in the Valley where his brilliant campaign occupied and deterred large numbers of Federals which might have joined McClellan.

Once the city was partially fortified, Lee was not disposed to await the Union commanders' attack. He reorganized his army into six divisions. Maj. Gen. Daniel H. Hill would lead one division of five brigades. Maj. Gen.

Ambrose P. Hill, Maj. Gen. James E. Longstreet, Maj. Gen. Thomas J. Jackson, Maj. Gen. John Magruder, and Maj. Gen. Ben Huger would command the other five. Lee determined to turn McClellan's right, threatening the Union army's attachment to its White House Landing base on the York River.[71] McClellan would thus be forced to leave his extensive fortifications and face battle on open ground.

Robert Rodes, recovering from his wound, suffered restlessly through weeks of inaction and idleness. For a major portion of his recuperation Rodes returned to Lynchburg, residing with his stepmother, Fanny Rodes, and her young family. Virginia Rodes, a distraught wife, hurried north from Tuscaloosa. Robert's father, David Rodes, had succumbed of paralysis in February of 1862 after a lengthy confinement to his bed.[72] Robert wrote to Superintendent Smith at the Virginia Military on June 17, that "my arm is nearly well as this is the first letter I have written. I will return to duty soon."[73] After enjoying the company of relatives and friends Robert left for Richmond and on May 24 reported for duty, anticipating action soon.[74] In his absence the brigade had experienced some alterations, becoming an all-Alabama unit. The 12th Mississippi and 4th Virginia Artillery were transferred and replaced by the 3rd Alabama of Lt. Col. Charles Forsyth from Mahone's Brigade and the 26th Alabama of Col. Edward O'Neal from Rains' unit. Robert was still weak as his wound was badly infected and was having difficulty riding, but stoutly determined to participate in whatever actions might occur.

Finally Lee was prepared to begin his offense. He could little anticipate just how violent the series of battles he was unleashing would become. He planned to attack on June 26, but fighting actually was begun by Federal initiative on June 25, 1862. The next week was marked by three days of intense action, one day's respite, and another three days of ferocious combat. The scope and intensity of these actions was beyond the comprehension of the combatants. Some thought it similar to Seven Pines, but repeated six times in seven days. Those few soldiers who were still naive enough to believe combat was yet an honorable contest between respectful foes and an endeavor worthy of man's noblest efforts, abruptly altered their attitudes. The plastic wrappings were removed and the cost of maintaining their ideals became very apparent. These two volunteer armies underwent a transformation in the seven bloody days as they contended each other along the sultry, steamy Chickahominy River bottoms. The butcher's bill was high, exorbitant, and those that survived could no longer be labeled amateur soldiers; they were now professionals.

Early on the morning of June 25, gunfire erupted from the Seven Pines battlefield. Lee had scheduled his attack for the following day and he wondered if the Federals had learned his plan and perhaps launched a preemptive advance.[75] Maj. Gen. Joseph Hooker deployed two brigades and smartly advanced, bands playing loudly, down the Williamsburg Road toward Richmond. He collided with two regiments of Brig. Gen. Ambrose Wright's Brigade, Huger's Division, and these two rookie units, who had been ridiculed for their non-participation in the Seven Pines fight, had something to prove. Soon a fierce little action developed with regiments charging bravely, fighting for a period, and then precipitously sprinting for the rear. Lee rode to the front for a time, assuring himself that the Federal advance was a limited one, its objective a grove of trees on a slight rise beside the road.[76]

Undaunted, Lee proceeded with his plan to launch four divisions against the Union V Corps on June 26. This Union corps was strongly entrenched at Beaver Dam Creek near Mechanicsville. Confederate attackers would be forced to cross open fields, wade a swamp, and scale an embankment to get at the enemy trenches. In addition, Federal Brig. Gen. Fitz-John Porter's three divisions were augmented by twenty batteries of artillery and a reserve division was nearby. Lee, aware of this strength, did not plan to attack Porter directly but instead would surround his works and rely on Jackson's appearance on Porter's right flank, forcing the Federal commander to abandon his strong earthworks. [77] For various reasons, some never explained, Jackson's men did not appear. Both Longstreet's and D.H. Hill's Divisions were delayed by failure of Confederate engineers to bridge the Chickahominy, and when A.P. Hill's impetuous brigades attacked Porter in late afternoon they were repulsed with heavy losses.

During that evening, a nervous McClellan visited Porter's front and fearing Jackson's arrival, instructed the V Corps to retreat six miles to the rear, near the Federal river bridges.[78] Porter's men skillfully executed the extensive withdrawal and the next morning found them in another strong natural position on the farm of Dr. Gaines. Confederates, particularly Lee, were amazed when at sunrise the strong Beaver Dam works were deserted. Lee began a pursuit, for although checked the day before, McClellan's nerve was shaken, and he seemed to be relinquishing the initiative to Lee. Once that occurred the gray-bearded Confederate would not relinquish his advantage, for he would become as if a tiger, scenting his prey's weakness and seeking an opportunity to attack. Lee dispatched Longstreet's Division down the Chickahominy's north bank, A.P. Hill's troops on the easily recognized trail of Porter's Corps, and D.H. Hill's soldiers to swing wide to the north, searching for a junction with Jackson and hoping to locate the Union right flank.

Hill's men made excellent time, marching hard in hot weather on the Old Church Road. Dust rose high in columns and the soldiers took on an ashen appearance. Passing Bethesda Church Rodes' Brigade, their thin commander riding in front, turned south toward Old Cold Harbor on the heels of Garland's leading brigade.[79] As the long column neared Powhite Swamp on a narrow land bridge between bog and marsh, Garland's skirmishers and his leading regiment received a sudden, heavy, accurate artillery cannonade from Union guns stationed in the trees ahead. The Jeff Davis Artillery was summoned and, eager to assist, galloped their guns and caissons past the waiting infantry. Unlimbering four guns they prepared to subdue the Union guns. But almost before they could open, a storm of shot and shell swept the road, overwhelming the Alabama artillery unit.[80] The Confederate gunners held their position for almost twenty minutes but were forced to retire, the surviving gunners riding their weapons back through the open ranks of Rodes' and Garland's infantry.[81] Hill decided to await Jackson, who was in overall command on the left. He and Rodes pondered their only avenue of advance, straight ahead and into the swamp and up a wooded hill. Rodes unsuccessfully attempted to approach the enemy position alone but was spotted and fired upon. The Confederates disbursed into the trees to recline in the shade or search for clear water.

When the Valley army commander arrived, he was little better informed than Hill, but he instructed Hill to form his units in the woods and await an expected general army attack.[82] A pale, weak Robert Rodes rode back and forth impatiently in front of his lounging soldiers, scanning the underbrush to his front. The hours dragged by as soldiers read, slept, or played cards. Rations were slim, for most men had consumed what they carried, and springs or streams of drinkable water were few. Finally at almost 7 P.M. with sunlight fading, galloping riders approached and the soldiers began to stir. The army would attack on all fronts, straight ahead and quickly, for Longstreet and A.P. Hill were already moving. Rodes summoned out his regiments to a loud ferocious cheer, and dressing the lines they advanced, flags snapping and measured treads striking the road. Forward the lines advanced, through a light artillery fire and into the thigh deep swamp. Alignment was impossible to maintain, regiments overlapped, others were halted and forced to find new routes. Rodes, his aides, and his regimental commanders worked diligently attempting to maintain contact between units and keep the troops moving forward.[83] The 5th and 26th Alabama regiments crashed out of the morass together almost atop a Union battery, capturing the guns and gunners in one rapid swoop.[84] Colonel Gordon's 6th Alabama raced past the battery and into an open field where they were plastered by ever present and always effective blue artillery. Garland's and Anderson's Brigades also forced their way through the mud and slime, and the three brigades realigned their lines under cover of a hillside. The brigade commanders were observing the enemy gun batteries when Rodes noticed the 20th North Carolina of Garland's Brigade, which had become lost, emerge from some trees directly on the enemy's flank and attack the batteries. It seemed a forlorn, attack but as Federal guns were moved to adjust, Rodes, followed by Garland and Anderson, unloosed every regiment along the swamp's edge in a wild charge which broke the enemy's line.[85] Lieutenant Park of the 12th Alabama recalled that at first the fire was so hot the soldiers lowered their heads as if leaning into a windstorm, but once they reached a deep sunken road near the gun positions they halted and thus sheltered, paid back the gunners. He remarked that the "men were not slow in execution and soon the batteries were standing silent."[86] Shortly, the soldiers went into the batteries with bayonets, remembering the gruesome wounds of their comrades, and woe to the artilleryman slow to surrender. One of Rodes' aides, the very capable Captain Webster, was shot through the head and slain in the charge. A Confederate unit discovered a neatly arrayed line of abandoned equipment including knap-sacks, haversacks, guns, and cartridge boxes. It appeared as if an enemy regiment had dropped all their accouterments in a neat row and fled precipitously.[87] The Confederate foragers enjoyed rifling the haversacks for reading materials, including letters and pictures of attractive ladies.

For once the entire Confederate army had surged forward as one, breaking Porter's lines in numerous places, and Federal captured were numerous although darkness probably prevented the complete destruction of his force. Two of Hill's brigades, Colquitt's and Ripley's, became lost in the swamps and were still missing at dark. But Hill was pleased with the punch of the three brigades on hand. He commended highly the brilliant performances of Rodes, Garland, and Anderson and their excellent troop control.[88] Hill later would contend that his division was in position to completely sever Porter's retreat route if General Jackson had allowed him to attack earlier.[89] Possibly a true statement, but prior to the attack Hill had no notion of exactly where he was located due to terrain.

The excitement and physical demands of the assault caused Rodes' arm wound to reopen as he became exhausted. Rapidly developing a high fever, he was, for a time, unaware of his surroundings. Rodes was evacuated by stretcher and placed in an ambulance for transport to the home of friends in Richmond.[90] His arm was so badly infected that for a time amputation was planned by surgeons, an alternative which he stubbornly refused.

The Confederate army was severely punished at Gaines Mill for its series of uncoordinated, head-long attacks against fixed Union positions backed by the artillery which earned the admiration and hate of every gray-back. Southern casualties were almost eight thousand men while Union forces lost seven thousand men and twenty-two guns.[91] Confederate killed and wounded reached high numbers while almost three thousand Federals were captured prior to dark, including Brig. Gen. John F. Reynolds who fell asleep and awoke a guest of D.H. Hill.[92] General McClellan fell back south of the river, burning his bridges to sever contact with Lee's pursuers.[93] This action, however, isolated him from his supply base and soon huge columns of smoke rose from White House Landing as explosions were heard for miles.[94] Mountains of Federal material were destroyed as McClellan retreated toward the James River and established his new base at Harrison's Landing.

Lee sent Longstreet and A.P. Hill southward in an attempt to cut off the Federal retreat as the long blue column fled toward the James. D.H. Hill's and Jackson's men attempted to follow the retreating troops. The capable and fearless John Gordon again took command of the Alabama Brigade. The weather was hot and progress was frustrating as no contact was established with McClellan's army, except for the sweeping up of prisoners from hospitals or road sides.

June 30 continued hot, humid, and windless in the foul-smelling swamps.[95] Lee's flanking column under Longstreet attempted to break the retreating blue column at the small village of Glendale, and a fierce engagement raged into the night on Frayser's Farm.[96] Longstreet's leading brigades, led by Jenkins, Wilcox, and Kemper, charging head-long into Union guns, tore open the Federal front, taking twenty-six more Federal cannon.[97] But the punch to crack the final Union line held by Kearny's tough Federal III Corps was missing, and five isolated Federal divisions slipped by the thinly held crossroads under cover of darkness.

By sunrise, July 1, an elated Union army was out of the swamps along the Chickahominy and onto an open plateau called Malvern Hill. There, with its artillery lined hub to hub, the blue coats felt they had escaped their persistent pursuit. Terrain approaching Malvern Hill was open and recently cultivated, difficult ground over which to attack.[98] But for a second time, through poor understanding and abysmal staff work, the Confederates launched a series of uncoordinated brigade-by-brigade attacks against the Union lines. Colonel Gordon led Rodes' Alabama Brigade to within close range of the leaping Federal guns but could go no farther and had them lie down and return fire. The 3rd Alabama lost thirty-seven dead and one hundred sixty-three wounded, 56 percent of those who advanced.[99] Another 400 casualties among the Alabamians reduced the brigade to a shadow of its former strength. Many officers were wounded, although the lucky John Gordon escaped with several bullet wounds in his clothing.

Yet when the sun rose, McClellan had again disappeared. He abandoned Malvern Hill and moved his army down to Harrison's Landing, encamping in the marshy, unhealthy lowlands alongside the James.[100] His supply needs were met by the steady line of ships which docked alongside, and the guns of the Union gunboats prevented Confederate attack.

The cost of these Seven Days of Battle was staggering both in human suffering and loss of life. From Oak Grove to Malvern Hill the Army of Northern Virginia lost 3,494 dead, 15,758 wounded, and 916 missing, for a total of 20,168 casualties.[101] By contrast Union losses were 1,734 dead, 8,066 wounded, and 6,055 captured,or 15,855 soldiers.[102] The Richmonders who had breathlessly listened to the roar of the guns, watched the wagon loads of dead and wounded driven through their streets, and helped tend the wounded, were overwhelmed that such a catastrophic event could occur. One young lady recalled that "day by day we were called to our windows by the wailing dirge of a military band preceding a soldiers funeral."[103] Soon interments were so frequent that bands were no longer used and services were conducted en masse. But if Richmonders changed, the combatants changed most. The shock of such sustained ferocious fighting hardened the most naive, the most gentle of men. Soldiers witnessed the mutilation, the death of others, even close friends, so often, they grew indifferent. Many questioned and criticized the leadership which placed them in perilous positions so ignorantly. William C. Dunn, Federal soldier, was anything but diplomatic when he said, "the fact is that we was outgeneraled and McClellan, to escape the blame, throws it on others."[104] Other soldiers were dazed and thankful to be alive as was Jesse Reid of the 4th South Carolina when he wrote his wife, "The greatest battle of the age is over and I am spared to write you."[105]

Lee was now in charge and the war would change. His will would force these alterations, even of his enemy. No longer would warfare see play-acting, posing participants who avoided the dirty and the dangerous. The conflict now became a fight to the finish between large armies possessing frightful destructive energy. There would be no quick victory or defeat: the realist could see the path was to be long, difficult, and bloody. The soldiers who wore blue and gray had displayed their bravery, commitment, and energy in the past month; now they must add persistence, for the days of the short-time patriot were over.

CHAPTER 4

ACROSS THE POTOMAC

South Mountain and Antietam

Robert E. Lee correctly deemed that George McClellan's Federal army, encamped at Harrison's Landing, was virtually unassailable but conversely powerless to threaten Richmond. Harrison's Landing was not a hospitable environment for McClellan's blue-coats, rather it seemed somewhat of a death trap. Oppressive heat and humidity, common to the James River bottoms in summer, became almost unbearable to the woolen-uniformed soldiers, and hordes of black flies and blood-sucking mosquitoes gathered about their camps. Drinking water was of poor quality, for the broad river which flowed so swiftly past their camps was tidal and unfit for consumption, and the shallow wells dug daily by soldiers, quickly turned sour.[1] Proper sanitation was impossible to maintain, and the scourges of diarrhea, dysentery, and malaria caused daily funeral parades and the daily notes of a dirge. Northern newspapers were in full cry, some insisting that Lincoln had abandoned his army by refusing to reinforce McClellan.[2] Other publications equally castigated McClellan's leadership and accused him of inept, even traitorous conduct.[3]

Lee ignored McClellan and moved north, leaving only Maj. Gen. D.H. Hill's Division in proximity to Richmond.[4] By late July, Robert Rodes' Brigade, under Col. John Gordon's command, was encamped below the obstacles at Drewry's Bluff as Confederate engineers continued to perfect the works and insure their invincibility. Rodes was still under his wife's nursing care in Richmond, while his brigade marched north to Hanover Junction.[5] Hill arrived at Hanover Junction by August 21, assuming command of his reassembled division and that of Maj. Gen. Lafayette McLaws.[6] Within days he received orders to march both divisions north to reinforce a Southern army fresh from a resounding defeat of General Pope at Manassas. As Hill's troops stripped to marching gear, a pale and thin Robert Rodes prepared to follow. Probably aware that Lee's request for additional troops indicated further campaigning, Rodes was determined not to be left behind. On September 1, he and Captain Whiting quietly departed the capital.

Hill, however, proved difficult to catch. He pushed his soldiers hard, covering sixty-three miles in three days, joining Lee's army near Chantilly, Virginia on September 2.[7] While his brigade was accustomed to his intense marches, McLaws' men were not and grumbled loudly. Brig. Gen. Howell Cobb, leading a Georgia brigade, became so incensed that he discussed with newspaper reporters the orders of "that incompetent and maybe plain crazy D.H. Hill."[8] Of course, Cobb's recent election to the Confederate Congress from Georgia and subsequent army resignation may have loosened his intemperate tongue.

While Hill and Rodes were moving north, Lee reached a noteworthy decision. He would cross his army into Maryland, searching for rations and encouraging increased support. Rodes' Brigade led Hill's Division toward the fords on September 4. The long, gray column marched a few miles north of Leesburg and began descending the steep banks of White's Ford. Wading across two arms of the Potomac and a sandy island in mid-stream they entered Maryland. Colonel Gordon halted the brigade to deliver a lengthy, patriotic oration as only he could.[9] Few soldiers would recall Gordon's exact words except to remember that he somehow compared this crossing favorably with Washington's similar endeavor on the Delaware.[10] Filled with optimism the brigade bands marched across to the thrilling and somewhat strange tune of "Maryland, My Maryland."[11] Confederate line troops were in rough condition. They were unbelievably ragged, underfed, unwashed, and unshorn. Their ranks were thin, both from Manassas casualties as yet unreplaced and the straggling of thousands with feet bloodied for lack of shoes. Most Marylanders ridiculed the filthy, gaunt men, but several remarked that their cartridge boxes and rifles were shiny and clean, a sign of veteran infantry.[12] A Maryland lady of Unionist sympathy told her friends that

> I could not believe these dirty, lank, ugly specimens of humanity with shocks of hair sticking through their hats....have consistently beaten and driven back our splendid legions with fine discipline, martial bearing, and color.[13]

Food availability increased in Maryland, although not always of a wide variety. Delicious apples and roasting ears of corn could be plucked alongside the road, and the soldiers gorged themselves with both cooked and uncooked corn. One trooper in the 6th Alabama recalled with a grin the scores of fellow soldiers with their digestive systems in open revolt, handing their weapons to a comrade, sprinting for nearby bushes or woods, then returning to locate their place in column.[14] As Hill's men neared Frederick, Maryland they swung into the fields of the Best farm and established camps along a ridge.[15] The soldiers were preparing their evening meal when Brig. Gen. Robert Rodes rode in and resumed command.[16]

White's Ford on the Potomac, Leesburg

The Confederate army streamed across the river on September 4, 1862, Rodes' Brigade leading Hill's Division as the bands blared "Maryland, My Maryland."

Robert Carter

The pace slowed for several days as soldiers relaxed in their Frederick camps. Haircuts, washing clothes, and even bathing their tired bodies in local streams were popular pastimes. Despite close supervision, many found reason to slip into Frederick City for purchases of needed items or sightseeing. Townsmen generally found their conduct excellent, certainly better than their appearance. Dr. Lewis Steiner, an ardent Unionist who wept openly when he heard that followers of the rebellion had set foot on sacred Union soil, stated that he talked to Confederates of all ranks and most knew their cause was a long gamble, but all believed fervently in themselves and their generals.[17]

Rodes found his brigade still consisted of the five Alabama regiments and the men were in good spirits. They were reasonably well equipped but far below strength, numbering only about twelve hundred soldiers.[18] Although the brigade missed combat at 2nd Manassas, few recruits had been added to the ranks so diminished at Seven Pines, Gaines Mill, and Malvern Hill. Their campsite was a pleasant one, alongside the camps of Lee, Jackson, and Longstreet, which were constantly visited by hundreds of gawking Marylanders. The heavily-laden fruit trees in Best's orchards were soon bare, requiring foragers to range further afield.

When Lee took his columns across the Potomac he purposely advanced east of South Mountain, for his army thus presented a threat to either Washington or Baltimore.[19] South Mountain, the dominant physical feature in the area, was more akin to a mountain range as it stretched fifty miles northward from the Potomac.[20] Its highest point was a mere 1,300 feet, but the terrain was rocky, rough, heavily wooded, and crossable by troop formations at only a handful of passes. The principal access was a National Highway which traversed the mountain at Turner's Gap. Lee planned to advance quickly up the eastern slopes to Frederick, then cross the mountain via Turner's Gap, and use the mountain as a barrier or screen while he plotted his next maneuver. After some deliberation he also decided to capture the border town of Harper's Ferry with its garrison of 11,000 Union soldiers and, more importantly, stuffed with supplies and military equipment.[21]

From a military viewpoint, Harper's Ferry was indefensible.[22] The town, fifty miles upstream from the Federal capital, was dwarfed by towering peaks on every side. While the Federal garrison seemed substantial in numbers it was actually little more than a glorified railway guard, for of its nine regiments only two, the 32nd and 60th Ohio Regiments, had seen action. Lee devised a three-pronged attack, placing Jackson in command. He envisioned three columns converging simultaneously at Harper's Ferry and sweeping up the garrison and its needed supplies.[23]

Dr. Steiner, Union Hospital director in Frederick, arose at 4 A.M. on September 10 as Jackson's three divisions of gray-coats were noisily marching out of town, their bands gaily pounding out "The Girl I Left Behind Me." Steiner bitterly recounted that the column seemed amply supplied with shiny new field guns, all displaying "U.S." stamps on their barrels.[24] He could not know that when Jackson exited Harper's Ferry more than seventy additional "US" guns would accompany his troops.

Calmly, Lee, twenty-six brigades dispatched to Harper's Ferry, faced McClellan's huge army, confident that be could read the Federal commander correctly and that there would be no Union attack. On the following morning, James Longstreet's and Daniel Hill's Divisions, led by Rodes' Alabamians, departed Frederick, leaving that small city and its large Union hospital to Brig. Gen. Wade Hampton's gray cavalry. The morning was overcast and rain began to fall as the long gray lines filed through the streets of Frederick. Curious, silent citizens of mixed sympathy lined the streets to watch their departure.[25] Almost leisurely the troops proceeded up the National Road, camping at nightfall on the eastern slopes of South Mountain.

Rodes' marchers, now swallowing the dust of Longstreet's Division, proceeded over Turner's Gap and down the mountainside to the picturesque little village of Boonsboro. Here they discovered acres of supply wagons and most of the armies' reserve artillery, parked in surrounding fields. Rumor of Federals in Hagerstown, a short distance west, brought a rapid response from Lee.[26] He pushed west with Longstreet's two divisions, leaving Hill's Division of five brigades to guard the mountain passes. At this moment, deep in hostile territory, the invading gray-coats were split into five widely separate parts. Lee was calm and unconcerned for he had faced an unsure and nonaggressive "Little Mac" before. Unbeknown to Lee, McClellan had recently discovered a new source of energy and courage, an inside track to Confederate plans of operation. Suddenly the Federal masses began to stir, as McClellan, utilizing this sudden knowledge, issued orders for a vigorous pursuit of the invaders.[27]

On September 13, as the Federal XII Corps paraded into Frederick, two inquisitive Union soldiers discovered a dispatch numbered 191 in the corner of a fence near D.H. Hill's old camp.[28] The order outlined the movements of the Confederate army for the next few days and clearly pointed to its division of force. Strangely, the message found its way directly up the line to McClellan's headquarters, transforming the commander almost at once. He shook off his indecision and apathy, and became aggressive and confident. "Little Mac" wired Lincoln that

> I have all the plans of the rebels and will catch them in their own trap if my men are equal to the emergency. I feel I can count on them as of old. Will send you trophies.[29]

For years, Southern veterans of the Maryland campaign argued vehemently over claims and countercharges as to who lost order #191, which so markedly affected the outcome of the campaign.[30] Whatever the real explanation, Lee's sojourn of more than one week in Maryland would change abruptly. The next day there would be fire and smoke on South Mountain.

Daniel Hill, the caustic yet talented divisional commander, now had full responsibility for protecting the army from sudden attack, as well as guarding the assorted wagons and guns parked about Boonsboro—a heavy burden and one about to increase as a result of the "lost order." Hill's brigades were scattered along the base of South Mountain, enabling Confederates to cover all incoming roads. About noon on September 13 he received a message from Maj. Gen. J.E.B. Stuart. The cavalry commander was falling back from Middletown toward Turner's Gap, and he reported that his riders were being vigorously pursued by two hard-marching Union infantry brigades.[31] Hill instantly realized the serious danger presented if Federal infantry gained possession of the passes on South Mountain, and he ordered a full brigade under Col. Alfred Colquitt to march east, climb the mountain, locate an advantageous position, and await Stuart. As Colquitt's men attained the mountain's crest, Stuart's gray-clad riders appeared, forcing the infantry to move to the side of the road, allowing the carefree riders to proceed west.[32] Colquitt conferred with the cavalrymen and was confused by Stuart's report that there was now only Federal cavalry behind him. Stuart also refused Colquitt's request that he leave two cavalry companies as assistance for the infantry unit. Stuart seemed unthreatened and unperturbed by Federal actions. Colquitt found an excellent position buttressed by a stone wall and encamped. He was close by the National Road almost at the crest of South Mountain in Turner's Gap. As night fell, Colquitt ominously observed thousands of Union campfires appear in the eastern valley.[33] This was Federal infantry and they were coming on in overwhelming numbers.

Sometime during the early morning hours, Hill, nervous and edgy, dispatched a second brigade up South Mountain, the North Carolina soldiers of dapper, young Brig. Gen. Samuel Garland, Jr. Two four-gun batteries accompanied Garland, the Jeff Davis Artillery, an Alabama unit commanded by Capt. James W. Bondurant, and Capt. John Lane's Georgia Battery.[34] Soon Hill followed, reaching the crest about daybreak. Using the observation deck at Mountain House, Hill gazed into the eastern valley for long minutes, then hurriedly dispatched couriers back to Boonsboro. He ordered up every brigade he had available.[35]

Garland's small brigade reached the mountaintop just before dawn, and the immaculately dressed officer dismounted at Mountain House to accept a cup of coffee with Colquitt and his staff.[36] The actual gap in South Mountain was quite wide, being traversed by two major roadways. The National Highway crossed at Turner's Gap while the Sharpsburg Road led across the peak at Fox's Gap, about a mile away. The two routes were connected on the crest by a narrow lane through the underbrush called locally "Ridge Road." Thus whoever desired to hold the crest was forced to defend two roadways.[37] Since Colquitt was already sitting in Turner's Gap, Hill instructed Garland to march south and block Fox's Gap. Within minutes Garland's leading units were double-timing down the Ridge Road followed closely by the bouncing guns of the Jeff Davis Artillery. When Lane's Battery arrived, Hill dispatched them to unlimber on a small knoll north of the National Road, in support of Colquitt.[38]

When Garland's men arrived at the road in Fox's Gap they discovered Union infantry quite near, advancing on a connecting road, which, if unchallenged, would soon flank the Confederates. Brig. Gen. Jacob D. Cox was advancing the Federal IX Corps' Kanawha Division, Col. Eliakim P. Scammon's Brigade in the lead. Garland immediately moved his regiments through Fox's Gap, continued out the Ridge Road, and deployed.

Garland dispatched skirmishers to his right front, feeling for the bluecoats, but they were rudely pushed back. Suddenly, the 23rd and 30th Ohio Regiments rushed Garland's line which stoutly resisted with the exception of the 12th North Carolina. This raw, inexperienced unit broke and fled.[39] Garland spurred his horse down the Ridge Road, attempting to rally the broken regiment. He was reminded by one of his regimental commanders that he should return to a safer position. But Garland persisted and as if for his efforts was immediately shot in the chest and fell from his horse.[40] Only an hour had passed since the enthusiastic young officer had halted for breakfast with his peers on the porch of the Mountain House. Now Garland's staff carried his body back to lie on that same porch.[41]

Garland's Brigade had been cut in two with Col. D.K. McRae of the 5th North Carolina and Lt. Col. Thomas Ruffin, 13th North Carolina, rallying portions of the brigade and continuing to pour fire into the advancing Union soldiers. Some survivors retreated up the Ridge Road following the artillery, but the 20th North Carolina and a part of the 23rd North Carolina were cut off and forced to find their way down the mountain toward Rohrersville.[42] A limited Federal success on one flank came to naught when the 23rd Ohio Infantry's Lt. Col. Rutherford B. Hayes was severely wounded.[43]

Despite stern resistance, the Ohio veterans, reinforced by Brig. Gen. Orlando Willcox's 1st Division of the IX Corps, steadily pushed Garland's survivors out of Fox's Gap, securing the crossroads. Bondurant's gunners hitched their weapons out before being overrun and fell back up Ridge Road. Reaching a clearing near a small cabin they unlimbered and prepared to

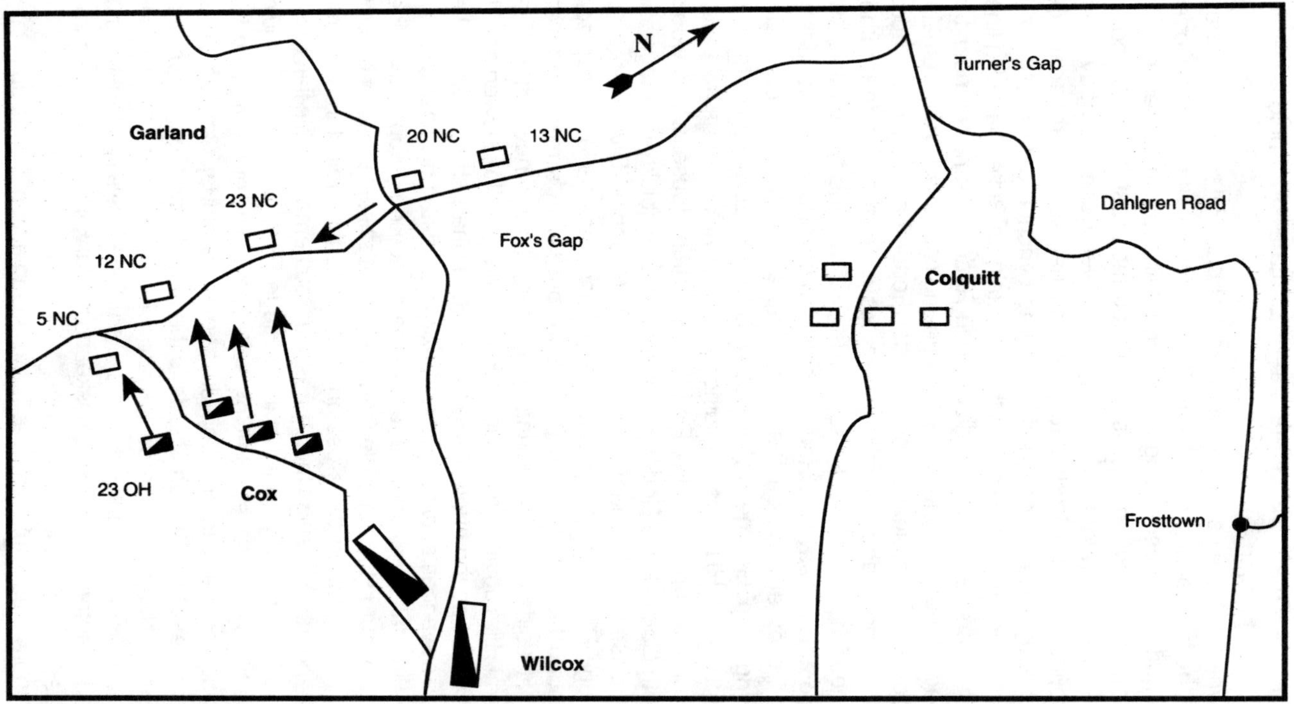

Battle of South Mountain, Fox's Gap, September 14, 1862

When Garland's Brigade arrived at Turner's Gap they were dispatched down the Ridge Road to defend adjacent Fox's Gap. Garland's scattered regiments were attacked and broken by units of General Cox's Federal Kanawha Division.

sweep the narrow road with canister. Underbrush was so thick that the brave Ohio troops were stymied, and the Alabama Battery held an entire enemy division at bay for almost an hour.[44]

Meanwhile in the west valley near Boonsboro, Hill's frantic couriers arrived, and the brigades of Brig. Gens. Roswell Ripley and Robert Rodes swiftly fell in and began ascending South Mountain, passing a descending stream of Confederate wounded. As he neared the crest, Rodes encountered Garland's staff, on foot, bringing their beloved general's body down the steep mountain road.[45] Rodes, removing his hat, stood at the roadside as Garland's body passed on its last journey to Lynchburg.[46]

When the two brigades reached the mountaintop Ripley halted in line, while Rodes' men swept past. Hill dispatched Rodes to a hillock near the National Road to support Lane's already smoking cannons.[47] After remaining in that position for almost an hour, under Federal artillery fire, Rodes was ordered to move about a mile left across a deep ravine to another small knoll near the Frosttown Road. So rugged was the terrain that this movement completely severed Rodes' contact with Hill's other brigades.

Violent action erupted back at Fox's Gap as Hill tried to retake the crossroad. Brig. Gen. George B. Anderson's Brigade had already attacked and been repulsed.[48] Hill began building another attack force as he feared Cox would continue up the Ridge Road to Mountain House, which would endanger both Colquitt and Rodes.[49] This new attack quickly disintegrated as Ripley and George T. Anderson of Gen. D. R. Jones' Division moved down the Ridge Road, took an incorrect turn, and became lost. Anderson eventually found his way back to the action, but Ripley's men stumbled around the back side of South Mountain all afternoon and never drew trigger, to General Hill's obvious displeasure.[50] Gradually, action slowed as Hill realized that Cox was too firmly seated on the Old Sharpsburg Road to be moved. Union advances also ceased as Cox consolidated his position; neither did the Federal commander attempt to advance his troops down the captured Sharpsburg Road into Pleasant Valley.[51] It's likely that Cox did not feel he had a firm grip on the crossroads and was thus reluctant to move men over the mountain, leaving the aggressive Southerners on his flank. Nor did he wish to blast his way up the narrow Ridge Road for to do so would surely cause heavy casualties. So Cox waited for news of the fighting he could hear beginning at Turner's Gap. Just before dark Maj. Gen. Jesse L. Reno, commander of the IX Corps, rode to the mountaintop to discover the cause of Cox's holdup. Reno rode forward with two aides to reconnoiter Confederate positions.[52] As they returned, a cry, "rebel cavalry," went up and a blue-coated infantryman fired his musket point-blank into General Reno's chest who died within a few moments.[53]

A little more than a mile north at Turner's Gap action heated up in late afternoon. When Rodes lost contact with Colquitt he realized his brigade would fight alone most of this day, and what a tough and desperate endeavor it would be. He could easily observe massive lines of blue-coats approaching the mountain, followed by a second wave and a third, all aimed directly at his position. Three divisions of first-rate Federal troops were approaching his lone brigade. The attack was led by the 3rd Division of the I Corps, commanded by the persistent perfectionist, Brig. Gen. George C. Meade, whose three-brigade division contained thirteen regiments of Pennsylvania Reserves.[54] Meade's first brigade, led by Brig. Gen. Truman Seymour, was aligned north of the Frosttown Road, and his remaining two brigades—those of Col. Albert Magilton and Col. Thomas Gallagher—moved up the mountain between the Frosttown and Dahlgren Roads.[55] Their advancing line was so wide and so overlapped his brigade that Rodes was forced to reposition his units. Moving with his left flank as far north as he dared, Rodes posted his best unit, Col. John Gordon's 6th Alabama Infantry, on another small hillock. He instructed Gordon to extend his men as far as possible to prevent Seymour's advancing units from turning his left and gaining his rear.[56] In a gorge or deep ravine which adjoined Gordon's position Rodes posted the 5th Alabama. This unit was placed on deplorable ground, but its position was necessary to maintain Gordon's key anchor position. The 3rd and 26th Alabama Regiments were aligned further south in fields of small mountainside farms, and Rodes placed his fifth regiment, the 12th Alabama, to his right flank on a hill near the artillery position being utilized by Lane.[57] His deployment thus covered a front of 3,500 feet. Due to the spread of distance, dense woods, and extremely rough terrain, none of the Confederate regiments could maintain sight contact with any of the

Turner's Gap, South Mountain

The view from the position in Turner's Gap where Rodes and his brigade held up a Federal division and immortalized themselves.

Robert Carter

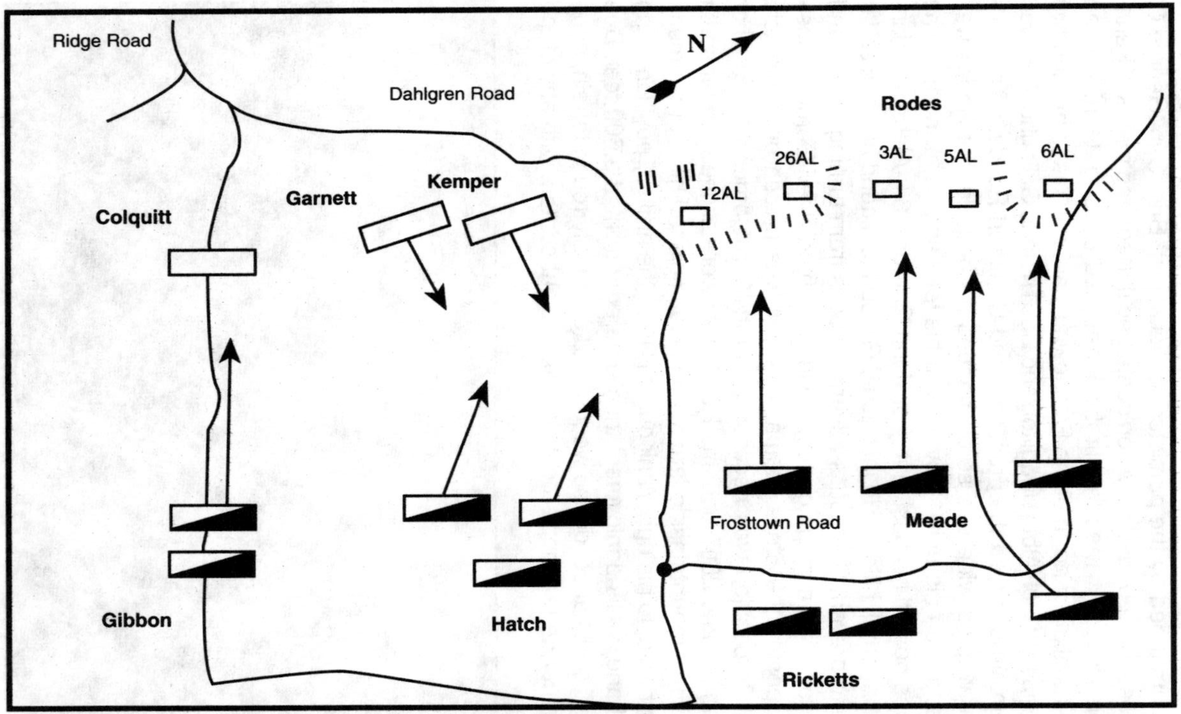

Battle of South Mountain, Turner's Gap, September 14, 1862

In late afternoon furious action erupted north of the National Turnpike. Initially, Meade assaulted Rodes' five regiments north of the Dahlgren Road with his division, then Hatch's Brigade collided with Kemper and Garnett. Finally, Gibbon attacked Colquitt directly up the National Pike. All three clashes continued until after nightfall.

other units.[58] Rodes' troops grew quiet and restless as they viewed the rolling waves of blue-coats moving directly toward them. When they glanced around, only a few hundred defenders could be seen. Even the novice soldier knew they were in a tough spot.

Rodes dispatched skirmishers from each regiment down the mountain slopes where feasible and moved one of Lane's guns left to support Gordon. Back near the gun positions, Colonel Bristor B. Gayle of the 12th Alabama directed Lt. Robert Park to select forty men and move down the slope as skirmishers.[59] Park was to slow down any Federal attack toward the artillery position and his adventures would prove critical to the entire defense of South Mountain. Nervous, riding up and down his lines, Rodes was certain assistance could not be expected to support his units. His only advantage seemed the steep, uphill terrain which Union attackers would be forced to traverse.

It was almost 4 P.M. when a grumpy, demanding George Meade, at last satisfied his regiments were prepared, launched his first line of brigades up South Mountain toward Rodes.[60] Grandly they began to advance, flags waving, mounted officers forward. Soon the difficult terrain broke the perfect line into three separate assault groups, each doggedly moving forward. A second division deployed and followed.[61] Brig. Gen. John Hatch's second line soon veered left, but Meade was closely supported by a third division under Brig. Gen. James Ricketts. A total of 15,000 men were available for use against Rodes' Brigade, but thankfully all could not be committed at once.[62]

Recognizing he could still be badly flanked, Rodes ordered Gordon to slide further left on his ridge top. This order was smartly executed by the 6th Alabama while under fire. A company of Gordon's men actually charged into the woodline, catching the 13th, 1st, and 2nd Pennsylvania Reserve Regiments of Seymour in the flank and forcing their temporary retreat.[63] The 9th Pennsylvania Regiment forced the skirmishers of the 5th Alabama to fall back and moved forward into the deep ravine. The two units, 9th Pennsylvania and 5th Alabama, exchanged fire at a range of fifty yards, both refusing to buckle. The 11th Pennsylvania emerged from heavy brush directly into a volley from the 3rd Alabama and were staggered backward. Meanwhile the 26th Alabama became engaged in a long-range fight with the 12th Pennsylvania. Each Confederate regiment was fighting its own battle and holding its position firmly and resolutely. A closely observing George Meade, however, sent for Brig. Gen. Abram Duryea's Brigade of James B. Ricketts' Division, and gradually the 5th and 26th Alabama Regiments began giving ground under Federal pressure.

On Rodes' right, Lieutenant Park and his skirmishers were well concealed behind trees and rocks near the Dahlgren Road. As the 8th Pennsylvania advanced jauntily upward, they were ambushed by Park's hidden soldiers with two volleys that Park estimated cut down fifty blue-coats.[64]

Three times the Federal regiment regrouped and advanced and each time Park and his riflemen drove them back in disarray.[65] The sun was now a Confederate ally, as the Pennsylvania infantrymen had trouble finding targets and were taking terrific punishment from Park's riflemen. Soon Park had his troops fire and fall back, then repeat the process, using the excellent ground cover. As they retreated, an outstanding sharpshooter, Corporal Myer was shot through the chest. Robert Park halted to give water to his friend. He then recalled:

> As I was about to abandon him to his fate, I found a dozen muskets pointed at me, and I was ordered to surrender....I was mortified and humiliated at the necessity of yielding myself as a prisoner....But certain death was my only alternative.[66]

He and his forty men had contested every inch of ground and delayed the advance of two or more Union regiments for an hour. Low casualty figures in the 12th Alabama speak to their superb performance. A retreat of adjoining Southern skirmishers permitted a section of the 7th Pennsylvania to get behind Park's unit, and most of his men were slain or captured. Park proved a disagreeable and unrepentant prisoner and was soon exchanged to greatly increase his combat experiences before war's end.

Several Union regiments retreated but Meade continued to feed in fresh regiments. Down in the ravine, the 5th Alabama was broken, but the brave and resolute Maj. Edwin L. Hobson led a sizable contingent which cut a path through Federal forces to unite with Gordon's 6th Alabama.[67] The 3rd Alabama, Col. Cullen Battle commanding, resisted so stoutly that Rodes contended if his line had been continuous, they would never have retreated. But when the 5th and 26th Alabama Regiments on either flank gave ground, Battle was forced to also give ground and suffered most of his casualties at this moment. The 4th Pennsylvania, in a resolute attack, shattered the line of the 26th Alabama, wounding Col. Edward A. O'Neal, its commanding officer.[68] Thus Rodes' flanks held solidly while the center, between the hillocks, began to melt away under blue-coat pressure.

Rodes had ridden to the right flank to confer with Col. Bristor Gayle of the 12th Alabama. He dismounted, joining the colonel and Lt. Col. Samuel Pickens as they advanced to a rock outcrop which overlooked the Dahlgren Road, attempting to ascertain if troops moving on that road were Federals or Longstreet's Confederate reinforcements. In the rapidly fading light, the officers peered down into the road. Rodes shouted, "What troops are these?"[69] Someone answered, "Pennsylvania Reserves." At that point Gayle drew his pistol and fired into the dark mass. A tremendous volley exploded in reply. Colonel Gayle was struck twelve times and instantly killed, Lieutenant Colonel Pickens was wounded by a ball through both lungs, but miraculously Rodes was untouched.[70] Several brave soldiers ran forward and assisted Rodes in dragging Pickens back to cover.

Hearing of the break of the 26th Alabama, Rodes vaulted into the saddle and spurred his black horse northward. Circling behind where he thought the 26th should be, he yelled, cursed, and threatened running soldiers, even drawing his revolver. Eventually he gathered sixty to seventy stragglers and marched north on the dark, tree-lined slope. Suddenly he confronted another large group of soldiers which, luckily, proved to be Colonel Battle with a hardcore of 3rd Alabama soldiers.[71] This cadre of 5th, 3rd, and 26th Alabama soldiers continued until united with the still cohesive 6th Alabama and pugnaciously repelled another Union onslaught. They pursued the shaken Federals for a short distance, then Rodes ordered the entire force to slowly retreat back up to the very crest of the mountain. There the defiant survivors continued to yell insults at the Federals below. Rodes then gradually worked the force southward until their left made contact with the National Road. At that point he spread the ranks widely to catch stragglers and allowed his soldiers to lie down and sleep in line of battle.[72] In his report Rodes states:

> We did not drive the enemy back or whip him but with 1200 men we held his whole division at bay without assistance during four and one half hours steady fighting, losing in that time not over half a mile of ground.[73]

While Rodes' units were struggling, isolated out on the Confederate left, another fight exploded nearer the National Road. Brig. Gen. John P. Hatch brought his large I Corps Division into the action. He advanced into a heavy wooded and ravined area between the Dahlgren and National Roads, covering Meade's flank and attempting to get to Lane's guns which had thus far been well protected. If Hatch could break through to the roadway he could swiftly advance and cut off Rodes' stubborn brigade. Fortune smiled on the gray-backs, for Brig. Gen. James Kemper arrived shortly with his Virginia Brigade of Longstreet's Division.[74] At about 5 P.M. Kemper aligned his small brigade and marched at an oblique angle down the slope from the National Road. The difficult terrain slowed progress, but accidently Kemper's men walked into the flank of Hatch's advancing blue-coats.[75] A brutal close-quarter firefight exploded with regiments and even companies fighting separately amid the trees and rocks. Two fresh Union brigades were rushed forward for support and a small brigade of almost four hundred Confederates under Brig. Gen. Richard Garnett also entered the fray. These units, fighting in tough conditions, pounded each other until well past 8 P.M. Garnett's men were routed while the Federal division commander, Brig. Gen. John Hatch, was shot down.[76] Little real advantage was gained and another stalemate was concluded, but one expensive in terms of human life and limb.[77]

Moments after this action began, a final Federal assault rolled straight up the National Highway. Brig. Gen. John Gibbon led his tough western brigade of Wisconsin and Indiana regiments up-slope until they ran into

Colquitt's Confederates. Colquitt's Brigade had been awaiting action all day, listening to battle rage all around them. The Federals ran into a stone wall and suddenly saw flame dance along its length. The 23rd Georgia, behind that wall, was a fighting outfit and in such an advantageous position they just could not be budged.[78] Casualties from the 6th and 7th Wisconsin Regiments collected in front of the wall as the two units were decimated. Attempts to flank the Confederates to either side failed, due to terrain as well as resistance. By 9:30 P.M. this action also ceased with the blue-coated attackers suffering the day's most clear-cut defeat.[79] Colquitt highly commended the performance of Colonel William P. Barclay of the 23rd Georgia.[80]

The fire on South Mountain slowly receded. Union forces would claim victory as the Confederates evacuated after midnight, leaving their dead and seriously wounded to the enemy. But Lee later stated, "the resistance that was offered the enemy at South Mountain secured sufficient time to enable General Jackson to complete his reduction of Harper's Ferry."[81] Hill's assignment, holding the army's rear, was ably completed. Never a man to issue compliments, Hill was positively glowing when he assessed his division's performance. Hill felt that Garland's, Anderson's, and Colquitt's Brigades had fought well; Ripley's had again become lost as at Gaines Mill; and he stated that Rodes' Brigade had immortalized itself.[82] Hill continued that Rodes "Handled his brigade in a most admirable and gallant manner, holding all key points until dark."[83] Gordon, a heavily involved observer, claimed that Rodes personally saved the brigade from complete destruction when, seeing his left-center fall apart as the 26th Alabama disintegrated, he established a new line higher up the mountain and changed his front, facing his entire brigade left, then falling back to the crest.[84]

Rodes did not fail to clearly credit those who had served him well. He felt Colonel Battle and Major Hobson as well as Lieutenant Park and the lamented Colonel Gayle had been admirable in their efforts. But he saved his greatest praise when he complimented the effort of Gordon and his 6th Alabama, who had served as a rock upon which he could rally his remaining soldiers. He remarked:

> Gordon's Brigade was kept well in hand and handled in a manner I have never heard or seen equalled during this war.[85]

At 11 P.M. Rodes awakened his exhausted men and led them slowly down the mountainside, taking the road toward Sharpsburg, eight miles away.[86] The soldiers straggled badly, almost sleepwalking, but Rodes and Maj. Green Peyton, his aide, followed the marchers, rousing those who lay down by the road. At Keedysville, Rodes halted for an hour but received an order to push on with his and Colquitt's Brigade as Federal cavalry was reported in Sharpsburg. The Alabama and Georgia soldiers staggered, sleepwalking through the night and reaching Antietam Creek to discover that the report was in error.[87] Since they were the first unit into town, and no commissary wagons had yet arrived, Rodes' tired veterans simply lay down by the roadside and fell asleep. After a short night, the sun rose, and with it the starving young soldiers began to awake. Soon they were on the prowl, searching through houses, basements, and barns for food, and their young brigadier for once did not interfere. Pumpkins, green corn, and apples were principally their findings, although a lucky group from the 5th Alabama broke into a cellar crammed full of cider which was soon consumed.[88] One soldier reported a cow wandering nearby at an inopportune moment was struck with ten bullets.[89] Cider and beef, although barely cooked, was a gourmet meal. After the wagons arrived, some meager rations were distributed and the brigade moved back through the village of Sharpsburg and into the center of a line Lee was spreading along the small stream. Sharpsburg seemed quiet, peaceful, and quaint to the tired Southerners. Many commented on the beautiful setting, too serene to be disturbed.[90] The Alabama Brigade, which had crossed the Potomac understrength at 1,200 effectives, had sustained 422 casualties at South Mountain, and when stragglers were added, moved into its positions at Sharpsburg with between 600 and 700 soldiers, less strength than any of its five regiments had totaled before Seven Pines.[91]

Lee decided to consolidate his scattered columns behind Antietam Creek near Sharpsburg, since the village was near the Potomac Ford from which Jackson's men would arrive, victorious from the capture of Harper's Ferry, 13,000 prisoners, seventy or more cannon, and mountains of supplies and small arms.[92] While the wide Potomac protected Lee's flanks, it also contributed to his vulnerability. The river was only scant miles from the rear of his army and a defeat would be disastrous, for the one ford available could not handle the rapid retreat of a fleeing army.

The decision to stand and offer battle was Lee's and he took full responsibility. Psychological considerations affected Lee's decision to draw his "line in the sand" and defy McClellan. While he respected the Federal commander, he felt McClellan was hesitant and timid. Lee was so sure of his men, his own ability, and McClellan's personality that he was not afraid to stand and bluff.[93] Lee was, at least at this point, not fully aware of the sudden decisiveness granted McClellan by his discovery of the "lost order."

Additionally, there were two fairly significant political considerations for the move into Maryland, and both demanded a victory north of the Potomac. Both he and Davis had vastly overestimated the response and support they would receive from their sister slave-state. Western Marylanders were strongly Unionist in sentiment and although no active opposition occurred, and locals were reserved but friendly, few recruits enlisted in the gray ranks. The second important political consideration involved the ongoing effort by Southern emissaries to gain recognition from European powers, particularly France and England.[94] While Lee was not an active participant in pursuing these options, he was surely not unaware of these developments. Confederate Gens. Braxton Bragg and Kirby Smith were driving into middle Kentucky with Confederate armies when Lee crossed into Maryland. Confederate military power seemed at its high point. While recognition by these nations on any basis may have been a pipedream, it was never so close as when Confederate armies raced north in the fall of 1862. This hope, which probably would have ensured Southern independence, disappeared forever on September 24, 1862, when Lincoln made public his Emancipation Proclamation.[95] European states might hunger for the products of Southern fields, but never would they dare to recognize a new nation fighting for the continuation of a system of human bondage.

So Lee spread his available force along a wide front following the winding stream, and awaited the return of his absent battalions. Less than 15,000 Confederates manned the lines as twenty-six brigades were still absent.[96] An aggressive attack by the slowly moving Federal army on September 16 would probably have shattered Lee's army. But George McClellan was accustomed to slow, methodical movements, and he spent the day bringing together his 87,000-man force with little thought of action. Confederate units marched in to Sharpsburg all day, gradually filling out the thin line. When completed, Lee's position would wander some four miles over the rural setting. Longstreet's Divisions would hold the Confederate right, Jackson's men the left, and Daniel Hill's five brigades were positioned in the southern center.[97] Hill's line was on flat, almost level, ground and included a sunken road which served as a connector between two turnpikes. Hill originally spread his units in a fan shape with G.B. Anderson's North Carolinians on the right, Rodes' Alabama brigade next, then Garland's badly depleted unit under Col. D.K. McRae, then Colquitt, and finally Ripley's Brigade. Hill thought his position decidedly weak and voiced this opinion to Lee and Jackson.[98]

Rodes' men lay in the shade where possible, munching on roasted corn, ducking when the sporadic Union artillery fire drew near.[99] As the sun went down, the soldiers gathered around their campfires, most being edgy and nervous. Large numbers of men and guns had arrived during the day and at night the trample of footsteps and rumble of caisson wheels continued to be heard by the sleepless. Most soldiers spent a restless night, even the horses were uneasy, and an eerie mist gathered close along the ground before dawn.[100]

Expectations were realized as at first light, Maj. Gen. Joseph Hooker launched an assault on Lee's left with a tremendous burst of noise. His I Corps, deployed in the dark mist, marched out aiming two assault columns at a quaint, whitewashed Dunker Church set in a clearing packed with Confederate reserve batteries.[101] A total of 8,600 blue coats swept noisily and confidently forward in the ground fog, searching for Stonewall Jackson's battle line.

But the ever alert Jackson had most of his two divisions on line. Ewell's Division, under Brig. Gen. Alexander Lawton, was positioned to dispute passage of the cornfield, while Jackson's old division, led by Brig. Gen. John R. Jones, was astride the Hagerstown Road. Two tough brigades under Brig. Gen. John B. Hood were still in camp back of the Dunker Church. Jackson's third division, that of Maj. Gen. A.P. Hill, was at Harpers Ferry paroling captives, thus Lee's temporary loan of Hood's Texans.

Charge and countercharge swirled over the disappearing corn stalks while artillery fired indiscriminately into the field from blue and gray batteries. Losses escalated from these point-blank exchanges and officers were shot down in large numbers. By 7 A.M. the cornfield quieted except for the cries of the wounded. Doubleday's massed brigades advanced primarily through the west woods. Each blue line that advanced found a fresh gray line singing their fearful yell. Soon, Union pressure was so great that Hood's men were summoned from breakfast and like an angry thunderbolt fell on the Union spearhead advancing through the cornfield.[102] By 7:30 A.M. Hooker's and Jackson's commands were in a shambles, having fought each other to a bloody stalemate. But the bloodletting in the cornfield had just begun.

Within minutes the Union XII Corps of Maj. Gen. Joseph K.F. Mansfield entered the arena.[103] More than 7,200 fresh blue infantry, rookie soldiers, many of which had never heard a gun fire in anger, anxiously approached the field of battle. Mansfield retained his troops in combat marching formation as he followed the trail into the cornfield already blazed by the I Corps. Hood's Texans lay in wait as Daniel Hill rushed Ripley's Brigade from his center position to Mansfield's left flank. The closely packed formation made excellent targets for Confederate guns, and they plowed holes in the ranks. When Mansfield attempted to deploy these green troops into line of battle the guns redoubled their fire. Suddenly Hood and Ripley seared their ranks with volleys and all at once the entire formation disintegrated. General Ripley was shot down and carried to the rear, but his brigade, stung by failure to locate the battle at South Mountain, fought on furiously.[104] Federals moved toward Ripley in large numbers, and Hill sent Colquitt's and McRae's men to assist. Colquitt's troops fought hard taking heavy losses, but McRae's demoralized soldiers broke and ran despite the taunts of Hood's veterans. Few Confederate infantry units remained and conditions appeared critical, but when Mansfield and Hooker, both corps commanders, were wounded, the brutal fighting ceased. Almost eight thousand men lay dead or wounded in the wheat field and west woods.[105] The first battle of three distinct attacks, any one of which would have qualified as a major engagement, was over.

Robert Rodes and his brigade could see little of this fierce early morning clash as trees, terrain, and the unusually low-hanging clouds of sulphurous smoke obscured their vision. But they could clearly hear the tremendous crash of musket volleys, the cheers of charging men, and the continual rumble of cannon fire. Those ever-active guns which fired all day and seemed to dominate the battlefield at Sharpsburg were recalled by every soldier who fought along the Antietam. Ripley, then Colquitt and McRae, had been ordered to move left to assist Jackson's hard pressed soldiers. When they began falling back about 9 A.M. Rodes moved his brigade toward the left front. Observing their rapid retreat, Rodes extended his brigade line to the rear of these units, forcing their fleeing remnants to halt and regroup.[106] Hill arrived and ordered Rodes to fall back to form line of battle in a narrow, sunken dirt road. Anderson's Brigade was ordered up on Rodes' right with the two units joining at an angle in the road which was sharp enough to create an elbow or salient. Although Colquitt's men had suffered some losses in their foray on the left, the remainder filed into the sunken road on Rodes' left.

Rodes' gray-clad soldiers tore apart the rail fence south of the road and piled up the rails to form a slight breastwork facing north. While the position appeared quite stout Rodes feared its vulnerabilities. The terrain sloped gently upward from the fence line for about eighty yards then fell rapidly, forming a ridge line which provided excellent cover for approaching attackers. A determined unit forming behind that defile could rush the fence line, taking only one volley. In addition the angle created in the salient made a portion of the Confederate line susceptible to enfilade fire from higher elevations opposite.[107] There was no artillery support in the orchard immediately behind the position. As Rodes and Anderson positioned their units for whatever might occur, a strange, almost overwhelming silence to their left was unnerving. After the loud continual roar which had existed in that sector, the eerie quiet seemed pregnant with danger.

At that moment a third Union corps was staging to enter the fight and quite by accident the thin gray line standing defiantly in the sunken road would be pulled into this maelstrom of death. Maj. Gen. Edwin V. Sumner roused the soldiers of his massive II Corps early that morning, expecting to move in support of Hooker's attack on the Confederate left. His three-division corps was the largest in the Union army, containing 15,200 soldiers. When he finally received orders to march, Sumner crossed the Antietam with two divisions, marching boldly to the beat of their drums, one division aligned behind the other. Sumner rode with Maj. Gen. John Sedgwick, the popular commander of the lead division. Following and gradually lagging further behind marched the division of Brig. Gen. William H. French. Sedgwick's troops presented a brave looking array as they entered the mutilated corn in Mr. Miller's field. The men struggled to maintain ranks in the "Killing Field" where the ground was covered with bodies of the dead and wounded as each attempted to avoid tramping these moaning, waterless, wounded, blue or gray.[108] A stiff Confederate artillery fire began to punch holes in the ranks but no gray battle line appeared in opposition. Entering the West Wood the Union line cautiously continued forward. Emerging from the trees the lead brigade was raked by a volley from a regimental size force rallied by Col. Andrew Grimsley. Then Brig. Gen. Jubal Early's

Brigade emerged from cover on one flank, and reinforcements from Tige Anderson's Brigade and Lafayette McLaws' Division slammed in fire from the opposite side. Sumner's leading division was caught in a cul-de-sac from which there seemed no escape. Unable to maneuver or fight, the ill-fated blue division was almost destroyed.[109]

Meanwhile French's Division had fallen so far behind that they lost contact with Sedgwick. For some unknown reason, French veered left toward those Confederates who were waiting in a sunken road that would ever afterward be known as "Bloody Lane." As they moved over open fields, French shook out his division into three well-drilled brigade lines, marching as if on parade.[110] Through the fields and past the barns of the Roulette Farm they continued, up a slight rise and to the crest of a ridge. At that point the leading unit, Brig. Gen. Max Weber's Brigade, sighted a small but aggressively shouting line of gray coats awaiting behind fence rails in a shallow, sunken road. Halting to fix bayonets, Weber's men moved smoothly over the crest and began marching downhill toward the fist-shaking Confederates. As the line reached a distance of sixty yards from the road, a sudden thunderclap occurred as if hundreds of triggers were pulled by one hand; a flash of flame was seen enwrapped in smoke; and the sickening thuds of bullets striking flesh followed. Weber's entire front rank disappeared and his remaining men fired once into the smoke and fled back over the crest, losing more than 450 men.[111] Col. Dwight Morris' Brigade now arrived and with flags waving and drums beating they passed through Weber's ranks. Morris' superbly drilled but unbloodied brigade approached to within fifty yards when Rodes' clear command, "Present and Fire," was heard. They absorbed two volleys of a more ragged nature before likewise falling back beyond the crest of the ridge.[112] Minutes later, French's third brigade of veterans under Brig. Gen. Nathan Kimball moved to the assault. These experienced soldiers jeered at the crestfallen rookies as they marched past and advanced at the double, but their efforts met with similar results and soon they also were seeking cover behind the crest line. By 10:30 P.M. French's 5,000-man division had suffered 1,817 casualties and two of Sumner's three divisions were broken.[113]

Longstreet, observing the action, noted the Union fire from soldiers lying prone behind the ridgetop was becoming effective on Confederates in the road, particularly those at or near the salient. He sent orders for Rodes to advance his brigade and clear the ridge of Federals. Longstreet was surely not aware of the large number of blue-coats behind the crest, and when Rodes moved out to attack he drew such fire that he immediately recalled his men back into the trench.[114] The soldiers did succeed in stripping Union dead of abandoned cartridges and rifles. Rodes sent word to Longstreet that only an all-out attack could clear the ridge, and that was not a certain outcome.[115]

The Sunken Road, Antietam Battlefield

Rodes' Confederate brigade occupied the left portion of the Sunken Road including the curve or angle pictured above where Gordon's 6th Alabama was posted—a strong yet vulnerable position.

Robert Carter

Rodes and his staff realigned the units, distributed captured ammunition, and prepared for further defense. Losses were mounting in the roadway with many officers down. Col. John Gordon of the 6th Alabama had already taken three bullets but refused to leave his regiment.[116] The soldiers were black-faced from their continual biting of the powder-filled paper cartridges, and throats were dry and water scarce.

Soon another blue wave could be observed advancing. Sumner was sending in his final division, that of Maj. Gen. Israel B. Richardson. The large Irish Brigade of Brig. Gen. Thomas F. Meagher led this division into battle. Marching behind their huge, billowing, green battle flags, these New York City Irishmen were determined to prove their mettle.[117] As they cleared

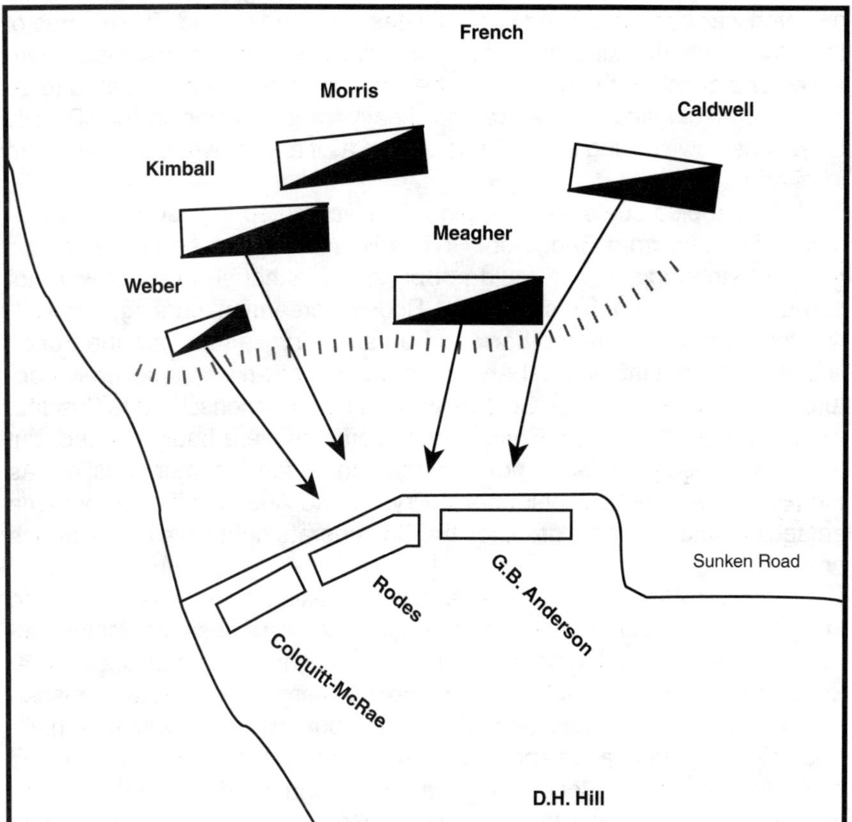

Battle of Antietam, Sunken Road, September 17, 1862

After repeated assaults and heavy losses by brigades of French's Division, a misinterpreted order led to a Federal breakthrough at the elbow of the Sunken Road between Rodes' and Anderson's Brigades.

the ridge, the unit broke into a run, but at forty yards' distance Rodes' thin Alabama Brigade delivered a killing volley into their ranks, then followed up with a rolling fire generated by use of the spare muskets retrieved earlier.[118] Even though their numbers were dwindling, the Alabamians possessed enough muskets to maintain terrific firepower, and they unleashed all they possessed on the Irishmen.

Lee was scrambling to scrape units from other sectors and already artillery batteries were arriving in the orchard. Federal fire was increasing and the line must be held, for penetration would sever the wings of the Confederate army. A fifth Union brigade was approaching. This unit was commanded by Brig. Gen. John C. Caldwell, although as the brigade prepared to attack, he could not be located. The onslaught was delayed while a search was conducted and subordinates prepared to lead. The residue of the other four attacking columns, particularly Meagher's Irishmen, were rallied and attached themselves to the Union front for what appeared to be one final all-out effort. Rifle fire was heavy, as the action in the "Bloody Lane" was now sucking in hundreds of men as if a giant whirlpool had them in its grip.

As the blue-coats were staging, Lee attempted to rush in reinforcements. Soldiers from Brig. Gen. Pryor's Brigade appeared in rear of the road but stood idle. Pryor could not be found, although this fact was not surprising to many of his soldiers.[119] Rodes, screaming, cursing, and spitting tobacco juice, charged back and ordered Pryor's men into the trench line. At that moment General Anderson was cut down with a severely fractured ankle while Colonel Gordon was knocked unconscious by his fifth wound, a ball to the face. Pryor's reinforcements were badly needed, but this was probably the worst possible moment to feed them into action. As the blue lines launched their attack, Pryor's and Anderson's men became entangled, and the entire group on the Confederate right gave up the trench and fled.

The 6th Alabama near the salient was taking heavy casualties, and Lt. Col. James Lightfoot rushed to Rodes, in Gordon's absence, for instructions. Rodes directed Lightfoot to pull back his right two companies in order to refuse the Union penetration. Lightfoot became confused and rushed back to order in a loud voice, "6th Alabama, About Face, Forward March."[120] The entire regiment faced about and moved to the rear, soon to be followed by Rodes' other units. Rodes and an aide, Lt. John Birney, started left when Birney was struck in the face by a bullet. Rodes caught Birney as he fell, pulling the lieutenant to cover behind a rock. As he turned to see his brigade falling back, Rodes was struck in the thigh and knocked sprawling.[121] Rising to find his wound minor, he found himself between the lines and grabbed Lieutenant Birney to drag him to safety.

Federal infantry moved into the roadline when the Confederates fell back inflicting casualties by firing into the backs of the retreating men.

Suddenly not a single gray infantryman stood between the blue masses and victory.[122] A thin line of Confederate guns formed the lone opposition. If Sharpsburg was truly artillery hell, these Southern gunners were bidding to gain admittance.

Capt. M.B. Miller's company of the famed Washington Artillery of New Orleans was first into action, soon to be joined by Capt. Richard Boyce's South Carolina Battery.[123] Soon the Jeff Davis Artillery, an Alabama Battery of South Mountain fame, arrived.[124] Bullets from the Federals sung through the orchard like wasps, but the pounding of the guns never ceased. As artillerymen went down, infantrymen, even Longstreet and his staff, served the guns. Boyce estimated his guns fired seventy rounds of canister into the Federal mass at a range of seventy yards or less.[125] The batteries were soon firing double charges of canister from red-hot barrels. Gunners avoided the time consuming task of swabbing the barrels after each discharge by "thumbing the vents," a dangerous process by which a gunner kept his thumb over the gun vent to prevent oxygen from entering the chamber and setting off the charge prematurely while the loaders tamped in powder and shot. When the gunner removed his thumb the cannon immediately fired. Firing these heavy double-canister loads, the guns recoiled four to five feet, and the gunner who was firing with his thumb had to ride the gun back, which required the agility of a monkey. This crucial fire was ultimately effective, for the blue coats were forced to grudgingly give ground before the storm of whistling, lethal, little iron balls. Lt. Col. Nelson A. Miles of the 61st New York commented that the artillery firing out of the orchard was the most effective he had ever experienced and that no one could survive its fire.[126] Rodes, meanwhile, rounded up by plea or threat several hundred soldiers which he spread out as skirmishers in the fields alongside the gunners.

Richardson's gradual withdrawal was frustrated by the Union officers' repeated and ignored requests for front-line artillery support. About 1 P.M. the battle for "Bloody Lane" diminished in ferocity after almost three and one-half hours of frantic combat.[127] Three thousand blue-coats had fallen alongside 2,200 Confederates. Richardson fell victim to a Confederate case shot, and when he was evacuated, action ceased and the guns finally fell silent. Richardson would succumb to his wounds six weeks later, still convinced that if he had been properly supported by artillery the entire Confederate center would have splintered. One Confederate expressed the beliefs of many when he declared himself "grateful to have escaped this mutual extermination." Another Federal corps had fought itself out without clear cut results.

Slowly, Rodes and Hill rebuilt a thin defensive line in the all but fractured Southern center.[128] Infantry units were regrouped as soldiers returned from assisting wounded, and those with slight wounds were recalled. When the Federals withdrew from the sunken road, it remained unoccupied in a sort of no man's land between the armies. Its roadbed was filled with dead, for the few wounded which sought cover there were by now surely decimated by the storm of Confederate canister.

The gallant Colonel Gordon, awakened in a dazed condition, found himself alone, for when his regiment fell back they believed him dead. Too weak to support himself, Gordon crawled some one hundred yards to the line Rodes was rebuilding.[129] His crawling probably saved his life as he was directly under the crackling discharges of the Southern guns. Gordon's loss of blood and severe facial wound that required the wiring of his jaw, left him incapacitated for months.[130]

Rodes' losses were substantial. Fifty Alabamians were slain, one hundred thirty-two wounded, and twenty-one missing, for a total loss of two hundred and three men. Many of these losses occurred when the unit abruptly retreated from the sunken road, exposing their backs to enemy rifle fire. When combined with the heavy losses at South Mountain, 631 of the 1,200, or 53 percent of the men who crossed the Potomac were listed as casualties.[131] Losses among officers were critical at the divisional as well as brigade and regimental levels. Hill reported three of his brigade commanders wounded: Ripley, Rodes, and McRae, while Garland was slain, and George Anderson would die of complications from his ankle wound.[132] Rodes lost one regimental commander, Gayle of the 12th Alabama, and had three, Gordon, Lightfoot, and O'Neal, wounded.[133] The Confederate army could not long sustain or replace these enormous losses in field leadership.

It was 1 P.M. and three large Federal army corps had been mauled, but the third and final phase of this long day's action had barely begun. Since mid-morning McClellan urged an advance on the Union left by the uncooperative Maj. Gen. Ambrose Burnside and his IX Corps. However, the Antietam was four to five feet deep and its banks were steep and muddy. The single bridge, a massive stone structure one hundred twenty-five feet long, was narrow and easily defended by the enemy. Confederates were dug in on the heavily wooded heights west of the creek and well supported with artillery. Originally two gray divisions had opposed the IX Corps, but Lee had borrowed heavily from this sector to support his left and center. Brig. Gen. David R. Jones' Division of about three thousand men was now the only opposition for Burnside's Corps of four divisions, or 12,500 men.

Col. Henry L. Benning's Brigade of Georgians successfully stalled each Federal attempt to take the bridge. The poorly coordinated rushes were easily repelled.[134] Eventually Union batteries moved up close and blasted the hillside, forcing Benning's retreat. A select Union strike force, led by the 51st Pennsylvania, bravely stormed the bridge.[135] Once the bridgehead was established, three full Union divisions crossed and began deploying for an attack. A delay of several hours for lack of ammunition was disturbing, but a little after 3 P.M. the ponderous and impressive Federal column moved forward.[136]

Almost forty Confederate cannon were waiting and blasted the Federal column with tremendous punishment, but the plucky blue lines continued their advance.[137] As had been the case all day, Confederate guns concentrated their fire against blue-coated infantry, while the well-served Northern guns concentrated on counterbattery fire, and played havoc with Southern artillerymen. Their losses were so severe that many Confederate batteries had to be completely reorganized after the campaign.[138] While the gray gunners enjoyed their finest day it was also their most costly. Lee deployed Jones' men wisely and moved other units to assist whenever he could. Gradually the Federal advance was slowed and when A.P. Hill's Light Division arrived from Harper's Ferry and counterattacked, defeat was again averted. A Confederate private exclaimed, "Finally, the sun went down."[139]

Thus ended the most costly one-day combat in the history of American warfare. The two armies had literally torn each other apart. Union losses were recorded as 2,108 slain, 9,540 wounded, and 753 missing, for a total of 12,401 casualties. Confederate losses were estimated as 1,546 killed, 7,752 wounded, and 1,018 missing, or 10,316 total. Neither army reported large numbers of prisoners, thus it's very likely that many of the 1,771 missing soldiers were actually slain.

Despite the critical condition of his army, Lee refused to leave Maryland. Straightening out his lines, repositioning his artillery, and issuing rations and ammunition, he prepared to receive additional attacks on the eighteenth.[140] Rodes estimated that he had accumulated 1,500–1,700 soldiers in the Confederate center by early morning, all that he could find of Hill's Division. [141] The day dawned quietly and grew hot and humid as the Confederates, waiting on line, realized the Federals were not coming again. About mid-morning, Federal authorities requested a truce to bury their dead.[142] As they dug, long wagon trains of wounded Confederates began leaving the barns and cellars which had served as hospitals, and began splashing over the river, starting the long jolting ride back to Winchester.[143] A soldier of Hill's Division recalled:

> We were in line of battle all day....then we buried our dead....It seemed very curious to see the men on both sides come together and talk to each other when the day before were firing at each other.[144]

During the night of September 18–19 Lee's army withdrew by Boteler's Ford, back into Virginia. No Federal opposition occurred when at dawn on the nineteenth the Confederate rear guard crossed the river.[145] The first serious Confederate attempt to take the war to the enemy's country thus concluded.

CHAPTER 5

A WINTER OF RENEWED HOPE
Fredericksburg

Within days of his return to Virginia, Lee gathered his tired, ragged soldiers near a rural intersection called Bunker Hill. This site, some five miles north of Winchester, provided an excellent camping area with level, open fields and groves of shade trees. Nearby were creeks and springs which provided ample fresh water.

The long wagon trains of wounded initially had halted in the Winchester hospitals, then those soldiers with serious injuries were shuttled further south to Staunton or Lynchburg, where hospitals could now handle more than 5,000 casualties.[1] Medical facilities, although still crude, were improving. Confederate troops possessed few tents or shelters, so they erected long brush shelters along roadside fences and among the trees, comfortable quarters for fall.[2] The weather remained hot and dry with regiments engaged at drill virtually obscured by clouds of dust. Lee's initial concern was for adequate rations, and through the generosity of the local populace considerable improvements occurred in quantity of foodstuffs. The badly needed shoes were, however, another matter. Although thousands were obtained, those imported of English manufacture were so poor in quality they soon fell apart, and the number of barefoot soldiers remained high.

Stragglers, slightly wounded soldiers, and some who had taken "French leave" began returning to the ranks. Additionally, a number of new recruits were added to some regiments. The overall strength of the army increased by more than 20,000 men in just a few weeks.[3] Many units, such as Rodes' Alabama regiments, were far from home recruiting bases, but a revision in the Conscription Act which extended the draft age to all males between 18 and 45 years of age abetted recruiting. A number of recuperating wounded and those few soldiers whom Rodes granted furloughs returned to Alabama with incentives of extra leave days for each recruit they could muster.

Despite competition with Alabama regiments fighting on the western front, Rodes' veterans brought back significant numbers of friends and relatives. Robert Rodes' regiments were never lacking in hours spent on drill, and assimilation of these newcomers was rapid. Regrettably, many of these deep South recruits suffered severely with illnesses during their first exposure to winter in Virginia.[4]

Rodes altered his campsites often, moving about the Bunker Hill area every few weeks. Medical officers may not have understood the causes of the serious diseases which ravaged the camps, but it was evident that changes in water sites and fresh latrines greatly reduced the episodes of sickness. The Confederate army improved dramatically in both its physical strength and its morale during these few weeks of rest and recuperation.

Lee was forced to reorganize his forces following the Maryland campaign as casualties among the officer corps had reached serious proportions. He formalized the corps' structure already being utilized by promoting James Longstreet and Thomas Jackson to lieutenant general and placing them in corps command. Each corps would contain four infantry divisions, with Jackson's 2nd Corps consisting of the divisions of Maj. Gen. Ambrose Powell Hill, Maj. Gen. Daniel Harvey Hill, Maj. Gen. Richard Ewell, temporarily led by Brig. Gen. Jubal Early, and Jackson's old division led by Brig.Gen. William Taliaferro. Harvey Hill's Division was assigned the same five brigades he had led into Maryland, although several of the units had new commanding officers. Rosewell Ripley, wounded in the throat, returned to South Carolina and George Doles of the 4th Georgia was promoted to brigadier general in his stead.[5] The highly regarded Stephen D. Ramseur, 25-year-old colonel of the 49th North Carolina, was promoted to lead the brigade of the mortally wounded George Anderson. Ramseur, however, seriously wounded himself at Malvern Hill, had not yet returned to duty and Col. Bryan Grimes of the 4th North Carolina temporarily commanded.[6] Alfred Iverson was named brigadier general to replace the slain Samuel Garland, Jr. The intrepid Col. John B. Gordon was recommended for brigadier by Rodes and Lee, but the War Department had already elevated Col. Alfred H. Colquitt.[7] Gordon had been so severely wounded in the sunken road at Sharpsburg that his recovery was doubtful. Colquitt and Rodes continued to lead Hill's other two brigades, Rodes now the senior brigadier.

This calm interlude was interrupted by a series of arguments, accusations, and formal charges among the general officers in Jackson's Corps. The recently elevated lieutenant general was at serious odds with Maj. Gen. A.P. Hill and several other officers. D.H. Hill, suffering spinal pain constantly, became more caustic and critical. His personal relationships seemed to deteriorate amid constant sarcasm as his disability increased. Hill had few friends, but was closer to those officers in his employ who shared his devout and pious nature.[8] Hill and Rodes shared a friendly, cooperative relationship despite Hill's deploring the lack of Christian commitment on Robert's part.

J.W. Ratchford, Hill's youthful chief of staff, was a loyal supporter of his commander, but on one occasion, Hill's biting comments convinced him that the major general desired to replace him with an older, more experienced officer. Ratchford went to Rodes "whom he admired greatly although regarding him as anything but a Christian man" and applied for a vacancy on Rodes' staff.[9] Rodes reacted by calling the young officer to his tent and in his uniquely direct manner inquired why Ratchford wished to leave Hill. When Ratchford explained, Rodes emphatically insisted that Ratchford approach General Hill and repeat his concerns. Rodes explained that if Hill truly wished Ratchford to leave, he would then consider him. As Rodes postulated, Ratchford's fears were unrealized as Hill assured him of his earnest desire for his continued services.[10]

Union Commander George McClellan continued to permit his potent Army of the Potomac to idly reside in camps north of the Potomac while Lee's troops rested, refitted, and reorganized. Lincoln pushed his commander in chief to advance into Virginia and initiate action. Finally on October 26, McClellan sent two divisions of the IX Corps across the river to invest Leesburg, and soon the I Corps and VI Corps followed.[11] In late October, Lee moved Longstreet's 1st Corps over the Blue Ridge Mountains and into the Piedmont near Culpeper. Jackson remained at Winchester with his 2nd Corps, marching north to destroy Federal railway lines every few weeks. Gradually, McClellan moved his entire force into Virginia but still resisted offensive movements, blatantly ignoring Lincoln's directives.[12] By November 5, the now irate chief executive decided to once more change army commanders. He relieved McClellan and replaced him with the popular Maj. Gen. Ambrose Burnside.[13] Opinions varied among Federal and Confederate officers on McClellan's removal as Robert E. Lee commented:

> I fear they may continue to make these changes till they find someone whom I don't understand.[14]

With uncharacteristic energy, Burnside organized his inherited army into three so-called grande divisions and issued a memorandum which revealed his campaign strategy:

> concentrate all forces near Warrenton and impress the enemy that we are to attack Culpeper or Gordonsville, and at the same time accumulate a four or five day supply for men and animals, then make a rapid move of the whole force to Fredericksburg, with a view to a movement upon Richmond from that point.[15]

By November 18, Burnside's entire army was on the march led by Sumner's Grande Division. Longstreet's 1st Corps moved eastward on a parallel track, and on November 20, Jackson's 2nd Corps broke camp near Winchester, marching out in cold, severe weather, with snow already covering the valley floor.[16]

The march from Winchester to Fredericksburg was remembered for its difficulty, especially for those many Confederates who lacked shoes. Sleet or snow fell daily and icy winds howled, turning the roads into sheets of ice.

Hill's Division utilized the service of a provost guard to prevent straggling. Behind each unit marched the provost accompanied by a surgeon and several ambulances. Those who fell out of ranks were examined by the surgeon and if sick or injured placed in the ambulances.[17] Those who fell out without cause were arrested and sentenced to hard labor in the pioneer corps. Straggling was reduced and possibly some deaths from exposure prevented. Hill's ailments forced him to turn over his division to his senior brigadier while on the march, and Rodes led the unit two hundred miles in ten days despite horrid weather. A misunderstanding occurred which Rodes regretted and quickly resolved.

Not aware that Rodes was in charge of the division, Col. Bryan Grimes, leading Ramseur's Brigade, rode up alongside Rodes who was calmly sitting astride his horse observing the troops wade the Shenandoah River. Grimes began complaining about procedure, commenting to Rodes concerning the order that forbade his men to remove their pants and shoes while crossing the icy river. Rodes listened for a while, then replied in sharp tones that he saw nothing hard in the order, that he was in command of the division, that the order emulated from him, and that Grimes had best see it obeyed. Silently fuming, Grimes crossed his troops, then halted to allow them to reorganize their belongings. Rodes rode up and asked why the troops were halted in disobedience to Jackson's standing orders to stack arms. As Grimes angrily passed that order, Rodes requested the unit remain there until an expected artillery unit passed. Hours passed and no artillery. At last a courier from Rodes arrived to ascertain the delay. Grimes sent word he was waiting for the artillery. Rodes then ordered him to proceed but was waiting on the hotel porch at Paris, the next village. Rodes asked, "What took you so long?" Grimes angrily replied, "Obeying your orders to await the artillery, I should have remained there until artillery passed or General Hill resumed command."[18] Rodes did not reply but stalked off and rode away. The two officers were decidedly cool to one another for weeks. But later, when each could recognize the fighting qualities in the other, Rodes glowingly recommended Grimes for promotion to brigadier, and eventually the two officers became friends.[19]

On November 30, Hill's Division reached the hills back of Fredericksburg. Next day Hill returned to resume command and was ordered to conduct his division twenty miles downstream to the small village of Port Royal.[20] Lee anticipated a Federal flanking movement in that area, but no blue-coated infantry appeared. Instead on December 5, Rodes' Brigade was ordered out, accompanied by the division artillery battalion, to shell five Union gunboats which were anchored in the river opposite Port Royal. After an exchange of cannon balls the vessels steamed away only to return with consorts primed for battle. Hill's batteries repelled them again despite Hill's comment that Confederate gunmanship was deplorable.[21]

On Thursday, December 11, Rodes' shivering men awoke to the rumble of gunfire upriver as Union artillery on Stafford Heights began feeling out

Confederate positions spread along the hills south of Fredericksburg. Lee had selected excellent defensive ground from where he would contest any Federal river crossings. Longstreet's 1st Corps was entrenched directly behind the city in a stout position, culminating in a stone wall behind which Confederate defenders could shelter in a sunken roadway. Jackson's men, downstream to the east, were in less natural strength but were ensconced in dense woodland where they were well concealed from the enemy.

Despite stubborn Confederate resistance, Burnside's blue-coats succeeded in completing six pontoon bridges over the Rappahannock. Three led into Fredericksburg and the remainder were downstream opposite Jackson's hidden soldiers. At dawn on the twelfth the Federals began crossing while at Port Royal; D.H. Hill's Division was ordered to prepare rations for three days and be ready to march.[22] The soldiers waited in columns all day, receiving no orders until dark when Jackson requested that they join his corps. A miserable, cold march of eighteen miles brought the brigades to a ridge on the Confederate extreme left about 3 A.M.[23] So severe was the cold that sleep was impossible. The soldiers pulled down and burned rail fences by the mile to avoid frostbite.[24] At break of day, Hill's units moved forward slightly, taking position in Jackson's third or reserve line on a semicircle facing the river. The Alabama soldiers, warmed up by the sun and bogus coffee, were in excellent spirits and full of fight. Rodes and Hill joined Jackson, riding forward to view the splendid array of blue-coats massed in the river bottom. They then slowly returned to their reserve positions. Rodes could hear each of four separate Federal lines attack against Jackson that morning, but so stout was the Confederate position that each was repelled. D.H. Hill's Division remained idly in reserve.[25] A small penetration by Maj. Gen. William Smith's VI Federal Corps into a railway cut near Deep Run Creek brought a call to Hill for support.[26] He dispatched his best brigade, that of Robert Rodes, and the troops excitedly moved out at double time in files of four, eager for action.[27] But Brig. Gen. E.M. Law's Brigade of Hood's Division was closer and counterattacked, sealing the breach. Rodes and his men reversed their march and returned to their reserve position.

After noon, Burnside altered his attacks to Longstreet's lines and Rodes' Brigade again listened to the cheers of combat coupled with the crack of rifle volleys. By nightfall some twelve thousand Union soldiers lay dead or wounded between Confederate lines and the Rappahannock.

General Jackson, impatiently awaiting further attacks, decided to organize an assault of his own. He would charge the Union soldiers in his front and hopefully drive them into the river. Jackson planned to lead with a tremendous artillery barrage, pushing his guns out of the trees into the open. Then a two-division assault would follow through the guns, utilizing D.H. Hill's and Taliaferro's Divisions to be supported by A.P. Hill's and Early's men.[28] Rodes moved his brigade forward and aligned his regiments promptly at dusk.[29] The attack lost its momentum when Jackson's A.A.G., Major

Pendleton, was wounded. The corps' staff seemed to fall apart with Hill receiving attack orders and beginning his advance while other units stood by awaiting commands. Jackson attempted to persist by delivering orders himself. But when his artillery batteries were rolled forward and opened fire, they were overwhelmed by Federal large-caliber guns north of the river. So severe was their punishment that Jackson called off his attack.[30] Soon all gunfire ceased and the field was alive with uninjured or slightly wounded blue-coats seeking their own lines under cover of darkness. Thousands more, seriously wounded and unable to move, were beginning the long attempt to survive the cold night.

Several hours after dark a brilliant, pulsing, white and red light spread across the northern sky. An aurora borealis, or northern lights, illuminated the frigid battlefield, a phenomenon which few of the Southern boys had ever seen.[31] The Confederates worked by the light display, deepening their trenches, for the repulse of Burnside's troops had been so easy that few Southern soldiers realized the tremendous damage inflicted on their foe. Federal losses at the foot of Marye's Heights were fearsome. Almost 8,000 blue-coats had fallen in piles three to seven men deep.[32] Longstreet had correctly surmised, when Lee expressed his concern over the vast lines of infantry marching at his position, when he replied:

> General, if you put every man on the other side of the Potomac on that field to approach me over the same line and give me plenty of ammunition, I will kill them all before they reach my lines.[33]

It was becoming evident to even the most uninformed soldier that recent changes in weapon design provided soldiers fighting defensively with a distinct advantage. Rifled muskets, now mass-produced, were the standard infantry weapon of both armies and had an effective range against massed troop formations of two hundred and fifty yards. Infantry tactics, however, were still based on defenders using the old smooth-bore muskets which required a capable marksman to strike a man-sized target at fifty yards.[34] Defenders could open fire with attackers so far away that veteran troops could deliver four or even five volleys before attackers could close, thus assaulting columns were often decimated before bayonets could be of any use. Colonel Fox of the Union army succinctly summarized the required change in tactics when he stated:

> there was a limit of punishment beyond which endurance would not go and the Springfield rifled musket was capable of inflicting it.[35]

So rarely were bayonets employed that many soldiers discarded them or utilized them as candle holders. Gen. John Gordon, a Confederate who experienced as much close fighting as any man, declared that to his recollection bayonets were almost never used as weapons.[36]

Artillery weapons were also evolving with rifled barrels which threw heavier shells a greater distance with more accuracy. With this rapid weapon development and a marked reluctance to change tactics of attack, casualty rates soared. Gradually, tactics dictated entrenchments or light earthworks whenever possible. Soon soldiers of both armies began to dig when halted in the near proximity of the enemy, realizing by thus working they increased their chance of survival.

Rodes and his men were sure Burnside would renew his offense on Sunday and concluded it was their turn to man the trenches. But the Federal army stirred very little on December 14. Sharpshooters traded fire but the two large forces simply stared at each other at close range. Confederate attacks were forestalled by the presence of the superb Union artillery, and Federals were not anxious to again advance into the forbidding-looking Southern trenchline. As rain began to fall, the Army of the Potomac recrossed its pontoons after dark, took up their bridges and marched back to their Stafford Heights camps.

As contact was effectively severed, the Confederate army began to prepare winter quarters. Horses and artillery were dispatched closer to Richmond, and Infantry units fell back from the Fredericksburg lines and began construction of log huts as pine forests disappeared overnight. Neat, orderly rows of snug cabins arose with canvas roofs and mud and log chimneys. Soon a steady stream of smoke spewed skyward, lending a domestic touch to the camp scene. Company huts, churches, and sutler's quarters completed the small villages which each brigade constructed. Officers usually rented nearby houses, particularly if their wives were expected to put in an appearance for the winter.

General Jackson established his headquarters near Moss Neck some nine miles below Fredericksburg in a location somewhat central to the camps of his divisions. Moss Neck Manor was the home of the wealthy, socially prominent Corbin family, and Jackson, while refusing rooms in the house, maintained headquarters in tents erected in their front yard. An amusing incident in late December was recalled by young McHenry Howard. The Maryland Confederate had arrived at General Jackson's headquarters seeking a letter of recommendation for a staff appointment. He remembered:

> Toward evening three general officers came in, one was Maj. Gen. Jubal Early, another Maj. Gen. Robert Rodes,[37] and the third I do not recall—and they were asked to stay to dinner. A turkey—I think it was—was placed on the table in a large tent in which we were, and at this moment General Jackson went out for some purpose....Dr. Hunter McQuire, who had been lying on his pallet, sprang to his feet with a suddenness which almost startled me and said, "Gentlemen, would you like a drink before dinner?" The officers made no reply....McQuire reached down and pulled out a canteen from under his bed and thrust it into the hands of one of the Major Generals, saying "Drink quickly, the general will be back in a moment," and these generals, high in rank, and I—longo intervallo—drank hurriedly, like schoolboys doing some wrong on the sly. McQuire

> hastily shoved the canteen back and we all straightened up just as Jackson reentered, whereupon we sat down to dinner. If Stonewall smelled anything, he made no sign.[38]

Rodes established his headquarters near Grace Church, southeast of Fredericksburg,[39] renting a small cottage so that Virginia could join him from Lynchburg. Many officers did likewise and even the stern Jackson was most anxious for his spouse, Anna, to join him at Moss Neck. The Jacksons had recently become parents of a baby girl whom Stonewall had not seen. He realized, however, the dangers of exposing an infant to the disease-laden army camps. Jackson was positively envious when he wrote Anna that he had recently seen Mmes. Generals Longstreet, A.P. Hill, and Robert Rodes riding about the camps, happy in the company of their husbands.[40] When Jubal Early, the corps' crusty old bachelor, complained about the number of women in camp, Jackson cut off his complaints with plans of Anna and young Julia visiting him in the spring. Again he wrote Anna that he had seen Mrs. Rodes in church and she was positively beaming[41]—undoubtedly over her success in getting her husband to finally attend services.

Despite the severe weather and the social obligations brought on by his wife's companionship, Rodes maintained his stern, uncompromising approach to daily drill. His brigade had grown by recruitment and his casualties at Fredericksburg had been minimal. He believed the new soldiers still needed drill whenever possible. The weather often curtailed his plans as a soldier wrote home:

> It's rained for five days in a row, but we are in snug winter quarters and I'm glad. Old Rodes will die for he can't drill us at double time for five hours a day.[42]

Winter in the Fredericksburg camps, although cold, was still recalled by many with pleasure. Morale was high; constant snowfalls prevented military exercises and provided ammunition for bitter snowball battles between regiments, brigades, and even divisions. Georgia and Alabama troops learned to ice-skate on homemade shoes. The religious revival that began in Winchester was rekindled in fervor and seemingly swept the camps. Even Robert Rodes, under the ministrations of his wife, Virginia, became a regular attender at services, to the surprise of his soldiers.

Rodes also attempted to host his share of the dinner parties with which general officers were expected to entertain one another. Often they received gifts with which their cooks would attempt to produce meals of superior cuisine. On one occasion Rodes invited a number of officers of Hill's Division to a well-prepared repast, the events being recorded by an officer of the 12th Alabama:

> A well-known corporal in the 12th Alabama named Henry Fowler was detailed with two others as Brigade Headquarters guard for General Rodes. Rodes had a twenty-five pound turkey given him and invited

> some of the officers to a dinner....this superb gobbler, done to a crisp, with dressing and gravy, was on a table in a tent adjoining the generals sleeping quarters, and while steaming hot the cook invited the company to the table. In some mysterious manner, before they could walk the ten or fifteen feet necessary to reach the table, the magnificent bird was wafted out of sight and never seen by Rodes or his company. The General was reported to have become very angry with Corporal Fowler and his two brother guards, expressing his displeasure in very forceful language, and during this talk he spoke of Fowler as belonging to the "damned chicken-thieving 12th Alabama." This not very complimentary appellation abided with the 12th Alabama from this time to the close of the war.[43]

Unbeknown to General Rodes, the 12th was perhaps the champion forager unit in Hill's Division. Their cooking pots were always filled with "freed pigs" or "liberated chickens," and Corporal Fowler was a giant among champions—somewhat akin to the proverbial fox assigned to guard a henhouse.

Soon serious organizational changes would involve the division. Gen. D.H. Hill, beset with an ailing back, displeased with lack of promotion, and listening to the urges of his wife, Isabella, abruptly resigned on January 1, 1863.[44] Hill had openly derided Lee's generalship, was critical of every possible movement of cavalry, and was never pleased with his artillery support. He was, himself, under fire, unjustly, for his actions at South Mountain. A capable, exceedingly brave, determined fighter, he could not overcome his personality deficits, and sadly his services were lost to the army. Not all of Hill's men regretted his departure. Maj. Eugene Blackford commented that "Hill was transferring to duty in North Carolina, much to our delight."[45]

With Hill's departure, Robert Rodes, the senior brigadier, assumed command of the division until such time that a new major general was appointed. He was well received by most of the men and officers. Many of the division officers knew Rodes well and had confidence in his abilities. His constant smile and down-to-earth, genuine friendliness convinced enlisted soldiers of his sincere concern for their welfare. The absence of pompous, superior behavior on his part was always appreciated by the soldiers who followed him. Captain Park recalled an incident which indicated Rodes' sense of fairness. Park had become involved in a controversy with brigade headquarters, after Rodes assumed division leadership, over the services of Jim, the 12th Alabama cook. Colonel O'Neal was attempting to confiscate Jim's services for his brigade mess, and Park galloped to division headquarters where he found General Rodes at Grace Church leaning on a pew near the altar. After carefully listening to Park's appeal, Rodes clearly and concisely adjudicated the case of Jim's services on its merits and not the rank of its participants.[46]

General Jackson actually preferred the appointment of Edward "Allegheny" Johnson to command Hill's Division, and he recommended that officer's promotion to major general. But Johnson's wound was slow to heal and he seemed to enjoy his avid pursuit of the young lasses of Richmond as he became a fixture in the drawing salons of the capital.[47] The division seemed secure under Rodes' leadership, for he administered its affairs using the same stern, fair, and consistent methods with which he had run his brigade.

CHAPTER 6

CHARGE TO GLORY
Chancellorsville

As squads of diminutive, gray-clad drummers paraded mud-packed streets, the reverberations of their blurred sticks echoed from sturdy mud-daubed walls of rows of log huts. From east and west of Grace Church the strident tattoo rose higher and higher in the cool morning air. Dogwood and redbud blossoms had already turned the somber forests brilliant with their color, and sprouting grass along the roadsides signaled the approach of spring. But the "long roll" of the persistent drummers awoke the almost 20,000 soldiers with another kind of message. The massive blue-clad foe camped across the Rappahannock was astir, signaling an end to the tranquility of winter camp.

Already the Federals were exiting their Stafford Heights camps under another new commander in chief. After his bloody repulse at Fredericksburg, Ambrose Burnside, subjected to much criticism from his subordinates, especially Maj. Gen. Joseph Hooker, had been relieved.[1] Reluctantly, the bearded Lincoln had accepted Burnside's resignation and appointed the aforementioned Hooker to replace him, effective January 25, 1863.[2]

Joseph Hooker was a gregarious, handsome officer, a graduate of West Point, Class of 1837, where he was famed for his academy high jinks while a cadet. A reputation for personal bravery during the hostilities with Mexico was somewhat offset by indifferent performances in the peacetime army. Hooker was fond of heavy drink, an avid gambler, and a resolute womanizer.[3] Joe Hooker was also an adept politician in an era when this talent was not yet a common route to high rank.[4] So successful were the clean-shaven officer's manipulations that he achieved the ultimate position, commander of an army, which in turn made him the target of the ambitious arrows of others.

On April 8, General Hooker staged a mammoth review of four of his army corps for President and Mrs. Lincoln. The soldiers presented a striking appearance, proudly striding past, flags aloft, footsteps in cadence to the music of their marvelous bands.[5] Regrettably he could only show off half his strength, for no available field could hold his entire force.

The Federal commander's plan of attack was simple, yet bold and ambitious. He would attempt to use each of his 130,000 soldiers in two enormous pincers which, hopefully, would either crush Lee's 61,000 Confederates or at least force their immediate retirement toward Richmond.[6] Hooker's intelligence was excellent and he knew that two of Lee's eight divisions were with Lieutenant General Longstreet in front of Norfolk, south of the James River.[7] Days earlier, Hooker dispatched most of his cavalry with Brig. Gen. George Stoneman on a raid into Lee's rear, hoping to cut Confederate communications with the capital.[8] After nightfall on April 27,

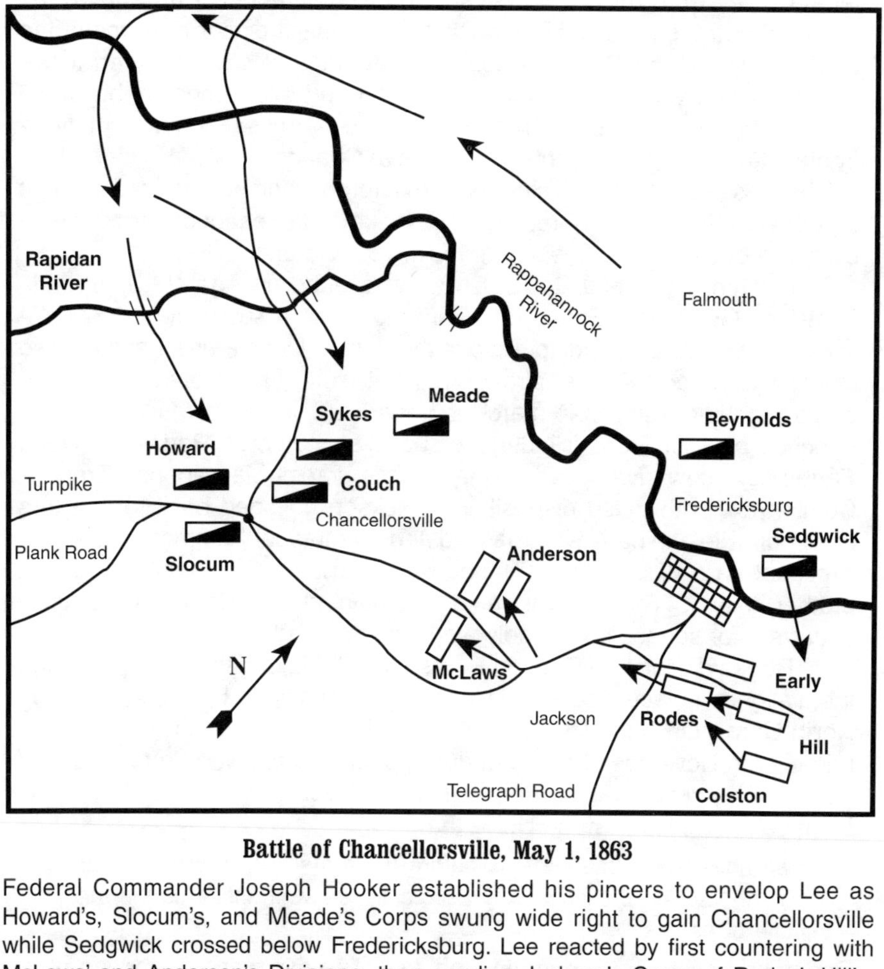

Battle of Chancellorsville, May 1, 1863

Federal Commander Joseph Hooker established his pincers to envelop Lee as Howard's, Slocum's, and Meade's Corps swung wide right to gain Chancellorsville while Sedgwick crossed below Fredericksburg. Lee reacted by first countering with McLaws' and Anderson's Divisions, then sending Jackson's Corps of Rodes', Hill's, and Colston's Divisions to assist.

Hooker put his infantry in motion. Three entire infantry corps were dispatched west, swinging behind screening hills until they reached and crossed the Rappahannock River at Kelly's Ford, some twenty miles west of Fredericksburg. This formidable force was led by Maj. Gen. Oliver Howard's XI Corps, followed by the XII Corps of Maj. Gen. Henry Slocum and the V Corps of Maj.Gen. George C. Meade.[9] To confuse the Southern army, a second force, led by the VI Corps of Maj. Gen. John Sedgwick, the largest corps in the Federal army, stormed across the Rappahannock some twenty miles below Fredericksburg at dawn on April 29.[10]

Hooker's grandiose plan was on schedule, the morale of his soldiers soaring, and their commander, brimming with confidence, loudly proclaimed, "I have the rebellion firmly in my breeches pocket and God almighty cannot take it away from me."[11] Hooker's bombastic statements of triumph assumed that the successful completion of this initial pincer movement had outmaneuvered the Confederates and now they would be forced to retreat.[12] In later years when Hooker reconsidered this campaign, he would avow that his real intent was not to crush Lee's army but to lure him into a frontal attack on his stout entrenchments at Chancellorsville.[13] Regardless of Hooker's true intent, all his plans were altered when he engaged in a test of wills with Robert Lee. In record time Hooker's demeanor changed from a cocksure braggart to a hesitant, fumbling spectator.

Lt. Gen. Thomas J. Jackson was awakened on April 29 by an aide from Maj. Gen. Jubal Early and within moments a suddenly wide awake Jackson was dressed and spurring to the front.[14] Upon arrival he found two officers, Early and Rodes, already hard at work, anticipating orders and preparing their divisions to march.[15] Soon Early's men were filing into the trenches back of Fredericksburg, and Jackson ordered Rodes to extend Early's right downriver, posting one brigade across Massaponax Creek.[16] Comfortable with these dispositions, Jackson galloped back to quarters and soon wife and baby were packed and en route for Richmond under the excellent care of Lieutenant Joseph G. Morrison, Stonewall's aide and brother-in-law.[17] Those few wives still remaining in winter camp hurriedly departed, for serious and deadly work was at hand.

Rodes dispatched Dodson Ramseur with his brigade forward, having them aligned to face a potential Union river crossing.[18] The intense, young North Carolinian had just returned to his brigade in March. Promoted to brigadier in November, he had endured a lengthy recovery from a serious wound.[19] Ramseur had married while convalescing and faithfully wrote his bride each day. He assured Nellie that

> we have a stupendous task before us, a task which will test our manhood and if successfully accomplished...will entitle us the full title of heroes.[20]

Rodes had every confidence in Ramseur. The two were embarking on a friendship that would grow and strengthen until the war's last few fateful months. Upon reaching his positions, Rodes ordered his soldiers to begin digging to strengthen the old trenches, for he fully expected the Federals to attack the next morning.

But suddenly, new orders arrived. At dawn, May 1, Rodes was ordered to move by the Military Road, a wagon trace which ran behind the Fredericksburg trenches, to its junction with the Orange Plank Road.[21] Lee had ascertained from prisoners that three Federal corps were across the Rappahannock at Kelly's Ford. He immediately perceived this march on his left flank as the primary Federal threat and ordered the divisions of Maj. Gens. Richard Anderson and Lafayette McLaws to march west and block the roads from Chancellorsville.[22] Lee then requested that Jackson proceed with three of his four divisions toward Tabernacle Church, taking charge of operations upon arrival. Jackson left Early with a reinforced division and several artillery units to hold Sedgwick in his bridgehead.[23]

As the sun rose, Ramseur's long-striding Carolinians led Rodes' Division up the military road. The Division of Maj. Gen. A.P. Hill and that of Isaac Trimble, now led by Brig. Gen. R.E. Colston, followed.[24] As the graybacks surged forward in high spirits, eager for action, a sweating courier approached General Rodes who was riding in the van with Ramseur. The rider proved a staff officer of Maj.Gen. Edward "Allegheny" Johnson who was approaching on the Telegraph Road from Richmond and was anxious to take command of "his" division.[25] Jackson had long intended to replace D.H. Hill with Johnson, and he had recommended the officer's promotion to major general for that purpose.[26] But Johnson's exceedingly slow recovery from his injuries had thus far prevented his assuming command. Rodes, focusing on the task ahead, never hesitated. Coolly and without rancor, he informed Johnson's envoy that, as he had begun this action, he respectfully refused to be relieved until it was over, unless placed under arrest.[27] The rider departed and no further messages were received. The infantrymen continued their march up the Plank Road for almost two miles when Rodes became aware of serious fighting on the turnpike to his right.[28] Several brigades of Anderson's and McLaws' Divisions had constructed breastworks across the road and were contesting Federal Maj. Gen. George Sykes' United States Regulars. By 11 A.M. Sykes was pushing hard on the Confederate units of Brig. Gens. Semmes, Mahone, and Wofford.[29] Southern resistance stiffened and despite the introit of Federal guns into the fray, Sykes' momentum ground to a halt.[30]

Rodes, finding no resistance on the Plank Road, rode forward to reconnoiter, leaving orders for Ramseur to continue his forward movement but to place skirmishers in the woods on his right. Soon Rodes overtook two Confederate brigades, those of Brig. Gens. A.R. Wright and Carnot Posey of Anderson's Division, engaged with elements of Maj. Gen. Henry Slocum's XII Union Corps.[31] General Jackson appeared in the roadway as firing escalated and requested that Rodes send support. Major Peyton raced back to bring Ramseur's men forward at double-time. Jackson inserted Ramseur between the two already engaged units, a difficult maneuver which they executed smartly.[32] Suddenly XII Corps' resistance faded and the Confederate units, proud to be under the eye of their corps commander, drove the Federals pell-mell for almost two miles, halting before stout-looking log breastworks within sight of the Chancellor House at 6:30 A.M.[33]

Rodes' remaining brigades were closed up on the Plank Road, ready for action. When Jackson terminated pursuit of Slocum, Rodes rode back down the track, directing each unit into open areas near Aldrich's Tavern, where they bivouacked.[34] Hill and Colston continued to close until they also encamped nearby. In the gathering dark, hundreds of campfires twinkled, but heavy woods shielded that sight from Union eyes. Hooker was unaware of the infantry power Jackson was amassing on the Plank Road.

Jackson had ranged up and down the front all afternoon. He was for a time near Catharine Furnace on the left where he and General Stuart searched vainly for a vantage point. Then he ventured north to the turnpike accompanied by A.P. Hill to witness McLaws' fight with Sykes.[35] Finally he galloped back to the Plank Road still earnestly seeking a weakness in Hooker's retracting lines. Near the junction of the Plank and Furnace Roads, Stonewall encountered General Lee and the two officers adjourned to a pine wood to avoid Federal sharpshooters.[36] Lee had also been scouting, searching for the Union left and had found the terrain impassable. There was no practical method of getting between Hooker and the river. Lee concluded:

> the enemy had assumed a position of great natural strength, surrounded on all sides by dense forests, filled with tangled undergrowth, in the midst of which breastworks of logs had been constructed....his artillery swept the few narrow roads by which his position could be approached from the front.[37]

Lee began questioning Jackson concerning Hooker's right. Stonewall, however, was firmly convinced that Hooker would continue to retreat and by morning would have crossed the Rappahannock.[38] Jackson had been apace of the rapid Confederate advance up the narrow road, and the ease with which the enemy had been driven convinced him there was little conviction in their efforts. While Lee expressed his hopes that his able lieutenant was correct, he did not agree.[39] So the two Confederate generals sat down on a pine log under a rising full moon to plan the next day's actions.[40]

Both wished to avoid a direct attack on the well-entrenched Federals, and concluded that they must find a way around the Union right, for Sedgwick's huge VI Corps would not remain idle in front of Early forever.[41] Lee was impatient but soon General Stuart arrived with good news. Brig. Gen. Fitzhugh Lee, commanding Stuart's 2nd Brigade, had discovered the Federal right flank was unanchored; it was "in the air."[42] Suddenly the point of assault and the method seemed clear, but could a route to the attack point be discovered? Soon a guide was found, one Charles Wellford whose parents operated the nearby iron furnace, and when questioned he convinced the officers he could find a route. Jackson fell to the task with his young guide and an array of maps, while Lee retired to complete a report to President Davis. Stonewall decided to get some sleep and retired, strangely, without notifying his division commanders of the next day's plan.[43] Rodes, however, must have received verbal confirmation of the plans, for he was up long before daylight. He awakened Iverson's Brigade and after they ate sent them to replace Ramseur's troops who were asleep in formation near the enemy. Ramseur marched his men to the rear and drew rations.[44] Rodes' entire division was prepared to march at 8 A.M. when Jackson appeared and ordered their advance. Earlier when Lee had inquired of Jackson what troops he would take, Jackson had replied he would move with his entire corps.[45] This conference and its conclusions have been so discussed that it almost appears as an electric moment in history, a moment actually frozen for posterity. Jackson's audacity in making such a request was only surpassed by Lee's commensurate audacious approval. The dangers

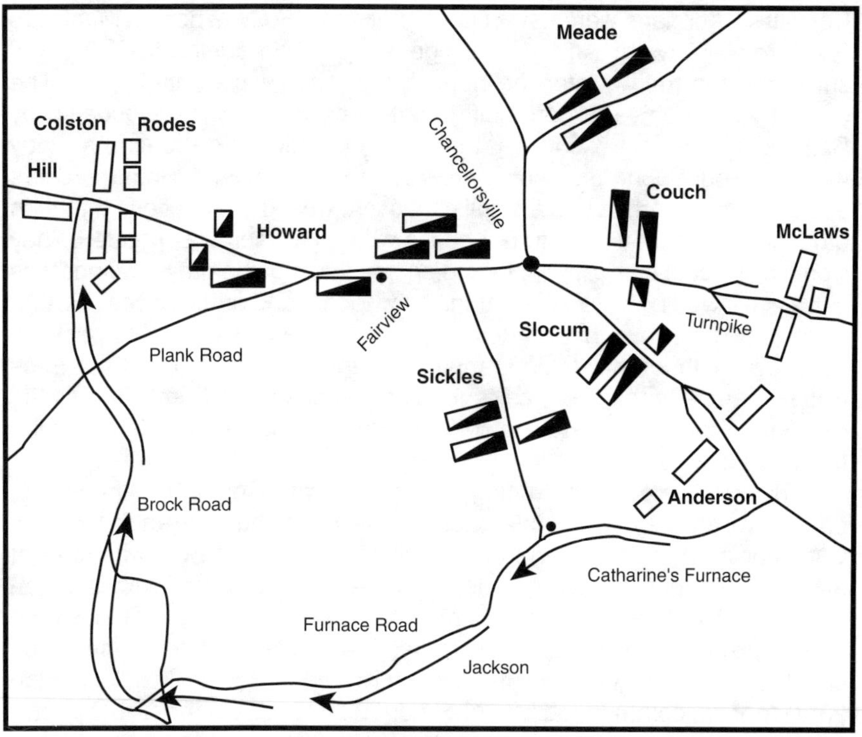

Chancellorsville, May 2, 1863

Lee and Jackson agreed to flank Hooker's right. The entire Confederate 2nd Corps undertook a winding 12-mile march on narrow roads to position itself in the woods opposite Howard's XI Corps.

inherent in Jackson's taking 28,000 men around Hooker's flank while Lee remained behind in place with 15,000 soldiers were well understood by both participants.[46]

Back at the Chancellor House, the mood of the Federal command suddenly was altered. Gone was the confidence of the previous day, replaced by uncertainty, disorder, and growing confusion. Hooker seemed uncertain of how to deal with the aggressive behavior of Robert E. Lee. Lee had not reacted as Hooker thought he should. Many have called this calm May morning Hooker's moment of truth.[47] Surely it was difficult to recall the empty boasts of yesterday while now under the foglike screen of his attempts to read Lee's reactions. Joe Hooker was smoking his cigars heavily, for he had foresworn drink for the campaign's duration.[48] But his nervous manner was so apparent that at least one of his corps commanders felt it was the wrong time to give up alcohol and that Hooker's nerve might return if he returned to his bottle.[49]

Rodes' veterans proudly led the snaking gray column. Shortly beyond Aldrich's the van turned left from the Plank Road onto the Furnace Road. Colquitt's Georgians were now in front, preceded by Col. Thomas Munford's 2nd Virginia Cavalry. An overnight gentle rain had settled the dust and smoothed the roadway for the hundreds of shoeless Confederates. The men of Anderson's Division, shifted left to cover the lines evacuated by Ramseur's men, sat silently by the roadside chewing on rations as they watched Rodes' long gray column purposely stride past.[50] Both marchers and observers were aware a significant event was about to occur, although probably neither could venture a guess where Jackson was headed. They were sure it booked no favors for the enemy. Each of the gray divisions was closely followed by artillery, ammunition wagons, and ambulances.[51] Other supplies would travel by a much longer, more secure route, but Jackson was never without bullets. In many places the roadway through the trees was so narrow that artillery caissons and wagons could barely egress the road, and firm orders were issued for broken vehicles to be pushed off the track and abandoned.[52]

Jackson and Rodes, riding in the lead with Colquitt's skirmishers, passed a roadway which intersected from the right. The track led past Catharine's Furnace and on to Chancellorsville. The roadway was straight and open, offering a view of Federal lines, and the officers knew their column could be observed at that point. With Jackson's approval, Rodes rode rearward and instructed Colquitt to detail a regiment to the flank which could call for assistance from the column if needed.[53] Colquitt selected the 23rd Georgia, commanded by Col. Emory Best. Best advanced three companies up the road as skirmishers, blocked the thoroughfare with one company, and retained the remainder in reserve.[54]

At Chancellorsville, Federal officers became aware of Confederate troop movements in the Catharine's Furnace area. Although a consensus of Union officers agreed that the Confederates were retreating, Maj. Gen.

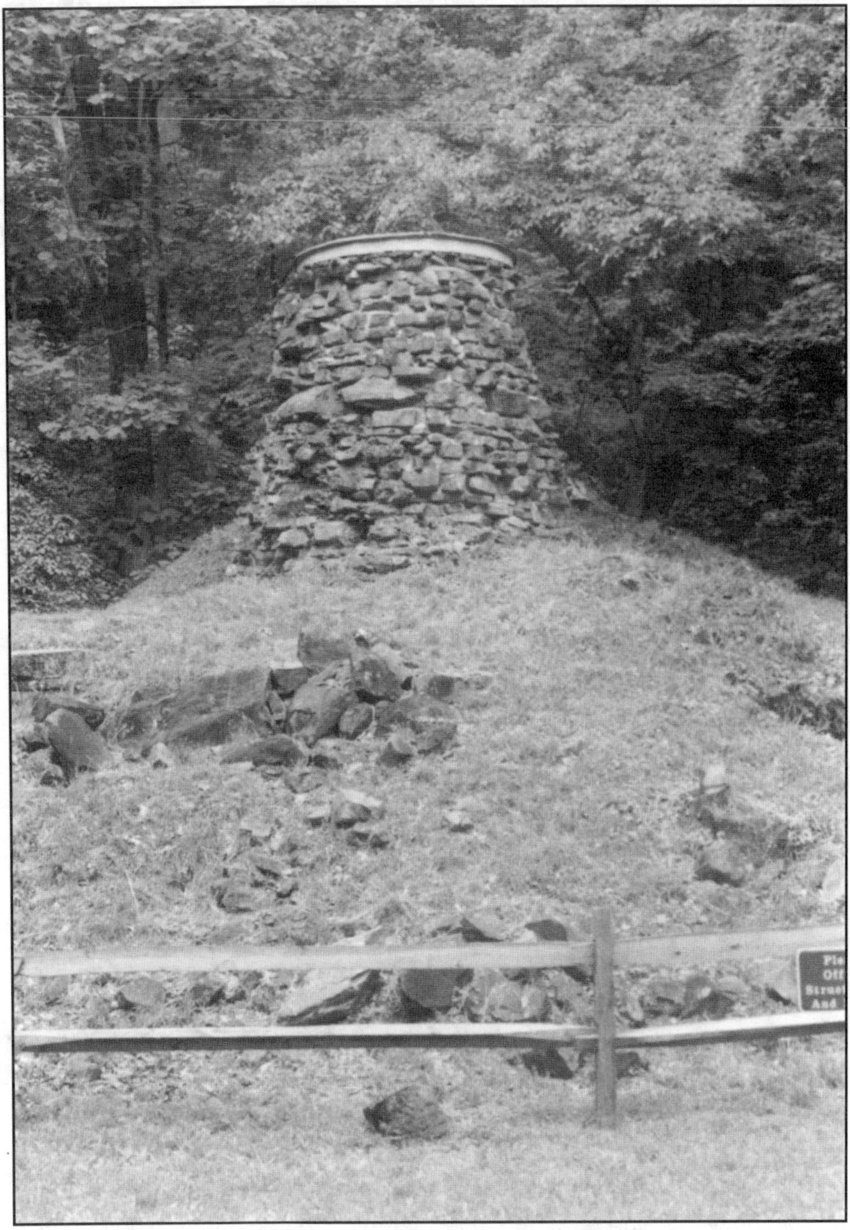

Catharine's Furnace, Chancellorsville

Robert Rodes, commanding D.H. Hill's Division, led Jackson's flanking force in a silent march past Catharine's Furnace and around Hooker's right, setting the stage for one of the most famed charges in Confederate military history.

Robert Carter

Daniel Sickles repeatedly requested permission that his III Corps be allowed to investigate.[55] About midday Sickles received approval and he dispatched Col. Hiram Berdan with the 1st and 2nd Battalions of United States Sharpshooters to probe the roadway. Sickles then backed Berdan with his third infantry division.[56]

Berdan advanced slowly, trading fire with Best's skirmishers. Berdan was unsure how close his lines approached Anderson's Brigades, and about 1 P.M. Best decided he could fall back since Jackson's column had safely cleared the intersection. He ordered his skirmishers to retire and problems then began. The skirmishers lost contact with Best's main force and with a sudden rush Berdan's sharpshooters captured the Georgia skirmishers.[57] Best sent to Anderson for assistance but before help could arrive the sharpshooters enveloped Best's command in an unfinished railway cut.[58] Surrounded and subject to a murderous enfilade fire, Best ordered every man for himself and the unit fell apart. As they scattered, most of the Georgians were captured, with Best and a handful of soldiers escaping.[59] Best reported:

> My loss in prisoners was 26 officers and 250 enlisted men....my colors were saved....I feel satisfied that every effort was made to save the train and extricate the command.[60]

A famed and hard fighting regiment was virtually destroyed. Colonel Best was later arrested and a court-of-inquiry scheduled, however Rodes postponed the proceedings when Colquitt's Brigade was transferred to North Carolina.[61] Subsequently, a court-martial found Colonel Best guilty of dereliction of duty and he was cashiered.[62]

Sickles' III Corps advance was arrested by the effective fire of Col. Thompson Brown's Reserve Artillery Battalion. Satisfied with Berdan's success and observing no further Confederate movement, the Unionists took a defensive posture, blocking access to Chancellorsville.[63] Most Federals were still convinced the gray-backs were retreating and laughed heartily at a ragged captive from the 23rd Georgia who sullenly drawled: "You may think you've done a big thing now, but wait until Jackson gets around on your right."[64]

As this action sputtered, Jackson's column continued to march, twenty-five minutes per mile, ten minutes rest per hour. The pleasant spring day grew hotter and the marchers began to suffer. Water was scarce and some fell out for a time. Jackson, Rodes, and other officers were constantly riding up and down the line of march, their energy and constant urging impressing the sweating marchers of the importance of their task. Soldiers recalled that all the officers, especially Rodes, were soaked through, but strangely Jackson wore his long, gum coat all day.[65] When the intersection with the Brock Road was reached, Jackson had Munford lead Rodes down a narrow trail, through an unfinished railway cut, and up a rough logging trail until they struck the Brock Road several miles north. This detour, although time consuming, provided security from Federal vendettas. As the leading elements reentered the Brock Road, Fitzhugh Lee was waiting. He urged Jackson to continue his march a few miles until he reached the turnpike and offered to take Stonewall to an observation post.[66]

Ordering Rodes to press on, Jackson rode into the woods with Lee, where he observed thousands of Federals at ease in their camps.[67] Excited, Jackson galloped back to find Rodes moving north with speed, all units closed up. Observing the silent columns gliding by him, Jackson peered around for a bit, and commented to young Tom Munford, "The Virginia Military Institute will be heard from today."[68] Jackson's comment encased not only Munford, Rodes, Colquitt, and himself, but a large cadre of regimental and field officers which filed past his post.

Rodes crossed the Orange Plank Road, moved on a few miles to the turnpike and began to deploy.[69] Maj. Eugene Blackford's skirmish line was so advanced that soldiers attempted to identify the contents of Federal cooking pots by smell. Rodes formed his battle line perpendicular to and astride the turnpike. Iverson's Brigade was placed on the far left, O'Neal's Alabama soldiers next, their right flank on the turnpike. Across the road Doles' Brigade was stationed, then Colquitt's. Ramseur's Brigade was aligned behind Colquitt and faced somewhat south to protect the flank.[70] The division commander traversed the lines twice, checking alignment and providing clear, concise instructions to each brigade commander. They were to guide on the road, storming directly through the Talley Farm and on to Chancellor's.[71] There was to be no stopping, no hesitation; flanks would be protected by following units. They were the tip of the spear and must penetrate and smash the enemy lines. As Rodes completed his preparations the soldiers dropped to one knee in formation and munched on whatever rations they had. Colston's Division arrived and started forming a second line, then A.P. Hill's units approached and began to form a third. No noise alerted the nearby Federal camps.

Silently, ominously, the thunderstorm which would wreck the Union right was positioned. At about 5:15 P.M. when Stonewall turned to Robert Rodes and softly spoke those famous words, "You can go forward then, General Rodes,"[72] he was releasing an onslaught unique in Civil War history. At no other occasion was such a mass of infantry power placed in such an advantageous position without prior warning to its foe. Maj. Gen. Oliver Howard, the one-armed old gentleman, who commanded the largely German-born XI Corps, was reviled for years, as were his soldiers, for the unseemly panic which swept their ranks under Stonewall's attack. Howard was well aware his flank was in the air and should have been curved back toward the river and Ely's Ford to be militarily sound.[73] But the blue-coats did resist, trying to stem the tide by company, regiment, and brigade in their recently constructed earthworks. Many Federal gun batteries fired until overrun. However, the sheer size and scope of the attacking line, falling with no warning from concealed woodlands, would have reduced to panic the soldiers of any Federal or Confederate corps and in virtually any formation.[74]

One of the most significant victories in military history was "almost" to occur on that late spring afternoon. A powerful well-led force would come very close to destroying another more powerful force.[75] The blue-clad army was probably saved that evening by two factors: the setting sun and its own ponderous size. Darkness certainly prevented the Confederates from fully exploiting their bold attack.[76] But it was also almost an impossibility to instantly destroy a force of 90,000 soldiers stationed in strongly entrenched positions. The sagacious Confederate attack completely panicked a substantial number of troops, but untested corps of veteran blue-coats never saw action that evening, and complete defeat of the Union force was simply unreasonable.

When Rodes turned and nodded to Major Blackford, the bugle notes ran clear as clarion calls, left and right through the forest. The first indication of trouble to the Federals, like the dust eddies which sweep before a storm, were the startled deer, rabbits, squirrels, and quail which wildly fled from the forest.[77] Closely behind, a dense gray line of soldiers emerged, many of whom wore clothing ripped to their chests from the race through briars and thorns.[78] Red, starry-crossed battle flags soared aloft and a fierce throat-clearing yell arose, half energy and part challenge.

Col. Leopold von Gilsa's Brigade of the 1st Division, XI Corps, was the first unit to suffer the impact. Running for their stacked rifles, knocking aside simmering pots of beef, they were shot down by Rodes' front rank or simply run over.[79] The initial objective, the breastworks at Talley Farm, were just ahead and Rodes tolerated no delay, just flush and drive the foe. Doles' and O'Neal's Brigades thundered along the roadway like runaway trains. Within minutes they surged over the Union works at Talley Farm.[80] Maj. Gen. Carl Schurz with his two-brigade division was next. Supported by two artillery batteries, Schurz attempted to change front and face the oncoming Confederates. He almost succeeded but von Gilsa's fugitives overran his line and his men simply joined the rout.[81] The runners were now a mass of blue-clad fugitives, throwing away haversacks, ammunition, even guns, as they raced for safety. Once spooked, like cattle, the Federal soldiers stampeded, impossible to rally.

Rodes rode from side to side urging the troops on faster and faster. A couple of his aides leaped from their horses in von Gilsa's camp, attempting to gulp down cups of coffee and found the beverage too hot to swallow.[82] Sprinting gray-clad soldiers expertly stooped to retrieve Federal haversacks which they rifled for food that they consumed without slowing their pace.[83] No food tasted sweeter. Schurz's brigades simply dissolved.

Only one error marred Rodes' exhilarating sweep. Colquitt, who was aligned on his right, was on open ground and should have outdistanced Rodes' other brigades. But despite Rodes' explicit orders, he became concerned over Federal cavalry on his flank and halted to investigate. This blocked the advance of Ramseur's closely following brigade, handicapping the entire division.[84] Rodes angrily surmised:

> During this glorious victory and pursuit of more than two miles, I had only three brigades involved....Gen. Colquitt halted his brigade....and Gen. Ramseur was effectively blocked from participation.[85]

The noise and din of attack thundered on into the twilight. Confederate veterans, firing, then reloading on the march, and firing again into the backs of fleeing Federals.[86] A well-constructed Union line, complete with rifle pits, was encountered near Dowdall's Tavern, and slowed the advance for a moment. Col. Adolphus Buschbeck had dug his men in well and was supported by three batteries. The guns punished Rodes' line with canister, but Colston's second line arrived and merging with Rodes', the attackers broke the Buschbeck line and raced after the retreating Federals. As they sprinted into a band of thick forest the various brigades became disorganized and confused.[87] Rodes halted both lines and dispatched a message to Jackson to send up A.P. Hill, then backed out of the trees to set up regimental rally points so that his brigades might swiftly reorganize.[88] Hill's brigades, in column, were marching up the turnpike in close support and began to deploy in near darkness.[89] An anxious Robert Rodes, leaving the sorting out to his staff, rode forward alone, almost to Chancellorsville and could find no Federal line of battle.[90] He little knew how fortunate he was to return, for although his observations were correct, large numbers of Federal cannon were trained on the roadway from both sides of the road.[91] A lone horseman riding in the moonlight was either unidentified or unworthy of their fire.

When Rodes informed Jackson of his finding, Stonewall was still intent upon continuing the advance and rode forward with his staff on the parallel Mountain Road. A.P. Hill's leading unit, a brigade under Brig. Gen. James H. Lane, was at this time passing through Rodes' line and deploying astride the Plank Road. Col. Stapleton Crutchfield advanced a pair of guns up the road and fired several rounds toward Chancellorsville, drawing such a storm of fire in reply that he fell back hastily.[92] Lane sent a regiment forward to act as skirmishers then spread his four remaining regiments with their center on the road.[93] The 38th and 7th North Carolina Regiments were south of the roadway while the 18th and 28th formed on the north side.[94]

Lane's men were edgy and tense. They had seen little action, not being participants in the charge, and were now stationed in an unfamiliar position. Federal refugees were everywhere; having sought shelter from the Confederate attack, many now sifting through the woods, attempting to return to their respective lines. Pickets fired at the slightest noise and artillery fire erupted spasmodically. Sickles' III Corps was on the move, having been ordered north to rescue the XI Corps, and a fierce Union cavalry charge had been severely repulsed on the Plank Road.[95] Jackson and his entourage started their ride back to Confederate lines when volleys fired by Lane's 38th and 7th North Carolina units whistled overhead. To avoid this fire the group crossed to the north side of the road. Amid shouts of "Yankee Cavalry" and "Friends," another volley was raggedly fired by the 18th North Carolina upon command of its major.[96] Two of the riders were slain at once while General Jackson, struck three times, would not recover.

Gen. A.P. Hill was soon at the scene to assist in Jackson's evacuation despite intermittent sweeps of Federal artillery fire.[97] Within moments Hill was struck by a shell fragment which cut through both boots and rendered him unable to walk or ride. A message was sent Robert Rodes to temporarily assume command of the 2nd Corps.[98] Rodes conferred hastily with Heth and Colston, and the three agreed to prepare to renew the attack at dawn.

But soon the dark forest would be the scene of a night attack by the foe. Advancing through the moonlight, bayonets glimmering, two brigades of Sickles' III Corps marched directly onto the turnpike. One of these units, that of Brig. Gen. Hobart Ward, veered off course and mistakenly charged and captured a Union battery of the XII Corps.[99] The second brigade, led by Col. Samuel Hayman, was more accurate, colliding with the right portion of Lane's line. A severe, confusing fight resulted in the dark woodland. Rodes brought Brig. Gen. Samuel McGowan's Brigade up on line to the right of Lane, but the Federals had already withdrawn.[100] While the Federal night attack was unsuccessful, it convinced the Confederate officers that there was plenty of grit left in the Union army.

Shortly after midnight, Maj. Gen. J.E.B. Stuart arrived at the front and assumed command of the 2nd Corps.[101] Rodes reviewed with Stuart the disposition of Confederate units and those Federal positions of which he was aware. There was some indecisiveness in the passage of command from Rodes to Stuart. A major on Jackson's staff sent the message to summon Stuart, although Stuart reported A.P. Hill had sent for him.[102] The exact sequence is impossible to reconstruct although many commented on Rodes' cheerful acquiescence to Stuart's assumption of command.[103] Rodes later expressed his feeling as:

> I deem it proper to state that I yielded the command to Gen. Stuart, not because I thought him entitled to it—belonging as he does to a different arm of service—nor because I was unwilling to assume the responsibility of carrying on the attack, as I had already made the necessary arrangements and they remained unchanged, but because, from the manner in which I had been informed that he had been sent for, I inferred that Gen. Jackson or Gen. Hill had instructed Maj. Pendleton to place him in command, and for the still stronger reason that I feared the information that the command had devolved on me, unknown, except to my immediate troops, would in their shaken condition be likely to increase the

> demoralization of the corps. Gen Stuart's name was well and favorably known to the army, and would tend, I hoped, to reestablish confidence. I yielded because I was satisfied the good of the service demanded it.[104]

Sleeping Confederates were awakened early on May 3 to heavy dew and a dense ground fog which obscured their view of Federal lines.[105] Nestled behind the second defensive line they had overrun the previous afternoon, the infantrymen began their eternal quest for food. Ammunition was plentiful but the supply wagons had not yet arrived. General Rodes, like all officers of serious mien, was an early riser and already was berating staff and commissary officers. Irritable, after only a few hours sleep, he railed that the troops must be fed, for action was imminent. Foragers began searching abandoned Federal equipment for eatables. Soon the awaited wagons arrived and cold rations were hastily distributed as the bugles blew assembly.[106] By 6 A.M. Stuart was aligning all three 2nd Corps Divisions. A.P. Hill's Division, now under Brig. Gen. Harry Heth, made up the first rank and would be followed by Colston's Division, and thirdly, Rodes' Division.[107]

Federal troops had not been idle during the night. Fresh, stout earthworks of log and dirt faced the assembling Confederates. Hooker had ringed the plateau at Chancellorsville with men and guns, as well as establishing two divisions of Sickles' III Corps in a salient at Hazen Grove, a cleared hilltop. His new trenches extended across the turnpike and some distance north. They were held in strength by William's Division of the XII Corps, Berry's Division of the III Corps, and French's III Corps Division.[108] A second line was erected near the edge of the woodland, and a third artillery line extended across a higher elevation. A formidable position, very compact, and packed with soldiers. Ample batteries of that superb Union artillery were interwoven in Hooker's line as well as Sickles' position at Hazel Grove.

As Stuart began aligning his corps perpendicular and across the turnpike, he requested the right portion of Heth's front line to move forward abreast of the other units of that division.[109] As brigades under Brig. Gens. James Archer and Samuel McGowan moved to comply they collided with troops of Sickles' Hazel Run salient whose lines bowed forward some distance from Chancellorsville.[110] Firing began simultaneously on the left, and brigades under Brig. Gen. Dorsey Pender, north of the road, charged forward over the enemy's initial line and pushed ahead until pinpointed by the Union artillery batteries. Archer methodically realigned his units to the enemy's position. McGowan, alongside, lost contact when Archer's troops charged resolutely with a yell.[111] After capturing several guns Archer was surprised to encounter Confederates of General Anderson's Division which were advancing from the reverse slopes of the ridge. Hooker had ordered evacuation of Hazel Grove and was pulling Sickles' units within his perimeter, despite the protests of his artillery officers.[112] A Confederate from Anderson's Division, who recalled listening to the sounds of Jackson's late afternoon flank attack, advanced the next morning with his unit into Hazen Grove and bragged that "they drove the Yankees into Rodes' men, who shot them down by the hundreds."[113]

The capture of the position at Hazel Grove proved very advantageous to the Southerners, for shortly Confederate guns massed there would enfildate the Federal lines.[114] Archer and McGowan could not progress much beyond Hazen Grove as Union resistance became fierce. Heth's other two brigades were forced to cover behind the captured Federal breastworks and struggled to repel Federal counterattacks on both flanks. The fire of the Union guns was devastating, and Stuart determined to send thirty more Confederate guns to Hazen Grove with hopes that Federal artillery could be silenced.[115] Soon, some of the finest gunners in Confederate service would be gathered there and for once would outgun and outfight their Union rivals.[116]

But Heth's infantry attack bogged down and Stuart ordered his second line forward. Colston's Division swept forward but quickly slowed and seemed to fall apart as Colston lost control.[117] Many of Colston's units moved forward under fierce artillery fire and simply joined the troops of Heth's Division who were hovering behind captured breastworks. The two Divisions became mixed; Hill's men were out of ammunition, and in a few rare instances units refused to obey orders to advance. Colston's Division was sadly lacking in field officers, being short every brigade officer but one, Brigadier General Paxton, who was soon slain by enemy artillery fire. Additionally, this was only General Colston's second occasion to lead men in combat. The confusing terrain and inexperienced leadership, combined with fierce enemy artillery, split the division into uncoordinated units, precipitating an ineffective performance. South of the road, McGowan's Brigade, their colonel a casualty, were sheltering behind the works almost out of ammunition. Colston recalled them massed six and eight deep, refusing to advance, and blocking movement of his other units.[118] The brigades of Paxton and Jones, ordered forward, were forced to move laterally to avoid the bottleneck, and in the process Paxton was slain as was Col. T.S. Garrett, who was leading Jones' unit.[119] The forward motion of both units faltered and they retreated to the breastworks, joining McCowan's men. Soon a South Carolina officer attempted to extricate McCowan's Brigade rearward for a resupply of ammunition.[120] Col. J.H.S. Fulk began to regroup the "Stonewall Brigade" but Jones' troops, all their leaders down, refused to leave their cover. The small momentum of Colston's second line was truly spent.

Rodes' Division was summoned shortly before 8 A.M. He carefully aligned his brigade just as he had done the afternoon prior. Iverson's Brigade was on the far right, O'Neal's Alabamians next, their right flank on the roadway, then Ramseur's, Doles', and Colquitt's Brigades.[121] Observing the stout earthworks and difficult ground which collected Southern troops in protected areas, Rodes clearly understood the difficulty of this assignment. His men would have trouble getting past the hiding Confederates and through the heavy brush, all the while being blasted by Union guns. Rodes called his brigade commanders together and gave specific instructions:

> each brigade was to push forward until the enemy was encountered and to engage him vigorously, running over friend and foe alike, if in the way.[122]

Federal artillery was sweeping the approaches and Rodes knew he could not hesitate or falter once the men had begun to advance. Colquitt was dispatched right to connect with Anderson's men, and the other four brigades prepared to advance, straight ahead in line. Stuart, impatient, sent another messenger, but the ever meticulous Rodes would not be rushed.[123] Then as coolly as with Jackson in the woods, Rodes waved them forward. Riding on the Plank Road between O'Neal and Ramseur, Rodes could only observe progress of those two units.

As they bounded forward, O'Neal and Ramseur soon approached the stalled second line of Confederates. O'Neal moved to his right to obtain Rodes' permission to pass through these troops. Rodes agreed and as O'Neal began to run back to his brigade he was shot down.[124] Rodes galloped across the front and taking the nearest regiment, the 3rd Alabama, passed through Colston's men. He then halted the 3rd, redressed the front and sent for Colonel Hall to assume command.[125]

On his far right, Iverson's unit drove forward smartly, passed through Colston's men and encountered Pender's Brigade. With these fresh troops Pender charged forward and into the enemy's second infantry line. But a Federal attack around his left flank forced Pender to give ground.[126] Short of ammunition, Pender and Iverson were in a critical situation. Rodes, riding left, had seen and anticipated the crisis. First he peeled off the 12th Alabama from O'Neal's left and sent that unit to assist. Then a staff officer, Major Whiting, dispatched by Rodes, arrived leading Colquitt's unit which had marched from the extreme right to the far left.[127] Rodes watched as Iverson's regiments and the 12th Alabama hung on gamely until Colquitt's men, at the double quick in column of fours, raced to assist. The Federal assault was repelled as Pender's men restocked their ammunition. Rodes was particularly thrilled with the leadership of Col. Daniel H. Christie, 23rd North Carolina, Iverson's Brigade, and recommended the young man's promotion.[128]

While Rodes was attending to these complications on his left, Ramseur and Doles advanced aggressively south of the Plank Road. They became separated slightly but continued forward despite heavy artillery opposition. Ramseur's troops soon arrived behind the massed soldiers of McGowan's and Jones' Brigades, sheltered behind the earthworks. The troops were leaderless and would not advance or retreat. Ramseur sent to Stuart, in Rodes' absence, for instructions. Stuart forcefully ordered Ramseur to "run over them," an instruction which Ramseur's regiments gladly obeyed.[129] Led by Col. Bryan Grimes and his 4th North Carolina, Ramseur's soldiers stepped on the backs of cringing Confederates as they crossed the trench and stormed into the 2nd Federal infantry line, capturing a lengthy segment. The attack, however, spurred a Union retaliatory attack and Ramseur's men were hard pressed to hold on to their gains.[130] Ramseur sent messages to Jones' men, even returning himself to plead for their assistance. He needed more troops and dispatched an aide to find his division commander who was at that moment returning from the left flank.[131]

Seeing Ramseur's desperate plight, Rodes spurred his huge, black horse into the mass of soldiers.[132] Some of Ramseur's units had been forced to fall back and the portly Colonel Grimes had passed out from heat exhaustion. Grimes was fortunate that an ambulance orderly from his brigade found him and poured water over his face to awaken him. As he awoke, Grimes heard General Rodes ask an officer, "Whose troops are these?" When the officer answered, Rodes asked further, "Why did they not join in the charge?" The officer gave some explanation that he had no such orders, but Grimes aroused himself and said, "That's a base lie, I heard the order from Stuart myself." Grimes described the remainder of the encounter as follows:

> Whereupon General Rodes took out his pistol, rode up to the officer, presented the muzzle to his head, and with an epithet of odium, told him to lead his men forward or he would blow his brains out.[133]

The frightened officer attempted to comply as Rodes watched, eyes flashing with anger.

Doles' Brigade survived heavy action and actually stumbled onto a route into the Federal rear near Chancellor House, but their numbers were so few they were forced to retreat. Rodes' entire division was now inside the Federal second line but receiving resistance so fierce they were unable to advance further. Suddenly this Federal pressure began to ease as Archer's and Anderson's units attacked from south of Chancellorsville. This fresh effort, combined with the deadly Confederate artillery, and Rodes' sustained pressure, compelled Hooker to retreat to already prepared trenches, giving up Chancellorsville. Shortly after 10 A.M. as the divisions met in the clearing at Chancellor's, Lee rode into their midst, and a rebel yell arose which surely shook the foundation of Joe Hooker's fast crumbling resolve.[134]

As Lee prepared to renew hammering on Hooker, hoping to prevent his escape across the river, he received news that altered his progress. Sedgwick had broken Early's lines at Fredericksburg and was moving on his rear. Realizing that Sedgwick must be dealt with at once, he ordered Stuart to draw a cordon around Hooker with the 2nd Corps which would contain the Federal chief in his earthworks.[135] Stuart ordered Colston to take whatever units he could reorganize and feel Hooker's lines north toward the river. Lee, undoubtedly, still was searching for a means to cut off the Federals. Colston sent scouts out and when they returned he heard their report and dispatched word to Stuart that "my division was not able to attack the position of the enemy with any prospect of success."[136] Stuart, already displeased with Colston's effort, was angered further by this and instructed Colston to place his units in entrenchments and report to General Rodes, who from 3 P.M., May 3, was placed in command of both divisions.[137]

Stuart assigned Rodes the arduous task of laying out lines of containment and insuring that they were well fortified. Rodes was engaged in this task for the remainder of May 3, and into the night. He posted Iverson near the Chancellor House and continued his line up the Plank Road with O'Neal's, Ramseur's, and Doles' units.[138] Doles' Brigade crossed the road at a 45 percent angle where it united with A.P. Hill's Division, now under Brigadier General Pender, since Heth also was wounded. Pender and Rodes set the lines on the left, and Rodes arranged Colston's Division as a continuation of his right with a gap of 200 yards between the divisions. This gap was an artillery salient, from which heavy gun fire could be maintained on Hooker's lines. Rodes then posted Colquitt's Brigade directly behind the artillery to prevent enemy sallies.[139]

The new lines were constructed primarily of logs, with earth and debris stuffed within where needed. Realizing the thin nature of these lines, and considering that they contained five Union corps or almost 90,000

Hazel Grove, Chancellorsville

Confederate guns lined hub to hub at Hazel Grove played a major role in the May 3 assault by Rodes on Hooker's lines.

Robert Carter

men, Rodes maintained a strong line of skirmishers and sharpshooters as close to Union lines as possible.

Federal trenches were also well made and their sharpshooters active, thus a deadly game took place in the dense woods. Rodes' primary advantage was the continued effective fire of Confederate artillery from Hazel Grove. Col. Porter Alexander was now in command and his skills became immediately obvious. Union troops were forced to add traverses to their trenches for protection from the hail of iron balls from Alexander's guns, and it was impossible for Federals to assemble in large numbers preparatory to attack.[140]

But Hooker had no offensive thoughts remaining. His objective was to get his massive army back over the Rappahannock in one piece. Years later, Hooker was questioned as to why he did not assault Rodes' lines when he well knew that Lee had weakened those lines to confront Sedgwick. Hooker replied probably as honestly as he could:

> it would seem reasonable....but the enemy had strongly fortified all egress and his artillery was formidable....accordingly, when my eight days ration was exhausted, I retired across the river.[141]

A few miles downriver, in the largely unpopulated town of Fredericksburg, Maj. Gen. Jubal Early's pickets watched the blue-clad men of Brig. Gen. John Gibbon's Division, Union II Corps, gather ominously across the Rappahannock. Towering, gaunt chimneys attested to the violence already visited upon this colonial trading post, and an eerie mist hung over the ruins, making sentinels nervous and quick triggered. Sedgwick sent Colonel Alexander Shaler's Brigade of Newton's Division marching up the Stage Road to Fredericksburg. Shaler drove Confederates under Brig. Gen. William Barksdale out of the city so Gibbon could erect bridges at Fredericksburg and cross his troops.[142] Newton marched his men directly at the stone wall at the foot of Marye's Heights, the very position which had been so invulnerable in December. The Confederate Washington Artillery, a capable New Orleans outfit, was awake and alert. Well dug in on Marye's Heights they had a perfect field of fire and opened as soon as the blue-coats emerged from cover. The gunners tore huge gaps in the Federal lines and the lone Mississippi Regiment behind the wall fired only two volleys to complete the repulse.[143] Soon, however, more troops arrived opposite the wall and the brave 18th Mississippi requested assistance. A Union officer approached with a flag of truce, requesting permission to evacuate his wounded. Colonel Griffin mistakenly agreed and the Federal discovered just how weakly held was the position.[144] Within minutes, heavy Federal guns opened a barrage and four columns of Federal troops moved to attack. Two of the columns were decimated by the Washington Artillery and a third was repelled by the Mississippians' rifle fire. But a fast-moving flank column led by the 7th Massachusetts blasted a path into the roadway and engaged the defenders in hand-to-hand combat. Additional Federals arrived from all over and soon fully half the Mississippi Regiment was captured.[145] Swiftly the blue-coats were ascending Marye's Heights, capturing gunners and weapons of the Washington Artillery. By a sudden, concise action the door to the Plank Road had been kicked open by the sturdy Union soldiers.

An exasperated, tobacco-chewing Jubal Early was angry. Gradually he was forced back onto the Telegraph Road, which led south, therefore isolated from the remainder of Lee's army. His losses were not high, but the veteran brigades of Brig. Gens. R.F. Hoke, John Gordon, and William Smith were completely cut off from the army whose rear they were charged to defend.

The Alabama Brigade of Cadmus Wilcox was on its own between Lee and Early at Banks' Ford. When Wilcox observed the blue-coats had donned knapsacks he realized they were preparing to move, thus when artillery sounded downstream, he made his first fateful decision. He moved his whole brigade toward Fredericksburg.[146]

Cadmus Wilcox then made a second important decision when he encountered advancing Federals. He decided to stay in front of Sedgwick and delay Federal progress as long as possible. He formed his brigade at a right angle to the Plank Road, placed two rifled guns of Lewis's Battery on either flank, and resolutely awaited the foe.[147] Wilcox, a native North Carolinian raised in Tennessee, was leading a gritty unit of Alabama soldiers. A West Point graduate, class of 1846, Wilcox was destined to be far outshone by classmates such as George McClellan and Thomas Jackson. But on this spring afternoon he took a back seat to no man. His astute decisions became the proof that one lone brigade, courageously and wisely employed, could play a significant role in any engagement.[148]

Newton's Division, which had broken Early's line, was exhausted, so Sedgwick ordered Brig. Gen. William Brooks and his 1st Division to assume the lead, moving up the Plank Road.[149] Sedgwick, a crusty old veteran, was intent on maximizing his good fortune to Lee's discomfort. As Brooks pushed forward he deployed two regiments of New Jersey troops and confidently advanced, but the artillery began tearing holes in his lines, and then he observed a gray battle line drawn across the road, red flags awave.[150] Brooks halted his troops and sent back for a brigade and artillery units. After an exchange at maximum range, Rigby's Federal guns opened and Wilcox faded his line back into the woods. Wilcox repeated this scenario several times, using each ridgeline to make Brooks deploy his brigades. The actual fighting was minimal, but Brooks' advance was so slow it was almost 5:30 P.M. when Federals sighted Salem Church on the ridgeline. Sedgwick's advance was three miles from Lee's rear.[151]

Lee dispatched forces to Wilcox's assistance, then followed up by ordering Lafayette McLaws and two more units to report. On arriving near Salem Church these units found Wilcox well deployed on a ridgeline.[152] The all-Georgia Brigade of Brig. Gen. Paul Semmes moved on line alongside

Wilcox as Brooks' Federals suddenly struck hard, driving to the very walls of the church. After twenty minutes of tough exchanges Brooks fell back.[153] Newton's Division moved up alongside Brooks on the right side of the road.[154] A series of sharp Northern attacks rekindled rifle fire around the church and on the wooded slopes nearby. McLaws was on the field and assumed command but Wilcox and Semmes did most of the fighting.[155] Just before dark the two Confederate brigadiers sent their men screaming into the blue ranks in a counterattack which cleared the field. They enjoyed some success until Union artillery halted their wild advance. Darkness closed the encounter, but soldiers, blue and gray, slept on their arms in line of battle.[156] Casualties were high in the units involved: the 121st New York of impetuous and gallant Col. Emory Upton's, Brooks' Division lost almost half its roster.[157] The door to Lee's rear, so abruptly opened by brave old John Sedgwick, was slammed shut by the timely actions of an obscure and brave brigadier, Cadmus Wilcox.

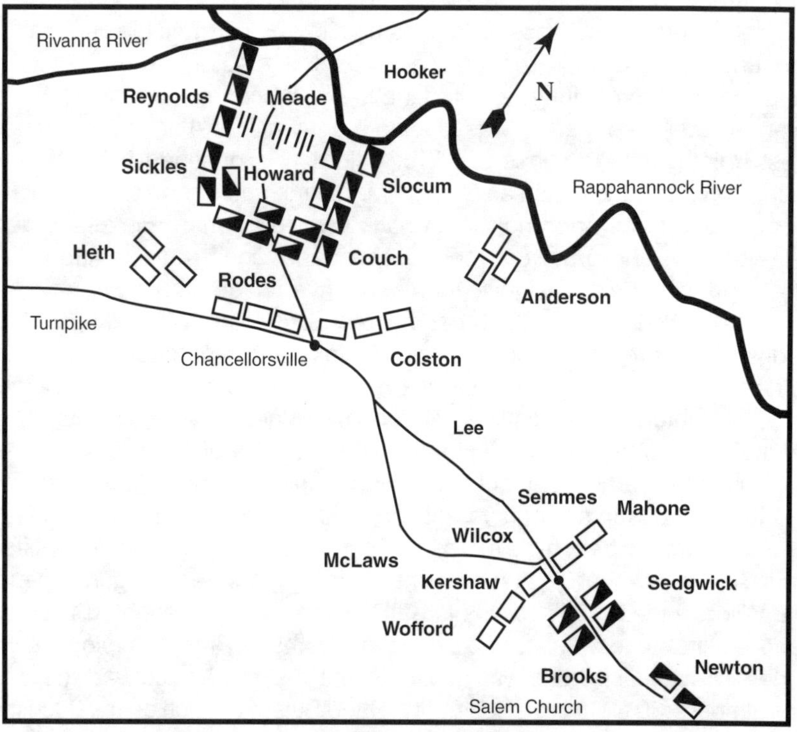

Chancellorsville, May 3, 1863

After his defeat Hooker pulled back into prepared defensive positions with the river at his back as Lee dispatched McLaws to assist Wilcox in stopping Sedgwick's threat to his rear. A sharp action resulted near Salem Church.

Somewhat later that evening, Lee began consideration of an attack at dawn to isolate and destroy Sedgwick and his giant VI Corps.[158] Turning his back on Hooker, and leaving Pender and Rodes to contain the Federal commander's forces, he dispatched McLaws' entire division as well as that of Richard Anderson in concert with Early to encircle Sedgwick.

Sedgwick, however, was beginning to reconsider his position. He was now positioned in a large horseshoe, both flanks on the river.[159] He could ascertain no action from Hooker's lines and was surely not strong enough to fight Lee's army by himself. He received a note from Hooker which was full of retreat instructions and did not mention any combined assault. Sedgwick, by the afternoon of May 4, began sliding his units toward the open crossing at Banks' Ford.[160]

Early on May 5, again leaving Early to guard the fords, Lee attempted to consolidate his army against Hooker's lines. He was still intent on attacking those lines, however formidable they might appear. Rodes' incursions had convinced that officer that Hooker was in very great force with extremely formidable entrenchments.[161] Colonel Alexander thought Lee never had a more audacious resolve than when he determined to attack Hooker in those earthworks.[162] On the afternoon of May 5, a tremendous thunderstorm broke over the area with heavy rainfall and vicious lightning. Movement of units was delayed by deep water which covered the roads and fields. About dusk another torrent broke and under cover of this storm Hooker evacuated his massive force to safety, despite the perils of traversing pontoon bridges on a rapidly rising Rappahannock. Early on May 6, Rodes threw his skirmishers forward, based on outpost reports, and found the enemy gone.[163]

The battle around Chancellorsville concluded with both Union wings being arrested and driven back across the Rappahannock River. The world's newspapers would proclaim this action Lee's ultimate victory, and future critics would assert that from a Confederate point-of-view, Chancellorsville was more nearly a flawless battle than any planned and executed by an American commander.[164] Certainly the Confederate chieftain demonstrated another facet of his leadership, a willingness to take long, calculated risks against formidable odds. Lee's ability to use his influence, his very personality, upon his foe and actually dictate his enemy's response was comparable with Napoleon and Alexander, the greats of history. At Chancellorsville, the aggressor, with a solid battle plan, a march to the flank, was in turn, surprised by the same maneuver.[165] In boxing parlance, Hooker's right hook was topped by Lee's left.

Jackson's display of pure nerve in requesting Lee's approval of his large flanking force and leaving his chief with so few, also contains an implication that he believed Lee would approve. And with that proposal Jackson took ultimate responsibility for its success. He managed, supervised, encouraged, and drove the marching column, for Stonewall was well aware of the odds he and Lee were facing. Then at the climax of his attack, his greatest day, his most significant achievement, he was suddenly removed from the stage. Mistakenly gunned down in the dark woodland at the very zenith of his prowess.

Among those other Confederates who contributed most to the victory, Robert E. Rodes was mentioned after Lee and Jackson. Few mistakes and much credit were attested to his initial performance in divisional command. His leadership on the march and management of the initial attack wave on May 2 were almost unmatched. On May 3 his constant attention to progress, his adjustments, and leadership of troops literally produced success in a fluid front where others had already failed. His ability to keep his various brigades well in hand and yet not hamper the aggressive, individual style of his brigadiers was the sign of a confident division commander. A.P. Hill, who observed most of the two days' fight, commented that "Gen. Rodes distinguished himself much and won a proud name for himself and his division."[166] Jackson, told of Rodes' success, simply said, "He is a soldier."[167] Lee remarked on several occasions of Rodes' abilities and the recommendation he received from the wounded Jackson.[168] On these high words of praise, Rodes was promoted to the rank of major general on May 7, 1863, this action being the nearest approach to promotion on the field for valor ever approved by the Confederate government.[169]

On May 6, the scavengers of Rodes' Division enjoyed an excellent haul in knapsacks, tents, oilcloths and other sundries always appreciated by gray-backs. Ordnance officers recovered much small arms ammunition but little edible was abandoned in the Federal camp. In a steady rain, over swollen streams, Rodes' Division moved out the afternoon of May 6, returning to their old quarters near Grace Church. In a week's hard action the division, which had totalled almost 10,000 men, had suffered 2,900 casualties, or about 29 percent, of its force killed, wounded, or missing.[170] Total army losses were almost as serious as the Army of Northern Virginia reported a 22 percent casualty rate, losing 12,800 soldiers from an engaged force of about 60,900.[171] The opposing Army of the Potomac suffered losses of 17,278 men, but that was only 13 percent of its 133,868 effectives.[172]

Back in camp, the soldiers began attending to their daily routine: drill, work details, and an occasional review. During late May, Special Order #136 from Lee changed the composition of the division which had now been formally assigned to Robert Rodes. Colquitt's Brigade was detailed to Goldsboro, North Carolina and replaced by the North Carolina unit of Brig.Gen. Junius Daniel.[173] This untested brigade was so large its numbers made up almost one-third of the 8,910 men Rodes reported in field returns of May 20, 1863.[174] Daniel's men were eager and proud to be included in such a veteran division. An officer from the 53rd North Carolina wrote home after a divisional review on May 29:

> We had a review of Roads Division. I suppose of some 10,000 troops where I saw Gen'l Roads and the Alabama coon himself. Gen. R.E. Lee, it was a grand seane to look upon.[175]

It's uncertain as to which general Lt. James Green was comparing to a nocturnal animal from the deep South, but the new division member was obviously proud to be associated with both. Such was the attitude and temper of Rodes' Division in May 1863, as they lazed in their camps awaiting the next plans of their trusted commander in chief.

CHAPTER 7

THE GREAT INVASION
Lee Sweeps North

Handsome, vain Joe Hooker, coerced into using his powerful army at Chancellorsville, had implemented a solid battle plan and executed the initial portions successfully; but was then rebuffed, repelled, intimidated, and forced to sneak across the rising Rappahannock at night by a grey-bearded Confederate general who seemed to take every chance, incur every gamble, and coolly and assuredly win every toss of the dice. However, the true measure of this failure lay not in the Army of the Potomac but in the mind of its commander.[1] Hooker would later explain that his army lost no honors at Chancellorsville, that there really was no battle, and that weather, position, and supplies forced him to withdraw and abort confrontation. These deluded statements really bring to question Hooker's grip on reality.[2]

The Union army was developing an esprit, a pride of its own ability which rivaled that of its gray-clad opponent. Despite repeated misuse by its leaders, the blue-clad troops that recrossed the Rappahannock were humiliated and even embarrassed by their defeat, but not severely injured. Casualties were heavy, even critical, in a few units; but their ranks were no more depleted than the victors'. A blue army as strong and proud as this force was becoming, would only succumb to physical defeat, not mere embarrassment.

As Lee assessed his losses, the wounding and subsequent death of Lt. Gen. Thomas J. Jackson was foremost in his mind. He wrote to his wife, "I know not how to replace him."[3] The Confederate nation mourned as muffled drums led the funeral procession, amid booming minute guns, into Capitol Square where Stonewall's body would lie in the Virginia Capitol.[4] Also missing were scores of regimental, brigade, and divisional officers of high reputation and ability. Rodes' Division, which had borne so much of the fighting, suffered thirty officers slain, and one hundred forty-eight wounded.[5]

Lee immediately was confronted with the necessity of reorganizing his army. The critical question seemed, who would lead Jackson's famed 2nd Corps? Certainly no one could replace Stonewall but where could an adequate commander be found? When Longstreet arrived with his two 1st Corps divisions, Lee's infantry would total about sixty thousand soldiers. Would they not be better handled in three corps of 20,000 rather than the previous two? The answer seemed obviously positive but compounded Lee's deliberations for he would thus need two corps commanders rather than one.[6] After deliberation and consideration of four or five candidates, Lee recommended to President Davis that Maj. Gens. Ambrose Powell Hill and Richard Stoddard Ewell be promoted to lieutenant general to serve as corps commanders alongside James Longstreet.[7]

A.P. Hill was, at least in Lee's opinion, the most proficient divisional commander in the Army of Northern Virginia. He was usually energetic, intelligent, and inspired his men in combat. Despite a prickly personality which landed him under arrest while serving both Longstreet and Jackson and a disturbing tendency toward poor health, Hill was well respected within the army.[8] Some thought him impetuous in that at Gaines Mill and other occasions his thunderboltlike attacks were loosened a bit recklessly, but Lee liked a fighter and Hill would fight.

Lee's other selection, Richard Ewell, was a little more of a gamble. Lee didn't know Ewell well since most of old "baldhead's" service had been with Jackson; besides he had seen no action for almost eight months or since his severe leg wound. During his convalescence, after amputation of the limb, Ewell married the wealthy widow Brown.[9] Since that marriage, Ewell had sincerely embraced the Episcopal faith and as an ardent churchman had forgone his previous liberal use of profane language. Ewell's lack of self-confidence was well concealed.[10]

Chancellorsville casualties and corps expansion also necessitated widespread reorganization of divisions and brigades. Lee desired to realign the army into nine divisions, three per corps, and this necessitated numbers of transfers and promotions. Richard Ewell's 2nd Corps would contain Jubal Early's Division, that of Edward Johnson, who was assigned the transferred Colston's Division, and Robert Rodes, newly promoted to major general and assigned to permanent command of D.H. Hill's Division.[11] Rodes' advance in rank was dated from his flank assault at Chancellorsville, based upon the death bed recommendation of Thomas Jackson. This action constituted as near a promotion for valor as the Confederate Congress ever approved.

The artillery was likewise reorganized with the army's cumbersome general reserve being eliminated and fifteen fairly equal artillery battalions established, each battalion consisting of four batteries of four guns apiece.

Five battalions were assigned to each corps, one battalion per division and two designated as corps reserve.[12]

The cavalry arm was also not ignored. The flamboyant Major General James E.B. Stuart now commanded three brigades of riders under capable brigadiers Fitzhugh Lee, Wade Hampton, and W.F.H. "Rooney" Lee. For the anticipated invasion William E. "Grumble" Jones' Brigade was added as was Beverly Robinson's small North Carolina Brigade. Additionally, two irregular cavalry commands would assist Lee's army, although not assigned to Stuart. Six batteries of horse artillery completed Stuart's command.[13]

The division which Robert Rodes would lead north was somewhat altered from that he led at Chancellorsville. Brig. Gen. Stephen Ramseur still led his outstanding North Carolina Brigade and Colonel E.A. O'Neal would continue to command Rodes' old Alabama Brigade. Iverson's Brigade was unchanged and George Doles formally took over command of Ripley's Brigade which was now an all-Georgia unit. Colquitt's Brigade was transferred and replaced by Junius Daniel and his untried but eager North Carolinians. The artillery battalion assigned Rodes was led by his firm friend, Lt. Col. Thomas H. Carter.[14]

On May 29, near Guiney's Station, a grand review of Rodes' Division was conducted by General Lee. Each regiment marched several miles to a wide level field, took long hours to properly align, then passed smartly in review before the commanding general, Rodes beaming alongside.[15] Several days later the movement north began, and by June 7, Rodes' Division was encamped alongside four additional Confederate divisions around Culpeper Court House.[16]

Robert Rodes, realizing hard campaigning was about to begin, reorganized his baggage trains to eliminate excess. He loaded divisional trains with three days' rations, brigade trains with an additional three days' supply, and issued three days' rations directly to the troops for their haversacks.[17] His soldiers would thus march with nine days' rations and plenty of ammunition but a minimum of wagons.

North of Culpeper, Cavalry Commander Stuart encamped most of his 9,500 riders near a large, grassy field and decided to conduct a grand cavalry review. He organized and carried out an elaborate ceremony, and when he discovered that General Lee was in the area, scheduled a repeat performance for his superior on June 8. The scene was grand for the thousands of spectators who rode out on the railway to view the affair, although those infantrymen present tended to deride cavalry capers. Lee commented that Stuart was "in all his glory."[18] Concluding the stirring ride-by, complete with artillery discharges and much yelling, the riders slowly returned to their scattered camps preparatory to moving north on the following morning. But early on June 9, they were rudely interrupted by the blue-clad cavalry of Maj. Gen. Alfred Pleasonton who came a'calling. Splashing across two Rappahannock River fords, brushing aside Stuart's vendettas, they moved in force to flank Stuart's camps.[19] The day-long conflict which followed was filled with reckless excitement as cavalry units charged and countercharged around Fleetwood Hill, the dominant terrain feature on the Brandy Station Battlefield. About midmorning Lee contacted Stuart offering infantry support but only if absolutely necessary. He wished to continue concealing his concentration of infantry from enemy eyes.[20] Rodes, camped nearby and anticipating orders, moved his division toward Brandy Station, sending Battle's men forward to support Stuart but not close enough to be sighted by the enemy. Stuart eventually held his lines with much effort and considerable lost pride as Pleasonton slowly withdrew across the river behind his own infantry support.[21]

Lee's army now began swinging wide across the Blue Ridge Mountains into the Shenandoah Valley. Ewell's Corps led by Rodes' Division moved northwest over difficult roads. Having crossed the mountains through Chester Gap and forded the Shenandoah River, Rodes and Ewell met on June 12 to clarify movements.[22] An advance was planned on two fronts with attacks on Federal garrisons at both Winchester and Berryville. Rodes, reinforced by the 1,600-man cavalry battalion of Brig. Gen. Alfred Jenkins, was to advance on the Millwood Road and assault Berryville while the remaining two divisions accompanied Ewell to reduce Winchester.[23] When Rodes captured Berryville he was to dash for Martinsburg, eventually capturing the fords of the Potomac.[24]

Rodes moved rapidly up the Millwood Road, utilizing the services of a local guide. He sent Jenkins forward to secure all nearby roads thereby screening his infantry approach. Federal Colonel Andrew T. McReynolds, commander of the outpost at Berryville, was well entrenched with a brigade of Maj. Gen. Robert H. Milroy's Winchester garrison. He possessed some cavalry and artillery, a total of about eighteen hundred men, a large garrison force entrenched behind good earthworks. He was, however, no match for Robert Rodes' large division. McReynolds suspected Confederate movements and was uneasy as Rodes bivouacked at Stone Bridge, planning to move on Berryville at first light.[25] But Union cavalry sighted the Confederate infantry and fled back to Berryville. Jenkins' failure to occupy Millwood exposed Rodes' van to prying Union eyes. When Rodes reached the environs of Berryville he found Jenkins' force checked by fire from a Union battery.[26] Rodes assumed Union infantry was still in the village in support of the artillery, and dispatching Jenkins to circle the town, cutting off any escape route, sent a brigade to either flank, and ordered O'Neal to assault Berryville directly down the Millwood Road. But McReynolds was long gone, with his infantry leaving one battery supported by cavalry to use the earthworks as a delaying tactic. This force unceremoniously fled at the sight of Confederate infantry.[27] So rapid was their flight that Jenkins' cavalry was outdistanced. A small Confederate force under Major James W. Sweeney made contact with McReynolds' cavalry just outside Winchester.[28] A disgusted division commander secured a few stores and started his van toward Martinsburg, his second objective. Confederate soldiers were excited by the discovery of large supplies of dried beans abandoned by the defenders. This was their first experience with this new stable, and when they moved on, all were well supplied.[29] Bean pots boiled at every campfire that night.

Rodes bivouacked that evening near Summit Point, pushing on the following day, to arrive near Martinsburg in late afternoon. Again Rodes discovered Jenkins' gray riders skirmishing with Federal defenders, but this time Rodes sent his lead brigade, Ramseur's, straight at the defenders. They bounced forward with enthusiasm, however the Federal troops were nervous and fled at once. Ramseur's Brigade had marched approximately twenty miles, and led by the persistent 14th North Carolina, they sprinted in pursuit for over two miles. While the spirit was willing the men were tired, and repeated vaulting over stone fences was just too much. Five cannon, several hundred prisoners, and an assorted collection of small arms and ammunition were captured by the Confederates.[30] The guns were three-inch rifles of excellent quality and were equipped with caissons and horses. Rodes turned these weapons over to a grateful Alabama battery which was still employing smoothbores.[31] Jenkins had failed Rodes a second time, exchanging fire and seeking loot rather than serving the role of cavalry when supported by infantry. Thus with open exit roads, a large part of the 1,200 Federals at Martinsburg escaped down the river to Harper's Ferry.

The division had marched hard, perhaps well enough to please "Old Jack," averaging twenty to twenty-five miles a day in oppressive heat. Rodes allowed the men to rest on the fifteenth, but receiving a message that Winchester had fallen, pushed his tired and foot-sore troops on to Williamsport and command of the fords of the Potomac River. The roads were rocky, rough, and difficult for two-thirds of the soldiers who had no shoes. Many attempted to follow the columns through nearby fields. They waded the Potomac in good spirits, strolling through waist deep water, singing and laughing. One of the Georgia bands attempted to cross while playing "The Bonnie Blue Flag," quite nude, with their clothes piled atop their heads.[32] Large crowds of spectators gathered to watch the division cross, but whether due to the serious occasion or the impromptu strip was unknown. Rodes was extremely concerned about his men's physical condition since they had marched hard every day since departing Culpeper and he stated:

> It was not until this day that the troops began to exhibit unmistakable signs of exhaustion, and that stragglers could be found in the line of march....A halt at Williamsport was absolutely necessary from the condition of the feet of the unshod men. Very many of these gallant fellows were still marching in ranks with feet bruised, bleeding, and swollen and withal so cheerfully, as to entice them to be called the heros of the Pennsylvania Campaign. None but the best of soldiers could have made such a march under such circumstances.[33]

Meanwhile in Winchester, Milroy had drawn in his outposts and consolidated his garrison in excellent entrenchments. He probably could have escaped on the night of June 13 as advised by his superiors.[34] The roads north were open although Rodes was camped at Summit Point, in a direct line to Harper's Ferry. Milroy felt the few gray-clad soldiers which his patrols had encountered were simply part of a smaller raiding force. In the few skirmishes which resulted, his men bested the Confederates and this indicated to Milroy that the battle for Winchester was over.[35] In reality, it had hardly begun. Hooker was gradually moving his army north to protect the Federal capitol, but seemed more intend in his arguments with Army Chief Halleck over the evacuation of Harper's Ferry, than he was in pursuing Lee. At length Hooker repeated his demands on Halleck and insisted he would resign if refused. Halleck refused, Hooker resigned, and a collective sigh of relief resounded through Washington.

Ewell utilized his advantages in numbers at Winchester wisely without allowing Milroy to ascertain the real size of his forces. He sent Edward Johnson's Division to demonstrate forcefully against Federal defense lines at a number of points east and south of the city. Jubal Early and his division were dispatched on a circuitous route, unseen by the enemy, to emerge opposite the northwest corner of Milroy's defenses, in position to attack West Fort, key to the entire position.[36] Early secluded his troops in a wooded area while reconnoitering carefully and placing his artillery. At 5 P.M. he unmasked and rolled forward twenty guns which began pounding West Fort.[37] Soon the Federal artillery was silenced and the fort's interior reduced to wreckage. This rapid use of masked superior guns overwhelmed the Federal artillerymen before they could be supported. Harry T. Hays' Louisiana Brigade moved up close by use of a nearby ravine and the moment the guns fell silent, dashed for the fort, absorbing a volley before reaching the walls. Union defenders resisted for several minutes, but as the graybacked color guards planted their blood-red flags on the parapet, they surrendered or fled.[38] Nightfall halted any further advance but it was obvious to each commander that the key to Winchester had fallen and the city must surrender at dawn.

Milroy planned his escape, abandoning his large hospitals, and starting his forces toward Harper's Ferry about 1 A.M. Ewell anticipated this movement and dispatched Gen. Edward Johnson with a strike force, reinforced with artillery, to block the main route north. Johnson's force was delayed in leaving, but still reached their planned position in time to collide with Milroy's van in pitch darkness near Stephenson's Depot. Several furious Union charges almost broke through Johnson, but artillery support buttressed the Confederates. The few Federal units whose officers enforced strict discipline seemed more able to escape this trap in a defile where the only light was from cannon muzzle-blasts or the flash of rifle volleys. Some units surrendered en masse while others disintegrated with each soldier seeking his own safety. General Milroy escaped with a cavalry unit of three hundred who sifted quietly into the woods and made their way to Harper's Ferry. General Johnson, who personally captured thirty Federals, reported a net bag of 2,500 captives.[39]

The initial phase of Lee's plan was complete. Winchester and the lower valley were cleared; he had broken contact with frantically searching Federal forces; and Rodes with his lead division was holding open the fords of the Potomac for his fast-moving army to initiate the second phase of invasion. The largest, most experienced Confederate field army ever assembled was poised to cross the river. Harper's Ferry, isolated and battened down, was bypassed as the hungry, enthusiastic, gray-clad infantry waded the wide Potomac, their bands playing the soldiers' favorite, "Listen to the Mockingbird," and swept unceasingly and unopposed north to Pennsylvania.

Crossing the river was significant to some, but most Confederates considered Maryland a sister Southern state, forcefully retained in the detested

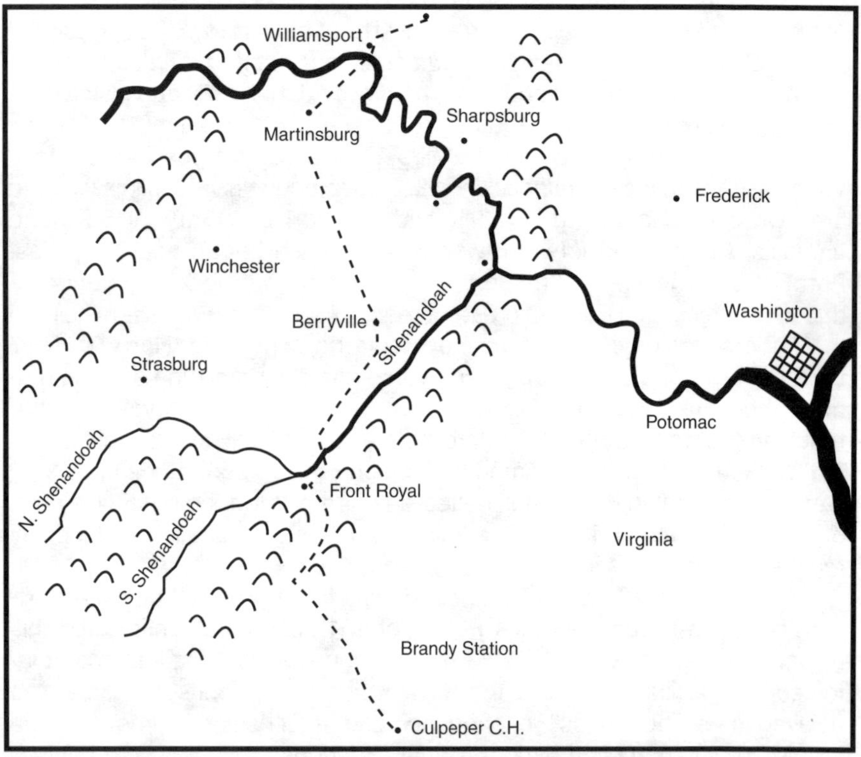

Route of Rodes' March North, June 10–25

From Culpeper Court House, Rodes' Division proceeded north via Berryville, Martinsburg, and Williamsport. Ewell's other two divisions captured Winchester, then joined Rodes at the fords of the Potomac. The 2nd Corps then strode purposefully up the Cumberland Valley to Carlisle, Pennsylvania, hence south to Gettysburg on July 1, 1863.

Federal Union. Many of the old veterans, also, had crossed this river before with high hopes and inauspicious results.[40] True invasion would occur, in their minds, when the Mason-Dixon line was crossed into the Keystone State.

Despite their lack of foot gear, the Confederate soldiers who entered Maryland were in excellent spirits. Their morale was soaring as they fearlessly strode the alien roads with light hearts and steady tread under the starry crosses emblazoned on their red battle flags. Almost to a man they were awed, even enchanted, by the bounty, the lushness, of this strange land unfolding alongside the well-fenced roads. Neat, well-maintained farms were often characterized by small, trim houses paired with huge, freshly painted red barns bearing colorful hex signs under their eaves. The almost perfectly maintained little farms were a constant amazement to the many farmers in Confederate ranks.[41] Big overfed, powerful horses were plentiful and admired until it was discovered they were useless for military purposes. Food, particularly bread and dairy products, was readily available and abundantly consumed.[42]

The men developed schemes for coping with Lee's orders against looting so as to obtain the fruits of the land. They were not adverse to approaching well-groomed houses and simply asking to be fed. Their very appearance encouraged a positive response for they were gaunt, bearded, fearsome-looking, and intimidating to the unknowing. They walked with a swagger, confrontation in their bold eyes, belying the half-smiles on their faces. In truth, they appeared to the peace-loving Pennsylvania farmers as "outlaws," and they did not disclaim the term. In a word, they were "rebels" and damn proud of it.[43]

Rodes' Division, safely across the river, established comfortable camps in groves of trees alongside the Potomac, and for several days enjoyed the respite to bathe, wash clothes, and soak aching, stone-bruised feet.[44] Quartermasters were busily engaged in purchasing supplies and equipment with Confederate script, while pioneers inflicted as much damage as possible on bridges, culverts, and tunnels of the Baltimore and Ohio Railroad. By June 18, Ewell's entire corps had arrived and he instructed Rodes to move north but to maintain a leisurely pace, allowing Lee's other troops to close up. Rodes moved directly toward Hagerstown with one slight diversion. Several miles outside his objective, he turned east for a time, feinting a march on Harper's Ferry.[45]

As the division moved through Hagerstown on Sunday, an adventurous Confederate officer ducked out of the line of march to attend services at the Methodist Church. Afterwards he was invited to take tea by an attractive young lady professing pro-Southern sympathies.[46] The regiments paraded down Hagerstown's main streets in column of fours and once through town broke into route step and began to move north in earnest. On June 22, a momentous day, they went over the line and into Pennsylvania, stopping that night to camp near Greencastle. A small number of Greencastle locals advocated "bushwhacking" Southern columns, and a few attempted such actions, then disappeared into the crevices of South Mountain.[47] Little damage or reaction resulted but no mercy need be expected if captured.

Ewell then broke up his long column, dispatching Jubal Early's Division on a more eastern route alongside the shoulders of South Mountain. Jubal maintained a stiff pace except for a foray to burn the Caledonia Ironworks, property of Thaddeus Stevens, United States Congressman and leader of the Radical Republicans.[48] Early declared the foundry a legitimate military target as it may well have been, but the incident was surely costly to the Southern states during the later years of reconstruction, for the powerful Stevens was not a forgiving man. It would appear the headstrong Early initiated this action fully knowing his commander would not approve. Fortunate it was for the citizens of Pennsylvania that Lee led the Confederate army and not Jubal Early.

The Divisions of Johnson and Rodes were ordered to proceed straight up the center of the Cumberland Valley, parallel to Early, gathering horses, cattle, and supplies, all properly paid for with Confederate money. A few militia units were called out, but they were not capable of confronting the Southern professionals and confined their activities to skirmishes with Jenkins' cavalry. Early captured almost two hundred militiamen and lining them up, took their shoes, lectured them on meddling, and sent them home.

Jenkins led his riders as far north as Chambersburg, but hearing rumors of 40,000 Union soldiers under McClellan marching to confront the Confederates, retreated. So convinced was Jenkins of a Union threat that when he reached Rodes' marching infantry at Greencastle, he reported the rumor as fact, and Rodes had his leading brigade deploy, knocking down fences on both sides of the road to shake out artillery on either flank. When Rodes found the report untrue he was irately displeased and so informed the lackadaisical Jenkins.[49] By now Rodes was attempting to get rid of his unsolicited responsibility for Jenkins, but both Lee and Ewell had assigned Jenkins to the strict Rodes in an attempt to control his wayward tendencies, and he was stuck with him.[50]

Once Jenkins retreated from Chambersburg, a suddenly optimistic city attempted to raise a defense force. Federal General Joseph F. Knipe, already in Chambersburg, assembled a force based on two small regiments, some regular cavalry units, and militia.[51] He planned on delaying the Confederate advance until assistance arrived, but wisely abandoned that plan when discovering that a returning Jenkins was closely followed by two large gray divisions barrelling up the Chambersburg Pike as fast as cavalry and would steamroll whatever meager force he placed in their path. Knipe entrained his men north for Carlisle and eventually moved on to Harrisburg.

General Order #72, issued by Lee as the army moved north, was strictly enforced by both Ewell and Rodes. This edict forbade looting, stealing, or destruction of private property.[52] Many infantrymen resented their close supervision on this matter versus the freedom of action they believed enjoyed by cavalrymen whom they observed with chickens and hams slung upon their saddles. There was little concern for losses suffered by Northern citizens as these soldiers had experienced firsthand the deprivations and destruction in Virginia initiated by Northern troops. In reality most Confederate soldiers believed that Northerners should taste the fruits of invasion, but most obeyed Lee's order because he was simply to be respected. Rodes supported Lee's order, suppressing irregularities, and he felt that most officers and men cheerfully obeyed. He did discover, while at Greencastle, some cases of violence to property which he traced to Jenkins' cavalry. Long after the invasion Pennsylvania citizens would reflect that gray-back soldiers indeed were restrained in their looting; they simply took what they needed and paid in worthless Confederate script. Only two items were considered exempt and fair game. They were bread and hats. One Georgia soldier remembered bread as so plentiful that he lived the entire campaign on fresh, light bread and Pennsylvania apple butter or "red spread."[53] The second item coveted by Southern infantry was the hats of the civilians. The sun was hot and head coverings a necessity, so they engaged in wholesale "hat swapping." Any civilian close to the line of march was fair game and in a flash their hats would disappear to be replaced by a ragged, old Southern cap.[54] Swapping reached such proportions that most regiments presented a comical appearance on parade due to a wide variety of strange headgear.

General Ewell, accompanied by his staff, travelled closely behind the troops in his trim two-horse carriage. Other officers such as Rodes and Johnson would report to confer with him and simply crawl into the carriage, and he could keep rolling while planning his next move. Ewell jokingly commented concerning the sullen looks they received as they moved deeper into Pennsylvania when he wrote his cousin:

> It is like a renewal of Mexican times to enter a captured town. The people look as sour as vinegar and, I have no doubt, would gladly send us all to Kingdom come, if they could.[55]

On June 24 at 9 A.M., preceded by Jenkins' cavalry, Rodes' Division entered Chambersburg. As the long gray lines proceeded up Walnut Hollow Road and turned into Main Street their bands struck up "The Bonnie Blue Flag," and the marchers laughed and joked with bystanders. A private of the 4th Georgia remembered the high spirits of his regiment, as they called out "Here's Your Played Out Rebellion," in reference to month-old Northern newspapers which had predicted the rebellion as almost played out and soon to be over.[56] Rodes hurried his brigades through Chambersburg and on north toward Carlisle, stopping to camp overnight near several large man-made fish ponds which provided water as well as supper for the more adept fishermen. The following morning the column reached Carlisle as Doles'

Brigade turned into the trim little campus of Dickinson College where his men encamped, constructing huge barbecue pits on the lawn for their captured beeves. Several alumni were present in the Confederate column and damage to the college buildings was minimal. The division commander led the brigades of Ramseur, Iverson, and Daniel out to Carlisle Army Barracks where they settled down in comfortable surroundings.[57]

Once again Lt. Robert Park of the 12th Alabama found an occasion to attend church services, this time at the Episcopal chapel. Park remarked that although he lifted his cap to all the well-dressed ladies he received little encouraging response.[58] The Alabamian can be commended on his faithful church attendance, although one might suspect his motives were primarily to meet members of the opposite sex.

Gen. Richard Ewell had been stationed at Carlisle while serving as a United States Dragoon, enjoying fond memories of the area. Several days later, when preparing to depart, Ewell commented that he trusted it would be remembered that his men did not damage or burn the hundred-year-old military post.[59] Actually, Rodes was forced to place a provost guard about the storehouses to drive away civilians intent on looting.[60] Several days later when Stuart's cavalrymen came through looking for Lee's army, an exchange of cannon fire resulted in extensive damage and the riders fired several buildings.

The Confederate Army of Northern Virginia was encamped in hostile territory, yet Rodes' troops recalled Carlisle with fondness. Rations were plentiful, shelter easily available, the weather pleasant, and the surliness of civilians did not frighten them; but none could foretell that in a few days almost 3,500 of their number would lie dead or wounded in a small town a few miles south.

CHAPTER 8

HIGH TIDE AT THE CROSSROADS
Gettysburg

In the sunshine of a Sunday afternoon in June 1863, the massed fife and drum bands of Maj. Gen. Robert Rodes' Confederate Infantry Division beat assembly on the parade ground of the United States Army Cavalry Training Center at Carlisle, Pennsylvania.[1] Gray-clad infantrymen flocked to align in precise formation at this, the northernmost point of Confederate invasion. They assembled to raise the infant nation's new flag, the "Stars and Bars," over the captured Federal post. The 32nd North Carolina Infantry was honored to hoist the banner overhead with appropriate pomp and ceremony, preceded by martial music.[2]

The veteran soldiers, dressed in natty, new uniforms, had enjoyed a relaxing day interrupted first by the lengthy divine service discourse of the Reverend Mr. Lacy. The flag raising was then accompanied by a number of lengthy orations, tolerated in reasonably good humor.[3] For one day, at least, the soldiers could forget that they were encamped in hostile territory dependent only on the guile, logic, and will of their trusted commander and their own considerable fighting talents.

General Rodes and his staff discovered a supply of captured Pennsylvania Lager Beer to be of excellent quality although rather strong. A member of Ewell's staff members swore the beer was spiked with whiskey.[4] Another witness declared Rodes tipsy for the first and only occasion so recalled or a least recorded.[5] Carlisle's grassy quadrangle resembled an artillery park with gun caissons and limbers scattered about among the large oak trees.

Late that evening General Rodes hosted a dinner in the Carlisle Mess for a number of officers. Candlelight and torches glistened in the hallways and windows of the hundred-year-old buildings as the laughing officers completed their repast with whiskey and ice water.[6] Outside, the troops, lounging about their campfires under the trees, joked, gambled, and read until a sudden rainstorm forced them to seek cover. They were eagerly anticipating the next day's march on Harrisburg and expected spoils. None were aware that General Lee, camping in Chambersburg, was about to alter those grandiose plans.

Lee was most concerned over his missing cavalry brigades, from which he had received no firm news for days and no reliable information on the Federal army.[7] Maj. Gen. J.E.B. Stuart, cavalry chief of the Army of Northern Virginia, had successfully screened the mountain passes in Virginia, keeping prying eyes and questioning tongues away as the gray infantry raced north,[8] but that task complete, he decided to combine scouting duties with a raid around Hooker's army, and he disappeared behind the northward marching bluecoats. This action isolated Stuart and his horsemen from contact with Lee. Stuart had taken his three best brigadiers and most of his veteran cavalrymen.[9] While such a decision could prove critical in any campaign, it was decidedly more so here in Pennsylvania, where suspicious locals provided little reliable information for the worried Confederate general. Lee's orders to Stuart provided the hard-driving cavalryman broad discretionary powers[10] in determining his route north, but this prolonged absence surely bordered on outright abuse of that discretion. Stuart left a subordinate, Brig. Gen. Beverly Robertson and his small brigade, to remain in the mountain passes, implying that Robertson inform Lee of all Federal movements observed. But Robertson either discarded Stuart's orders or misunderstood, and Lee's informational needs were not served. Lee's constant referral to Stuart's welfare betrayed his dire concern for relevant information.[11] Filled with concern, Lee repeatedly told Harry Heth, "I hope no disaster has overtaken my cavalry."[12]

But Lee soon received news from a rather unexpected source. General Longstreet had long employed a gentleman named Harrison as his spy or agent. Henry T. Harrison, a thirty-year-old, stoop-shouldered Mississippian, was recommended to Longstreet by Secretary of War James A. Seddon.[13] Although a heavy drinker, Harrison could keep his lips sealed even when in the cups and had always provided Longstreet with accurate, reliable information. Prior to leaving Virginia, Longstreet dispatched Harrison, with a supply of gold dollars, to enter Washington, frequent the bars and bawdy houses, and determine Union marching orders if possible.[14] Suddenly, the resourceful agent appeared, experiencing difficulty in convincing Confederate sentinels of his bonafides, but finally was ushered into Longstreet's tent.[15] Longstreet rushed Harrison into Lee's nearby tent and as he began to relate his news both men were shocked.[16] Harrison informed the two officers that Hooker was no longer in command of the Union army but had been replaced by Gen. George C. Meade. Additionally, the Army of the Potomac was on the march toward South Mountain and the Confederate supply line behind the mountains. Lee began issuing orders for delivery to his scattered divisions; they were to consolidate at once, near Cashtown, Pennsylvania.[17]

Based on Lee's comments, two assertions appear clear. Firstly, that the change in army commanders was of serious significance for he knew George Meade well, didn't fear him, but felt Meade was a fundamentally prepared soldier who would make few mistakes and would utilize any advantage he recognized, a marked measure of respect over Hooker.[18] Also, Lee was tethered to a long supply line stretching from the valley of Virginia to his present position west of the Blue Ridge and Meade was nobody's fool; when he located that supply line, he would soon be astride the umbilical cord.[19]

Thus Lee's questions as to Meade's intentions and his concern for his supply line exasperated his lack of cavalry assistance. Under this increased pressure Lee's style changed, for instead of becoming more conservative, more cautious, as most military commanders probably would, Lee became markedly more aggressive. Now that Jackson was gone, he was certainly the most offensive-thinking of Southern generals, and he remarked that he must find and meet the Army of the Potomac as it moved north, corps by corps, demolishing each in turn.[20] He could not permit Meade to feint and parry, dancing across Pennsylvania, and neither could he allow the Union general to pick a strong position and entrench. So Lee, not knowing Meade's location or his intentions, seemed to wave a hand aloft, calling the Federal forces to come and drive him away.[21] Lee's strategy of threatening Northern cities while collecting the bounty of the land changed to that of a challenger. Invading an enemy land was in effect an offensive maneuver, precluding or a least limiting defensive strategy. Lee was as if a blind man, in danger of isolation and destruction, and his instincts dictated he close with his foe.

Lee's formidable army was scattered across the countryside on June 28, taking advantage of supply and forage opportunities. The 2nd Corps Divisions of Robert Rodes and Edward Johnson were poised at Carlisle and were preparing to force a crossing of the Susquehanna River into Harrisburg, Pennsylvania. From that location they could threaten Philadelphia, Baltimore, or Washington; all connected to the Pennsylvania capital by good hard-surfaced roads and the firstmentioned two cities, defended by raw militia units, sure to run at the sight of Southern infantry. The remaining 2nd Corps Division, under Maj. Gen. Jubal Early, was at York. Lt. Gen. A.P. Hill's 3rd Corps was camped at Fayetteville and Lt. Gen. James Longstreet's 1st Corps about Chambersburg.[22]

Rodes' men at Carlisle were shocked at Lee's urgent message which canceled their Harrisburg adventure.[23] Ewell, upon receipt of Lee's new orders, gave the men another day's respite, issuing early marching times for June 30; so at 3 A.M. Rodes awakened his troops to a cold breakfast and a hard march. These veterans marched light, carrying only that which they deemed essential. Northern citizens often commented that lean, lank, bearded, and unbelievably dirty Confederates carried less than half the load of Union soldiers. Usually a canteen, blanket roll, and occasional knapsack, accompanied by their rifle completed their equipment.[24] When food was issued they usually ate it; up to three days' supply, reasoning that it was easier to carry inside than out. Few bands or drummers interspaced their ranks when cleared for combat since officers had issued orders concerning band transfers of "more shooters, fewer tooters." The regiments moved at route step, talking incessantly, four abreast, fifty minutes to the hour, as Jackson had taught. All demonstrated fidelity to the Southern cause but perhaps none more so than Pvt. James Mullens. This young man was a native of Harrisburg, Pennsylvania, but had relocated in the South and enlisted in Company B of the 21st Georgia Infantry, Rodes' Division. He proved to be a dauntless, fearless soldier, fighting in every battle in which the regiment was engaged. While at Carlisle, within twenty miles of the home of his parents and sisters, James was punished quite severely for a supposed infraction of regimental regulations. He proclaimed loudly his innocence and appealed his case first to Brigadier General Doles, then to Major General Rodes. But neither general would interfere. His fellow soldiers were soon taking bets that he would skip out and return home. But Private Mullens surprised everyone by remaining with his unit, fighting throughout the battle, then returning to Virginia. He surrendered at Appomattox in a great rage over being defeated and returned to Georgia to reside until his death.[25]

No cavalry being available, Rodes detailed an advance guard of infantry to lead the march and he closely followed.[26] As the initial ranks reached the toll-house gatekeeper's home just after exiting Carlisle, lights were burning brightly in John Mott's kitchen. His wife had risen early to bake bread. The delicious aroma drew the soldiers and soon the kitchen was crowded with hungry men begging for bread, butter, and molasses. Sarah Mott, John's young daughter, was awakened by the noise and slipped downstairs to witness a scene which she remembered for many years. The crowd in the kitchen suddenly parted and General Rodes entered, dashing in full uniform with clanking sword and spurs, and seeing the clamor over food, ordered the men to cease at once and leave Mott's kitchen. Sarah was impressed that Rodes issued his orders, not in stern, harsh language, but in soft, gentle tones; yet obedience was immediate. He turned to Mrs. Mott and, smiling, remarked, "Madam, my men must not annoy you!"[27]

The long column filed through the gap in South Mountain as a gentle rain began and the roads turned muddy. They took the York Pike into Petersburg. Bushwhackers fired on the infantry column in the mountain passes, causing minor delay.[28] The sun burst through and the day turned unusually humid, so the marchers were pleased to reach Heidlersburg in late afternoon and encamp. Ewell, riding in his two-horse carriage, met Rodes and Early, who had ridden cross-country, to review his new orders. Lee had instructed the new lieutenant general to use varying routes as "circumstances might dictate," and the three officers attempted to interpret Lee's desires. Ewell and Early seemed quite agitated as Rodes remained silent, doubtless concerned by Ewell's frustrated reaction to Lee's expectations. Early spoke vociferously, agitating Ewell's indecision. This apparent self-imposed pressure and indecision would have serious consequences in the next few days.

The following morning, as the sun rose blood-red in the east, Ewell turned south, utilizing two roads. Rodes moved through Middletown and Early marched on a parallel route.[29] When Rodes' lead regiments reached Middletown they could continue on to Cashtown or turn toward Gettysburg. The trek led past green fields filled with grazing stock and wooded glens, revealing the lush, unsoiled Pennsylvania countryside. The soldiers chattered as they marched, remarking on the fine brick and stone buildings and discussing the local lasses whom they observed by the roadside in numbers, for since these "rebels" had proved well mannered, large crowds now gathered to observe their passing. Sometimes infantry regiments moved four abreast through grain fields which bordered the road to avoid artillery and ordnance wagons. This practice resulted in broad paths being trampled through the wheat to the protests of the "dutch" farmers.[30] As the column approached one dwelling, the lead elements witnessed a bizarre occurrence. As General Ewell, in his carriage, and General Rodes, on horseback, rode past, a man with a Bible in hand leapt from his porch to a rail fence alongside the road. In a high voice, speaking in strange tongues initially, he began to belabor the two officers. Stating that he was of a sect that disapproved of war, he demanded he and his property be protected and that the "devils" depart at once and return to their Southern homes. Ewell became flustered and red-faced while Rodes, giving the man a sideways glance and a wry smile, spurred his horse and moved on.[31] Arriving at Middletown in mid-morning Ewell received a note from A.P. Hill that he was moving on Gettysburg and that Union forces of unknown size had been sighted at that location. Rodes immediately turned his men toward Gettysburg and after a few hot miles of marching, was surprised to hear the sounds of cannon fire.[32] He excitedly spurred his horse to the front of his column and urged his men on to the sound of the guns. The veteran infantrymen shed their blanket rolls and knapsacks in piles on the roadside to be retrieved by the wagons as they broke into double-time toward the growling thunder.[33]

Gettysburg, Pennsylvania was an unimportant little village until several key military factors were considered. The town was easily reached from almost any location with ten roads radiating from its locale as from the spokes of a wheel, creating an excellent point of concentration for a military force. The nearby countryside was open, with many fields, cultivated fruit orchards and a few forested areas, offering good visibility, thus, a military commander from a well-selected location could observe any approaching threat. But best of all, the ridges provided excellent defensive positions. West of town, from which the Confederates were approaching, were a series of ridges including Herr's Ridge, McPherson's Ridge, and Oak Ridge, to be called Seminary Ridge as a small college building implied. South and east of town ran Cemetery Ridge anchored on its right by Cemetery and Culp's Hills and on the left by Little and Big Round Top. Cemetery and Seminary Ridges were roughly parallel.[34] Maj. Gen. Harry Heth's Division of A.P. Hill's 3rd Corps approached Gettysburg in early morning via the Chambersburg Pike. As Heth neared the village, artillery rounds began to crash around his column's van, so he deployed two brigades to push forward and disburse what Heth believed were dismounted regiments of Brig. Gen. John Buford's Federal cavalrymen.[35] Heth, the courtly gentleman, was an amicable companion and a well-trained soldier. But the fortunes of battle never seemed to smile on him and his luck that day would be no better. His marching orders that morning were to proceed by camping locations and Heth's leading two brigades were probably his weakest.[36] Brig. Gen. James Archer's tough Alabama and Tennessee veterans had experienced hard fighting and high casualties at Chancellorsville and were far under strength. The second brigade was a newly formed Mississippi unit under the president's nephew, Brig.Gen. Joseph Davis, who was as green as were his soldiers.[37] In support were twenty guns of the reserve artillery under the renowned Willie Pegram.

Maj. Gen. John Reynolds, first on the field and initially in charge of Federal forces as they arrived, made a momentous and farreaching decision. Realizing the tactical importance of the heights south of Gettysburg, Reynolds dispatched Buford and his cavalry west of the village to fight and delay Confederate infantry. He then reinforced Buford as soon as Union infantry arrived.[38] Reynolds determined that the longer he could delay Confederate approaches to the Southern heights, the more force he could amass there. He expertly managed his blue-clad defenders until he was slain by a sniper's bullet in mid-morning. Gen. Abner Doubleday, upon Reynolds' death, continued to fight in the same manner, and in the critical moments ahead provided outstanding field leadership to Federal troops fighting on heavily wooded McPherson's Ridge.[39] When the remaining I Corps brigades arrived, Doubleday wisely stationed two of them in reserve on Oak Ridge.[40] As Maj. Gen. Oliver Howard's XI Corps came up they were assigned to the right flank to support Buford's cavalry in covering the Mummasburg, Carlisle, and Harrisburg Roads.

Pegram sighted his guns on the woods ahead[41] and quickly silenced Federal artillery fire as Heth's brigades bounded forward eagerly. Archer's men cleared a stream and moved uphill into a murderous volley from a concealed line that could only be delivered by veteran troops. They had collided with the "Iron Brigade" of the I Federal Corps under the command of Brig. Gen. Solomon Meredith.[42] One of the Union regiments maneuvered onto Archer's flank and the Confederate veterans raced for cover in the rear. A furious Archer was tackled by a big Union private and became the first Confederate general officer captured since Lee had taken command. Archer spent some time in Federal prisons and died of ill health soon after being released.[43]

On the other side of the pike, Davis enjoyed some initial success driving Union troops until he reached the deep cut of an unfinished railway, ominously concealed by high grasses which grew about the rim. Davis thought he could use the cut as protection for his men and emerge on the flank of the Iron Brigade facing Archer. Gray-backs of his 43rd and 2nd Mississippi Regiments started through the cut, but suddenly Federal regiments moved up to the lips of the defile on three sides, and the Mississippians were like fish trapped in a barrel.[44] A charging 6th Wisconsin reached the lip of the cut and Major Rufus Dawes of that regiment recalled:

> I found myself face to face with hundreds of rebels whom I looked down upon in the railway cut, which was about four feet deep....we began shooting into the massed Confederates and they began to surrender....almost the entire 2nd Mississippi were made prisoners.[45]

Scores were shot down or captured, since the sides of the cut were too steep to scale, and within minutes the fighting ability of Joe Davis' Brigade was wrecked.[46] Heth's setbacks were sudden and he brought up his remaining two brigades. Archer's regrouping veterans, angry despite the loss of their general, reformed on the two fresh units.[47] Heth, remembering Lee's reluctance to bring on a general engagement, waited for Hill.[48] John Buford's dismounted cavalry had blustered, bluffed, and delayed the Southern advance with their breech-loading carbines until Union I Corps veterans arrived to give Heth a bloody nose.

Shortly after 12:30 P.M. Rodes' Confederate Division, 8,000 strong, came booming down the Middletown Road, skirmishers three deep, red battle flags unfurled. The division marched in column with the exception of Iverson's Brigade, which was fully deployed in the lead.[49] Robert Rodes, immediately behind Iverson's skirmishers, spurred to Oak Hill where he surveyed the clash on his right front and began to deploy. Rodes swung his units into the woods on the left rear of Oak Hill, hoping he could deploy without Federal discovery. He stated, "I could perhaps then strike the force of the enemy with which General Hill's troops were engaged on their flank."[50] His division was forced to move by its right flank and alter front after reaching the ridge.[51] Rodes detached Doles' Brigade to his left, directing that trusted brigadier, assisted by Maj. Eugene Blackford's Corps of Sharpshooters, to stretch his formation toward the Heidlersburg Road where Early's brigades were momentarily expected. Next Rodes dispatched Lt. Col. Thomas Carter to install his guns on Oak Hill and open fire, there being no further need for secrecy.[52] He then aligned two brigades to sweep down the ridge and possibly drive a wedge between the Federal I and XI Corps.[53]

Oak Hill, Gettysburg

On July 2, 1863, George Doles' Brigade, supported by Page's Battery, was dispatched by Rodes to command the small valley left of Oak Hill, holding open Jubal Early's expected route of arrival.

Robert Carter

Gettysburg

Lieutenant Colonel Carter established his guns in excellent position atop Oak Hill, July 1, 1863.

Robert Carter

Gettysburg, July 1, 1863

The route of Iverson's advance from Oak Hill. Aimed toward the trees at center ridge where Cutler's Brigade was positioned, Iverson advanced into an ambush and was decimated by Baxter's Federals who were hidden along the roadway to left center.

Robert Carter

Rodes' old Alabama Brigade, commanded by Col. Edward O'Neal, was deployed in the center while Brig. Gen. Alfred Iverson's North Carolina Brigade was aligned alongside. The raw, unbloodied brigade of Brig. Gen. Junius Daniel deployed behind Iverson, the unit being so large it overlapped Iverson's right substantially.[54] Brig. Gen. Dodson Ramseur's Brigade formed in reserve.

Doles' widely spread soldiers were soon threatened by an enemy force emerging from the village on Rodes' left. The Federal XI Corps of Maj. Gen. Oliver O. Howard had arrived and was moving into position. Since a wide gap existed between Doles, located on lower terrain, and O'Neal, Rodes retained the 5th Alabama of O'Neal's Brigade under his personal control to cover that opening if needed.[55] Doles had four Georgia regiments and Blackford's fine unit to cover more than one-half mile, and his line was being probed by elements of Brig. Gen. Alexander Schimmelfennig's Division of the XI Corps.[56] Aligning O'Neal's and Iverson's Brigades, Rodes pointed out to each their point of attack, then ordered the units to move forward.

The wooded ridge which lay ahead was not as lightly held as it appeared, however. Brig. Gen. Lysander Cutler's Brigade of the I Corps had moved up Oak Ridge until reaching the corner of a tree line and established an L-shaped position. While Rodes was aware of Cutler's presence and aimed his advance at their line, he was unsuspecting of another I Corps Brigade, the large six-regiment unit of Brig. Gen. Henry Baxter. This key unit was marching north on a lane concealed by the ridge and discovered Confederates on Oak Hill. Baxter had his troops creep up the slope and conceal themselves behind a stone wall at the crest.[57] The blue-coats lay prone, flags and rifles down behind the wall, no skirmishers out or officers standing.[58]

O'Neal's Alabama Brigade moved out, emerging from the woods three regiments abreast, the 12th, 26th, and 6th Alabama units from left to right, the 5th Alabama still in reserve and for some reason the 3rd Alabama received orders to attach itself to Daniel's Brigade, an order O'Neal never clarified.[59] Colonel Battle of the 3rd Alabama reported that just before the advance he received orders to move adjacent to General Daniel's Brigade and to keep alignment on that unit.[60] From its inception the attack seemed disjointed as O'Neal moved forward early and set an inaccurate line of direction. Soon the Alabamians ran head-on into the 90th Pennsylvania which Baxter had detailed to refuse his right. When a XI Corps Regiment, the 45th New York, appeared on O'Neal's flank and opened fire, the entire Confederate unit retreated within fifteen minutes of stepping off.[61] Rodes, noting the confusion, started forward with the 5th Alabama but was too late, meeting the brigade in full retreat. Rodes was amazed to discover that O'Neal had not accompanied his men in their attack but remained behind.[62] No real closeness existed between the two men, but Rodes grew red-faced as he sat on his prancing black horse and listened to O'Neal explain that he had no horse and could not advance with his men.

However, O'Neal's gross negligence was only the first problem Rodes would face this afternoon. Suddenly Iverson's Brigade, which had started forward minutes later, suffered an even worse fate. They continued to march forward, disregarding O'Neal's quick retreat, and thus opened themselves by an uncovered left flank. As the formation neared the stone wall, still marching at an oblique angle, five of Baxter's regiments arose as one from their seclusion and at about fifty yards' distance loosed a blast as if from one trigger which decimated Iverson's Brigade.[63] Grey-coats fell as tenpins, hundreds seeming to lie in a single line.[64] Many attackers, not struck, lay down in a gully which accorded some shelter and, waving white handkerchiefs, signalled their willingness to surrender.[65] Cutler's Brigade advanced from the trees to take a perpendicular line to Baxter's crossing Iverson's front. As Rodes fell back with O'Neal's men he met an envoy from Iverson who informed him that one of his regiments had defected to the enemy.[66] Rodes' unprintable reply is fortunately forgotten. His rage was monumental. He had no sooner blasted O'Neal for inappropriate conduct than he was faced with Iverson's breakdown. Iverson's excitable message was incorrect, probably spurred by his witnessing large numbers of men waving white kerchiefs. But there was another shock for Rodes: Iverson

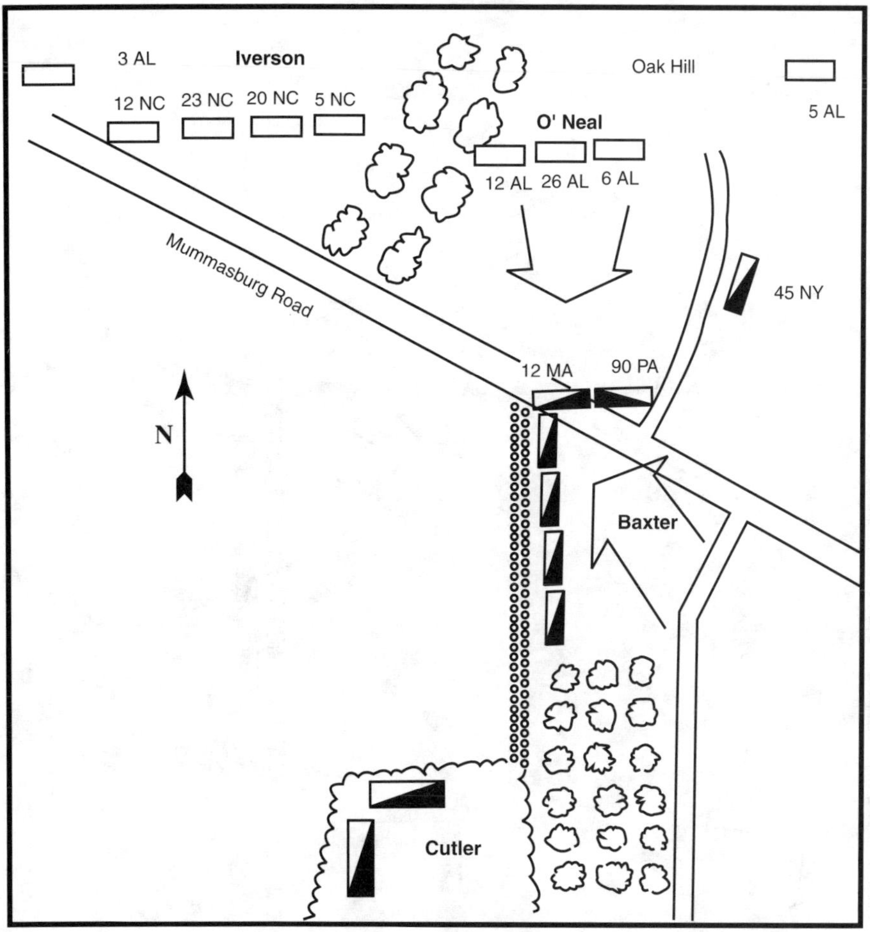

Gettysburg, July 1, 1863

Rodes' initial onslaught, designed to clear Oak Ridge, became disjointed as O'Neal attacked prematurely and was rapidly repulsed by two of Baxter's regiments assisted by the 45th New York. Baxter's troops, marching north, had wisely and stealthily deployed behind a stone wall on the crest of a hill.

also had not accompanied his regiments for whatever reason. A furious Robert Rodes relieved Iverson on the spot, appointing Capt. Donald P. Halsey, A.A.G., to command of the unit.[67] Iverson's unsuspecting soldiers were as nearly ambushed as could occur on a field of battle.

The large, untried brigade of Brig. Gen. Junius Daniel, 2,150 men strong, moved forward on Iverson's right. Daniel split his force at first, sending three regiments to assist Iverson and advancing with the remaining two upon the railway cut.[68] Suddenly attacked from three sides the two regiments fell back. But an intrepid Daniel rallied his men and using all his

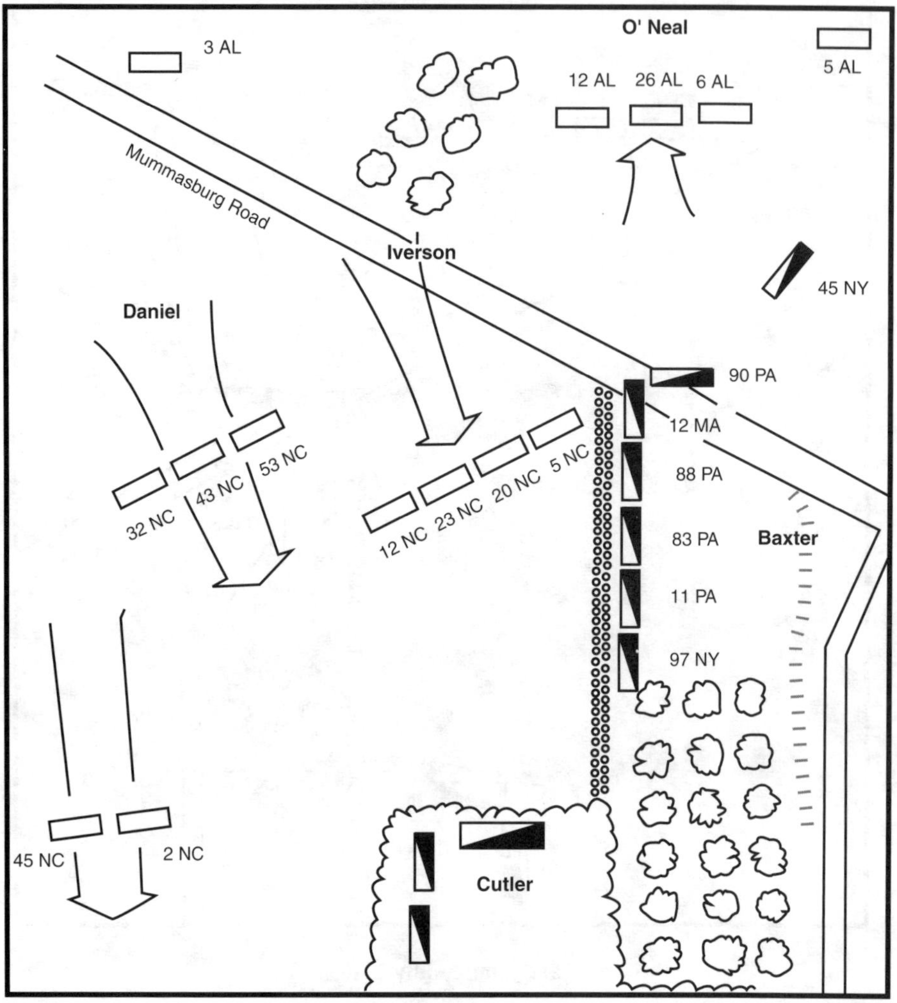

Gettysburg, July 1, 1863

As O'Neal retreated, Iverson's Brigade stepped off, moving obliquely into Baxter's well-concealed ambush and was decimated. Daniel attempted to support Iverson as two of his regiments swept south toward the unfinished railway cut.

regiments forced Federal evacuation from the rail cut. The large flag raised so proudly at Carlisle Barracks, with its long white tail, had been presented to General Lee, and he had passed the banner down until it finally became a possession of the 32nd North Carolina. Soon that huge banner flew over the railway cut.[69]

Meanwhile the irrepressible George Doles sparred with numerous Federal units, changing fronts on several occasions and succeeding in maintaining contact with Rodes' hard-pressed division while keeping Early's arrival route open.[70] Pressure by the XI Corps forced Carter to move three batteries from Oak Ridge around to the base of the hill to support Doles' effort.[71] Gunfire from these pieces curtailed Federal advances on Blackburn's sharpshooters. Doles experienced an unusual occurrence when his horse suddenly bolted for Federal lines, and no matter how hard he attempted to turn or stop the animal, the wild ride continued. Doles was forced to jump clear, receiving a hard fall, then an ungainly sprint to the rear resulted in his safety.[72] Fighting in the ranks of Doles' Brigade was Pvt. John B. Countess who had risen through the ranks from private to captain but had been court-martialed for insubordination just prior to the battle. Reduced to the ranks, Countess fought for three days so well as a private and was so conspicuous he was noticed by General Rodes and restored to his previous rank.[73]

Now Robert Rodes, who had so confidently cleared for action about midday, found his plans in serious trouble.[74] One brigade was wrecked, his center crushed, and Doles still isolated on his left. He had, thus far, been defeated by a combination of inept Southern brigade leadership and excellent use of terrain and fire discipline by the enemy. Rodes had opened the action with a weak blow and now, countered, he prepared to deliver another.

He dispatched orders to gunners Carter and Fry to increase their fire on the Union center, then he sent for the reserve brigade, that of Stephen Ramseur. Ramseur smartly marched his brigade directly into the center, advancing toward Brig. Gen. Gabriel Paul's Brigade which had relieved Baxter's men. Rodes gathered the remnants of Iverson's Brigade and Col. C.A. Battle's 3rd Alabama, adding these units to Ramseur's little force.[75] Ramseur massed his force on Paul's right and fell like a thunderbolt on the Union line. On his conspicuous grey horse, Ramseur seemed an inviting target, but his fortune held.[76] Ramseur hammered on the Federal lines until it slowly began to crack, leaking blue-coats to the rear. Federal Division Commander Robinson ordered Paul to slowly withdraw his command, leaving the 16th Maine to hold until the brigade was withdrawn. This action simply sacrificed the Maine Staters as they lost 232 of 298 men engaged.[77]

Daniel's Brigade, on Ramseur's right, swung wide to take another crack at complete capture of the railway cut, despite fierce opposition from the 143rd and 149th Pennsylvania Regiments. While Daniel welcomed the assistance of the 12th North Carolina of Iverson's Brigade he could not entice the Mississippians of Davis' unit to join his effort.[78] As his line swept forward past the cut a horrendous noise occurred when the 43rd, 53rd, and 2nd North Carolina units collided with Cutler's Pennsylvania regiments. Casualties mounted and when the 149th Pennsylvania charged across the cut Daniel's entire line was shaken. But the resolute Daniel, whose conduct won high praise from both General Rodes and his own men,[79] rallied his brigade and led a sprint to the lip of the cut that resulted in decimation of the Pennsylvanians as they attempted to retreat.[80]

Pressure was building on the Federal defenders. Maj. Gen. A.P. Hill released Maj. Gen. William Pender's Division to advance on Rodes' right

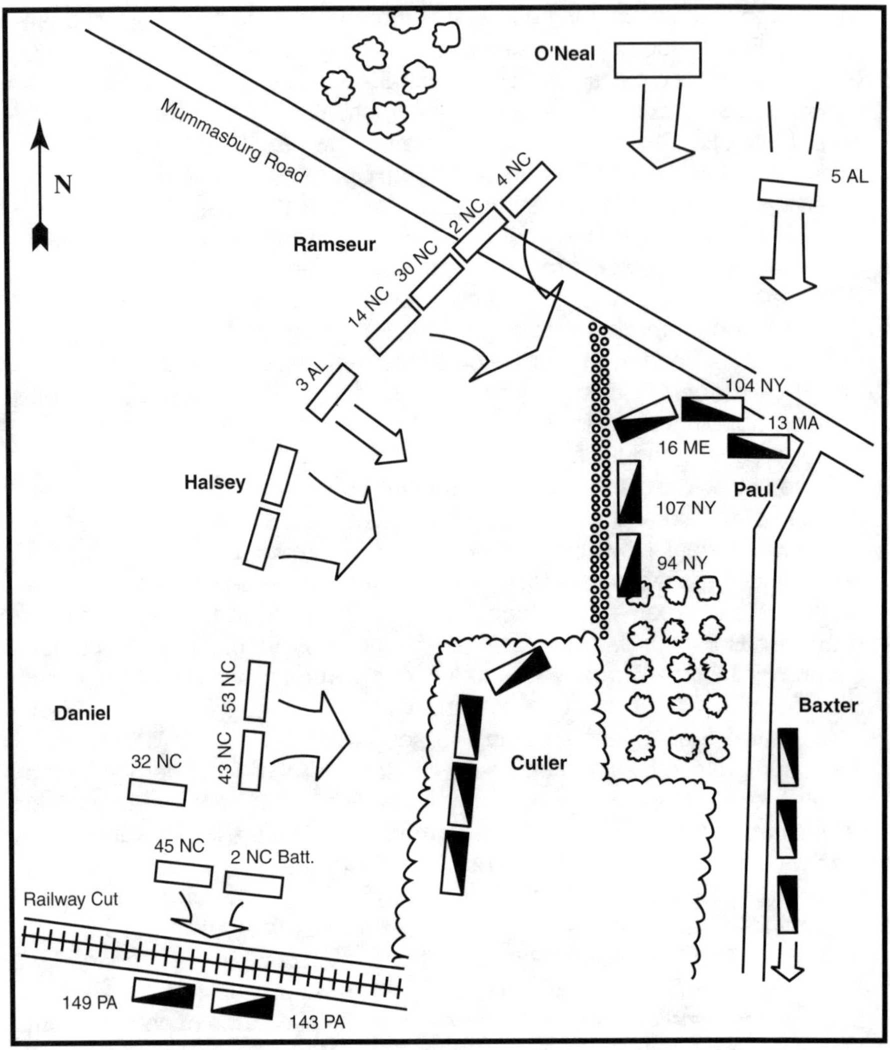

Gettysburg, July 1, 1863

Rodes marshalled his entire division, led by Ramseur's fresh brigade, in smashing Paul's Federal Brigade, newly arrived in relief of Baxter. Assisted by Doles' and Gordon's onslaught on his left, the entire Federal force collapsed and raced for Gettysburg.

alongside Daniel, Ramseur continued his drive into the Federal center, and Doles was joined by Brig. Gen. John Gordon's lead brigade of Early's Division in an assault on the Union left. As Doles and Gordon charged with a piercing "rebel yell" the Federal XI Corps panicked and ran for the second consecutive battle, the 21st Georgia routing an entire Union brigade.[81] Despite the arrival of the Union III Corps, the combined Confederate push was irresistible. Abandoning their wounded, Federal withdrawal, at first orderly, became rout. The small, narrow, tree-lined streets of the village could not contain all those attempting to push through, and soon yards, alleys, and cellars were full of blue-coats, and the exultant scream of the victors resounded throughout the town. One Union sergeant who recalled the sprint into Gettysburg, disgustedly likened the infantrymen to a "herd of cattle."[82]

The Union "Iron Brigade" was wrecked on McPherson's Ridge for the first and last time, and the survivors were decimated as they retreated into the village.[83] As the victorious gray-backed raced for Gettysburg, Early's aide, Maj. John Warwick Daniel, rode through lines of slain blue-coats and recalled that within just a few minutes of the passage of the Confederate battle line, none of the dead blue-coats had shoes or unrifled pockets.[84] Several units attempted to regroup within the town's protection, but despite a few sharp exchanges the rapid advance and continual pounding of Southern guns precluded a rally. Between 3,000 and 4,000 prisoners were taken in the town, primarily by Doles and Ramseur. Rodes remarked that the division captured so many prisoners as to hinder its further movements.[85] Many of these Federals simply gave up in exhaustion after long sprints in the heat and humidity.[86] A majority of the Federal soldiers who fled across the lots and fields were successful on their escape, while most who went through the town were captured. Those who escaped through Gettysburg could see safety in III Corps troops arriving on the heights south of town.

General Ramseur's horse was slain by a straggler as he rode casually into Gettysburg.[87] Ewell rode into Gettysburg with General Gordon, suddenly hearing the thud of a striking minie ball. Gordon asked the corps commander if he were injured and Ewell replied laughingly, "No, I'm not hurt, they shot me in the wooden leg."[88] Rodes, with Ramseur's assistance, took charge of the village, securing a line and setting skirmishers as he observed hundreds of Federals climbing Cemetery Hill and new Union forces arriving on its forbidding crest. He did not prepare for an immediate pursuit, as in the midst of the previous action, Rodes received a message from Ewell that General Lee did not wish a general engagement brought on.[89]

Early appeared and, together, he and Rodes approached Ewell concerning the possibility of further pursuit of the enemy, even an attempt to scale Cemetery Hill. But Ewell demurred conservatively, deciding to await the arrival of his third division, that of Maj. Gen. Edward Johnson.[90] The three officers rode out of town to observe Federal preparations and while so engaged a report arrived from Brig. Gen. William Smith of Early's Division that Federal infantry was in rear of the Confederate left flank. An amazed Early dispatched Gordon's tired men to investigate what proved to be erroneous information. The false alarm seemed to sap whatever resolve Ewell possessed to continue the fight. When Ewell reentered Gettysburg, Lee was waiting. Ewell summoned Early and Rodes and together they adjourned to a shady little arbor behind Ewell's headquarters where they avoided the oppressive heat.[91]

The conference which followed seems surreal in its proposals and lack of decision. Lee felt he had achieved a victory that afternoon but with no appreciable results except high enemy casualties and many prisoners. But gray-clad losses were also high, almost 3,000 in Rodes' Division alone, and the Union soldiers on Cemetery Hill seemed resilient and defiant. Ewell said very little, allowing the loquacious Early to dominate the discussion with his punctuated opinions. Rodes remained silent but nodded agreement when Early stated that an attack on Cemetery Hill the next day would be a risky undertaking.[92] Lee rode away after an hour without a decision, but contemplating a movement of Ewell's Corps by the right flank, as the unit was poorly aligned and facing a bend in a Federal fishhook.[93] Many experienced observers, then and later, felt that any attack on Cemetery Hill, that night or over the next few days, was doomed to fail.[94]

Lee and Ewell met later that evening and Ewell talked Lee out of moving his corps, convincing Lee that he would be able to put troops on Culp's Hill, which was to the right rear of Cemetery Hill. After more discussion Lee queried Ewell as to his ability to attack Cemetery Hill, *if possible*, the next day in conjuncture with an assault by Longstreet on the enemy left.[95] After Lee departed, Ewell decided to send Johnson's men up Culp's Hill when they arrived, but Johnson arrived late and when he sent out scouts after dark, he found Federals on the crest.[96] This significant nondecision seemed meaningless until the ring of federal axes was heard on both prominences in the night.

Rodes rode away from the meeting with Ewell and Lee somewhat confused as to what actions the following day would bring. He was surely depressed over the loss of so many fine soldiers in his division that afternoon. Of greater concern to him must have been the performance of his division. Three of his brigadiers had performed magnificently, worthy of the highest accolades, their dogged persistence earning the costly victory. But what of the other two, O'Neal and Iverson? Both had performed well in the past and both had been wounded at Chancellorsville. These facts did not explain nor predict their sending units into combat without proper leadership. O'Neil's actions had upset whatever timetable the attack possessed and led to his rapid repulse which, in turn, endangered, even doomed, Iverson. O'Neal's behavior was unbending, defiant, and uncommunicative. O'Neal was permitted by Rodes to complete the campaign but upon return to Virginia was passed over for permanent assignment. Iverson's Brigade had been chopped apart when it marched directly into a Federal trap, in part caused by O'Neal's failure. But Iverson's absence, together with the fact that his regiments were led by inexperienced officers, prevented any reaction to the Union ambush. Iverson was heavily criticized by his men, some stating they would not serve under him again.[97] Others accused him of cowardice for standing by and telling his soldiers to "Give Them Hell" and then walking calmly to the rear.[98] Rumors of drunkenness were circulated. Already removed from command he could not be reinstated and upon his return to Virginia was reassigned to his native Georgia to organize cavalry.[99]

A prideful soldier such as Robert Rodes must also have thought of his own performance on July 1. He was, of course, not personally responsible for the serious indiscretions in behavior of two of his brigadiers, but the division's overall performance had been less than desired: uncoordinated, jerky, and spasmodic, and those matters were in his immediate charge. Rodes' desire to rapidly move to assist Heth's Division was creditable and the quicker the better if the attack were on an uninformed enemy. But once his division was discovered, and he was aware that it was, then the need for such urgency in attack was alleviated. The meticulous, highly organized Rodes should have reorganized his assault, using all of his units, thereby maximizing his firepower at the point of attack. Baxter's men presented a critical surprise that he could not prevent, but if he had redeployed to organize a crushing attack by his 8,000-man division, time was available for a more thorough reconnaissance than his cursory ride forward into the fields. In short a sloppy attack was delivered principally because Rodes tried to deliver a quick-hitting surprise attack on a prepared enemy, instead of taking the time to prepare a divisional effort.

Rodes would move at once to correct the serious deficiencies in brigade command. His own development as divisional commander would also see much change but in a slower, more subtle nature. This, his first experience in control of a fight, would teach Rodes a great deal. As weeks and months passed and his confidence in divisional command grew, Robert would become much more demanding, more exacting of his brigadiers. In addition he would learn to temper his aggressiveness with prudence and wisdom, taking the role of a divisional leader more than the chief of a brigade.

At sunrise, Ewell's Corps was still arranged around the Union fishhook. Rodes' Division adjoined Pender's Division on the right, extended through Gettysburg and met Early's lines on his left. Johnson's Division curved around Culp's Hill. Maj. Eugene Blackford, in command of Rodes' sharpshooters, placed his riflemen in a row of houses facing Cemetery Hill. Sniper fire was wicked and Blackford's men cut doors from house to house, and enclosed the windows with mattresses, leaving loopholes from which they could maintain a steady fire on the hilltop.[100] Three of Rodes' Brigades, those of Doles, Iverson, and Ramseur, were strung down Middle Street from Baltimore Avenue to the edge of town.[101] O'Neal's Brigade was aligned to the right rear along a railroad bed while Daniel's men were positioned on the ridge near the seminary, in support of the division artillery.[102]

Ewell's plan of attack, designed to coordinate with Longstreet's onslaught, was simple. Johnson would attack Culp's Hill with his division; Early would attack East Cemetery Hill; Rodes would move directly at the center of Cemetery Hill; and Pender's Division of Hill's Corps would advance alongside Rodes. Instructions were issued to prepare the formations to move off at 9 A.M., then 11 A.M., and finally 4 P.M.[103] The day passed slowly in the steaming hot village, as the Confederates kept their heads down and listened to the continued sounds of Federals chopping trees on the heights above.[104] Longstreet, however, was far from prepared to attack on the Union left. Two of his divisions were camped some distance from the field and faced a lengthy march, and the third, that of Maj. Gen. George Pickett, was so distant it could not possibly be available for action on July 2. The roads which Longstreet's men must employ were packed with wagons of other units, for much traffic was funnelled onto a few narrow thoroughfares.[105] A continued difficulty of all Confederate units was the lack of competent staff officers. An observer reported that "scarce any of our Generals had half of what they needed to keep constant and close supervision of the execution of important orders."[106] This constant weakness of Confederate arms was never solved. All staff work seemed to devolve on a few capable officers.

Lt. Gen. James Longstreet and General Lee were at odds as to just what sort of attack should be launched. Longstreet deemed the Federal position too strong for frontal attack and favored a flanking or turning movement around the Union left.[107] Lee envisioned an assault through the wheat field and onto the "Round Tops," the dominant physical feature on the line. Longstreet became irritated when Lee did not follow his advice and insisted on his attacking the Federal left.[108] While the struggle on the Confederate left in the Peach Orchard, the Wheat Field, and Devil's Den is a story in courage and sacrifice, it was to have occurred in coordination with Ewell's assault on Culp's Hill to hopefully prevent Union forces, on their interior lines, from rushing in troops to reinforce weak points. So Ewell's men waited and their officers stared at the formidable Union works above. After all these delays it was almost 4 P.M. when Hood moved to attack.[109]

When the noise of action rolled up the ridge Ewell ordered his artillery to open on Culp's and Cemetery Hills. Maj. Joseph W. Latimer's sixteen guns opened at once and were on target, but strong, accurate, Federal counterbattery fire made their continued firing impossible.[110] Union artillery batteries with superior guns and better ammunition were, in addition, usually superbly served and, consequently, Confederate batteries were often overwhelmed. Ewell now instructed his division commanders to advance their men in demonstration and if they saw signs of Federal weakness or a location where Federal units had possibly been moved, to attack. Ewell's responsibility-avoiding orders offered his subordinates the ultimate discretion: to execute an attack if they saw an opportunity.

Rodes certainly was aware that his brigades were aligned poorly for an assault.[111] There on the edge of the village, they faced down a valley and not Cemetery Hill. To align properly they were forced to turn at an angle of 45% to the left and move about one-half mile before reaching an attack position.[112]

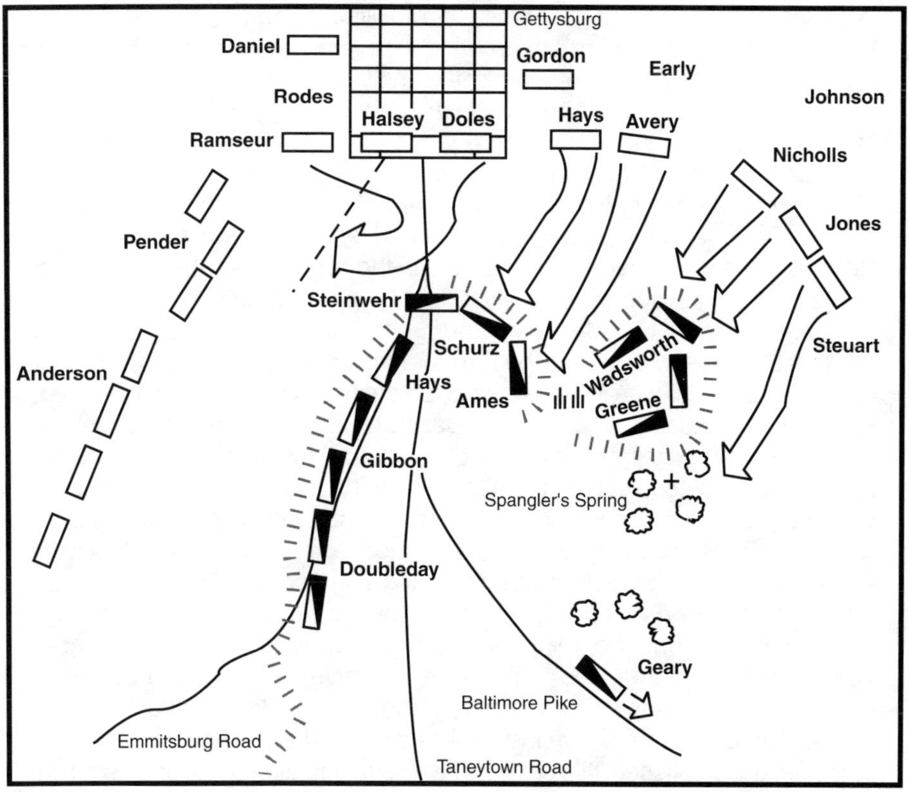

Gettysburg, July 2, 1863

Just prior to nightfall Johnston launched an attack against the backside of Culp's Hill, with Steuart's Brigade gaining penetration almost to Spangler's Spring. Early sent two brigades up East Cemetery Hill, briefly gaining a foothold in Ames' line. Rodes' move to attack was late and Early was withdrawing, thus he withdrew his troops to a sunken road.

When Rodes began to shift his units it was already too late as the orders from Ewell reached him last.[113] It is probable that Rodes was caught unaware since the attack had been delayed all day and his last conversation with Ewell had stressed a demonstration; he thus probably assumed no attack would be made and disdained from exposing his brigades to artillery and sniper fire. When Rodes received orders to advance he learned what he should have known, that disengaging from the streets of Gettysburg would take much longer than the preparations of Early and Johnson.[114] But he could not simply mass his brigades and allow them to wait in artillery fire.

Edward Johnson sent three of his brigades, those of Nicholls, Jones, and Steuart to overrun Culp's Hill.[115] They were slowed somewhat due to the rough ground at the foot of the hill and underestimated the steep face of the slope. However, a mistake by Union Brig. Gen. John Geary in that he mistakenly moved two brigades off Culp's Hill, created an opportunity and Brig. Gen. George Steuart's men seized several trenches.[116] The works captured were near the bottom right rear of Culp's Hill. Little further advance was made for night had fallen and the only light was from the rifle flashes. Early sent in two brigades, those of Hoke and Hays, on the left flank of Cemetery Hill. Federal artillery had wisely placed white range stakes at the foot of Cemetery Hill and they proved of great value.[117] Several units of Hays' Brigade slipped through a crack and penetrated into the guns atop Cemetery Hill. They were unable to hold in the face of overwhelming Union forces on the crest and were rudely kicked from their perch.[118] Early did not commit his reserve brigade under Gordon.[119] Early's men were falling back as Rodes' Brigades arrived, prepared to attack the right flank of Cemetery Hill.[120] Rodes, who was ill that evening, delegated to a brigade commander, Ramseur, an unusual responsibility. Based on Ewell's "Demonstration" order, Rodes instructed Ramseur to observe the strength of Federal lines before determining to pursue the attack.[121] In the moonlight Ramseur could see that the hill bristled with Union guns and men, probably resulting from Early's foray. Ramseur consulted with Doles; the two brigadiers decided further action would waste men's lives and so informed Rodes.[122] Rodes agreed and issued a recall, for he thought the Federal position impregnable, but placed his front lines along a sunken road, called Long Lane, nearer the enemy front and from which a morning attack could be easily launched.[123] No support issued from Pender on Rodes' right as was expected. The Confederate attack at dusk had created lots of noise and flashes of fire but accomplished little save Johnson's occupation of several trenches on Culp's Hill.

During that evening, Lee and Ewell decided that Johnson's lodgement on Culp's Hill was a real advantage that should be exploited come morning. Since Rodes' Division was confined by its poor alignment, they determined to loan two of Rodes' brigades and one of Early's to Johnson for a massive effort.[124] This would make seven brigades available for an assault on Culp's Hill. In the early morning, Rodes rose and led O'Neal's and Daniel's Brigades through Gettysburg far out to the left flank position to find Johnson's men had risen and were preparing breakfast.[125] Lee left instructions with Ewell that he should attack at daylight, in concert with Longstreet, but this time Ewell's movement was to occur first as a signal to action.

Edward Johnson, ever-present oak stick in hand, opened the action with the sun.[126] He hurled wave after wave of screaming gray-clad infantry at Culp's Hill with no appreciable effect. Johnson had ample troops but the terrain prevented him from bringing most to action at one time. O'Neal's brigade tried and was repulsed as was James A. Walker's Stonewall Brigade. In late morning Daniel and Steuart were ordered to attack in concert, and both officers protested, but to no avail. The 2nd North Carolina Battalion with Daniel's lost 200 of its 240 men.[127]

On the crest so many Federal regiments were available that defenders fought in shifts.[128] The 2nd Division of the XII Federal Corps had been shifted to atop Culp's Hill, and these experienced woodsmen took advantage of the profusion of trees to erect stout ramparts that turned Culp's Hill into an impenetrable position.[129] Like many of the positions held by Federal infantry at Gettysburg, Culp's Hill was extremely good defensive ground. Noise and smoke obscured the crest and heat exhaustion was as much a danger as bullets. Only the extremely rough terrain, offering ample cover behind rocks, trees, and in gullies and ravines prevented horrendous Southern casualties.

Rodes' three remaining brigades lay in the sunken road listening to the roar from Culp's Hill. Occasionally exchanges of rifle fire grew heavy and artillery barrages continued spasmodically.[130] Thousands of soldiers lay on their arms in the heat that afternoon, facing enemy soldiers and wondering what would happen next. Suddenly the stillness was broken by the guns of E. Porter Alexander, and the greatest cannonade in North American history was under way.[131] So fierce was the noise of the exchange that it seemed to block all thoughts from the minds of the waiting infantry. Alexander fired as long as possible and when he finished, Pickett and Pettigrew took their 13,000 men up Cemetery Ridge.

A frustrated and powerless Robert Rodes paced his lines, chewing the ends of his mustache as he watched Pickett's men charge and be repulsed. His hard-won victory of July 1 seemed meaningless and his hopes for another opportunity, another critical chance, never materialized.[132] As evening came, the groans of the wounded and maimed replaced the thunder and smoke, and as if the roar of the guns had disturbed the gods, a light rain began to fall. About an hour after dark Rodes received orders to fall back through the town to Oak or Seminary Ridge, where rifle pits and entrenchments were constructed.[133] Fortifications were erected on either side of the railway cut, concealed in the tree line to invite attack, but no enemy movement was forthcoming.[134]

As the great battle at Gettysburg concluded, Southern fortunes were significantly impaired although few realized this fact that night. The Army of Northern Virginia licked its wounds and took care of its own.[135] Meade's Army of the Potomac had suffered like losses and the commanding general correctly surmised that the Confederate army was still a formidable opponent. Later estimates of considerable accuracy placed total Confederate losses at 23,000 and Federal at 20,500, a total of 43,500 casualties in three days' fighting.[136]

Robert Rodes, in his second action as a division commander, had been severely tested. He was surely perplexed as the army withdrew. When Rodes, advancing toward the cannon fire on July 1, 1863, reached the crest of Oak Hill, he all at once faced critical decisions and he made them in the best manner he knew. He ventured forward to reconnoiter, placed

Carter's guns in a tremendous artillery position, and recognizing Heth's heavy engagement could be relieved by a movement on the flank, he attacked. Deploying Doles in good position, Rodes moved forward with two brigades. The failure of the initial assault and his inability to alleviate the mistakes seemed to make him a slightly less confident, more hesitant commander. His responses to Lee's and Ewell's pursuit questions became more conservative, less daring, and his support of the second day's assault was inadequate due to improper preparation. Longstreet's delay with Ewell's corresponding puzzling orders, with all the attendant complications, created a strange procession of orders to a methodical and logical individual. But despite the fallacy of the decision to attack, whoever ultimately decided, and regardless of his feelings of the orders being impossible to implement, he should have been ready to move his division from his most advantageous position upon orders of the corps commander.

While Robert Rodes could not even dream that two experienced brigade commanders would send in their troops unaccompanied, the lack of coordination which so plagued the division's effort must be laid at the feet of its commander. Rodes assuredly did not exercise, over the three days, the sort of field management he displayed at Chancellorsville and in later actions. His instincts and his appraisal skills seemed adequate, but his divisional control and coordination were poor, his weakest day on the army's weakest three. There is little question he was aware of these shortcomings; although never openly discussed, Rodes, like General Lee, changed his style to fit those he led. He became less passive as a leader, less delegatory, more directive and more demanding of others.

CASUALTIES—GETTYSBURG—RODES' DIVISION

	Present		Killed		Wounded		Missing		
Brigade	Offs.	Men	Offs.	Men	Offs.	Men	Offs.	Men	Total
Daniel	171	2,123	15	150	48	587	0	116	916
Doles	129	1,275	2	84	11	113	0	31	241
Iverson	114	1,356	12	118	33	349	20	288	820
Ramseur	119	971	5	18	7	122	2	42	196
O'Neal	138	1,656	5	68	38	392	7	186	696
Total	671	7,381	39	438	137	1,563	29	663	2,869[137]

The Army of Northern Virginia experienced on the hills of Gettysburg its worst days since Malvern Hill. Coordination of even the simplest action became a seemingly impossible task.[138] The new three-corps structure seemed to hurt rather than increase efficiency by lowering the span of control. Perhaps the actual size of the army and the scope of its operations was beyond the capabilities of many of its officers. Divisional leadership was good at times, and in other cases mediocre or even poor, but in all instances divisional and brigade officers at Gettysburg outshone their corps commanders. Charges and allegations in later years often alibied a defeat and attempted to isolate blame, but few facts can be clearly delineated and perhaps in truth, blame was due many.

Lee's attempts to lead his assortment of new corps commanders in his well-proven style was unsuccessful. He could not simply identify aims, goals, and objectives, leaving wide discretion in their method of implementation. His inferences and even his direct orders were sometimes disobeyed. The army commander accepted responsibility for the setback and he wisely recognized his style must change for he would become more precise, more exacting, in his orders. Gradually the officer corps of the army grew tighter, more capable of working as a team, and this improvement may more than ever have been a function of Lee's adaptability.

On the 4th of July the Confederate army readied its withdrawal. Rodes toured the hospitals and commented on the wounded who could not be transported in wagons or ambulances when he stated:

> ...near one-half of them, say about 760, were in the hands of the enemy. This painful result was of course unavoidable. Four surgeons, six assistants, three hospital stewards, and ninety-four attendants were left to tend the wounded and with them ten days supply of such food and medicines as were needed. This was all we could do for them.[139]

Some of those left behind would survive their ordeal in Union hospitals, where they were well treated, and vile Union prisons, where they were not. Officers were still being exchanged for Union captives of equal rank, but that selection was made by Union surgeons. Several irate Southern officers accused the surgeons of:

> ...sending only those who have lost an arm or leg, fearing the others, if allowed to breathe once more their free Southern air, may recover too speedily, and soon return with fresh ardor to their places in the Confederate Army.[140]

The ambulances, intermingled with supply and ordnance wagons began to roll westward before nightfall into a driving rainstorm. The route was toward Cashtown, then south to Hagerstown, heading for Williamsport on the Potomac. Brig. Gen. John Imboden and his 2,100 cavalrymen, who had seen little hard service on the campaign, were entrusted with escorting the seventeen-mile-long column.[141] General Rodes dispatched Brigadier General Iverson with infantry to support Imboden and they, in fact, did succeed in repelling Union cavalry near Hagerstown. Several of the severely wounded general officers such as John Hood, Wade Hampton, and Dorsey Pender refused to be left in Northern hands and endured the wet, bone-jarring ride back to safety, although Pender died of his wounds and subsequent infection.[142]

About 1 A.M. on July 5 the army began its evacuation. A.P. Hill's III Corps followed the wagons with Longstreet's I Corps close behind. The II Corps under Ewell brought up the rear with J.E.B. Stuart and a cavalry brigade on the left rear and Fitzhugh Lee's troopers on the right rear.[143] Rodes' Division bivouacked two miles from Fairfield on the night of July 5, having experienced a difficult march in mud and rain.[144] On the sixth, Rodes' Division took over the rear guard assignment and was forced to halt and deploy Doles' and Daniel's Brigades on several occasions as Maj. Gen. John Sedgwick's VI Corps drew close.[145] Wright's Division of the VI Corps advanced a heavy skirmish line but all attacks were minor and easily repulsed.[146] Sometime that afternoon the marchers passed the charred remains of a Confederate wagon train. Kilpatrick's Cavalry had caught and burned the wagons the previous day. The most serious loss was the forge and repair equipment for Carter's Artillery Battalion. A number of teamsters and attendants of the Jeff Davis Artillery were also captured.[147] By July 7 the rear guard reached Hagerstown where Rodes deployed his entire division, expecting a Union onslaught and determined to buy several days' respite. Pursuit was still minimal, however, and the rear guard waited for several days while Lee selected a defensive position near Downsville, south of Hagerstown, which covered the Williamsport Road. When Lee reached Williamsport he discovered the long wagon trains of wounded stalled north of the river. The rains had produced high water so there with its back to a flooding river the army constructed strong earthworks in a wide arc with inner works around the fords of the Potomac.[148] When the works were complete, Rodes fell back from Hagerstown and occupied the extreme left side of the defensive arc. Meade's army grew close, skirmishing was constant, but the Federal general did not attack despite constant pressure from President Lincoln. The pontoon bridge had been destroyed by Federal cavalry and had to be rebuilt at Falling Waters which took several additional days. Upon completion the wagons of wounded and supplies plus the reserve artillery crossed at once. On July 12 Meade held a war council and polled the opinions of his corps commanders concerning an attack on the Confederate lines. Seven of these gentlemen vetoed the idea, and after Lee crossed they inspected the works and were thankful they desisted.[149]

On the night of July 14, Ewell's II Corps fell back and forded the Potomac. Rodes' artillery made use of so-called port fires to aid the crossing. These were long paper tubes filled with a combustible substance which burned slowly with a beautiful flame. These previously useless pieces of equipment thus lit the way for the guns to slowly traverse the steep approaches and then the pontoon bridge, which was swaying in the dark river.[150] The operation was not without hazards. One soldier remembered his regiment wading across four abreast with arms interlocked to prevent men from being swept away.[151] Robert Rodes, in concluding his Gettysburg

Report, described vividly the night crossing and the conclusion to the great invasion. He stated:

> It was very dark, raining and excessively muddy. The men had to wade through the aqueduct, down a steep bank of mud, in which numbers lost their shoes and down which many fell. The water was cold, deep, and rising, the lights on either side of the river were dim, just affording enough light to mark the places of entrance and exit. The cartridge boxes of the men had to be placed around their neck some small men had to be carried over by their comrades—the water was up to the armpits of a full size man. All the circumstances attending this crossing combined to make it an affair not only involving great hardship, but one of great danger to the men and company officers; but be it said to the everlasting honor of these brave fellows, they encountered it not only promptly but with cheers and laughter. We crossed without the loss of a single man but I regret to say, with the loss of some 25000 to 30000 rounds of ammunition, which was unavoidably wetted and spoiled. After crossing, I marched by orders a short distance beyond "Falling Waters" and then bivouacked and there ended the Pennsylvania campaign, so far as this division was concerned.[152]

CHAPTER 9

KEEP TO THE RANKS
The Mine Run Campaign

Despite the successful withdrawal from a precarious position in Pennsylvania, none but the most optimistic of Confederates could look upon the recent invasion as other than a bitter and disappointing defeat. Coupled with the surrender of Vicksburg, key to the Mississippi River, the darkest of days fell on Southern hopes and aspirations. At no other time during the brief existence of the Confederacy were such optimistic dreams for a successful culmination of the conflict so abruptly dashed on the rocks of despair. Maj. John W. Daniel felt the emotions of the soldiers were raw as "they had experienced the height of anticipation until July 2 and then had plunged into the depths."[1]

Maj. Gen. Robert Rodes, masking his personal disappointments, attempted to stimulate troop morale by issuance of dispatches which complimented the marching performance and battle accomplishments of his soldiers. In official reports he praised the performance of men "who day by day sacrificed self....who with bloody and swollen feet, kept to their ranks,...for weeks."[2] Additionally, Rodes remarked on the performance of officers under his command who distinguished themselves, especially Brig. Gens. Junius Daniel, George Doles, and Dodson Ramseur, as well as Lt. Col. Thomas H. Carter, chief of artillery, and Capt. Donald P. Halsey, assistant adjutant general of Iverson's Brigade.[3] Rodes also lamented the loss of officers such as Col. Daniel H. Christie of the 23rd North Carolina and Lt. Col. D.R.E. Winn of the 4th Georgia, both potential brigade commanders.[4] Rodes focused his reorganization efforts on removal of the incompetent, promotion of those deserving, and obtaining needed supplies of shoes, tents, and clothing.

After recrossing the Potomac, Rodes' Division was retained near Hedgesville for some time, in an abortive attempt to ambush Union pursuit, but ultimately moved on to camp at Darkesville in Berkely County. On June 22 the division proceeded up the valley to Winchester. The following morning Rodes marched rapidly to assist Brig. Gen. Ambrose Wright's Brigade of Anderson's Division, charged with the defense of Manassas Gap.[5] Wright was down to six hundred effectives and was deployed in a lengthy skirmish line, attempting to delay a Federal force estimated as almost 20,000 strong.[6] Rodes' Division marched twenty-three miles at a rapid pace. Upon arrival, Rodes dispatched Blackford's sharpshooters to join Wright, then deployed his Alabama Brigade on a ridge three hundred yards to Wright's rear. Finally, he spread the remainder of his division across a spur of the mountain in formidable position and in clear sight of the enemy. Union soldiers in compact blue masses marched confidently at Wright's elastic line, bending it backward. But Rodes unloosed Carter's guns whose plunging fire, combined with the obvious presence of a fully deployed Confederate division, convinced Union officers that the pass could not be forced. Rodes' main battle line was never engaged and his total casualties were only fifteen.[7]

After nightfall the troops fell back near Front Royal to bivouac, moving on into the beautiful Luray Valley the following morning. Several days of relaxation followed about Luray amid cool shade trees and delicious spring waters, while some of the more adventurous spirits explored several of the famed caverns with which the limestone hills abounded. A swift march via Thornton's Gap brought Rodes and his men to Madison Court House on July 29.[8] Here they encamped, sprawled in fields around Madison throughout August and into September, resupplying and recuperating.

Rodes was compelled to address the disposition of the two brigade commanders who he adjudged had performed so inadequately at Gettysburg. General Iverson, already removed from command, had performed significant volunteer service on the retreat to Virginia. In his battle report, Rodes complimented Iverson's prompt response in bringing forward infantry support to assist the hard-pressed Confederate cavalry which was attempting to protect wagonloads of wounded at Hagerstown.[9] Iverson had commanded the North Carolina Brigade since General Garland was slain at South Mountain, and prior to Gettysburg his army record was impeccable. Both Maj. Gen. D.H. Hill and Lt. Gen. Thomas J. Jackson had urged his advancement to brigadier.[10] But the lack of confidence in him now evidenced by soldiers dictated that he could not be retained in brigade command, so his North Carolinians were turned over to Brig. Gen. Robert Johnston.[11]

Iverson returned home to his native Georgia and in 1864 was recalled to lead a cavalry brigade under Maj. Gen. Joseph Wheeler in defense of the Georgia capital.[12] Both before and after July 1863, Alfred Iverson enjoyed a reputation as an honest, sincere gentleman. Whatever the cause of his failure on July 1, his later military and civic career was honorable.

Col. Edward O'Neal's appointment as brigade commander was temporary. After consultation with Ewell and Lee it was determined to pass him over for promotion. The forty-five-year-old Alabamian, a graduate of LaGrange College, was an attorney and a powerful force in his state Democratic Party. He had risen through the ranks of several Alabama regiments to become colonel of the 26th. Lee had earlier recommended that O'Neal be promoted, and the colonel must have learned that Rodes disagreed and had instead suggested three candidates for Lee's consideration, omitting O'Neal's name from that list.

Rodes' first recommendation was John Gordon, but he could not be spared from Early's Division. Next he submitted the name of John Tyler Morgan from Alabama, who had briefly commanded an Alabama regiment, but resigned and returned home when defeated in officer elections.[13] Following Gettysburg, Lee agreed to the promotion of Morgan, but when contacted he refused, remaining in the western army. Rodes' final recommendation was that of Col. Cullen A. Battle of the 3rd Alabama who was promoted to brigadier on August 25, 1863.[14] O'Neal protested vigorously to Lee, who then permitted the dissatisfied officer to return with his regiment to Alabama. The 61st Alabama was transferred into the brigade to complete Battle's troops. But this did not conclude the affairs of Col. Edward O'Neal. In the spring of 1864, Senator James Phelan of Alabama filed a protest with President Davis that O'Neal had been treated unfairly.[15] Davis forwarded the letter to Lee who answered as follows:

> I concur with the Hon. Mr. Phelen that Col O'Neal is a most true, brave, and gallant officer. Still I believe Cols. Gordon, Morgan and Battle give promise of making better brigade commanders, and therefore recommend them before him.[16]

Months later when O'Neal's Regiment returned to Virginia and promotion was again proposed for that officer, Lee absolutely refused to endorse him, questioning the officer's ability to command.[17] Without doubt, O'Neal blamed Rodes for his lack of promotion, protesting and meeting with every congressman or government official. But Lee's support of the major general, in his usual tactful manner, precluded O'Neal's appeals. O'Neal was particularly successful in politics after the war, being elected governor of Alabama in 1882 and 1884. In addition one of his six children ran also for that office.[18]

In late August, Rodes was in Richmond clarifying his position on the O'Neal case to the War Department. Upon his return and as he dismounted the train at Orange Depot he encountered an officer of the brigade whom he knew well and informed him that O'Neal had been transferred west and General Battle had been appointed to command.[19] The appointment of the thirty-four-year-old Alabama native was popular among the soldiers. The devout Battle had risen from major to colonel in the 3rd Alabama, surviving wounds at Seven Pines, Sharpsburg, and Fredericksburg, and was an officer of widespread respect.[20]

Lee, in permitting this late-summer respite, was attempting to rebuild an army which he knew was badly wounded, physically as well as emotionally. He anticipated the return of stragglers, those slightly wounded in the Gettysburg campaign, and new recruits; all of which would, hopefully, increase the strength of many badly depleted regiments and brigades. However, serious desertion rates threatened to offset those gains. Despite Lee's liberal furlough plan, notoriously individualistic Confederate infantrymen often made their own decisions regarding leave. On many occasions, as this surely was, solid veterans determined by intuition or smell of powder that no serious action was forthcoming, and slipped away for a visit home to see the family, check the crops, or obtain new clothes. They simply disappeared and after a time would reappear just as mysteriously.

Despite the lack of shoes, clothing, hats, and horses, once established in camps, the soldiers enjoyed the luxury of plentiful rations for a time. Bivouacked in a productive farming area as harvest approached, they were able to obtain potatoes, flour, fruit, berries, beef, and bacon in abundance. Their general, however, did not believe that troops should long be idle, and drill at regimental and brigade level soon became a part of daily life. Inspections were instituted frequently and Rodes appeared often in their camps and on their drill fields. His soldiers grew accustomed to observing his tall, lithe form stalking through the camps, and his friendly, unpretentious smile earned their friendship. New recruits were constantly being integrated into the regiments and during the winter of 1863–64, while checking picket lines, Rodes found a rookie lounging on the ground, his rifle leaning on a nearby tree. Rodes stopped and asked the young man if he knew he could be court-martialed for his action.

"No, I did not," the boy replied, still lying on the ground.

"When did you enlist?" Rodes snapped.

"Last week."

"When were you assigned to picket duty?"

"This morning," answered the recruit.

"Do you know who I am?" the general asked.

"No sir."

"I am General Rodes."

The boy leaped up, ran over to Rodes and, offering his hand, said, "Glad to meet you General Rodes, I'm Dick Maness. How's your folks?"[21] The general tactfully withdrew.

Rodes was overjoyed on September 2 when his wife, Virginia, delivered a son, Robert Emmett Rodes II, born in the military hospital in Charlottesville.[22] The thirty-four-year-old first-time father was doubly pleased that his son arrived during a relatively quiet period when he could anticipate the enjoyment of his family for the next few months.

Lee initiated several military ceremonies, reviewing the entire 2nd Corps on September 9 and the 3rd Corps on September 12, intent upon stimulating the military ardor of the troops by having them realize their power. The review was recalled as a brilliant affair with the magnificent dress of the officers, who managed to keep one good uniform, contrasting markedly with the poorly clad soldiers. [23] In addition, strong religious revivals swept through the camps in September, improving spirits and inspiring commitment to God and country. Soldiers seldom attended divine services in churches; in good weather they simply lay upon the ground in groups while the minister delivered his sermon. Many brigades formed Christian Associations with members, including the newly promoted Battle, signing pledges they would avoid liquor and the use of profanity.[24] Rodes did not so pledge.

Lee was still desirous of initiating offensive actions against a, thus far, passive Federal army under Maj. Gen. George Meade. But these ambitious plans were curtailed by President Davis' decision to dispatch Lieutenant General Longstreet and his 1st Corps west to reinforce Gen. Braxton Bragg's Army of Tennessee, now facing a large Federal army in front of Chattanooga. After enjoying a decisive initial success at Chickamauga on September 19 and 20, failures and disappointments in the sleet and cold of the East Tennessee Valley concluded Longstreet's campaign. Controversy and acrimony within the command would rage as the campaign floundered to an inglorious ending before Knoxville.

In mid-September Rodes led his brigades out of their camps and moved toward Summerville Ford on the Rapidan River, supposedly to assist Confederate cavalry, but despite sharp artillery exchanges no action occurred. The division then established camps in position to contest Morton's Ford on the Rapidan, a favorite crossing point for Union cavalry. On October 12, in reaction to a request for support by Gen. J.E.B. Stuart, Rodes moved the division rapidly toward the Rappahannock. He advanced through Jeffersonton, driving out a Union cavalry outpost, then to Warrenton Springs on the Rappahannock where a brisk, little action occurred. Lieutenant Park of the 12th Alabama recalled the fight:

> General Rodes ordered Battle's Alabama and Doles' Georgia Brigades to push rapidly across and it was promptly done amid a sharp fire from musketry and cannon. Battle's Brigade was moved down the Warrenton Pike by an old, burnt hotel. Right there gallant J.E.B. Stuart galloped by with the 12th Virginia Cavalry and charged right royally upon the Yanks, posted strongly upon a hill in front but the Virginians were to few in number and were forced to retire. General Battle was ordered by Rodes to send a regiment to dislodge the enemy, and he selected the 12th Alabama for the honorable though dangerous task....we moved under a heavy fire....when within forty yards the regiment fired a volley into them....and followed it by volley after volley until the enemy turned and fled.[25]

The willingness of dismounted cavalry to contest Confederate infantry was an insult to the gray-backed veterans, but also pointed to the changing nature of the war. Union cavalry were now led by better officers of a stouter nature than previously, and their repeating rifles made them more than a match for any opponent. Rodes' infantrymen contented themselves with the capture of some of those guns that were loaded on Sunday and shot all week. No further assistance was necessary as Stuart's troopers pursued the enemy north, so Rodes, the ex-railway engineer, assigned his men the task of wrecking the Orange and Alexandria Railway.

Meanwhile, Lee called out A.P. Hill's 3rd Corps and sent them moving north in an attempt to flank Meade, force him to retreat, and perhaps attack at an advantage while the blue-coats were on the march.[26] Ewell's 2nd Corps was to follow and support Hill, so Rodes moved by way of Auburn and Greenwich. An officer recalled: "The weather was magnificent and the crimson foliage of the woods rivalled the tint of the red battle-flags, fluttering above the long glittering hedge of bayonets."[27] Hill's column passed Culpeper, looping toward the Orange and Alexandria Railway. Their slight, bearded, red-shirted corps commander was soon convinced that Lee was correct: the Federals were in retreat and now he must catch and punish them. Hill enjoyed a reputation as an outstanding divisional commander, but was as yet unproven at corps level. He had been ill at Gettysburg, taking little part in combat, thus this was his initial assumption of corps command.[28] Scouts reported blue-coats moving north in large numbers near Broad Run Church, and Heth's Division led the chase.[29] Delighted Confederate soldiers followed a trail of knapsacks, blankets, and even guns, indicators that the Union retreat was actually flight. The anxious urging of their commander and the thoughts of their favorite plunder, Federal sutler's wagons, changed the nature of their pursuit to a fast march with no stragglers, akin to a pack of hounds on the trail of their quarry. As the Confederate column neared Briscoe Station, Hill emerged onto high ground and saw spread before him thousands of Federal soldiers milling about, waiting to cross the narrow bridge over Broad Run.[30] Instant action seemed the answer and Hill hit them at once with Poague's cannon fire, then ordered Heth to send his leading brigades at them, head-on. Impulsive and aggressive Ambrose Powell Hill!!!

True, those Federals in view were retreating, revealing a confused appearance, and their situation at that moment was indeed precarious. Across the stream most of the Union army's transport vehicles were massed in an open field, and a Confederate breakthrough could cause incalculable damage.[31] A thirty-minute delay by Hill would have permitted Rodes to join him, and a reconnaissance would have prevented the mini-disaster which followed. Hill's cursory glance did not mean the plodding and careful George Meade was unprepared. Part of the II Federal Corps, 3,000 men under Maj. Gen. G.K. Warren, were entrenched behind a railway embankment, three full Union divisions awaiting two charging Confederate brigades.[32] Artillery was also in position across the stream.[33] The brigades of Brig. Gen. John R. Cooke and Brig. Gen. William Kirkland raced to the assault, screaming their rebel yell, intent upon quickly pushing across the little stream and falling on the unprepared enemy milling in the open fields. But they were shocked and literally slaughtered by Warren's unseen troops who were behind an embankment on their flank.

Rodes' Division, marching hard, heard the rifle-fire and picked up the pace believing Hill was "into" the Union column. But the battle was over in a few minutes and the 2nd Corps would be too late to assist.[34] Cooke and Kirkland lost more than 1,300 men in the hasty and ill-conceived pressing of the enemy. General Hill, in his report, manfully accepted blame as he stated that he made the attack too hastily, although he added that in a half hour there would have been no enemy to attack.[35] Lee, after surveying the damage, made only one comment which surely seemed a rebuke, when he remarked to Hill: "Well, well, General, bury those poor men and let us say no more about it."[36] Federal forces continued to fall back as the weather grew cold and a hard rain began. Robert Rodes again put his men to destroying cross ties and rails. As night fell, the brigades dried out and slept in captured Union tents near Catlett's Station.[37] On September 19 Rodes placed his men in motion toward another river crossing but for once was forced to surrender to the weather. A terrific storm produced such heavy rain and sleet, amid winds so fierce that a man could scarcely stand, that the brigades were forced to seek cover in the woods and thickets. Straggling back to camp, avoiding flooding streams, they were ordered by the commanding general to proceed to Kelly's Ford on the Rappahannock to prevent a Union advance in that sector.

Robert Rodes rode back into Charlottesville whenever possible to steal a visit with his wife and newborn son. Virginia was staying with Robert's uncle in the university town, and when Robert arrived on October 30 he was surprised to find a group of native Lynchburgers on hand with a beautiful black mare as a gift from his friends.[38] Knowing his preference for black horses, a public collection had been undertaken to purchase the fine animal.

To threaten the flank of an enemy assault on Kelly's Ford, Lee rebuilt a complex of old redoubts further upstream on the north side of the river near the unusable Rappahannock Railway Bridge. These redoubts formed a bridgehead connected to the Confederate bank by a lone pontoon bridge. Both Lee and Ewell thought the works strong, but Early, whose men held the bridgehead, disagreed.[39] On November 7, Brig. Gen. Harry T. Hays' Louisiana soldiers held the bridgehead, although Hays was away on court-martial duty and twenty-seven-year-old Col. Davidson Penn, a V.M.I. graduate, was in command.

Before noon, Federals in force stormed across the river downstream at Kelly's Ford, capturing soldiers of Rodes' guard regiment and more graybacks from a regiment which arrived to relieve the pickets, and drew up in battle order.[40] The 2nd North Carolina of Ramseur's Brigade was on guard and poorly supported by the 30th North Carolina. Their brigade commander was not present having received leave for his long-delayed marriage on October 28. Doubtless the intense young Dodson Ramseur was crushed by Rodes' appraisal that the 30th had not upheld its reputation in losing almost 300 prisoners.[41] Soon Rodes' entire division thundered up and aligned itself facing the enemy, exchanging sharpshooter fire and artillery rounds. But Rodes immediately realized that the Union force did not intend to venture beyond the protection of its stout artillery which was firing from the heights north of the river. He notified Ewell, correctly, that he believed the enemy movement was purely a demonstration.

Upstream at Rappahannock Bridge, the Union V and VI Corps were closing in around the bridgehead. Early rode across the pontoon bridge, analyzed the situation, and upon returning, sent reinforcements.[42] As the November twilight gave way to darkness, a nervous Early could discern rifle flashes growing closer to the redoubts, but Lee and Ewell assured Early that Federals never attacked at night. Suddenly surging soldiers of Russell's Federal Division, paced by the 6th Maine, swarmed over the walls and into the salient. For one of the few recorded instances men in both armies died of bayonet wounds. Fighting was hand-to-hand and fierce until Union numbers overwhelmed the defenders. Early, watching from the opposite bank, dispatched his aide, Maj. John W. Daniel, to investigate. When Daniel reached the pontoon bridge he could not get across as it was packed with fleeing Confederates. Soon firing ceased and loud Union huzzahs were heard. A horrified witness, Early finally torched the pontoon bridge. Early lost a total of 1,674 men, most being captured when surrounded with no hope of succor. Colonels Penn and Godwin were captured along with eight colors and 2,000 stands of arms.[43]

Strangely, after his success, Meade retained his army in camp until late November. He then launched a more ambitious plan to turn Lee's right flank and force Confederate abandonment of their winter line on the Rapidan. Ewell was ill and Maj. Gen. Jubal Early temporarily led the 2nd Corps. When Meade crossed the Rapidan Fords on November 26 under cover of heavy fog, Early marched north, his division under Hays followed by those of Rodes and Johnson, each eager to repay the Federals for Rappahannock Bridge. Rodes' leading brigade encountered Federals near Locust Grove and he shook out his men into battle order. Hays deployed alongside and Rodes urged advancement. But Lee had arrived, viewed the strong Federal position, and decided to await Johnson who was marching by another road. Employing sharpened oak poles, bayonets, and tin cups the two divisions began entrenching, rapidly throwing up walls of earth and stone, for by now they were experienced and one remarked: "considerable earthworks could be expected in a short time, particularly if the diggers were in peril."[44]

Johnson's men, on the march, were assaulted by Union skirmishers on their flank, then they collided with the III Federal Corps near Payne's

Farm. Johnson wisely rode directly to the point of contact, formed line of battle and advanced.[45] A brief but sharp encounter produced high casualties for the small numbers involved, but his check of the Federal III Corps while Rodes and Hays held firm at Locust Grove, completely disrupted Meade's plans.

Lee realized the entire Army of the Potomac was in his front, and not favoring his position, he moved his two corps back several miles and began construction of new earthworks between hills and behind Mine Run. Meade followed slowly in heavy rain, halted, and also began entrenching. Artillery fire was exchanged and as both armies dug furiously, a cold penetrating wind began to whistle through the trees as temperatures plummeted.[46] The soldiers built fires behind their earthworks and huddled close to stay warm. One Confederate was told by Union prisoners that some of their pickets actually froze to death on guard duty.[47] Meade planned an assault on both Confederate flanks for November 30, dispatching Maj. Gen. G.K. Warren's II Corps on a wide swing around the Confederate right while Maj. Gen. John Sedgwick massed the V and VI Corps on Lee's left. Warren was to sever the Confederate line of communications and supply while Sedgwick charged the gray line. Warren, however, cut short his flank movement, was then observed by gray cavalry, and when prepared to attack faced formidable earthworks.[48] Warren hesitated, then determined an attack was useless, and retreated. Meade, in an ill humor, redressed Warren severely, then called off Sedgwick's planned assault.[49] Lee's men remained quietly behind their now extensive earthworks hoping for, even inviting, enemy attack. Thus the thirtieth passed quietly, much to the satisfaction of the soldiers seeking cover from the cold wind. Their only real shelter was underground, but digging was difficult since heavy rains produced bottomless mud which cold weather turned into ice each evening. When Meade didn't move on December 1, Lee decided to initiate a limited advance. But when Rodes sent his sharpshooters sprinting forward, the enemy was gone. Bitterly disappointed, Lee dispatched Rodes and his division in pursuit. Rodes pushed hard in terrible conditions back to the river fords on the Rapidan, picking up hundreds of shivering prisoners; however, Meade's men had disappeared back into their waiting winter camps. Icicles formed on the beards of Confederate soldiers and one recalled that "such cold winds eighteen months ago, would have caused colds, coughs, and pneumonia, but now we are accustomed to rough conditions and thin clothing."[50]

Rodes moved his men into winter quarters on the Plank Road, six miles below Orange Court House.[51] The soldiers were so hungry they were eating acorns on the return to camp. But realizing the army was now in winter camp, they fell to work constructing shelter. On a bright, unusually warm day in January, Rodes' Brigades re-enlisted for the war en masse in a public parade, most regiments stepping forward the required two paces as one man. Pleased, Rodes published a general order in which he congratulated the unit as he stated:

> The significance of this movement...will not be underrated, either by the enemy or our own people. They will, as I do, see in this the beginning of the end, the first dawn of peace and independence, because they will see that these men are unconquerable.[52]

In late February, Rodes turned out his division and marched toward Charlottesville in a blinding snowstorm, responding to an enemy threat. Later he unlimbered several brigades on the Plank Road in a vain attempt to intercept Union Gen. Judson Kilpatrick retreating after the failed Dahlgren raid on Richmond. Leaving Johnston's Brigade at Hanover Junction to prevent further raids, Rodes returned to winter quarters. Johnston's Brigade was subsequently attached to Gordon's Division.[53] Gov. Zebulon B. Vance of North Carolina visited Rodes' camps, in an effort to inspire Confederate soldiers.[54] On the twenty-eighth Vance made a lengthy oration which, when Stuart, Early, and Rodes added their comments, lasted for four hours. Reaction of most of the troops was unrecorded.

Despite these interruptions, Robert Rodes enjoyed the cold winter in the company of his wife and newborn son.[55] General Ramseur returned from North Carolina and was joined by his new bride. He and Rodes had contemplated sharing a house but could not work out a satisfactory site, nevertheless, the ladies added needed domesticity to pleasant evenings by the fireside. The Rodeses entertained other officers frequently and quite a lively social season ensued. One amusing incident disturbed this tranquility. Several soldiers, desperate for lack of meat, made a raid upon the cowpen of General Rodes and killed the milk cow of the Mrs. General.[56] This action incensed both General Rodes and his wife since the cow was a supplier for the younger Rodes, but despite valiant attempts the culprits were never identified. In early April wives and families departed as husbands again prepared for battle.

Rodes and Ramseur long enjoyed a close relationship, personally and professionally, despite the fact that they were ambitious young officers in an extremely competitive environment. Both were conspicuously brave in battle, choosing to lead from "in front," a fact that would later prove fatal to both. But their personalities differed in that they were almost complements of one another. Ramseur was an intensely devout Presbyterian, searching for God's meaning in every endeavor including his military career. His views and moods could vary from the extremely enthusiastic to quite dour, somewhat dependent on his view of God's approval of Southern arms. Rodes, while not overtly religious, was more evenly optimistic of Confederate victory. Both men of high ambition, they desired advancement in their profession; but Ramseur more openly courted the support and assistance of those in the political arena, particularly from his native North Carolina. Rodes shrank from these efforts as Capt. Thomas H. Carter explained:

> I asked the reason such splendid qualities as a soldier should have received less than due distinction in a great war of long duration

> and in an army which, though rich in good division generals, was poor in good corps commanders. I should ascribe it to his profound sense of responsibility as to his command, and his duty, and his refusal to countenance army correspondence in his own behalf. Every contempt of counterfeit merit was his, every instinct of a true soldier was his. His laurels had to rest solely on the eternal foundation of truth.[57]

Loyalty was a characteristic of both men. Rodes had a better opportunity to display this trait when widespread resentment to Ramseur's promotion to command of Early's Division developed and Rodes came to the young officer's defense.

Longstreet's 1st Corps returned from its Tennessee campaign and encamped near Lee's other two corps. The officers and men were pleased to be reunited and eager in anticipation of a coming clash with blue-coats. They had heard rumors that a new Federal general, Ulysses S. Grant, had come east to match his wits with Lee's, and his soldiers' prowess with theirs. But other Federal generals had started south with huge armies and Marse Robert had always prevailed.

CHAPTER 10

A NEW OPPONENT
Into the Wilderness

On March 9, 1864, Ulysses Simpson Grant was commissioned a lieutenant general[1] and three days later appointed to succeed Henry Halleck as commander of Federal armies. In less than a week following his second inauguration President Abraham Lincoln determined that he had found the commander to terminate this wretched war, and he placed his trust in that officer. At once, Grant transferred his headquarters east, camping alongside Maj. Gen. George Meade, who commanded the Federal Army of the Potomac. Soon this force would be known as Grant's army, presenting some difficult and awkward moments for the mercurial Meade despite Grant's constant attempts to alleviate the problem.

Throughout March and into April, Grant conferred with Lincoln, the secretary of war, and other senators as he formulated a strategy for the spring of 1864. He even journeyed to Nashville, spending several days conferring with Maj. Gen. William Sherman, the fiery redhead who commanded Federal armies in the western theater.[2] Aware that his biggest advantage was numerical superiority, Grant determined to utilize that advantage by simultaneously advancing on all fronts. Gradually, he devised a plan which included advances by five separate Union armies on five widely scattered fronts. These initiatives, if pursued with persistence, would lead to an inevitable outcome: subjugation of the Confederacy by defeat of her armies. A second portion of that strategy entailed persistent hammering at the enemy.[3] If all five armies committed themselves to action by constantly engaging the enemy then the Southern armies would eventually be worn into submission.

The armies which Grant would utilize to implement this strategy included Meade's army, augmented by the powerful IX Corps. This tremendous force of almost 120,000 men would move across the Rapidan and engage Lee's army in daily combat. A second large Federal force, containing seven army corps, under Sherman would move south from Chattanooga.[4] While these two major advances were occurring, three minor offensive movements were also initiated. Maj. Gen. Nathaniel Banks was to move from his base in New Orleans to attack Mobile, Alabama, one of the South's few remaining ports which still accommodated blockade runners.[5] Maj. Gen. Franz Sigel was to lead a small force south up the Shenandoah Valley, and Maj. Gen. Benjamin Butler's Army of the James was to advance from Hampton Roads up the south side of the James River, threatening the Confederate capital. If all moved as one, pressure on the Confederates would be tremendous.

Grant issued orders forbidding sutler's wagons from accompanying the army, an order which incensed veteran Confederate infantry, as they considered Federal sutlers their personal and private commissary. All Union units were stripped down to essential, necessary equipment as the new commander found the army too slow on the move, unable to keep pace with its more agile Confederate counterpart. Finally, Grant was instrumental in alterations of the system whereby prisoners of war were exchanged.[6] He terminated exchanges, condemning thousands to the horrors of Libby and Andersonville in the South and the equally foul Northern pest-holes of Elmira, Camp Chase, and Johnson's Island.[7] Prison administration was a novel science in both armies, usually staffed by those unsuited for combat, provisioned only after each government fed and clothed its own troops, and envisioned as a temporary restraining pen awaiting exchanges. Without parole or exchange, untold numbers perished in the filth, stupidity, and utter brutality of Civil War prisons, but Grant correctly surmised that this favored Northern purposes with their unrestricted resources in manpower—a brutal, cold, but effective policy entitled "war to extermination" by Confederates.[8]

Grant had no tremendous record as a tactician, although he enjoyed superior moments at Vicksburg, but he was a doggedly persistent man[9] who focused on his determined goals and never deviated. Confederate Lt. Gen. James Longstreet, who knew Grant well, issued a warning to his contemporaries when he stated:

> We must make up our minds to get into line of battle and to stay there, for that man will fight us every day and every hour until the end of this war. In order to whip him we must out-maneuver him and husband our strength as best we can.[10]

The battleground which Lee and Grant were soon to employ was a large, barren, inhospitable area below the Rapidan River known locally as the "Wilderness." The Army of the Potomac was camped north of the Rapidan and to move south without a wide detour via Fredericksburg was compelled to cross the stream and slide east toward Richmond, hopefully, clearing this underpopulated waste area as soon as possible. Although the area was basically flat, it was cut by ravines, gullies, and marshes or bogs. Most of the large timber had been harvested years earlier, and the second growth covering of scrub-oak, pine, cedar, and sweet-gum was unbelievably thick and strangely stunted at a height of ten to twenty feet. These small trees were interlaced with bushes, briars, and grapevines which presented a thicket difficult for a man to penetrate and impossible for horsemen. Infantry units found formation movements exceedingly difficult throughout the entire area except for the few cultivated fields. Artillery was useless except along the two roads or in these cleared fields. It was spring and the profusion of budding greenery further reduced this already limited visibility.

Within this warren of brush, trees, and vines there were a few cleared fields or glades as stubborn settlers had continued to fight the encroaching jungle in their attempt to scratch out a living from poor soil. As military units began to deploy in the Wilderness, these few fields became, at first, a welcome area of maneuver and artillery placement, but soon they became the "killing zones." Units in the openings were decimated by riflemen crouching in fringes of undergrowth. Eventually each clearing was surrounded by infantry units entrenched in the woods, and advances across these no-man's lands simply resulted in additional layers of the carpet of dead and wounded. Once action became intense, bullets cut branches from saplings which sagged into the maze, then the underbrush caught fire and smoke hung low over the vegetation almost eliminating already meager visibility. Soldiers loaded and fired into the smoke and the air was alive with unaimed bullets.

On the night of May 4, Grant launched his offense and by morning declared himself pleased with his "great success."[11] He had evidently expected difficulties in crossing the river with his three large corps in the face of the enemy and was pleased to find himself initially unopposed. Maj. Gen. Gouverneur K. Warren's V Corps supported by Maj. Gen. John Sedgwick's VI Corps forced a crossing of the Rapidan, splashing across at Germanna Ford. Downstream Maj. Gen. S. Winfield Hancock's huge, 27,000-man II Corps crossed on pontoon bridges at Ely's Ford and approached Chancellorsville.[12] Dust clouds obscured the sky as columns of infantry and wagons poured southeastward. Grant emphasized speed, get the troops over the river, march southeast, clear the Wilderness, then look for a fight.[13]

But Lee understood Grant's dilemma and moved rapidly to exercise options which reduced Grant's advantages. To oppose the mammoth Union army he had three corps of eight divisions or about 64,000 of all arms.[14] On the night of May 3–4 the signal station on Clark Mountain sent word that the enemy was stirring, and by dawn they confirmed Federals were moving over Germanna and Ely's Fords. Lee's anticipation resulted in rapid reaction, and he decided to hit the enemy while they were moving through the Wilderness under conditions more favorable to the Confederates.[15] He launched two columns down the principal thoroughfares crossing the area, the Orange Turnpike and the Orange Plank Road. Both roads led from

Orange Court House east toward Fredericksburg, so both Confederate columns, moving parallel, would attempt to hit the Federal forces in the right flank as they marched east. Lt. Gen. Richard S. Ewell was ordered to start his 2nd Confederate Corps east on the Orange Turnpike as Lt. Gen. A.P. Hill would lead his 3rd Corps east on the Orange Plank Road, both feeling for Union contact. Lee planned to gain the initiative with this double thrust, pinning Grant down in the Wilderness, then Longstreet's 1st Corps would arrive and deliver a killing blow.[16]

By 10 A.M. Ewell was moving east hard, unknowingly camping that evening near Locust Grove, only about two miles from the flank of Brig. Gen. Charles Griffin's Federal division. Edward Johnson's Division led Ewell's advance, followed by Rodes', then Early's men. Federal scouts correctly reported the advance but Griffin, oddly, was not told.[17]

Rodes was worried that some of his best and most experienced soldiers were absent. Brig. Gen. Robert D. Johnston's Brigade was still stationed at Hanover Court House and a portion of Brig. Gen. George Doles' fine Georgia Brigade was on assignment in North Carolina. Additionally, just prior to leaving winter camps, Ewell had instructed Rodes to leave Brig. Gen. Dodson Ramseur's Brigade as a rear guard for the corps. Thus Rodes, riding with Brig. Gen. Cullen Battle's leading brigade, was advancing with about two and one-half brigades, or about 50 percent of his fighting strength.

Warren's V Federal Corps marched early on May 5, and was crossing the Orange Turnpike on an intersecting road, aiming to turn east on the Orange Plank Road. A glance west by members of Brig. Gen. Joseph J. Bartlett's Brigade observed Confederate infantry, recognizable by their distinctive slouch hats, swarming down the Orange Turnpike, as Ewell's men had also marched early in heavy dew and low hanging fog.[18] Bartlett deployed across the road and Griffin sent him support from available brigades. Johnson, cursing loudly, deployed his leading brigade, that of Brig. Gen. J.M. Jones, to face Bartlett. Maintaining alignment was extremely difficult in the underbrush, and once deployed the two forces, only one and one-half miles apart, could not see each other except along the roadway.[19] Hearing movement to the north, possibly Sedgwick's VI Corps closing up, Johnson became concerned about his left flank and swiftly dealt his remaining brigades, those of Brig. Gens. Steuart, Stafford, and Walker, north of the road to extend Jones' line. Rodes, dashing forward, realized the absolute necessity of Jones holding the road, for otherwise Johnson's whole division could be cut off, and ordered Battle to deploy behind Jones and slightly to his right. This would be Cullen Battle's initial fight in command of a brigade, and the former colonel of the 3rd Alabama was anxious to prove his capabilities.[20]

Rodes sent Doles' understrength brigade south of the road to extend Jones' right and Brig. Gen. Junius Daniel's North Carolinians to Doles' right. Early's Division was well closed up, led by Brig. Gen. John Gordon's Brigade,

Wilderness, May 5, 1864

A determined Union assault along the edge of Saunders Field broke Jones' Brigade and threatened to split the 2nd Corps until repulsed by Gordon, Doles, and Daniel under Rodes' direction.

Robert Carter

Wilderness

In ensuing days Rodes' Division dug miles of elaborate trenches through the woods and thickets.

Robert Carter

which remained poised on the turnpike to move wherever needed. Federal commanders, blessed with abundant troops, decided to strongly probe the Confederate position. Brig. Gen. Romeyn B. Ayers' Brigade, accompanied by Bartlett and supported by Colonel Sweitzer's Brigade, moved on Jones and Steuart, crossing Saunders Field, a rather large cleared area. Ayers' regiments swept smartly forward, striped ensign slanted forward, but had no chance in the open field. Led by the 146th New York in natty blue pants, white gaiters, and red sashes, which made excellent targets, they marched toward Steuart's men who were concealed in the thickets. Ayers was smashed when Stafford was able to turn his brigade to enfilade the well-dressed New Yorkers.[21] Sweitzer fared no better and for a time neither did Bartlett. But suddenly, south of the road where a grove of trees protected the advance, Bartlett's men broke Jones' front, and when the Confederate regiments fled they collided with Battle's men, causing momentary confusion. Rodes, witnessing the retreat, coolly sent for Early's leading brigade, that of John Gordon. Brig. Gen. Lysander Cutler's Federal "Iron Brigade" had rushed forward into the breach, feeling for an opening. But Doles' men stood firm on the shoulder and poured a stiff fire into Bartlett and Cutler. As if on parade, Gordon's men, with a piercing yell, smashed into the Federals. The Iron Brigade was repulsed and Bartlett suffered heavy losses. Two additional Federal brigades, those of Col. Roy Stone and Brig. Gen. James Rice, were moving hesitantly forward, but Rodes, noting their movements, sent Daniel's men running forward in a charge into their flank. As Daniel's Brigade advanced, smoke from brush fires hung heavily along the ground, obscuring visibility. When Union fire began peppering them from within the smoke, Daniel halted the brigade and fired a volley at shadows in the smoky haze. Charging forward they emerged from within the smoke to discover Federals fleeing to the rear, leaving dead and wounded in their wake.[22] Soon the entire Federal force was rolled up and running, caught between Daniel, Gordon, and Doles. Hundreds of Union prisoners were taken as many of the attackers refused to run the gauntlet of Southern fire to return to their lines.[23] Sadly, Brig. Gen. John Jones and his aide-de-camp, Capt. Robert Early, a kinsman of Jubal Early, were both slain when they attempted to rally their broken brigade.[24]

Robert Rodes had handled the fight on the turnpike in exemplary fashion, and with the assistance of Gordon, Daniel, and Doles, had inflicted a stinging defeat on a number of Union brigades. His cool analysis of enemy intent, and reaction by dispatching his available force to unerring position keyed the dramatic Southern success. Once action ceased he readjusted the lines, withdrawing Jones' Brigade, and instructed his men to begin entrenching, for his instinct predicted the day's fight was not done.

About 3 P.M. Sedgwick's VI Federal Corps made its awaited appearance well north of the turnpike. Brig. Gen. Horatio G. Wright deployed his division of Colonel Upton's, Colonel Brown's, and Brigadier General Neill's Brigades with Brigadier General Seymour's in reserve and assaulted

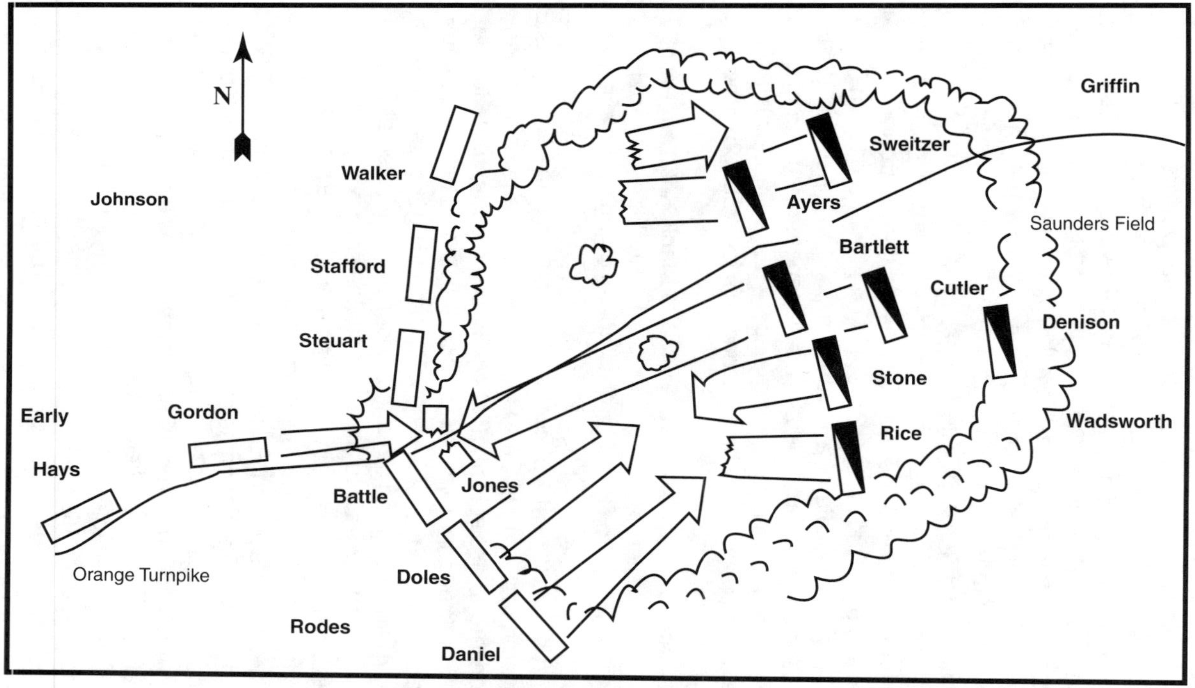

Wilderness, May 5, 1864

As Johnson's Division collided with marching Federal forces he deployed north of the Orange Turnpike. Rodes, arriving, deployed south of the roadway. The Federal V Corps launched an attack across Saunders Field, a large cleared area. Ayers and Sweitzer, to the north, were repelled, but Bartlett and Cutler broke Jones' Brigade and confused Battle's troops. Gordon quickly drove to restore the line as Daniel and Doles disrupted Stone's and Rice's reinforcing units.

Johnson's line. Undergrowth was much thicker north of Saunders Field and preliminary alignment was difficult. Upton, attacking across Saunders Field, could make no progress, but further north in the heavy brush Neill and Russell, assisted by Seymour, managed to get to close quarters with Stafford and Walker. Walker's famed "Stonewall Brigade" suffered heavy casualties when caught in a poor position. Brig. Gen. Harry T. Hays' Louisiana Brigade was dispatched to assist Walker, and in savage hand-to-hand combat the two gray-clad units were able, just barely, to hold off the determined Federals in terrain so terrible that the first sight of an enemy was usually at bayonet range. After an hour or more of such combat, both sides returned to their respective lines and, although exhausted, began to improve their trenches using whatever logs, rocks, or earth that was available. Since so much material was at hand, the ramparts grew swiftly, stout and strong.

Late that evening on Rodes' line, Private Leon of the 53rd North Carolina, tired of the close pot-shots of a Union sharpshooter, decided to slip out and confront this sniper. Thirty minutes later Leon returned carrying the body of his adversary. He discovered the sniper was a Canadian Indian complete with scalp lock, and Leon brought back his foe's body to prove his discovery.[25]

Meanwhile, three miles south on the Orange Plank Road, an entirely separate but even more ferocious fight erupted. Maj. Gen. Harry Heth's Division, leading A.P. Hill's 3rd Corps, struck Federal outposts, driving them back and colliding with Federal Brig. Gen. George Getty's 2nd Division of the Union VI Corps. Grant sent Hancock's men back into the Wilderness and action escalated rapidly. Maj. Gen. Cadmus Wilcox rushed his Confederate Division forward to assist Heth. Fighting became gun-muzzle to gun-muzzle as men kept firing into smoke so thick they could scarce see the enemy. The hum of bullets in the air was constant, sounding like the swarming of bees, the roar of artillery being strangely absent.[26] Grant also attempted to push Sedgwick and Warren into an advance against Ewell on the turnpike, but Sedgwick's half-hearted advance was mauled by Early's Division. Warren seemed intimidated by the whipping his division had received from Rodes earlier, and his attacks on Rodes' line were feeble. Around 8 P.M. darkness fell and rifle fire slackened as the sounds of wounded men crawling in the woods were heard. Pickets fired all night and false alarms of enemy assaults were continual. Many Confederates crawled over the works and slithered out into the open fields, where they searched among the dead and wounded for valuables. One gray-back returned with six pairs of Union boots draped around his neck.[27]

When dawn broke on May 6, two unsubdued and unbloodied divisions of Hancock's II Corps awoke Hill's Confederates, attacking up the road in the rays of the rising sun, bayonets agleam. By mid-morning the situation was desperate. Driven back a mile, the Confederate front was hanging on behind twelve cannon under Poague which had located a good position on the edge of Widow Tapp's farm and were being served with super-human effort.[28] Hancock's excited blue-coats surged forward, victory in their reach. Then, suddenly, Longstreet was there. Dramatically advancing two divisions eight abreast down the Orange Plank Road, they flowed through the broken ranks, then divided right and left, deploying in column of battle to both sides of the road.[29] Soon the tide turned and Federals were in turn fleeing down the Plank Road, although the wounding of Longstreet by fellow Confederates slowed the onslaught.

North on the turnpike the bloodletting was not yet over. Sedgwick continued to probe Early's Brigades although both forces had entrenched so well that frontal attack was virtually impossible. Warren deployed and demonstrated stoutly, as if advancing, on Rodes' now almost impregnable trenches. Shortly after noon a serious danger arose when an always tardy Ambrose Burnside led two divisions of his IX Corps into the unoccupied area below Rodes' right and midway between the twin battles.[30] Rodes had returned Gordon's Brigade to Early, but his reserve unit under Ramseur had arrived and was wisely held in reserve.[31] He posted sentinels in the leafy Wilderness and they discovered Burnside approaching near a small farm. When they returned and reported to their lanky commander, Rodes reasoned that he must attack at once, for if Burnside obtained the flank of either Confederate force, he could cause havoc. So he immediately sent for Dodson Ramseur.[32] Rodes rode alongside Ramseur as the brigade moved at a rapid pace toward the enemy. Once he reached the small cleared field, Ramseur deployed his regiments and furiously assailed Burnside's van. The Confederates smashed through the skirmish line and into the battle line with so much impetuosity that Burnside was confused, believing the force he confronted to be much larger. Some of his inexperienced men fought well at first, then panicked and fled. This was not unusual behavior when troops like these, who had been sedately stationed on North Carolina's outer banks, met veteran Army of Northern Virginia troops in slugging matches. Garrison troops were unprepared for the ferocity with which veterans could attack. One brigade, well led by Ramseur, had defeated two divisions by smashing headlong into an enemy column and planting seeds of doubt in the mind of its commander. Burnside's men drifted southward and soon Ramseur was able to connect his right with some of A.P. Hill's brigades, and the gap was closed.[33] Rodes had witnessed Ramseur's charge and complimented the brigade as he called the charge one of the finest he had seen.

Action settled down in mid-afternoon, but the serenity was suddenly broken when Lee ordered an all-out charge against Hancock's rampartlike line. While almost breaking through, the attack cost Longstreet's 1st Corps heavy casualties. Save for a successful enveloping attack by Gordon on the far Union right, activities were to fizzle to a close. Gordon's charge shattered several Union brigades and captured irate Federal Generals Seymour and Shaler, but seems to have begun too late in the day for significant success. Controversy later swirled around just who delayed this movement and why, Ewell or Early?[34]

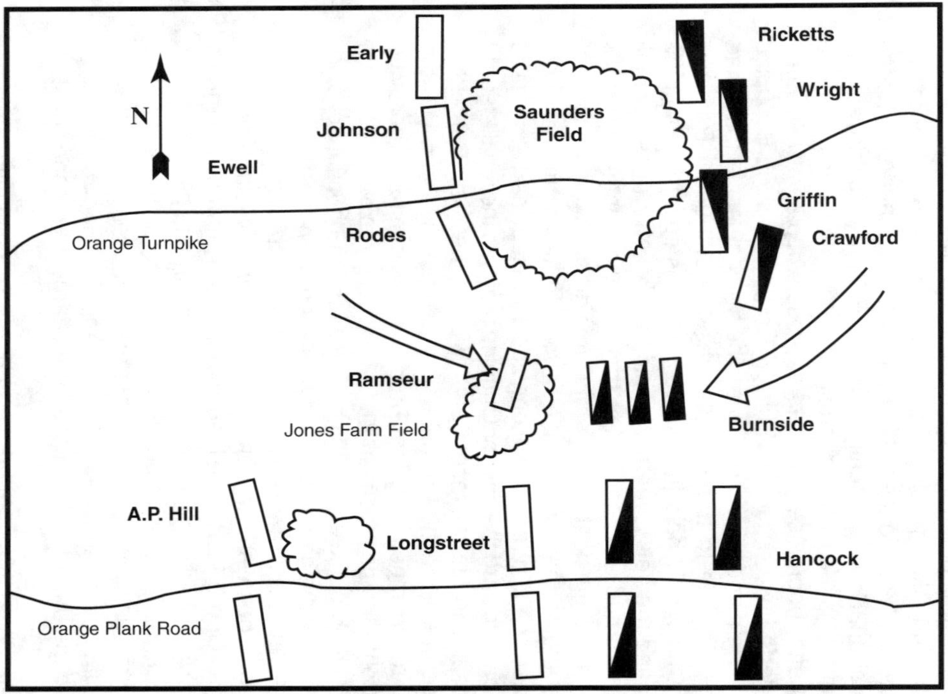

Wilderness, May 6, 1864

As the furor of twin battles subsided on the Orange Turnpike and the Orange Plank Road, both armies fell to construction of stout entrenchments. In late afternoon Federal General Burnside led two divisions of his IX Corps into the gap between the two battlefields, threatening Rodes' and Longstreet's Flanks. As the Unionists neared the Jones Farm, Rodes dispatched his last brigade under Dodson Ramseur in an impetuous charge, crashing into Burnside's leading unit and stopping cold all further progress of the XI Corps.

On May 7 heavy entrenching continued and light skirmishing was the action of the day in both armies as the contest seemed stalled, with each side hoping in vain that the other would attack their formidable works.[35] Grant's attempt to get through the Wilderness without fighting had been disrupted by Lee. While it might seem that Lee had won a significant victory, in reality the scales of measurement had changed. Grant's objective was the destruction of Lee's army and the survival of his. On that yardstick, there was no victor, just yet. Grant intended to fight day after day until the issue was resolved, regardless of the consequences in human life.

Lee's strategy was executed in better fashion than at Gettysburg. Ewell proved capable in defense, but reluctant to initiate offensive action. His three strong division leaders upheld the corps' reputation for hard marching and fighting.[36] Longstreet's performance was outstanding. His troop dispositions were perfect and he truly saved Hill's Corps. His wound was a blow to an already wounded army.

Robert Rodes had performed well, demonstrating anew that he was confident, decisive, and worthy of trust. He handled his portion of the battlefield with impeccable skill and precision. Disposition of his units into combat were correct and prompt. His recognition of Federal designs was unerring and he countered astutely. Rodes now realized he must operate within Ewell's low risk quotient, but he truly liked the outgoing corps commander and felt Ewell would back his decisions when questioned. Unlike the caustic Early, who chose to intimidate and bully Ewell,[37] Rodes quietly and unobtrusively learned to obey his own judgment, initiating action and conferring when appropriate. Rodes might have wished for the strong, directive leadership of Thomas Jackson or even D.H. Hill, but the reality of this leadership change demanded his personal growth as a divisional commander in battle and in camp.

The Wilderness fight was a battle of brigades, regiments, or even companies more than of corps or divisions.[38] The terrain and conditions dictated small-scale movements and placed a premium on the decisions of squad, company, and regimental officers. Gordon, Daniel, Doles, and Ramseur performed in outstanding fashion in Rodes' view, and he astutely recognized their contributions, recommending promotions for each. While not lacking in personal ambition, Rodes never understated the contributions of subordinates in his division's successes. Company officers actually made the Wilderness fight, and Rodes commented that in many instances they were simply too stubborn to be whipped.

Late on the night of May 7, noises arose from the Union lines which indicated movement. Dawn showed no further attack was coming, for the Federals were gone and had abandoned equipment and materials highly valued by the gray-backs.[39] Grant had disappeared, sliding east again. Except for stragglers, a few oversleepers, and the dead and wounded, the blue-clad army was on the march.

CHAPTER 11

AN ANGLE TO REMEMBER
Spotsylvania Court House

On May 7 Ulysses S. Grant issued a directive to Gen. George Meade which began: "General, make all preparations for a night march to Spotsylvania Court House...."[1] This introductory statement confirmed two assertions by the new commander that were not lost upon the blue-clad soldiers manning the ramparts in the Wilderness. Firstly, that Grant was abandoning his assaults upon the entrenched Confederate army in the tangled thickets and, secondly, and more significantly, intent on further action, he was moving left, forcing Lee to follow. He intended to hammer at Lee and if he failed, not be deterred, simply step left and hammer again. There would be scant time for regrouping between clashes with Grant as an opponent.

Union officers worked all night, untangling and reassembling badly mixed units, while Southern units continued to dig, strengthening their already formidable ramparts in expectation of further Federal attacks on May 8. Details of gray-backs had collected discarded Union weapons, and most Confederates sat behind earthen and log walls with four or five loaded rifles, hoping for another onslaught.[2]

Confederates began probing Union lines north of the turnpike at daybreak. Lee had already ordered work begun on a rough road which cut through the woods southeast of his position, considerably shortening the route to Spotsylvania, and he dispatched cavalry units to seek Union movements on all roads leading east.

Disengagement from a position in close contact with an enemy is a difficult military maneuver, but exactly what Grant was determined to execute. First he withdrew Warren's V Corps, entrenched on the Orange Turnpike opposite Rodes. Warren pulled back his brigades and moved in rear of the Federal IX and II Corps as he proceeded toward Spotsylvania, primarily using the Brock Road. Lee, anticipating Grant's move, instructed Anderson to start his 1st Corps toward Spotsylvania that night.[3] He would move cross-country, using the newly cut road, until it intersected with the Shady Grove Church Road. As his regiments were aligned that evening they seemed to stretch forever on the narrow road and, as usual, were forced to stand idly, awaiting movement by the leading units. Suddenly and spontaneously a loud cheer began near the column's front and swept down its length, was picked up by the 3rd Corps on the Orange Plank Road, then relayed up the entrenchments of the 2nd Corps until it reached the Rapidan. The eerie, high-pitched yell seemed to wrap itself around the Union army and echo and linger in the dreary forests. Three times it was repeated. One Confederate recalled it as "the grandest rebel yell of the war."[4]

Robert Rodes' Division led Ewell's 2nd Corps south behind Anderson, by a slightly different route, and A.P. Hill's 3rd Corps would follow. Hill was too sick to ride and Lee placed Jubal Early in command of Hill's Corps while John Gordon took charge of Early's Division.[5] Ewell was still hesitant and seemed to rely excessively on Early for advice, but Lee concluded that with Rodes, Johnson, and Gordon leading Ewell's Divisions, the 2nd Corps would not be weakened.[6]

The race for Spotsylvania now began. The Confederate 1st Corps, marching most of the night, was not bothered by heat, but instead by poor visibility due to the uneven terrain and extensive roadside fires. Rodes marched at 8 A.M. and the heat and humidity was soon debilitating.[7] One 2nd Corps marcher recalled the torture of the march:

> Our Brigade moved like a race horse down a new road cut by our pioneers through a grove of large oak trees. The woods were on fire on each side of the road and it was suffocating marching through the smoke and fire. Men fainted, broke down, and fell out all the way. The sun shown hot and we suffered very much. After 3 or 4 hours through this purgatory we came in sight of a field of wheat....A welcome sight. We rested here about 20 minutes.[8]

Warren's Federal V Corps halted for several hours' rest in mid-morning, and about noon his leading brigades were challenged by sharpshooters and horse artillery as they approached the crossroads at Alsops. Federal skirmishers deployed and collided with slouch-hatted, barefoot, butternut infantry. Anderson had arrived. Warren hesitated, then requested assistance, which was hurried forward from Maj. Gen. John Sedgwick's VI Corps. Grant sent word that when the two corps united they were to push on through the Confederates into Spotsylvania Court House.

Back near Shady Grove Church, a tireless Robert Rodes was charging up and down his column of brigades, calling for more effort. The soldiers had been on the road since 8 A.M., and many were falling out from exhaustion, but Anderson, who was blocking two Federal corps at Alsop, sent an urgent dispatch for assistance.[9] Daniel, Ramseur, and Rodes yelled, begged, and urged already exhausted men to pick up the pace despite the rising heat. Every soldier felt the day depended on him and most responded by discarding rations, blankets, everything but guns and bullets, as the long gray column sped to rescue Anderson.

Grant and Meade arrived as Warren and Sedgwick were forming their troops for attack, and they noted that General Eustis could not seem to maneuver his brigade. Upon investigation he was found to be quite drunk and was summarily relieved.[10] Finally, by 6 P.M., the Union force was prepared. They would move astride the Brock Road with Brigadier General Neill's and Brigadier General Eustis' Brigades aligned with Brigadier General Crawford's two Pennsylvania brigades. James B. Ricketts' Division also was on the road and other Federal units were aligned east of the roadway.[11]

The attacking Union brigades advanced almost at the same moment that Rodes' units arrived, behind Anderson's Corps, emerging onto the field alongside Kershaw's Division. Rodes was forced to throw his units into action "onto run" or as they arrived.[12] Crawford's Pennsylvania Brigades encountered Ramseur first as the aggressive Southern brigadier drove his brigade into their right flank and the fight began. The Pennsylvanians broke with Ramseur and Daniel, following them closely on the run and capturing four hundred or more blue-coats. The two Confederate brigades traded point-blank volleys with Federal reinforcements until the sun went down. Battle's Alabama Brigade, charging around Ramseur and into the darkness, was repelled by mixed Federal units. A wild melee ensued where men fought hand-to-hand in every direction as order disintegrated. Battle, attempting to re-establish control, pulled back two regiments, dressed their lines and ordered a charge, but his troops would not follow.[13] Doles' Brigade swung wide right and collided with Neill's unit in another confused, hand-to-hand free-for-all. Rodes, riding up, disengaged his brigades, fell back a short distance and began construction of entrenchments. Isolated Federal units continued to roam around in the dark, colliding with and sometimes firing on each other. Union dead were piled in front of Rodes' position, and hundreds of Union captives were led away.[14]

Rodes arranged his line as an extension of Kershaw's and placed three brigades in line with Battle in reserve.[15] Soon Johnson's Division arrived and moved alongside Rodes, while Gordon's men formed a reserve. Cullen Battle was irate that his men had refused his commands.[16] He lost fifty men as prisoners and the flag of the 6th Alabama was taken.[17] Rodes reminded the angry brigadier that his men were exhausted from the tiring march, and the day's objective, the race for Spotsylvania, had been won. Privately, Rodes must also have worried over his old Alabama Brigade, so misused at Gettysburg by O'Neal and now reluctant to enter combat. Could a fine officer like Battle rejuvenate this excellent body of men?

Both armies began to dig entrenchments and Ewell was forced to make a decision which had farreaching consequences. Rodes had entrenched

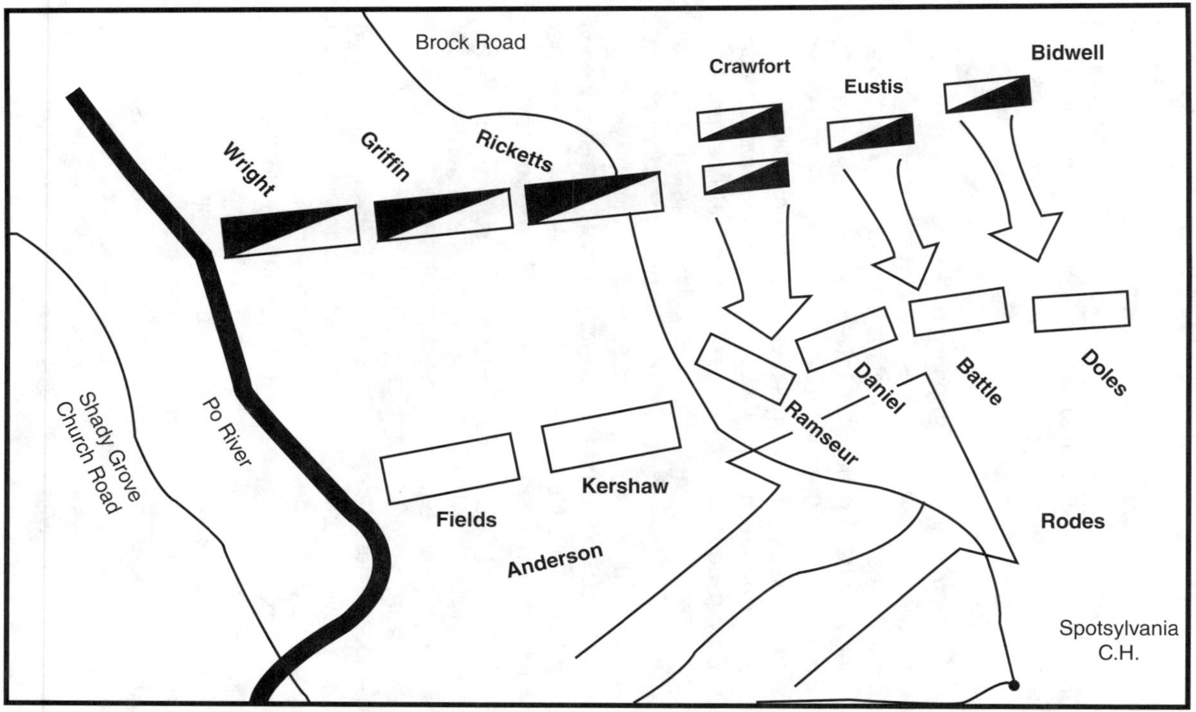

Spotsylvania, May 8, 1864

About 6 P.M. on May 8, Federal units east of the Brock Road moved to flank Anderson's 2nd Corps and drive on Spotsylvania Court House. After a hard, driving march down the Shady Grove Church Road, Rodes' Division arrived to rescue Anderson by suddenly appearing around his right and hitting the Federal advance on the run. Severe fighting raged until after darkness when both armies again began to dig trenches.

roughly on an alignment parallel to Anderson's Corps. To Rodes' right General Edward Johnson's Division began digging in on an arc which produced a large protruding salient. Later, much criticism would develop as to who selected this position and why. Firstly, the salient contained the highest terrain in the area and this, naturally, was the best artillery platform. Secondly, to fall back would not only give this advantage to the superb Union artillery, but if the position were abandoned the Southern army would be forced to retire beyond artillery range, thus uncovering the roads into Spotsylvania Court House.[18] Possession of these roads precluded easy flanking movements by Union forces.

At first light, soldiers of the 2nd Corps were digging in earnest. They constructed double rows of stakes, then filled the space between with logs and earth until the wall was three or four feet thick and breast high.[19] When Federal artillery began to fall in their midst, traverses were constructed and in some cases log walls were added in the rear. Head logs were added by many to protect themselves from sharpshooters. Gordon's Division, assigned to reserve, started erection of a reserve line which was not completed. Maj. Gen. Edward Johnson, nonetheless, felt the salient a very weak position. He complained that it was untenable unless supported by well-sited artillery.[20] While artillery colonel Thomas Carter agreed somewhat, he added that if defended with coordinated artillery and infantry support, the salient was impregnable.[21] Rodes was worried that extensive woods close to the lines threatened Doles' sector, and he left instructions that skirmishers should maintain outposts in the woods. Rodes took some minutes to pay his respects to his aide, Lt. Henry D. Yancy, whose body was being prepared for shipment home for burial. Yancy, a younger brother of Rodes' mother, was slain in the previous night's confused actions.[22]

Additional units arrived for both armies on May 9. Sedgwick's VI Corps dug in opposite Rodes' lines. Sharpshooters were active and infantrymen were forced to find cover where available. General Sedgwick, sitting on a cracker box, was observing Rodes' lines and several times was advised to seek cover. He disdained, jokingly replying, "those rebs couldn't hit an elephant at this distance."[23] Sedgwick rose and began pacing about, chiding good-naturedly those soldiers who were ducking. Suddenly a loud whistle was heard followed by a dull, heavy stroke. The general was struck in the right cheek just under the eye and expired within a few moments.[24] Sgt. Charles D. Grace, Company B, of Doles' 4th Georgia was acclaimed as the shooter. He made the one-half mile shot with a Whitworth scoped sharpshooter's rifle.[25] Sedgwick's loss was keenly felt, for whatever his abilities in command, he was widely admired and respected by the private soldiers in his corps.

Union efforts on the ninth and tenth centered left of the 2nd Corps' position, first against General Early's 3rd Corps, then General Anderson's 1st Corps. Several attacks were launched but with noticeable lack of persistence. One action saw Union troops advance southwest from the Brock Road across the Po River. Heavy casualties were suffered when they were forced to extricate themselves. Just south of the Brock Road, several divisions delivered a determined assault but were repelled by the units of Brigadier General Law and Colonel John Bratton.[26] Grant continued to probe and poke at Lee's lines, searching for an opportunity. The wooded terrain made reconnaissance difficult and dangerous. Small Union successes were often countered by Confederate artillery and spirited counterattacks. Rodes' Confederate infantrymen lay quietly in their shelters, smoking their pipes, and discussing the fighting qualities of the 1st and 3rd Corps. Artillery fire from the salient was often effective, but the counterbattery fire it drew was not appreciated by the lounging gray-clad veterans.

Unbeknown to the relaxed 2nd Corps veterans, Federal Generals Wright and Russell were developing a plan which would soon demand their utmost effort.[27] When these enterprising officers examined the salient, they noticed a distinct weakness. On the west face a corner jutted dangerously near a thick pine woods, behind which were excellent avenues of Union approach. Confederate skirmishers attempted, as Rodes had ordered, to occupy rifle pits in the woods, but they were repeatedly driven back inside their works since they could not be supported by their main line.[28] This point or elbow was defended by Doles' Brigade which had only three regiments: the 4th, 12th, and 44th Georgia Infantries.

Wright obtained Meade's approval of a plan to sneak a select force into the woods, charge quickly and overwhelm Doles' Brigade, then roll up the Confederate line. Union commanders chose twelve Infantry Regiments to carry out the attack, mostly from Neill's and Russell's Divisions, a total of 4,500–5,000 soldiers. Command was delegated to Col. Emory Upton, a twenty-four-year-old, highly aggressive officer.[29] Upton arranged his force in four lines of three regiments each, the first line to load and cap its rifles, all others to load only. All were to fix bayonets. So tightly packed was Upton's mass that intervals between lines were only ten feet.[30] Once the Confederate line was breached, the 96th Pennsylvania was to turn by the right flank and charge the supporting Confederate artillery battery. Slowly and quietly the regiments were led down a trail into the trees and lay down in order.

Concurrent with Upton's onslaught, Brig. Gen. Gershom Mott's 4th Division of the II Corps was to move on the apex of the larger salient.[31] This attack would, at the least, pin down Johnson's Division, preventing any assistance to Rodes should Upton succeed.[32] Mott's orders were unclear, at least to him, and his division made very little effort. Col. Robert McAllister, one of Mott's brigade commanders, reported simply that the men were enfiladed by Confederate artillery fire, stopped, and broke to the rear.[33]

Doles' skirmishers had been driven pell-mell from the woods about 4:15. The energetic thirty-four-year-old native of Milledgeville, Georgia was worried.[34] Federal artillery was landing on his brigade trenches, and skirmish fire from the woods was increasing in volume. The dense growth prevented sight of what was actually occurring, but Doles was sure the Federals were massing to attack somewhere and his line seemed the most likely. Doles had his men load their rifles, fix bayonets, and crouch under the breastworks.[35]

Suddenly, a few minutes after six, a loud cheer issued from the woods as files of Union troops emerged and sprinted for the Confederate works. Doles' men had time for one devastating volley and the blue-clads were over the wall. Upton described the attack as:

> Here occurred a deadly hand-to-hand conflict. The enemy sitting in their pits with pieces upright, loaded, and bayonets fixed ready to impale the first to leap over, absolutely refused to yield the ground....The first of our men who tried to surmount the works fell pierced through the head by musket balls....Finally numbers prevailed and like a resistless wave the column poured over the works.[36]

The Georgians ultimately were overwhelmed by numbers and forced to run or surrender. Soon the four-gun battery of Capt. B.H. Smith on Doles' right was surrounded and taken.[37] One member of the 44th Georgia recalled, "We were simply overwhelmed and forced to retire, every man for himself."[38]

Conditions were precarious, but Rodes' quick response erased the threat within minutes. He threw Battle's reserve brigade in front of the bridgehead, rolled back Doles' right hand regiment, to seal the front, and sent Major Peyton to Johnson requesting a brigade. Johnson pulled Col. William Witcher's small unit and moved it onto the Federal left. Moments later another brigade arrived from Gordon's Division. Upton thus found his force inside the trench line but surrounded with determined foes, and when he heard no evidence of Mott's supporting him, decided he would be wise to evacuate. Soon his rearmost units were sprinting for the woods amid rifle balls and grapeshot. The well-planned and smartly executed coup had been quickly neutralized by experienced Southern officers and soldiers. Colonel Upton received a battlefield promotion for his conduct in the affair.[39] Federal losses were recorded as in excess of 1,000 killed, wounded, or missing. The 49th Pennsylvania experienced the heaviest losses with 216 reported casualties out of its 479 engaged.[40] Confederate losses are more difficult to assess. Ewell reported them as 650 with 350 captives from Doles' Brigade.[41] Upton later claimed he took 1,200 prisoners. A realistic Confederate total is probably akin to the Federal loss of 1000, with more Southern prisoners taken and a higher count of Union dead.

Amid the wounded and dead, the Confederates again manned their trenches. The 4th Georgia Band, one of the Confederacy's best, began to play "Nearer my God to Thee," and as their notes died away a Union band countered with "The Dead March" from Saul. Soon this spirited competition evoked a concert as "Bonnie Blue Flag," "Yankee Doodle," "Dixie," and "The

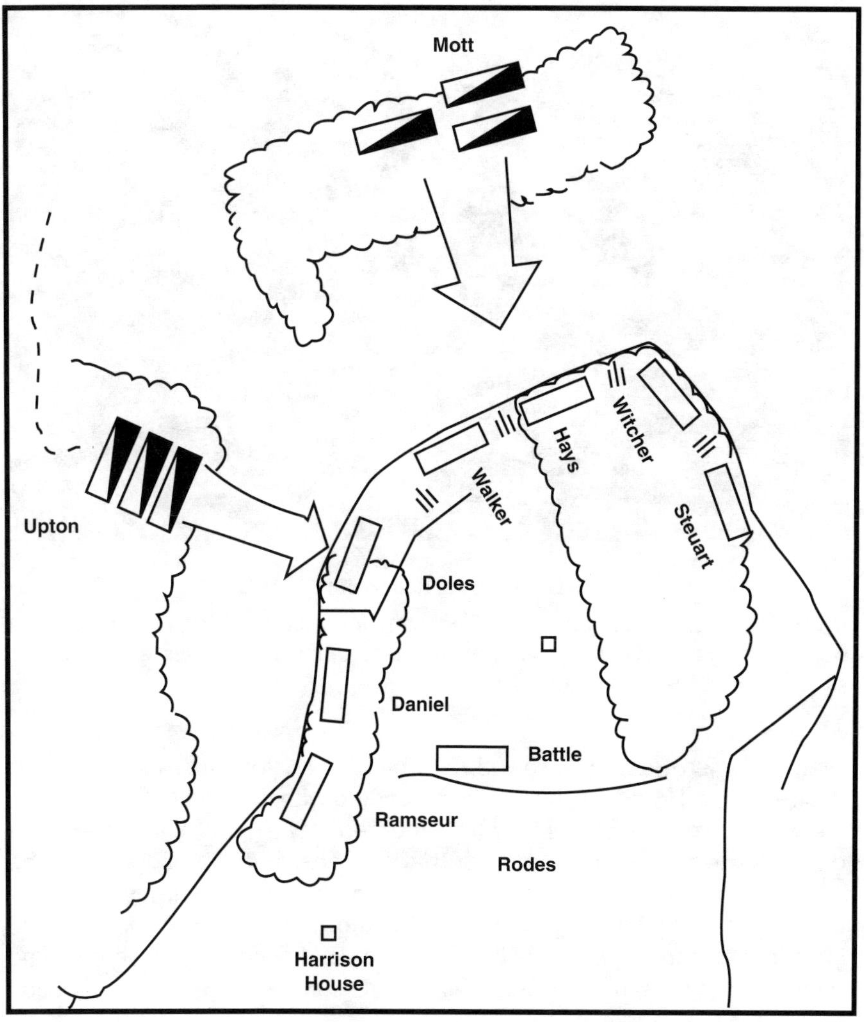

The Spotsylvania Salient, May 10, 1864

Federal Colonel Upton led ten picked Federal regiments as they burst out of the woods and attacked Doles' position in the Confederate salient. Rodes quickly pinched off the penetration with the assistance of a brigade from Gordon's Division and Battle's Reserve Brigade. When Mott failed to support Upton he was forced to abandon his hard earned foothold in the salient.

Spotsylvania Court House, May 10, 1864

Upton's Federal column swept out of woods to the left and overran the trenches of Doles' Georgia Brigade. After severe fighting, Upton's force was expelled by a force organized by General Rodes.

Robert Carter

Star Spangled Banner" followed. The bands concluded by jointly playing "Home Sweet Home" as the woods resonated with the singing of lonesome men. Many soldiers particularly remembered that night with fear and trepidation as they lay under arms in the trenches. Pvt. Hampden Osborne recalled his confidence in Rodes as on this anxious night his presence could be ascertained by a faint but well-known sound, the tinkling of the long Texas spurs which he habitually wore. This distinctive noise could be heard all night as he rode his entire front, for every trench and bastion received his personal inspection.[42]

At daybreak Rodes had the troops back at work. Abatis of sharpened tree limbs were added to the lines, particularly in areas where they neared the trees. Rodes pulled Doles' men to reserve duty, moving Daniel's Brigade right to adjoin the Stonewall Brigade with Ramseur's lines also adjusted.[43]

Late on the evening of May 11, after an inactive day and worried by the constant marching and countermarching of Federal units, Lee began to consider possible Federal withdrawal from Spotsylvania and a march to his right flank. Intelligence reports were confusing and J.E.B. Stuart was off defending against another Federal cavalry raid. Finally, Lee concluded his counterpart had experienced enough casualties in assaulting fixed positions and was falling back preparatory to sliding east again.[44] One of Lee's concerns involved the complicated positions of his artillery. Many of his guns, especially those in the salient, were enconsced in thickly wooded terrain with atrocious access routes. Necessarily, the guns had been placed near the front line for maximum effect, and often they had been hand-rolled into position. If Lee was forced to move quickly, he must be able to extract these weapons at once.[45] Thus, he issued orders through General Pendleton that where there was difficult terrain, all guns be withdrawn to a location behind the front whereby they could leave at a moment's notice. These dispositions were to be completed prior to nightfall.

Col. Armistead Long, in charge of 2nd Corps' guns, reluctantly withdrew twenty-two guns from the battalions of Page and Cutshaw out of the salient just before sunset.[46] Col. Porter Alexander later recalled that when the Federals rushed the salient and the twenty-two cannon were recalled, the guns were forced to re-enter in two long lines on narrow lanes. Only the leading weapons arrived in time to unlimber and fire, yet the entire two columns were captured save the rearmost two. The night turned very cold and raw as the rain increased and, eerily, Federal bands played loudly in the darkness.[47]

Grant was certainly not intent on moving east, but conversely, buoyed by the partial success of Upton's attack on Doles, Grant was preparing another, much larger, attack on the salient. He decided to assault the vulnerable looking section of salient garrisoned by Maj. Gen. Edward Johnson's Division.[48] First he had Meade move three full divisions of the II Corps from the army's right to a central position alongside Burnside's IX Corps. Hancock's Divisions under Brigadier General Barlow and Major General Birney shuffled endlessly along muddy roads, searching for their designated attack positions. Shortly after midnight the lead elements began arriving; however, it was minutes before the assault when the last elements were appropriately placed. Barlow deployed four brigades, two abreast.[49] Birney's two brigades lined up on Barlow's right while Brigadier General Mott and Brigadier General Gibbon placed their two-brigade divisions in close support. An entire Union corps would fall on the apex of the salient. Barlow's and Birney's front line totaled 11,000 men and the entire assault column contained 19,000 soldiers,[50] with unlimited reserves nearby to exploit any opportunity. The tired blue-coats lay down on the wet ground in formation and waited for dawn.

At 4:35 A.M. General Hancock ordered his divisions forward at right shoulder shift, bayonets fixed. They stepped off smartly in the pale light, soon emerging from the fog to encounter Confederate pickets who fired and fled.[51] Without firing a shot, the mass tramped steadily forward, through woods, fields, and ravines. At about two hundred yards they caught sight of the Confederate earthworks, raised a tremendous shout and dashed forward en masse, losing all semblance of formation. The blue mass veered a

Spotsylvania Court House, May 12, 1864

Gen. Edward Johnson's Division held these trenches which were stormed in a massive assault by Hancock's II Federal Corps, triggering 24 hours of constant fighting. Rodes and Gordon rallied Confederate opposition and were credited with saving the Army of Northern Virginia.

Robert Carter

bit and hit the trenches head-on despite desperate volleys by the defenders. Within minutes hundreds even thousands of blue-coats poured into the log works. Col. Porter Alexander, viewing the attack from a nearby redoubt, lamented the removal of the guns, stating that the Federal mob approaching the ramparts was the target of a lifetime for a gunner.[52] Capt. William Carter led his battery back into the salient, desperately whipping his horses. He managed to fire one round and looking around found himself surrounded by the enemy.[53] Brig. Gen. George Steuart's Brigade, defending the east face, had erected elaborate traverses with rear walls of logs, which simply became pens from which there was no retreat. Most were captured. General Johnson was almost shot down as he continued to swing his walking stick at Federal soldiers, ignoring demands to surrender. At last he gave in, as did Brigadier General Steuart. Also taken were twenty guns of Page's and Cutshaw's Batteries.[54] The Stonewall Brigade was rolled up in its trench line and large numbers of its veterans were led away to Union prisons. Thousands of blue-coats were milling about inside the Southern trenches. By 5:15 A.M. Federal infantry had overrun three-fourths of a mile of trenches and captured two thousand or more Confederates.[55] Victory seemed assured.

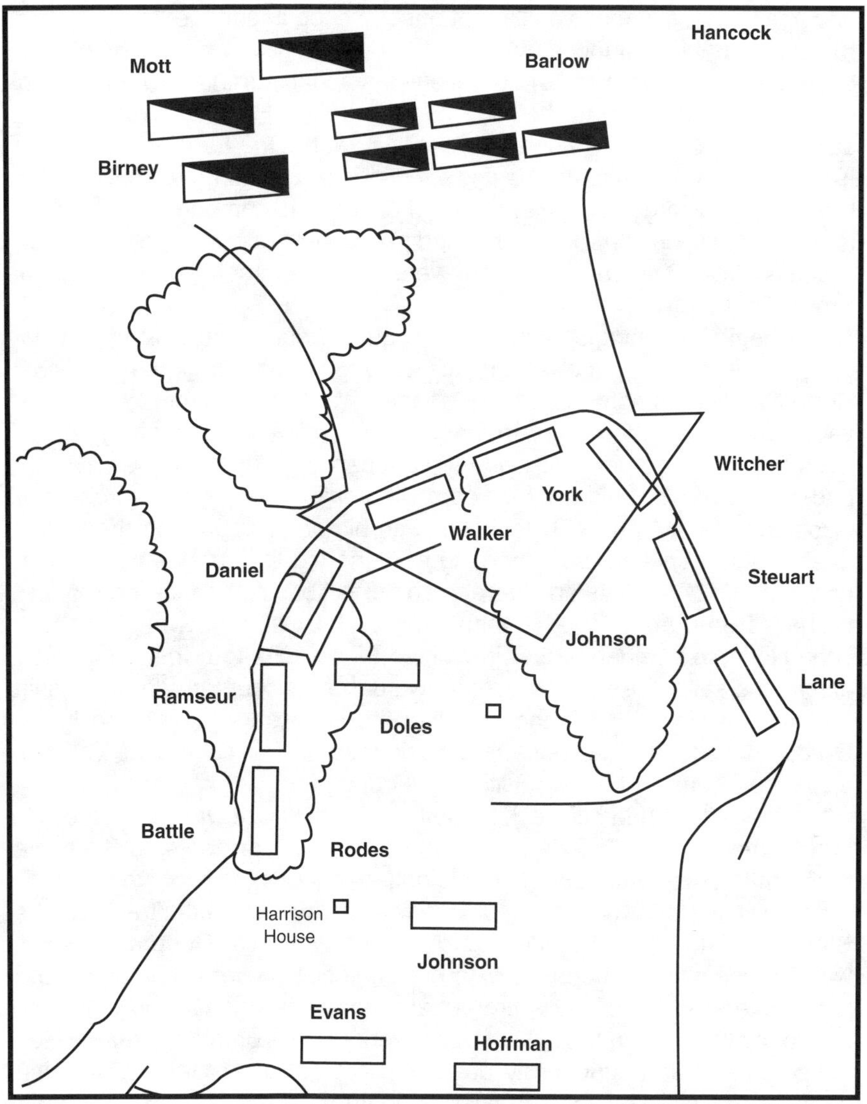

Spotsylvania, May 12, 1864

Encouraged by Upton's initial success, Grant sent Hancock and his reinforced II Corps to attack the apex of the Confederate salient in overpowering numbers at 4:45 A.M. on May 12. The huge Union corps of four full divisions fell on Johnson's Confederate Division, shattering the Southern line of well-prepared trenches.

Their initial success, however, actually overwhelmed the attackers. It had been easy, this mass onslaught out of the fog at sunrise. The men had run considerable distances over rough ground and were unbelievably disorganized and intermixed.[56] Federal officers began sorting out this mass of men and this delayed further action. Additionally, Federal officers in the salient seemed unsure of how to proceed now that the trenches were captured. Those who could provide this direction never entered the salient. The tremendous disorganization and lack of direction in company with two factors outside Union control all combined to counter Federal opportunities for success. These two outside factors were Robert Emmett Rodes and John Brown Gordon.

The first meaningful resistance occurred when Junius Daniel, his brigade adjoining the Stonewall Brigade, swung his right regiment, the 45th North Carolina, at right angles and opened fire, halting further Federal advance down the trench line. Gradually Daniel added more firepower to buttress the 45th. Gordon, temporarily commanding Jubal Early's Division, had posted most of his units in rear of the salient, heard the uproar, and dispatched Brig. Gen. R.D. Johnston with his brigade through the woods directly at the unseen din. Emerging from the fog they traded volleys with unnumbered blue-coats and were forced to fall back, and Gordon realized he had a real problem.[57] He then aligned Col. Clement Evans' and Col. John Hoffman's Brigades and instructed these units to sweep diagonally across the salient. As they moved forward they encountered a make-shift Federal line which broke and fled over the walls and out into the fields. Gordon continued to advance these brigades until, reaching the salient's east face, Steuart's former position, they dug in.

Rodes, spurring his black horse forward, saw that Daniel's maneuver had blunted Federal filtering down the trench line on the west face. He returned to order Ramseur out of his entrenchments to circumvent Daniel, drive down the salient to the west face wall and recapture the trench of the Stonewall Brigade.[58] An aide was dispatched to Major General Kershaw with a request for his troops to extend their lines to cover for Ramseur and join Daniel's left. This cross fire, established by Ramseur and Hoffman, forced the Federals in the salient back over the walls or into the rear-walled traverses. But they stubbornly dug in on the outside of the walls, using them as breastworks from Ramseur's right to Hoffman's left. Outside the Federal line reinforcements continued arriving and troops were packed twenty deep at some points.[59] Federal reinforcements from Neill's and Russell's units freed many of Barlow's assault troops who were low on ammunition and they retreated. Confederate artillery from other positions began to effectively play on reinforcements, forcing many Federals to lie down and remain still.

Rodes, realizing the Confederates on both walls were in an extremely precarious situation due to their proximity to massive numbers of the enemy, requested assistance to attack the walls of the apex. Lee dispatched the large Mississippi Brigade of Gen. Nathaniel Harris from Mahone's Division. As they marched smartly into the salient, Rodes rode back, and taking off his hat, waved them into action. They responded with a great cheer and charged through the maelstrom of fire to take the trenches to Ramseur's right.[60] Still taking casualties, the Mississippians began working up the traversed line and captured isolated blue-coats. Some of Ramseur's more adventuresome soldiers, crawled over the log walls and sprinted into the trees where they had excellent angles of fire on the thousands of enemy troops massed at the "Bloody Angle." Soon Rodes received more assistance as General McGowan's South Carolina Brigade arrived.[61] He dispatched McGowan to move up and join Harris. These movements reduced the Federal fire sweeping down the salient, but Harris', McGowan's, and Ramseur's men were fighting for their lives with equally determined Federals directly across the ramparts.

The savage melee now was to rage for hours with minimum change of position by the participants. Rodes assumed tactical command of the salient while Lee collected troops to start erection of a new wall of entrenchments across the foot or gorge of the salient.[62] Years later in conversation, Lee would admit that when Hancock's men broke through Johnson's entrenchments, Ewell was completely overwhelmed by the near disaster and was incapable of functioning effectively.[63] Actually, by removing himself from the field he created a command vacuum which Rodes, assisted by Gordon, filled effectively. This freedom from any interference and Lee's tacit support allowed these aggressive young officers to make decisions that saved the remainder of the 2nd Corps and the army. The reinforcements of Perrin, Harris, and McGowan added about 2,500 men to Rodes' Division, bringing his total to almost 10,000 soldiers. With this number, he held off fully one-half the infantry of Grant's whole army for another sixteen hours.[64] During this entire period, General Rodes could be found at the famed spring within yards of the line of battle.[65] As troops hurried from all directions to assist, Rodes coordinated defense of the line to hold back the blue torrent until a relieve line was constructed. All units reported to and were put into battle by Rodes.[66]

Rodes gradually reintegrated available artillery into the defensive positions. Guns were rolled in through the woods and unlimbered just back of the trenches, for only from that position could they use canister on Federal attackers. As the lines became more secure due to this artillery support, Rodes could slide more infantry toward the cauldron boiling at the apex. Soldiers remembered Rodes' constant exposure and his cool leadership. An artillery officer recalled:

> We saw nothing of the Major-General of our division. General Rodes of Ewell's Corps, was the only General officer we saw. He was a man of very striking appearance, of erect fine figure and martial

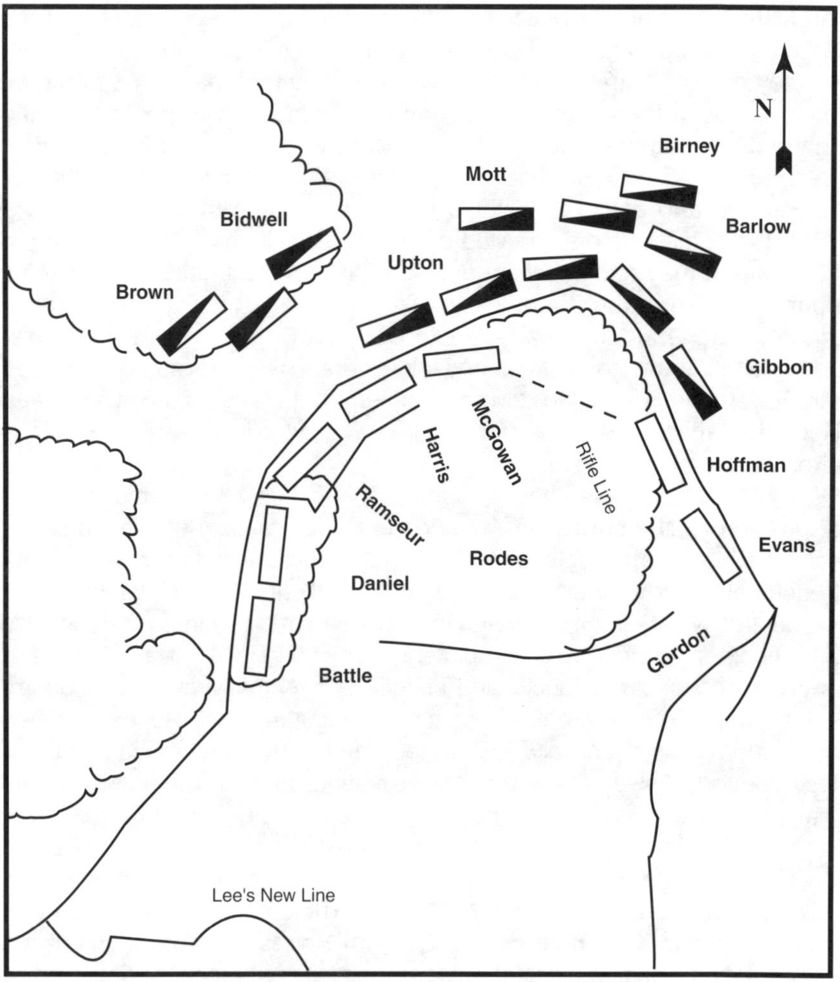

Spotsylvania, May 12, 1864

By 10 A.M. Confederate reactions had forced most of the Federal assault force outside the salient but the situation remained critical. Edward Johnson's Confederate division had virtually disappeared while Hoffman's and Evans' Brigades of Gordon's Division had retaken a portion of the east wall. Rodes used Daniel and Ramseur to recapture the west wall, then fed in Harris' and McGowan's reinforcements on the salient's face. He next deployed a rifle line across the center composed of survivors of Edward Johnson's Division, R.D. Johnston's Brigade and Perrin's Brigade to exchange fire with Federals massed behind the log barricades. The conflict would rage in undiminished fury for another 14 hours until Lee's new line across the salient base was complete.

> bearing. He constantly passed and repassed in rear of our guns, riding a black horse that chomped his bit and tossed his head proudly, until his neck and shoulders were flecked with white froth, seeming to be conscious that he carried Caesar. Rodes' eyes were everywhere, and every now and then he would stop to attend to some detail of the arrangement of his line or his troops, and then ride on again, humming to himself, and catching the ends of his long, tawny moustache between his lips.[67]

For eighteen long hours, Rodes' men fought on in the cold rain and mud. Soldiers fired over the log walls virtually into the enemy's face. Men were shot or stabbed by bayonets through chinks in the walls and, in a few cases, dragged over the walls by their foes to be dispatched or captured. On several occasions, men jumped up atop the ramparts to fire down into the enemy as fast as comrades could pass them loaded weapons, but these foolhardy souls were soon dispatched. Never had the two armies fought like this.[68] Soldiers became so exhausted they ceased firing and lay down in the mire to rest. Rifles were so hot they often burst. But Lee's line was not yet ready and Rodes' lithe figure, now horseless, paced up and down cajoling, "Not yet, men, not yet."[69] Ammunition was invaluable. Federal troops were supplied by pack mules which brought forward three thousand rounds apiece.[70] The boxes were dropped right behind the engaged troops. Some Federal regimental accounts claim that members fired three to four hundred rounds each during the battle.[71] Southerners were supplied by hand carrying of shelter halves loaded with ammunition. Artillery was devastating when it could be used, but the guns had to be manned in such close proximity to the enemy infantry that gunners and horses were prime targets. A Union gun in the process of unlimbering was caught by a point-blank Confederate volley and every man and horse slain. They remained in position, a tragic frozen tableau.[72]

Seldom in that era of military history was an action fought so savagely and ferociously for as lengthy a period. The trenches filled with water, and the wounded struggled to keep their heads afloat. Dead were trampled underfoot or hit so many times their bodies disintegrated. At the point of the "Bloody Angle" the conflict was truly sustained with the hearts of the soldiers of both armies. Once, men noticed that the "Stars and Stripes" and the "Stars and Bars" literally touched each other across the contended works.[73] Time passed slowly as Rodes held his men at their parapets, contesting every movement of fresh Federal reinforcements. Eight hundred yards behind the raging battle, out of sight but not hearing, Lee's drafted engineers labored to complete the new line of trees and earth.[74]

Sometime after midnight Rodes received word he could begin withdrawal, and he dispatched Major Peyton and aides to whisper such commands to each regimental commander. Slowly and skillfully, Rodes pulled his troops back, a regiment at a time.[75] By dawn withdrawal was complete, the final units moving back unopposed by an enemy equally exhausted. Both armies were glad to disengage as the rain picked up in volume. After such stupendous physical efforts the soldiers needed food and sleep, time to lick their wounds and clean their positions.

Federal losses for the twenty-four-hour period would eventually be reported as 7,000 men, and Confederate casualties, including 3,000 captured in Johnson's ruined Division, exceeded 5,000. In his official report, Grant remarked that the Army of Northern Virginia had offered such obstinate resistance that the initial advantage gained was not decisive.[76] He very well could have added that this "obstinate resistance" was primarily the work of Robert Rodes. Ewell estimated the size of his corps after the May 12 slug fest as 6,000 effectives. Just months before as Rodes moved on Gettysburg from Carlisle, his division alone was 8,000 strong. The Confederate army was bleeding to death from casualties it could not afford and losing officers it could never replace. Sadly, Brig. Gen. Junius Daniel was one of those casualties. The native of Halifax, North Carolina was shot in the abdomen and died the next day. Daniel was a West Point graduate and a seven-year professional soldier who resigned to run his father's plantations. He was elected colonel of the 14th North Carolina and promoted to brigadier on September 1, 1861.[77]

Early returned to take over his own division, and Gordon assumed command of a make-shift division of the few troops remaining from Johnson's Division and added brigades. The rains which had begun so suddenly, continued steadily for the next four days, curtailing action, to the relief of every soldier. They erected shelters and attempted to sleep as much as possible. The only activity of May 13 was a reconnaissance in force of the salient by Federals.

Just prior to dusk on May 17, Rodes led his division over the ramparts en masse and aligned them on their red battle flags. At Rodes' command "Guide Center, March," they moved forward, shaking out double skirmish lines.[78] Federal outposts were driven into the works occupied by Federal II Corps soldiers as Rodes pressed forward. About two hundred yards out, Rodes halted and redressed his lines, the division remaining motionless for a time. As night fell, he retracted his steps, mission completed.[79] Lee was desirous of locating the Union battle line in the salient, and Rodes' movement provided that information at some discomfort to his men but without losses.

The determined Federal commander in chief continued to search for avenues of approach around Lee's right. If he could hook around Confederate lines he would have a clean shot at the Confederate capital, but Lee continued to extend his right, preventing any Union advantage. Finally, Hancock carefully positioned his men to again assault the salient. He used a two-brigade front and had Gibbon do the same on his left. Gibbon's front included a newly arrived Irish Legion of 8,000 men who had never seen combat. Thus an assault force of 22,000 men was set to step off by 5 A.M. Three brigades of the initial line would proceed down the salient to attack the new Confederate line. The troops of Neill and Ricketts would move outside the old salient's west face, cross over the wall, and join the attack.

The newly built line at the salient's base was held by only two Confederate divisions, both under strength. Rodes' Division held the left portion and Gordon's the right part of the line. Rodes had aligned his brigades from right to left: Ramseur, Battle, Daniel, and Doles with Gordon's men adjoining. There were no reserves.[80] But the Confederates had used well the three days of rain in bringing their elaborate defenses to a point of near impregnability. A full one hundred yards of abatis, so thickly constructed as to seem impassable, preceded the works. Additionally, the Southern position was dominated by twenty-nine guns in prepared positions and served by some of the best artillerymen in Lee's army.[81] Thomas Carter's entire artillery division, newly reorganized, including the batteries of Dance, Griffin, Jones, and Smith, was ready.[82] These veteran artillerymen would be firing at infantry forced to advance over a long open field, unsupported by friendly fire. The Union infantry stepped out early in excellent formation and were at once hit by long-range solid shot that tore gaps in their ranks. As they advanced, Confederate guns switched to canister and entire rows of infantry were mutilated. Only a very few Union units progressed far enough to view the abatis.[83] Southern infantrymen never drew trigger, an easy victory. The Federals retreated as Rodes' infantrymen walked over to congratulate their gunners. A few wandered out onto the lanes of Union approach, searching for plunder, and were amazed at how mutilated and maimed were the Union dead.

Lee, still lacking reliable information as to Grant's dispositions, ordered Ewell to conduct a reconnaissance with his entire corps on May 18. Ewell assumed the point of the salient was still held in force, so he swung wide around the enemy's left flank. In mid-afternoon he marched out with his small corps, Rodes' Division in the lead.[84] Gradually the roads became so poor that Ewell sent his artillery back to camp.[85] As he approached the Harris Farm some contact occurred with Federal troops. General Ramseur observed a large body of blue-coats in a clearing and requested permission to attack. Soon Rodes sent word to proceed, and the North Carolinian lunged forward, easily driving the 1st Massachusetts Heavy Artillery, a unit recently converted to infantry service.[86] The noise from this encounter attracted Federal units from all over the area. Swarming onto Harris Farm they began to envelop Ramseur's exposed flanks. He was forced to fall back alongside the brigades of Bryan Grimes, who had replaced Daniel, and Battle. Birney's Division of Hancock's Corps arrived on the double and deployed, dispatched by Meade's headquarters. A full-scale battle seemed eminent, and Ewell with no artillery. Thankfully, a number of the Union units were untested recruits and their inexperience may have rescued the isolated

Southerners. Grant was sweeping the defense forces from Washington and other garrisons in order to replace his heavy casualties. The Federal units fired on each other as well as the 2nd Corps, and one Union officer claimed the Federal artillery caused most of the casualties among their own troops.[87] Much of Gordon's line was flanked and falling back in disorder, when a brigade now commanded by Col. Bryan Grimes, skillfully avoided a disaster, earning the plaudits of Rodes and a rapid promotion of Grimes to brigadier general. Rodes withdrew his other three brigades. Ewell experienced a hard fall from his horse and was led back to friendly lines dazed and confused. As intended, a reconnaissance to find Union positions, the affair was an abject failure. Much of the responsibility for the fiasco must fall on Ewell who neglected to check the trenches opposite him before proceeding—trenches that were empty, and would have answered Lee's questions without the sortie. The inexperience of the Federals and incompetence of their officers probably saved the 2nd Corps from complete destruction.[88] Ramseur had dashed off into an action that was at best an ill-advised gamble and surely not within the guidelines of the corps' mission. Rodes must share that blame, for he allowed him to go.

On May 20, Grant's infantry began evacuating their Spotsylvania lines and moved east, soon followed by Lee's tattered legions evacuating the miles of trenches which traversed woods, fields, and farms. Also remaining were unnumbered shallow graves where foemen, blue and gray, found their final rest. The cigar-smoking Federal leader had absorbed 18,000 casualties in the two weeks of intense combat, but his losses were already being replaced by units called from garrison duty. Lee's total losses of around 10,000 could not so easily be recouped. Confederate leadership was not always above par and casualties reduced the thin ranks further. The most conspicuous figures of the operation were, as Colonel Venable wrote:

> The restoration of the battle line on the 12th, was a wonderful feat of arms in which all troops engaged deserve the greatest credit for endurance, constancy and unflinching courage: but without unjust discrimination we may say that Rodes, Gordon, and Ramseur were the heros of this bloody day.[89]

The performance of Robert Rodes had saved this army to fight another day. He was growing rapidly as a division commander. When Douglas Southall Freeman years later compiled a list of the credits and debits of that critical day when the army's future teetered in the balance, he declared:

> Rodes conduct, like his military bearing, was flawless in the crisis, which allowed no time for deliberate reflection, he displayed the soundest economy of force. His tactics were those of protecting his flank by drawing a line perpendicular to the west front of the salient, while the greater part of his division fought its way up the salient.[90]

CHAPTER 12

CHECK AND CHECKMATE
From the South Anna to Cold Harbor

Down the dusty Telegraph Road they flowed in the moonlight. A river of butternut and gray-clad infantrymen, four abreast, moving at route step, swinging easily along while tobacco pipes glowed like an army of fireflies moving in column. On the cool, clear night of May 21, 1864, the 2nd Corps of the Army of Northern Virginia, long recognized as the army's premiere marchers, were elated to be rid of the stinking trenches and half-covered graves of Spotsylvania and again stretching their legs on the march. Invigorating weather seemed to spur the marchers as they sped past Mud Tavern and Mount Carmel Church, halting for a few hours' rest alongside the road at Dickerson's Mill. Soon, the veterans were back up and onto the narrow road, racing for the bridges over the North Anna River, Lee's next anticipated point of confrontation with a relentless Grant. The 1st Corps was close behind and Hill's 3rd Corps moved by a parallel route. By mid-morning, on May 22, all three Confederate corps were safely over the North Anna and resting in the fields and woods along the river's southern bank. For perhaps the first occasion since May 4, when this campaign began, the Confederate army was out of contact with its foe for a twenty-four-hour period.[1]

As Lee's veterans crossed the North Anna they were met by the first reinforcements they had received since May 4. Maj. Gen. George Pickett's Division, 4,800 strong,[2] arrived, accompanied by a two-brigade force of 2,200 men from southwest Virginia under Maj. Gen. John Breckinridge. In addition Hoke's Brigade of 1,200 men, part of Early's Corps, which had been on assignment in North Carolina, rejoined their division.[3] This total of almost 9,000 men would help replace some of the horrendous casualties suffered in the past three weeks.[4]

Late on May 23, units wearing Federal blue began appearing on the banks north of the river and an artillery exchange was initiated. Maj. Gen.

Gouverneur K. Warren, arriving with his V Corps, dispatched troops upstream and found a suitable, unopposed ford at Jericho Mills, about five miles upstream. Lee, seeing an isolated and unentrenched Federal corps, instructed A.P. Hill to attack at once. Soon superb Federal artillery appeared on Warren's flanks in sufficient numbers to preclude any Confederate success. An opportunity to cripple a portion of Grant's army failed miserably. Lee, ill and angry, sternly rebuked a chagrined A.P. Hill for the performance of his corps.[5]

Meanwhile, Hancock's II Corps had approached via the railway line and stormed across the river below Ox Bow. Thus two Federal corps were now across the North Anna: one, Warren's V Corps upriver, and another, Hancock's II Corps, downstream. That night Lee reformed his army, drawing back his wings and ordering heavy entrenchment. His formation took shape as an inverted "V" with both flanks secured. Col. Porter Alexander described Lee's unusual dispositions as follows:

> It rested on the river from a half-mile above the bridge to the Ox Ford, and hence, leaving the North Anna, it ran across the narrow peninsula one and one-half miles to the Little River, where it rested. Returning to the center, on the North Anna above the bridge, the line ran southeast across a large bend in the river and rested on its right six miles below, near the site of Morris' Bridge. In front of us the enemy formed with the V and VI Corps before our left flank, and with the II and part of the IX Corps' before our right flank. Their two wings, both south of the river, were unable to communicate without crossing the river twice.[6]

Lee's placements took advantage of natural terrain, anchored as it was on the commanding high ground opposite Ox Ford. From that point, A.P. Hill's 3rd Corps was drawn back on the left extending to Little River, and Anderson's 1st and Ewell's 2nd Corps bent severely on the right to a swamp just below Hanover Court House. The Confederate commander could easily reinforce one wing from the other and communicate rapidly with his entire force. The Union army was literally cut in two on the point of a wedge.[7]

Grant relied heavily on prisoners and Negroes who crossed the river for intelligence. While some of these persons reported accurately, many, for numerous reasons, were models of fabrication. This conflicting mass of information led to several erroneous Union assumptions.[8] Grant deducted that Lee was falling back over the South Anna and the action at Ox Ford was merely a Confederate rear guard activity. Federal corps commanders began advancing skirmishers to search for the Confederate position. When these attempts were rebuffed rudely, Grant resorted to forced reconnaissances of regimental or brigade size, feeling for Lee's lines. Hancock sent a brigade around the Confederate right, attempting to turn the position where Rodes' Division, which held the far right, abutted a swamp. Upon observing this move, Rodes doubled his skirmish line, and the advance was repelled before his main trenches were uncovered.[9] Possibly this effort was not vigorously pursued and simply strayed close to Rodes by mistake.[10] Rodes commented that he regretted the repulse was too easy and the enemy not properly punished.

Lee's position was simply too good, for it in truth defeated its own purpose, in that the enemy never dared to attack.[11] About 10 A.M. on May 26, Grant made up his mind to forego an attack and instead issued orders for an immediate evacuation across the river by all his units as soon as darkness permitted.[12] In his official report, Grant stated:

> Finding the enemies position on the North Anna stronger than either of his previous ones, I withdrew on the night of the 26th to the north bank of the North Anna.[13]

As dawn broke on May 27 the Federal army had disappeared, leaving only cavalry pickets at the fords. The Federal chieftain was flanking again, moving toward Hanoverton and a crossing of the Pamunkey River.[14]

Within hours the 2nd Confederate Corps was again the vanguard, moving south. Lee's cavalry scouts had found that the blue-coats were toiling east along the Pamunkey's bank. Lee rode up front, with Rodes and Ewell, followed by a long, sweating line of gray infantry. Ewell abruptly turned and informed his commander that he was too ill to continue and wished to turn his command over to his senior major general, Jubal Early.[15] Lee assented and Ewell slowly left the column while Lee and Rodes continued on, discussing a possible temporary commander for Early's Division. Obviously Lee considered none of Early's Brigade commanders qualified, and Gordon was already leading a division. Both agreed that Ramseur of Rodes' Division was the best officer available.

Grant's army crossed the Pamunkey, positioning themselves in line of battle.[16] But Grant soon discovered Lee well entrenched behind a creek and decided to forego an assault, still intent on catching the Confederate chief in open country. At daybreak on June 30, Union troops began vacating positions on the Confederate left, and all observations pointed to another slide to the left by the Federal army.[17] The ever aggressive Lee authorized Early to advance his corps and strike the enemy a blow if he was presented an opportunity. Early decided to move forward by the Mechanicsville Road toward Bethesda Church, Rodes' Division deployed in column of brigades in the lead.[18] Rodes' men stepped off smartly, immediately driving in Federal pickets and a supporting Federal brigade, sending prisoners to the rear as they rolled past Johnson's Farm and approached Bethesda Church.[19] William Nelson's artillery battery was accompanying and, finding a good position, unlimbered and opened a galling fire on the Federal flank. Suddenly fresh turned dirt indicated a stout line of earthworks, well-manned, and Rodes, searching for a flank approach, sent for Early.

But trouble had developed behind Rodes' advance. Ramseur, now leading Early's Division, was following Rodes on the road, undeployed. As his division moved along the road, Ramseur and Early riding at its head, a lone Federal cannon began to fire on the column from a nearby woodland. Ramseur at once approached Early about the gun and Lt. Col. Charles B. Christian recalled their conversation: "I heard General Ramseur say to General Early, Sir, let me take that gun out."[20] General Early vigorously advised against such action but Ramseur persisted. Early finally reluctantly acquiesced and moved on, following Rodes' advance.[21] Pegram's Brigade, now led by Col. Edward Willis, was in the van of Ramseur's Division, and Ramseur ordered Willis to clear the annoying gun from the flank. Willis, a cadet at West Point when the war began, had formerly commanded the 12th Georgia of Doles' Brigade, Rodes' Division, and was considered one of the brightest young officers in the army.[22] He shook out into line his five Virginia regiments and boldly advanced into the woods. The solitary Union gun crew limbered their weapon and retreated hastily, crossing the woods they proceeded over an open field and entered some small earthworks. Willis continued on, clearing the trees, and moved into the field beyond. Suddenly, the earthworks were alive with the enemy, and numbers of guns opened a tremendous barrage on the Confederate brigade.[23] Ramseur, hearing the artillery, begged some support from a Mississippi unit, but it was too late. Willis had but two choices, charge or retreat. Being halfway across the field he decided to attack.[24] As the men sprinted forward, taking gruesome casualties from the well-served Federal guns, two full brigades of blue-coats rose up behind the breastworks and delivered a crunching volley into Willis' Virginians. The 13th and 49th Virginia Regiments were almost destroyed.[25] Colonel Willis was slain, being hit six times, as was Colonel Terrill of the 13th Virginia. Lieutenant Colonel Christian of the 49th Virginia was wounded three times and captured.[26] The loss among officers was tremendous, yet some of the gray-backs charged into and atop the Union ramparts. One lanky, tall mountain boy from Amherst County carried the 49th Virginia battle flag, and he dashed into the gun muzzles, waving his flag defiantly, until a charge from a heavy gun blew him apart.[27] Federals considered the young man so brave they questioned the captured or wounded Confederates as to the brave youth's name.

Surely not an auspicious start as divisional commander for the eager Ramseur. He was heavily criticized by Early's veterans for his rashness and failure to reconnoiter,[28] charges he was hard put to refute.[29] In retrospect neither Ramseur nor Early seem to have exercised good judgment in allowing an insignificant activity such as a one-gun barrage to divert them from their principal mission. Rodes continued to probe until faced with a dug-in IX Federal Corps. Early forbade an assault and Rodes was unsuccessful in finding a means of flanking Burnside's men.

Grant was receiving ample reinforcements as two divisions of the all-Negro X Corps and two divisions of the XVIII Corps were shipped to his army from Butler's command.[30] These four divisions were grouped together and labeled the XVIII Corps, commanded by Maj. Gen. William F. Smith.

Thus Grant's army increased by 16,000 infantrymen just when he needed more force. He had run out of room to maneuver and must lower his head and bull his way through the Confederate lines. A clean breakthrough near Cold Harbor, with its road connections, could find the Federal army in the streets of the Confederate capital within a few hours. With these fresh troops, Grant determined he had sufficient force to effect a breach.

Lee leap-frogged Anderson and his 1st Corps over Early and sent him pounding south to join General Robert Hoke's Division. Unbeknown to Anderson, a real opportunity was being offered. General Smith and his newly called-up Federal divisions had been incorrectly routed, become lost, and were delayed in reaching Cold Harbor.[31] Therefore Wright's VI Corps was for a time alone to face Anderson's thrust. An enthusiastic attack would possibly have wrecked Wright's Corps.[32] But the effort made at dawn on June 1 was one of the most ineptly led attempts in the annals of the Army of Northern Virginia. When Anderson called off the attack, the effort had been so weak that most Federals never realized such a mass of Confederate were so near. Anderson and Hoke fell back, drew a line and began entrenching, perhaps a telling indicator of their offensive attitude.

As Confederate infantrymen were compelled to increase their dependence on earthworks to "even" the odds with their Union counterparts, they concurrently seemed to become less able to deliver the smashing attacks of past days of glory. Lee was undoubtedly frustrated: Early had tried on his left and found no opportunity, Anderson had failed on the right and Hill, who had returned to duty, was so lethargic as to exclude dependence.

It was well that they began digging, for about 4 o'clock that afternoon, Grant ordered a massive attack of his own. He sent the VI Corps and the barely arrived XVIII Corps in his initial attempt to drive over the Confederate Army.[33] As they reached about one hundred yards from the Confederate breastworks a seeming tornado of fire was unleashed, primarily by the men of Hoke, Field, and Kershaw. Enfilading fire was extended by Pickett and artillery all along the line, wherever guns could bear.[34]

The attack and rudely abrupt repulse was a shock to most Federal officers and men. The volume of fire these earthworks released was unlike any they had ever experienced and actually staggered their formations. Adj. Theodore Voill described it as: "A sheet of flame, sudden as lighting, red as blood, and so near it seemed to singe men's faces: burst from the rebel breastworks."[35] Some officers, such as Brig. Gen. Upton, instructed their men to lie down and dig holes or find other cover, for to retreat was fatal, and advancing out of the question. By nightfall fully 2,600 casualties littered the fields in front of the Confederate trenches.[36]

On the far Confederate left, Rodes' men continued to press back Union defenders, and his sharpshooters under Major Blackford intimidated the Federal trench lines. Confederate snipers found points of vantage from which they fired on any Federal movement. Burnside reported losses of more than two hundred men to snipers. Whenever possible, Rodes' artillery added their fire to the lines of Federals advancing in their view. The division took a serious loss on June 2 when Brig. Gen. George Doles fell, shot in the chest by an enemy sharpshooter.[37] Doles was a steady force in the Georgia Brigade he had commanded since this fine unit joined Rodes in January of 1863. This outstanding officer, perhaps at that moment the army's premier brigadier, and veteran of a score of battles, was strangely slain on a day when his death was the lone casualty in his brigade.[38]

Rodes was losing his best subordinates. Since May 5 when this campaign began, Daniel had been mortally wounded, Ramseur promoted, and now Doles slain, leaving only Cullen Battle among Rodes' brigade commanders. This was perhaps atypical of the attrition in gray officers' ranks in 1864.

Grant, undeterred, decided to renew his onslaught. Lee had adjusted his lines, and even though reserves were few, gray-jackets were now adept at digging, and the additional day produced earthworks so forbidding that Union observers grew wary. Thousands of Union soldiers watching the earth fly and realizing they would be ordered to attack, pinned white pieces of paper containing their names to their coats to identify themselves for the grave diggers.[39] Lee's line was slightly the arc of a curve with the concave side facing the enemy.[40] This produced a phenomenon in that every division which attacked swore that each line was enfiladed, with every commander accusing others of uncovering his flanks. Interlocked fields of artillery crossfired the Union columns.

At dawn on June 3 all Confederate trenches were manned and the waiters were not disappointed. Promptly at 4:30 A.M., with a rousing cheer three Federal corps filed out, dressed their lines and began moving forward. Hancock's, Wright's, and Smith's Divisions advanced simultaneously in the largest mass attack in the history of the Army of the Potomac.[41] As the huge mass of blue-coats moved forward, flags waving, the Confederates, crowded into their trenches, chewed tobacco, talked, and watched with amazement. When leading Federal units reached about one hundred yards distance a cloud of smoke and a sound like thunder cracked from the trenches as almost every trigger was pulled at once. Within a short, awful eight minutes almost every Federal soldier still alive realized they were not going to reach these ramparts today or any other day.[42] Despite Meade's continued messages to advance, most survivors simply lay down in line and attempted to survive amid the puffs of flying dirt.

Brig. Gen. Evander M. Law commented that "It was not war, it was murder."[43] Law also remarked that he had never witnessed his men so confident and unconcerned when in action. They were laughing, joking, and talking as they fired, reloaded, and fired again.[44] A Union soldier of the 12th New Hampshire recalled his regiment was physically staggered with the first volley, and men went down in rows like blocks.[45] But as terrible as the infantry volleys and the long-range artillery fire which fell on the flanks were, numerous batteries were dug in on the Confederate front line. One Confederate gunner recalled firing double-shotted canister at a range of 100 yards and "at every discharge of our guns; heads, arms, legs, and rifles were observed flying in the air."[46] He remembered that "as they closed the gaps we created more." Federals recalled with horror the clearly heard commands of the Confederate gun captains, attesting that if you could hear the order you were too close to survive.

The Federal repulse was so complete that Col. Charles Venable, one of Lee's aides, remarked that it was the easiest victory ever given to Confederate arms by the folly of their Federal opponents.[47] Thousands of blue-coats, both wounded and unhurt, lay in the rising heat of the sun without water, and their cries were as of a lamenting chorus, but Confederate sharp-shooters were unrelenting and to move was to invite a bullet.[48] Yet no flag of truce was issued from Union lines to relieve the suffering. For three full days the armies lay facing each other with no respite from the high pitched "whip" of minie balls. Grant's pride would not permit his asking for a truce, for to do so would admit his defeat.[49] Lee had no need for a truce, as his casualties were within his trenches and treatable. By the time a truce was arranged on June 7, most of the Union wounded remaining on the field were beyond caring for.[50] Fully 7,000 Federals had fallen on June 3 and most were now dead. When added to those lost in the assault on June 1, 10,000 soldiers were lost in futile and useless assaults against impregnable positions.

The effects of these attacks were felt in Union morale and spirit for months.[51] Further, these actions would be discussed excitedly in the halls of Northern politics. Many expected Grant's dismissal, but Lincoln stood four-square behind his low-key commander and deflected all assaults. Somewhat obversely, this continuation of Federal official confidence in Grant affected morale in the Confederate army. Sgt. Maj. Gary Eggleston of Lambkin's Battery, Confederate Artillery, very astutely commented on the new kind of war which gray-coats were forced to face. He wrote:

> ...Cold Harbor marked a new phase of the war. By the time we got there, we had gotten over our surprise and disappointment at the conduct of General Grant....we discovered after the Wilderness that he was not going to retire....instead he had the temerity to move by his left flank to a new position....By the time we reached Cold Harbor, the men in the ranks realized that Grant was never going to retreat, that he was not going to be removed from command because he failed to break Lee's resistance; and that the policy of pounding had begun and would continue until our strength should be utterly worn away....Grant had taken hold of the problem of destroying Confederate strength in the only way that the strength of an army, so commanded, could be destroyed, and that he intended

> to continue until the task be accomplished wasting little time or strength in efforts to contest wits with Lee. We at last began to understand what Grant had meant by his expression of a determination to "fight it out on this line if it takes all summer."[52]

These sobering thoughts were disturbing to Confederate soldiers accustomed to Lee's sweeping triumphs earning time to rest, regroup, and enjoy the spoils of their efforts. All veteran Confederates could now recognize the growing disparity in numbers and the change in tenor brought on by Grant's arrival. Early, Ramseur, and Rodes openly discussed this change in the war. Early and Ramseur were somewhat gloomy as they considered the future actions of an enemy commander who could lose 54,926 men in a campaign from May 4 to June 3 and seemingly not blink.[53] In that month, Grant's casualties almost exceeded the total army which Lee commanded.[54] Rodes was more optimistic as he felt Lee capable of prolonging action until such time as political pressure in Northern climes would bring a close to the festering conflict. Ultimately, he felt, or more realistically hoped, that Northern politicians would let their sisters depart in peace.

Suddenly, in a bold strategic move, Grant was gone from Lee's front to emerge south of the James. Rodes' Division which had 6,987 men available for duty on May 4, 1864,[55] was now under half that strength by June 10, and by August 31 would report 3,103 soldiers.[56]

CHAPTER 13

CHASING BLACK JACK
Campaign to Rescue Lynchburg

After Grant abruptly crossed his army over the James, Confederates enjoyed several days of rest near Cold Harbor. But at 3 A.M. on June 13, hours before a blood-red, hazy sunrise, 2nd Corps soldiers fell into formation preparatory to departing their encampments. The understrength corps of three infantry divisions and two battalions of artillery was led by the best the army had left to offer. Maj. Gens. Robert E. Rodes, John B. Gordon, and Stephen D. Ramseur commanded the three infantry divisions and it's doubtful any Confederate army corps ever boasted three officers who had seen more real fighting. Brig. Gen. Armistead L. Long commanded the guns, with the 2nd Corps itself led by the newly promoted Lt. Gen. Jubal Anderson Early.[1] Early had conferenced with Lee the previous evening and was forewarned about the need for absolute secrecy[2] as he prepared to undertake an independent assignment: Maj. Gen. David Hunter's Federal force must be cleared from the Shenandoah Valley.

Unaware of these discussions, the gray-backs were pleased to exit the trenches and again be on the move. Rumors concerning their mission were widespread, with most old rankers certain they were embarking on another grand flank movement by which Grant would be outgeneraled by Lee.[3] Battle's Brigade of Rodes' Division set the pace as the long gray column streamed past Mechanicsville and, ignoring the growing heat and towering dust cloud, proceeded rapidly northward to make camp that evening on the banks of the South Anna River.[4] Sunrise found the column turning west, Ramseur's Division in front, and suddenly the soldiers realized their destination was the Shenandoah. Spirits rose and strides lengthened. Camp that night for Rodes' men was at Gardner's Cross Roads.[5] On June 15 Gordon's men set the pace past Louisa Court House and toward Trevilian's Station. A sharp two-day cavalry engagement had raged about Trevilian's on June 11 and 12. Gen. Wade Hampton's outnumbered gray riders had successfully repelled the raid of Maj. Gen. Phillip Sheridan's blue-coats. The marchers could observe the cost by viewing the shallow graves and hundreds of dead horses.[6]

Before daylight on June 16, General Early spurred ahead to Charlottesville, searching for news of Hunter's progress while attempting to locate rail transportation from Charlottesville to Lynchburg. Early's previous experiences with the Orange and Alexandria were not pleasurable, and all his considerable attempts to cajole, pressure, or coerce the railway personnel produced no appreciable results. Finally an irate Early threatened to hold all employees responsible with their lives,[7] and this extreme threat brought about a begrudging response.

Rodes' Division led the army's march and set a torrid pace. By nightfall his soldiers were resting near Shadwell at Keswick Depot.[8] The tough veterans had covered eighty miles in four days of intense heat and humidity.[9] Early established headquarters near the University of Virginia, and while awaiting rail cars he met friends who escorted him to a local hotel bar where some excellent apple-jack was acquired.[10] Early's Ordnance Officer, Col. William Allen, found the frolicking general somewhat tipsy, and with the assistance of other staff officers took "Old Jube" to a professor's house for tea.[11] Soon the general was sober as a judge and hard at work. By sunrise, Early had a collection of dilapidated locomotives and cars waiting on the tracks. First Ramseur's Division was entrained, then two brigades of Gordon's Division were loaded. Rodes was ordered to march his division and the remainder of Gordon's men along a narrow roadway parallel to the tracks until the trains could return.[12]

A heated argument arose between the two hot-tempered officers when Rodes approached Early with a request that his units be permitted to lead the 2nd Corps to the city's rescue.[13] Rodes' wife and son were in Lynchburg and he was anxious for their welfare. Additionally, having been reared in Lynchburg, Rodes felt his knowledge of the area and its terrain would prove advantageous for the army. But Early refused to listen to Rodes' appeal, rapidly demonstrating his reticence to hear advice from subordinates. The two men, although never close, had worked well together in the past. But on this occasion the air was soon blue with the epithets of both men.[14] Early stalked off to board the leading locomotive, leaving a disgruntled Rodes to continue his march down the tracks as he headed for the railroad depot at North Garden.[15]

Railway equipment was in terrible condition. The sixty-mile journey took Early a full five hours, about twelve miles per hour.[16] As the initial convoy of trains chugged into Lynchburg, one of the units derailed on a bridge. In the accident several soldiers were killed and a number injured. Ramseur's men began unloading from boxcars alongside the river about 1 P.M. on June 17.[17] To the cheers of the populace they marched up Fifth

Street and out the Salem Pike some two miles beyond the city limits.[18] Rapidly they began to turn earth and erect works, for Hunter's confident blue-coats were advancing on the pike.

Maj. Gen. David Hunter had replaced the popular but incompetent Maj. Gen. Franz Sigel in late May.[19] The Virginia-born, sixty-two-year-old West Pointer, who dyed his mustache to match his toupee, may have been the most unpopular of Civil War commanders. The son of a Presbyterian minister, Hunter was highly religious, a teetotaler, and a non-smoker. Yet he possessed so violent a temper that he fought and won a number of duels while on active duty and survived a court-martial sentence of dismissal from the service.[20] A fanatical abolitionist, Hunter revealed his unforgiving vengeance in constant acts of retaliation against Southern citizens.

As requested by Grant, Hunter began to move his nine thousand-man force up the Valley Pike. As he neared Staunton, a make-shift force opposed his further advance at a sleepy little hamlet called Piedmont. Confederate Brig. Gen. William "Grumble" Jones had collected about five thousand men, mostly militia and cavalry, and blocked the pike, inviting attack.[21] On June 5, Hunter obliged, attacking and routing Jones' little army, Jones being slain on the field.[22] Hunter estimated his prisoners at more than 1,000.[23]

Hunter's troops marched into Staunton early on June 6, bands blaring and flags flying. His men rifled and burned factories and warehouses.[24] On June 8 Brig. Gen. George Crook marched in with his infantry division, and Brig. Gen. William Averell brought in his cavalry division.[25] These elements increased Hunter's total force to a quite respectable 18,000 soldiers. Just before departing Staunton, Hunter received a telegram from Grant who insisted he proceed to Lynchburg, for "it would be of great value to us to get possession of Lynchburg for a single day."[26] The Union commander in chief was well aware of the value of quartermaster, commissary, and medical goods stored in that city. In addition, destruction of the several railroads into the city and the James River and Kanawha Canal could be devastating to a Confederate transportation system struggling to survive.

On June 10, Hunter's reinforced army left Staunton, moving south in four columns[27] and reached Lexington by noon on June 11.[28] The V.M.I. cadets were repaid for their gallantry at New Market by the burning of every building at the military school on the express orders of General Hunter,[29] as was the modest home of Virginia Governor John Letcher.

Back in a panic-stricken Lynchburg, Breckinridge arrived with his small force and assumed command. Brig. Gen. Francis T. Nicholls, a former commander of Taylor's Louisiana Brigade, was post commander and delighted to witness reinforcements. Breckinridge's tired infantry marched down from the Amherst Heights and crossed the Ninth Street Bridge into the city.[30] His slim battalions joined the home guards and cadets which were summoned from their mountain lookout near Balcony Falls. As Breckinridge attempted to organize local defenses he was bedridden by recurring pain from a fall he had taken from his mount at Cold Harbor.[31] Maj. Gen. Daniel H. Hill and Brig. Gen. Harry T. Hays volunteered their assistance, and Breckinridge turned over command to Hill prior to Early's arrival.[32] A rather large and formidable array of Confederate officers was in Lynchburg, many recovering from wounds or injuries. While their assistance was appreciated, all the gold leaf in the Confederacy couldn't make up for the lack of soldiers.

Hunter advanced through Liberty, crossed both Big and Little Otter Rivers, and when Early detrained on June 17, Hunter's advance had reached the Quaker Meeting House, on a hillock about five miles outside the city.[33] Early toured the defensive lines with General Hill, a somewhat uncomfortable situation, for Early and Hill were not on friendly terms.[34] Early immediately recognized that the lines were too near the city and that the town was wide open to shot and shell from enemy guns. He feared that Hunter would merely bring up his artillery and pound the city into submission.[35] So Early drew up new lines well outside the city in a westerly direction.[36]

McCausland's and Imboden's riders had constructed a defensive line using wooden rails to supplement a stone wall which encircled the Quaker Church Cemetery.[37] About 4 P.M. Averell's troopers, most dismounted, moved

Quaker Meeting House, Lynchburg

This small chapel, five miles outside the city, marked the scene of substantial fighting as McCausland's and Imboden's troopers delayed Hunter's advance.

Penny Swisher

against this seemingly benign Confederate line. But Imboden had concealed several artillery pieces, and when these guns opened, the blue-coats wavered. A ragged volley from behind the wall produced a number of casualties and Averell's men retreated.[38] General Crook, observing the action, grew angry and waving the cavalry aside deployed his two leading infantry brigades.[39] Slowly the pressure by blue infantry on both flanks cracked the defense and caused the defenders to precipitously flee for safety.[40]

Meanwhile, Alfred Duffie's Cavalry Division slowly advanced on the Forest Road. McCausland's men were dispatched to assist the defenders and retreated until a railroad bridge was reached over Ivy Creek.[41] Skirmishing and artillery fire increased at that point until darkness fell. Early spread his 2nd Corps brigades and Breckinridge's regiments over his new outer line while the cadets, dismounted cavalry, and militia units manned a second, inner line along the city boundaries.[42] Early was agitated over the delay in arrival of Rodes and his brigades. Despite their hard words, Early knew he could rely on Rodes to drive his units hard, but he was much less certain of the railroad efforts.

Hunter first demonstrated on the Salem Pike, using both infantry divisions. When little reaction occurred, Hunter pulled Crook's men off line and swung them wide right, seeking to turn the Confederate left.[43] Suddenly Southern attackers charged and Sullivan's men fled. Crook's steady infantrymen were forced to quickly return and reestablish the Federal line.[44] After repelling the Confederates, a counterattack almost broke the Southern lines. The 116th Ohio planted its flag on the Confederate works and maintained its position there for some time.[45] The humid, sultry afternoon soon brought a halt to significant action. Sharpshooters and artillery exchanges continued to pile up casualties. The trench-wary Confederates and their long-range Whitworth Rifles enjoyed a distinct advantage, while Early was content to await Rodes' reinforcements.

Spectators gathered in numbers on sites which offered some view, at a real danger to themselves. From College Hill, Mrs. Susan Blackford watched much of the artillery exchange of the afternoon of June 18. She recalled:

> It was very exciting to see the cannon fire from both sides and the explosion of shells on the opposite side. It was fascinating beyond description....and then the fearful reality was forced upon me by the lines of ambulances which were kept busy bringing our wounded into town.[46]

About 4 P.M. the long drawn-out whistles of approaching trains could be heard north of the river. The train voyage had seemed endless to Rodes who was fretting over breakdowns and delays. Pulling across the bridges into the depot, the train cars were literally covered with troops hanging to sides and roofs. Quickly they detrained and dressed their ranks, then began moving at a brisk pace up the steep Fifth Street Hill amid cheering crowds of relatives and citizens. Maj. Eugene Blackford, chief of sharpshooters in Rodes' Alabama Brigade, recognized his sister-in-law in the onlookers, then found himself on line in a cemetery alongside his father's grave.[47] On they raced, past the fairgrounds, turning west onto the Forest Road. The commotion and clouds of dust were observed by Duffie as the gray-coats moved straight toward his position.[48] Once he had several brigades on line, Rodes advanced these units to the crest of the hill and opened a heavy artillery fire. Duffie's troops fell back as the stirring strains of a military band could be heard escorting more Confederates to the front.[49]

All three Confederate division commanders were anxious to attack before sunlight faded, and they urged Early to throw caution to the wind. But Jubal decided to wait for morning, believing that Hunter would renew his attack at daybreak, and with his additional troops Early could break the Union force and rout Hunter's Divisions.[50] His decision was perhaps wise although Rodes and Gordon disagreed, both predicting Hunter's flight before daybreak. Rodes turned over command to Colonel Grimes and rode quickly back down to Harrison Street to see Virginia and young Robert.[51]

In truth, the yelling, cheering, and music heard on the arrival of Rodes' Division had been the final factor in Hunter's decision to retreat. He was now aware he faced Confederate professionals and not simply home guards. He started his wagons on the road west and ordered his troops to pull off line between 9 and 10 P.M.[52] When Rodes returned he could hear the movements of Union forces on his front, and he dispatched a message to Early that Duffie was gone and only sentinels remained to stoke the campfires. No reply was forthcoming and the night passed fitfully for the listening Confederates.

Long before light Rodes' brigades rolled out on the Forest Road, vainly attempting to catch Duffie's Cavalry, while Ramseur's Division led the chase on the Salem Pike.[53] The sun rose warmly and soon the troops were sweating freely and looking for water. Early sent McCausland's riders toward Buchanan, with plans to cut the road over the Peaks. The Forest Road and Salem Pike merged at the town of Liberty, and when Rodes entered town he could hear Ramseur's advance driving Hunter's rear guard.[54] The officers pursued until Hunter stopped a few miles west and unlimbered Capt. Henry A. DuPont's guns. Early arrived and decided not to waste his infantry but rather to await his own artillery, delayed at a destroyed bridge over Big Otter.[55] Finally Early sent his tired infantry into camp and the Federals slipped away. The Confederate commander was still confident his cavalry would cut the Federal escape route.

Gray infantry was awake before sunrise and marching by first light.[56] Soon they learned the enemy had moved most of the night, opening a gap between the two forces. In addition, the blue-coats were continuing due west toward Buford's Gap and Salem and not turning north.[57] Early had no cavalry units at hand and was forced to depend on his infantry to catch up.

By mid-afternoon Hunter's units were safely on line in Buford's Gap, flanks anchored on the steep mountainsides and artillery in position.

Early approached and deployed Ramseur in his center, Gordon to his left, and Rodes on the right. Rodes' men drove in skirmishers and moved in close, feeling out the enemy line and exchanging heavy volleys with Crook's Division. Early was not anxious to attack the fortified pass, so he dispatched Gordon left and Rodes right, each to search for a route around the pass. But there was no road or even trail and the divisions were forced to climb over the precipitous slopes.[58] All formation was lost and the movements of Rodes' units were hampered by darkness, when the men experienced real difficulty in descending the steep passages. Meanwhile, Hunter departed with half his army, leaving Crook and Averell to hold the pass.[59]

The following morning Confederate pursuit was slow to develop. An angry Early had intended Rodes' men lead the chase but Rodes was unaware of that decision. While General Rodes was extracting his troops from the mountainside on the previous evening, Early had dispatched a single courier with a verbal message to him, but the man was unable to locate Rodes. An artillery officer who knew the messenger commented that he never understood Early's selection of that courier, for he was well known to be the dumbest man in the army.[60]

Hunter was now moving rapidly through Big Lick and on into Salem by June 21.[61] Duffie's cavalry was leading the column and already were into the mountain passes at Hanging Rock. Rodes' soldiers, leading the pursuit, were struggling and in a surly mood, having no rations issued for three days.[62] Their only food was that handed out by Lynchburg citizens as they detrained. Once, near Salem, when Rodes and Early rode by the marchers a cry of "Bread, Bread" was raised to the embarrassment of both officers.[63] Confederate cavalry cut the Union column at Hanging Rock with McCausland's troopers scooping up fifteen cannon and a number of wagons.[64] But Averell soon rode up with infantry support and disbursed the gray-coats.[65] Some eight cannon were disabled by the gray cavalrymen and had to be abandoned.[66] Early was unaware of the action and sent no infantry to support McCausland. As Hunter's column cleared Hanging Rock, Early gave up the pursuit. Moving northward, the Confederates staggered into nearby Botetourt Springs where the soldiers relaxed in the healing waters.[67] The equally exhausted Federals reached another famed spa, White Sulphur Springs, on June 24, and they also paused to recoup.[68]

The first phase of Early's assignment was completed. Lynchburg was preserved from Hunter's torches as the invader was repelled, without causing severe damage. Actually, Hunter's retreat was to become more important than his defeat.[69] By moving into the mountains, he removed himself and his soldiers from the stage of war for a lengthy period.

Early had demonstrated energy, drive, and some promise in his initial attempt at independent command. He was aggressive in his movements, demanded a great effort from his infantry, but was prudent in their employment. But he was never one to solicit or heed advice. Already experiencing a tense relationship with Gordon, his relationship with Rodes was now precarious, and soon Ramseur would join this list. These three excellent officers were the real strength of his little command, and the caustic Early needed their wholehearted support and cooperation. However, Early's most obvious weakness was his continued criticism of his mounted force. He probably never met a cavalryman he liked, but his continued abuse of their efforts only alienated this important part of his command. In his pursuit of Hunter, Early was served very poorly by his mounted arm, but it's questionable as to how much of this fractionalized effort was actually the fault of the commanding officer.[70]

The other source of Early's frustration was the Federal general, David Hunter. Despite his distasteful personality and vindictive nature, Hunter's troop dispositions were well executed and his retreat was masterful. Only his initial delays in Staunton and Lexington prevented a great and significant victory for David Hunter. But when his troops faced the hard professionals of Early's 2nd Corps, Hunter's nerve failed. He chose to retreat rather than cross swords with veteran soldiers. Years later Hunter would blame Averell for all his ills on the Lynchburg Campaign, but in reality David Hunter simply became too timid to succeed.

CHAPTER 14

SHAKING THE GATES OF WASHINGTON
Early's 1864 Invasion

Lines of lean, veteran infantry moved steadily down the valley pike at route step. Cavalry covered the front and mountain passes on either side of this Virginia breadbasket. As the leading units neared Lexington, they grew strangely quiet as they observed the destruction of railroads, canals, and homes, which had been ignited by Hunter's skillful burners.[1] Robert Rodes' thin brigades entered the small valley town, turning left into the village cemetery. While an accompanying band played softly, the regiments dipped their starry flags, reversed arms, uncovered, and marched slowly by the grave of Stonewall Jackson.[2] No headboard or marker was visible, but the resting place of the first commander of the 2nd Corps was bedecked with a mound of flowers.[3] One marcher stated that "I felt I was stepping on Holy Ground, the last resting place of a Christian Hero."[4] As his division continued through Lexington, Rodes sadly observed the blackened, twisted ruins of his beloved Virginia Military Institute.

On June 27 the marchers reached Staunton to discover new uniforms accompanied by a real luxury, unlimited undergarments. Early had spurred ahead the previous day searching for supplies: food, clothing, and shoes.[5] Rodes' Division drew new uniforms and rations, but the always badly needed shoes had not yet arrived.[6] Early reorganized his little army for the hard campaign he was preparing to initiate. He eliminated wagons for personal possessions, and consolidated Brig. Gen. Long's artillery batteries, mainly to conserve horseflesh.[7]

Early also reorganized his infantry into four divisions, although each was little larger than a brigade of a year hence. Early was confident in the divisions of Robert Rodes and Dodson Ramseur. He based ready reliance on the trust exhibited for the tall, blond Rodes by his soldiers, and Ramseur led his old division.[8] But his other two divisions were not so well disposed.

Gordon's Division contained the remnants of fourteen regiments from five brigades.[9] Hays' and Stafford's Louisiana troops were combined into a brigade under transplanted Northerner Brig. Gen. Zebulon York, whom the rowdy soldiers disliked. In addition, Brig. Gen. William Terry led a brigade in that same division composed of survivors from Gen. Allegheny Johnson's Division, including the skeleton of the old "Stonewall" brigade, and their morale was low.[10] Gordon's difficult task was further complicated by strained relationships between Early and himself.[11] Breckinridge's small division was composed of local mountain dwellers who would fight hard for their homes but didn't like to leave their valley. Early appointed Breckinridge to command a small corps consisting of Gordon's Division and his own under Brig. Gen. John Echols. Rodes and Ramseur would continue to report to General Early.[12]

Thus the army that marched from Staunton on June 28 was a lean, mean little force of experienced soldiers. They had fought many battles, conducted numerous campaigns and were accustomed to hard, difficult marches, short rations, and variable weather. Their uniforms were new, equipment clean, and for once they were well fed, carrying five days' rations in their wagons and two days' supplies in their haversacks.[13] Shoes were still their major deficit as evidenced by the trail of blood which followed their passage.

The units marched steadily and unopposed down the valley, almost as if on a training mission. On June 30 they reached Mt. Jackson, were in Strasburg the next day, and on June 2 camped on Opequon Creek near Winchester.[14] The 12th Georgia of Phillip Cook's Brigade undoubtedly pointed out scenes of combat from Jackson's Valley Campaign as the columns passed Front Royal, Port Republic, Cross Keys, and Kernstown.[15] On July 2 the Valley Army marched through Winchester to the excited cheers of this pro-Southern town so often occupied by the enemy.[16] Breckinridge led two divisions northwest toward Martinsburg while Early accompanied Rodes and Ramseur through Halltown advancing to capture Harper's Ferry, Ramseur on the railway, Rodes on the Charlestown Pike.[17] Early's ploy to trap Union Major General Sigel and his 6,000 men at Martinsburg came to naught as Sigel became aware of the Confederate advance and abandoned the supply warehouses in Martinsburg, falling back to Harper's Ferry.[18] There he combined his force with that of garrison commander Weber and they consolidated on Maryland Heights.[19] Rodes closed on the village but could not enter as heavy guns on Maryland Heights controlled the streets. When darkness fell he dispatched Brigadier General Battle and his Alabama troops into Harper's Ferry to destroy all public property.[20] An angry Rodes was forced to arrest a number of soldiers from other units who crept into the town seeking alcohol.[21]

John Gordon's men were more fortunate; they opened the warehouses of Martinsburg.[22] Despite his best efforts, a number of Confederates became intoxicated on medicinal alcohol. Breckinridge crossed his divisions into Maryland on June 5 while Rodes and Ramseur marched on to Shepherdstown.[23] Both divisions crossed the Potomac on the following day. As Rodes marched through Sharpsburg, the soldiers could witness scars of the tremendous battle which had occurred there in 1862, and many surely recalled brave comrades who still rested on the banks of the Antietam.

An audacious, aggressive Early had skillfully maneuvered his little force across the Potomac, but was now in enemy country and must place his trust in his Valley Army's abilities. Maj. Kyd Douglas commented that "Jackson being dead, it is safe to say that no other general in either army would have attempted an invasion against such odds."[24] He ignored Sigel by swinging north through the gaps in South Mountain, concealing his objectives. As the gray-backs advanced, concern rapidly spread in Washington, Baltimore, and other Northern cities. The governors of Ohio, Pennsylvania, and Maryland activated their 100-day militia.[25]

On July 7, the wagons reached the army with the long awaited shoes and once distributed, Early ordered the advance.[26] On a hot, humid July day Rodes moved his division across Pleasant Valley and began to climb up South Mountain at Crampton's Gap.[27] Breckinridge took his soldiers through Fox's Gap.[28] One Confederate thought the view from South Mountain the finest he had seen, the farms being laid out in regular squares and from the mountaintop seemed like a big garden.[29] Early's columns rejoined at Frederick City. Despite a lack of clear information on Federal opposition, the tobacco-chewing Early pushed on further into Maryland.

The lone Union commander between Early and Washington was Maj. Gen. Lew Wallace, the thirty-seven-year-old chief of the Department of Maryland. Wallace had been made the scapegoat for a near Federal disaster at Shiloh and shuffled out to this backwater assignment. His Federal VIII Corps contained only 2,500 soldiers, mostly guards and clerks.[30] But the courageous Wallace boarded a railcar in Baltimore and rode toward Monocacy Junction where he discovered an excellent defensive position and decided to delay Early as long as possible. He summoned his regiments, some Maryland national guard units, and found a support battery of 3-inch cannon.[31] Fortunately for Wallace he soon received unexpected assistance. On July 8, Brig. Gen. James B. Ricketts arrived at Monocacy with 5,000 veterans of his 3rd Division, VI Army Corps, recently arrived in Baltimore by steamship from Grant's army.[32] Ricketts found Wallace in a strong position, a river in his front and good roads to his back and decided to throw in his lot with the defiant blue-coat.[33]

On a beautiful summer day the Confederates advanced from Frederick City across a level plain toward the Monocacy River, utilizing two principal roads. Robert Rodes advanced on the northernmost road, the Baltimore Pike. Cook's and Cox's Brigades led, skirmishers three-deep in front, with Battle and Grimes following.[34] About 8 A.M. Rodes' units neared the "Jug" or Stone Bridge as Ramseur, advancing on the Washington Pike, closed on a wooden covered bridge. A railway trestle spanned the river alongside the wooden bridge. Both bridges were heavily defended by strong blockhouses. Rodes deployed, shook out a battle line, and probed the Federal line with rifle fire. Soon similar action could be heard from Ramseur's men on the Washington Pike. But Early, now up, and studying the ground, did not like what he observed. Deciding that a frontal attack on either bridge would be costly, Early searched for a flank to turn and decided it must be on Wallace's left, for Early needed the Washington Pike.[35]

Suddenly Early saw gray cavalry splash across the Monocacy about a mile downstream. General McCausland spurred his men into an attack on Ricketts' line and was sternly repulsed.[36] Early sent for Gordon's Division, relaxing in reserve. Gordon led his men quickly across the ford, up the steep bank, and deployed them under fire.[37] Ricketts' Federals changed fronts smartly and met Gordon's charge head-on in a brutal stand-up fight. The Louisiana Brigade of General York broke two Federal lines before falling back to regroup, then assisted by Terry's Virginians broke the third Federal alignment.[38] The Union position became unhinged as Ramseur crossed men on the railway bridge, and Rodes flanked and captured several hundred of Tyler's men.[39] Wallace withdrew toward Baltimore and Early allowed him to escape. Confederate losses, mostly in Gordon's Division, were about nine hundred while Wallace and Ricketts' reported 1,300 casualties.[40]

Early was extravagant in his praise of the Louisianians, but privately York was unimpressed. He remarked that "the compliments were fair coming from the most cross-grained and fault-finding general in the entire Confederate States Army."[41] Within hours panic gripped the citizens and officials of Washington. Early's army had brushed Wallace aside and now most sources accurately reported him advancing on the Federal capital. President Lincoln revealed his concern when he stated: "Let us be vigilant, but keep cool. I hope neither Baltimore or Washington will be sacked."[42]

On June 10 Early's Valley Army moved east led by Breckinridge's troops, followed by Rodes. Ramseur's rear guard was constantly harassed by Union cavalry which trailed his marchers, often causing his units to deploy.[43] The humid, hot weather was intensified by a lengthy drought which turned the roadways to ankle deep dust so fine that it wrapped around one's ankles. Huge clouds enveloped the sweating marchers who were soon gasping for air.[44] On June 11, Rodes' men set the pace, marching at 3:30 A.M. A battery of artillery followed Rodes' leading brigade and a battalion of guns trailed his division.[45] Rodes' vanguard closely followed McCausland's riders down through Silver Spring, approaching Washington on the 7th Street Road.[46] As Federal artillery opened about 1 P.M. from Fort Stevens, McCausland's men dismounted and, moving from rock to rock, darted forward. Riding at the very point of his first brigade, Robert Rodes deployed his skirmish line, but that was all he had, for the soldiers

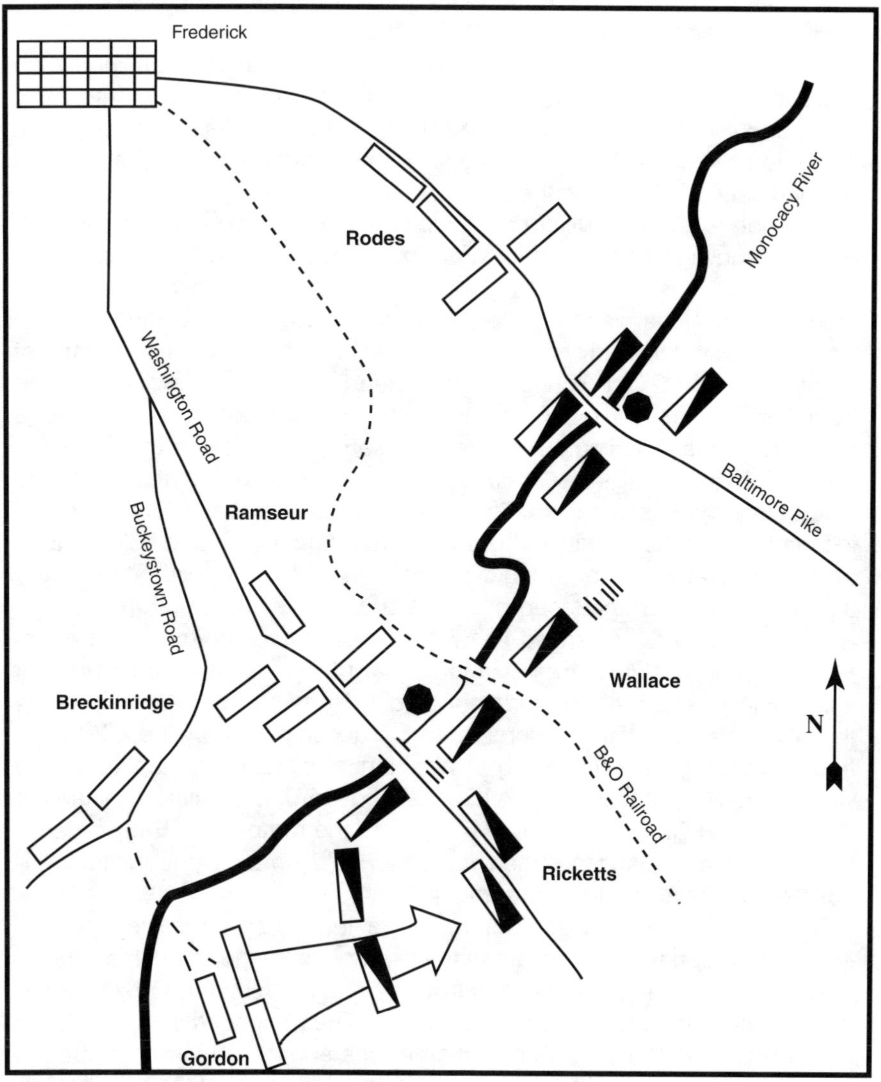

Battle of Monocacy, July 9, 1864

Federal General Lew Wallace, in a superior defensive position, attempted to delay Early's move on Washington, D.C. Rodes and Ramseur pressed the Federals at formidable, heavily defended bridges while Gordon moved around the enemy left, forded the Monocacy, and uncovered the Washington Road.

behind were almost in single file.[47] The struggling soldiers had been on the dusty roads for more than nine hours in the torrid heat and only the very strong could keep up. Rodes awaited their arrival.

One Alabama soldier recalled their initial appearance; out of breath and ducking the 100-pound shells thrown from the fort, suddenly they gazed at the unfinished dome of the United States Capitol.[48] As Rodes stared at the Union ramparts through field glasses he noted a long file of soldiers wearing deep blue entering the trenches. The blue-eyed division commander opened long-distance artillery fire as the 5th Alabama spread into skirmish lines and moved forward. A single Federal company rushed from the works, attempting to destroy a dwelling which could harbor Confederate marksmen, but the Alabamians repulsed them easily as the sun went down.[49]

After nightfall, Early convened a council-of-war at the palatial home of Frances Blair in Silver Springs. After a hearty toast of wine appropriated from Blair's cellars, and much teasing of ex-Vice President John Breckinridge on his return to Washington, the officers seriously reviewed their options. With much debate all four divisional commanders agreed that, despite the inherent dangers, an attack at dawn was in order.[50] Most, including Rodes, felt they could take the city but probably would not be able to hold it. However, appreciable damage could be inflicted in a brief occupation. Early agreed to attack but prefaced his decision with a statement that if further Union reinforcements arrived he would not assault. He knew that a defeated or badly injured army would be hard to extricate from its present vulnerable position. About midnight a report arrived from cavalry scouts that the remainder of the Federal VI Corps, accompanied by the XIX Corps from Louisiana, were unloading at Washington piers. Early slept little, and was on the lines at first light. He, Rodes, and Gordon identified the flags of the veteran VI Corps which were flying from the ramparts.[51] Early ordered the two officers to stand their men down; he would remain in position throughout the day, then withdraw after nightfall.

The humid day passed quietly, characterized by artillery salvos and exchanges of sharpshooters, while the infantrymen rigged blankets or tarps to escape the boiling sun. Federal troops were harassed by crowds of onlookers which included President Lincoln.[52] The prolonged inactivity of the Confederates led to a sortie by Union troops about 6 P.M. Preceded by a heavy cannonade, a brigade of the VI Corps, led by Col. Daniel Bidwell of the 43rd New York, advanced in line toward a low wooded hill held by Rodes' Alabama Brigade. A long ripping volley from the tree line repelled the bluecoats who called for reinforcements. Rodes sent for another brigade, and it seemed, to Early's dismay, that a major action might develop, but darkness concluded the sortie.[53] Bidwell suffered about two hundred fifty casualties or 25 percent of his attacking force.[54]

Shortly before midnight, Early smoothly and rapidly withdrew his divisions. The Blair house burned furiously, lighting up the sky. Many suspected it was fired by looters to cover their thieving as they entered the house the moment Rodes' provost guards were withdrawn. Thousands of dollars were circulated among the marchers of Ramseur's Division, the bills being drawn on the bank of Monroe, Michigan.[55] Marching speed was hampered by large herds of horses and cattle.[56] In addition about one thousand Union prisoners were escorted back into Virginia and to Confederate prisons.[57] The long column marched most of the night, halting near Darnestown, then proceeding over the majestic Potomac at White's Ferry, wading the waist deep river easily, cartridge boxes held high to keep powder dry. They then moved into camp on July 14 near the little Southern town of Leesburg.

The VI Corps of Maj. Gen. Horatio G. Wright belatedly pursued Early's retreating army, and attempted to trap the Confederates by utilizing David Hunter's reappearing Army of West Virginia which had reached Harper's Ferry on July 14. But Early's sweating files were a full day ahead of Wright's pursuers, although unaware of Hunter's position. The Union VI Corps and four brigades of the XIX Corps forded the Potomac at White's Ferry and marched through Leesburg on Early's trail.[58] Soon Maj. Gen. George Crook led Federals from Hunter's force to assist Wright.

The Confederate column, laden with captured livestock and supply wagons, proceeded from Leesburg west toward Berryville via a road through Purcellville and Snicker's Gap. Aware of this movement, Crook requested that Duffie, his cavalry commander, attempt to intercept the wagon train. Hard riding blue troopers cut into the Confederate column without warning at Purcellville, driving off the cavalry escort and capturing about two hundred wagons and one hundred fifty Confederate teamsters.[59] Rodes, riding some quarter mile back, saw the commotion, and discerned the cause. He dispatched his leading two brigades which raced forward to intercept the raiders.[60] The two infantry units recaptured most of the wagons and a majority of the prisoners. Federals were able to burn about forty of the wagons before fleeing. One Southern brigade chased the Union cavalry for two miles at double-time before conceding the race. Several gray-backs commented that despite Rodes' angry utterings, "Union cavalry, when frightened, just could not be caught by Confederate infantry."[61]

The Pike between Leesburg and Berryville passed through the Blue Ridge Mountains, in a narrow defile known as Snicker's Gap. When a marcher emerged from this gap the powerful Shenandoah River was at one's feet flowing northward parallel to the mountain range. Travelers descended from Snicker's Gap directly to a ford and ferry called Castleman's Ferry. The Shenandoah, flowing forcefully toward its junction with the Potomac is a swift, four- to six-foot-deep stream at Castleman's Ferry.

The Confederates crossed, cavorting in the cold water, and slipping on the uneven river bed.[62] Once his divisions were over the Shenandoah, Early spread them behind the river with all fords picketed.[63] Rodes' Division moved downstream to Rock's or Island Ford while Gordon's Division camped back of Castleman's. Rodes' tired soldiers relaxed in the parklike wooded groves near the crossroads of Gaylord, about two miles back of the river.[64]

On Sunday both Federal and Confederate armies rested, gray-backs killing and cooking beef in their pots. After noon a Union cavalry unit under Alfred Duffie rode down the narrow trail through Snicker's Gap. They discovered heavy gray pickets at Castleman's Ford and brought up guns to shell the sentinels.[65] After several failed attempts to get across, General Duffie decided to bull his way over, and aligned a cavalry regiment four abreast to charge across, sabers high.[66] The splashing horsemen successfully reached the western bank, but heavy rifle fire scorched their ranks, and a lone Confederate cannon sprayed them with canister. After a loss of fifteen or more, Duffie sounded recall and withdrew back up the gap at dusk.[67] It was certainly clear that the Confederate pickets at Castleman's Ferry were numerous and determined to resist.

Flags unfurled and whipping in the strong wind, the Federal column marched down the pike on June 18, then filed into the narrow gap and out onto a small plateau overlooking Castleman's Ferry and the beautiful valley beyond. The Federal soldiers broke ranks, stacked rifles, and ate lunch. Appropriated Confederate beef and corn were an enjoyable change from army rations.[68]

About 2 P.M. Generals Wright and Crook determined to flank the Confederates out of Castleman's Ferry. Crook ordered Col. Joseph Thoburn to take his two-brigade division, reinforced by a third brigade and move downstream, find a ford, and cross. Thoburn was then to march back upstream on the west bank and clear the ford at Castleman's for the remainder of Wright's soldiers to cross.[69] Thoburn discovered a small road north screened by trees and hills, and began his circular movement.

Col. George D. Wells' Brigade led Thoburn's column toward the Island Ford and was fired on by Confederate sentinels at about 3 P.M. After an exchange, Thoburn ordered Wells' 34th Massachusetts further downriver where they braved the swift current of chest deep water and splashed across.[70] Confederate pickets were flushed, with a handful being taken captive. Colonel Thoburn then crossed his entire force to the west bank and deployed in double lines, back to the river. Wells set up his brigade on the left flank, Col. David Frost's Brigade aligned in the center, and Thoburn's Brigade filed in on the right.[71] A low stone wall ran beside a rutted road which paralleled the river, and Thoburn had his first rank deploy in that road. He advanced the second rank of all three brigades about seventy-five yards toward a wheat field and halted behind cover of a small bluff or bank. The position faced gently rising ground through wheat fields to a crest of small hillocks.[72] Thoburn questioned his captives and discovered they were Confederate infantry of Rodes' Division. Becoming concerned, he forwarded this information to Crook, who replied at once, ordering Thoburn to find a good position, dig in, and await reinforcements.[73] This presented a rapidly changing situation for Crook and Wright, for they had not anticipated Confederate infantry this far downstream.

As Thoburn realigned his troops, Confederate reaction to his incursion was swift and decisive. Gen. John Gordon extended his division northward from Castleman's toward the Cool Springs Farm, while Brig. Gen. Gabriel G. Wharton, now commanding a small three-brigade division, hurriedly deployed on the line of hills opposite Thoburn's lines. Wharton's force aligned, left to right, brigades of Col. August Forsberg, Col. Thomas Smith, and Col. George Patton.[74] All three units advanced skirmishers which drove in Thoburn's skirmishers. As they settled into their lines, the Confederates looked down from a fifty-foot elevation across a waving field of wheat at Thoburn's advanced line, entrenched behind a bank and his reserve line at a stone wall on the river's edge.

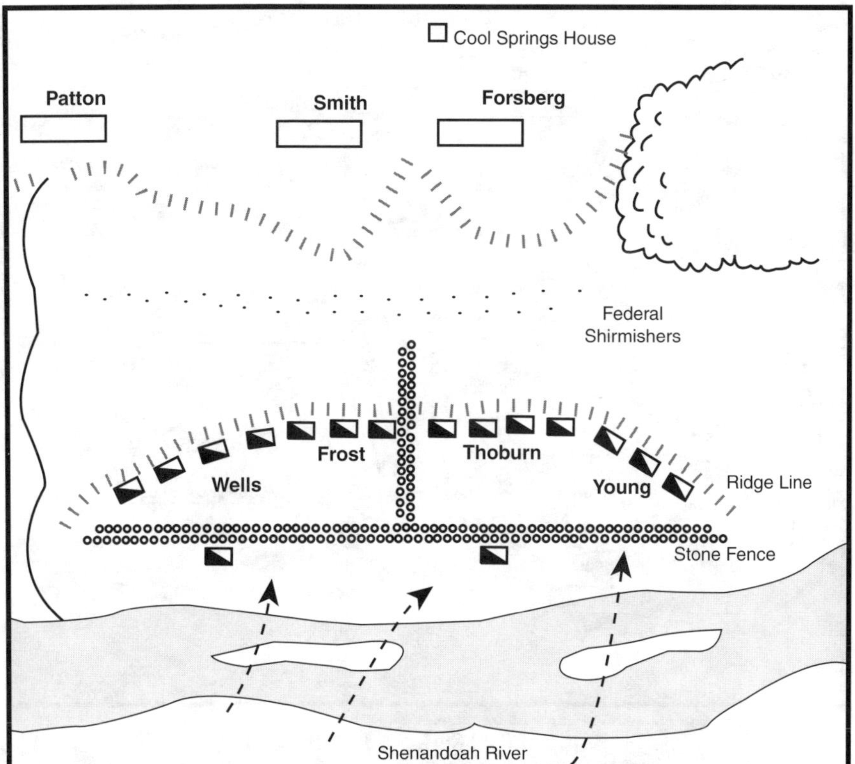

Battle of Cool Springs, July 18, 1864

By 5 P.M. Thoburn's heavily reinforced division was across the Shenandoah River and had established a defensive position in the shelter of a slight ridge. Skirmishers were sent forward and began to exchange rifle fire with arriving brigades of Wharton's Confederate division under Smith and Forsberg.

Within mere minutes, Federal artillery found Wharton's line. First, VI Corps batteries on the plateau at Castleman's began lobbing long-range shells onto the Confederates. Next, Battery C of the 1st Rhode Island opened from an elevated position directly behind the Island Ford.[75] As the Union skirmish line was driven in and Thoburn's line began a long-range exchange of rifle fire with Wharton's men, suddenly, an entire Confederate Division emerged from the wooded hill on the Federal right, marching in battle formation, starry flags aloft, en echelon, aiming directly at the Federal right flank. Rodes' Division had arrived.

Rodes had hurried his men toward the river when he found that Federals were crossing. Turning left they filed down a country road behind Wharton's line and emerged to the rear and north of the Cool Springs Manor House. There, in an open field, the division deployed in battle array.

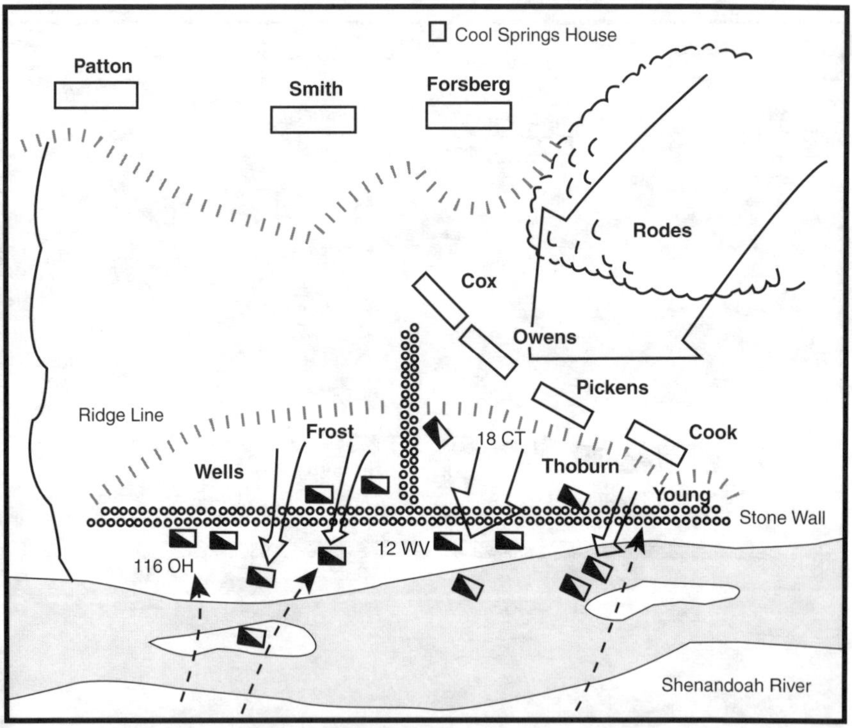

Battle of Cool Springs, July 18, 1864

Rodes' entire gray-clad division suddenly assaulted Thoburn's position, appearing in battle order from the trees and sweeping downhill at left oblique onto the Federal right. Young's dismounted cavalrymen broke at once as scores of Union soldiers were shot down or driven into the Shenandoah and drowned. Only a gallant effort by the 12th West Virginia, 18th Connecticut, and 116th Ohio, supported by massive Federal artillery fire from the east bank, prevented total destruction of Thoburn's force.

Advancing through a parklike woods of large oak trees, Rodes turned the formation slightly left and dressed ranks to emerge from the trees in perfect alignment. Magically, the 3,000-man division appeared in view of the Federal lines.[76] Rodes advanced his division four brigades abreast in double or triple ranks. Brig. Gen. William Cox's North Carolina Brigade made up the right unit with Col. William Owens alongside, leading Byran Grimes' Brigade. Adjoining Owens was Col. Samuel B. Pickens commanding Battle's Alabamians. Col. Phillip Cook with Doles' Georgia Brigade on the far left completed the deployment.[77] Despite a crescendo of artillery fire, Rodes' Division sliced into Thoburn's position like a knife.

Cox's troops raced across the battlefield to take a position behind a stone wall which ran up the slope perpendicular to the river. This quick movement forced Federal regiments on the left to change front and face right, becoming vulnerable to Wharton's long-range fire.

Lt. Col. Samuel Young's dismounted brigade of blue-coated cavalry was positioned on the Federal right flank. Composed of transfers from various disbanded regiments into a conglomerate brigade of displeased and unhappy soldiers, this unit was the first to run.[78] Almost as Rodes' lines emerged from the treeline, the entire unit turned and rushed into the water. Numbers of men drowned in the deep, treacherous pools of the Shenandoah. Bodies of short-jacketed cavalrymen were pulled from the river downstream for days.[79] The next Federal unit, the 4th West Virginia, was forced to fall back to the riverbank. Facing the rifles of Doles' and Grimes' Brigades with an exposed flank caused them to quickly fold.

Col. William Ely's 18th Connecticut were then left exposed from front and flank. Changing front and refusing their right, the 18th attempted to rest one flank on the stone fence at the riverbank and the other on a perpendicular stone wall. Thus aligned they resisted in determined fashion until the units on their left broke, permitting Cox's riflemen to flow into their rear. They fell back, fighting to unite with the 12th West Virginia which was firing furiously from the reserve line. Colonel Frost, holding the center, attempted to turn his brigade to face echelon right but when he was mortally wounded his troops fell back in confusion, carrying their wounded colonel.[80] Within thirty minutes of the appearance of Rodes' Division the entire advanced line had disintegrated, and hundreds of the second line blue-coats were attempting to flee into the water. Large numbers of wounded Federals were abandoned on the field as the survivors rushed to escape. But as minie balls zipped overhead it was considered too dangerous to assist them.[81] Just as the Confederates reached the crest of the bank previously occupied by the Federals, additional Union batteries joined the barrage with vigor. As the blue-coats fell back to the riverbank, Union gunners had a clear field of fire.[82] Col. W.A. Owens of the 53rd North Carolina was mortally wounded as he realigned Grimes' Brigade. This highly respected officer had just returned to duty, arriving from home that morning, having been wounded at Spotsylvania on May 12.[83]

Cool Springs, July 18, 1864

Rodes' Confederate Division appeared suddenly from the tree line on the left, marching echelon right and falling upon Thoburn's reinforced Federal Division positioned below with backs to the river.

Robert Carter

Cool Springs Battlefield

Rodes' Division continued down the slope and across the wheat field, cutting through Thoburn's front line like a knife through butter.

Robert Carter

Battery G of the Ist Rhode Island Light Artillery joined the aforementioned Battery C. The gunners plastered the ridge line with canister and case shot; sparks flying from the limestone formations scattered throughout the wheat field. Gray-clad infantry continued to fire into Union soldiers attempting to recross the river. An Alabama soldier recalled his regiment firing volleys by the numbers according to the manual of arms for the first and only time during the war.[84] The 12th West Virginia and the 116th Ohio maintained some order as the battle settled into an exchange between Rodes' infantry and the Union guns. Three Union batteries were firing at close range, barely preventing Rodes' veterans from driving Thoburn's entire force into the river. As Union infantry evacuated they waded the river with only their heads above water as minie balls splashed into the river surface.

General Ricketts' Division of the VI Corps joined the action as they approached the river on the east bank, spread out and opened fire to cover Thoburn's evacuation. Despite earlier orders, Ricketts refused to attempt a crossing to assist the trapped Federals. When his leading units approached the ford, Ricketts observed the Federal forces in a cup surrounded by the enemy and decided that further crossing would only increase Union losses.[85] Considerable animosity developed between Crook and Ricketts over this decision. Wright supported Ricketts' decision. In so doing, Wright admitted the fallacy of his plans.[86]

As daylight faded, a furious artillery duel exploded. Infantrymen searched for cover, then enjoyed the fiery exchange. Federal losses in the brief, fierce engagement were reported by Colonel Thoburn as 422, although other sources estimated them as much higher.[87] Confederate losses, almost entirely in Rodes' Division, were about two hundred. A majority of Rodes' losses were from artillery fire. Rodes was disappointed as were many of his men. While the Confederates won an easy victory by driving the Federals rudely back across the river, the fight had been primarily a one-division matter: Rodes' men against the Federal bridgehead. Better use of the entire available Confederate force and rapid deployment of gray artillery would likely have resulted in the destruction or capture of Thoburn's entire force.

Rodes' troops slept on the battlefield and began digging graves for the casualties come morning.[88] Captain Park recalled encountering the remains of a gallant North Carolina soldier, his tall, elegant silk hat at his side. Park remembered that comrades had long warned the veteran that wearing such a conspicuous headgear was dangerous, yet he smiled and persisted and now lay shot in the head.[89]

At sunrise July 20, Federal troops awoke to find the Confederates gone. About noon the Federals waded across at Castleman's Ferry in a tremendous rainstorm. They camped that night in the trees near Rodes' old encampment. The encounter with Rodes' troops did impress Federal decision makers. Confederate ranks might have been thin, divisions were mere brigades and brigades composed of regimental numbers, and graycoat morale somewhat dimmed by the near-miss at Washington; however, Early's tattered veterans were hard professionals who could march hard and long, handle their Enfields, and hit like a thunderbolt, and they were still led by capable, aggressive, and skillful leaders.

CHAPTER 15

IN THE FOOTSTEPS OF JACKSON
Defeat and Death on the Opequon

Lieutenant General Early dispatched orders to Maj. Gen. Stephen Ramseur on July 19, to proceed with his infantry division, assisted by Brigadier General Vaughn's cavalry, toward Winchester, then to turn north and intercept Federal forces moving south from Martinsburg.[1] As Generals Wright and Crook attempted to force their way through Snicker's Gap, Brig. Gen. William W. Averell moved toward Winchester with his cavalry division and an infantry brigade under Col. Hiram Duval, a total of 2,350 soldiers.[2] Ramseur marched that afternoon, and the following morning was two miles north of Winchester, advancing behind a cavalry screen. About 4 P.M. Ramseur heard heavy firing on his front. When a message arrived that Vaughn's Cavalry was attacked by a regiment of infantry and another of cavalry, Ramseur deployed into a two-brigade front and moved to support his cavalry.[3] He aligned Brig. Gen. Robert Johnston's Brigade on his right and Brig. Gen. William Lewis's Brigade on the left, while Brig. Gen. Robert Lilley's Brigade was in reserve. As they moved forward, a lengthy Federal line suddenly appeared, sweeping down on the Confederate front overlapping Lewis' left.[4] Ramseur ordered Lilley's reserve unit to extent his left, but before Lilley arrived Lewis' two right regiments broke and ran. Soon Lilley's Brigade also broke and within minutes the entire division was in rout.[5] Ramseur vainly tried to rally his men, using his sword over their backs as he wept in humiliation, but his efforts were for naught. His losses were four guns, and more than two hundred and fifty captives, including the wounded Lilley.[6]

Early was withdrawing south when he learned of Ramseur's defeat and, taking Rodes' Division from Newtown, started back toward Winchester to rescue his subordinate. Upon arrival, Early and Rodes discovered that Averell had not pursued the fleeing Confederates, being satisfied with their defeat. Collecting stragglers, the units fell back to Middletown.[7] By July 22, Early's entire force was consolidated in a strong position on Fisher's Hill near Strasburg.[8]

Ramseur received much criticism, both within and outside the army, for his rash and impulsive conduct. Ramseur countered by censoring Vaughn for bearing false information, Lilley for tardiness in advancing, and Lewis for failure to make his regiments fight.[9] The *Richmond Examiner* demanded an investigation, citing the wounded Lewis that Ramseur had even been arrested. Soldiers complained that Ramseur calmly advanced up the road with no idea of what lay ahead, just as at Bethesda Church. Early and Ramseur were observed exchanging sharp words, and the soldiers momentarily expected Ramseur's removal.[10] Gordon and Rodes reassured Ramseur. Rodes, in addition, wrote to General Ewell, then serving in Richmond, to appeal for assistance in preserving Ramseur's good name. Rodes explained the circumstances and commented:

> urged by a natural desire to shrink the responsibility for this disaster, and the less laudable one inspired by their dislike of Ramseur...the men and main officers concerned have succeeded in winning public opinion to their side and have very nearly ruined Ramseur. He, of course, is perfectly powerless. He degrades himself to a newspaper controversy, or is driven to ask that a court of inquiry be called. In the meantime his reputation is ruined, and he is deprived of his permanent promotion.[11]

As Early retreated, a strong Union force of two additional infantry divisions and three artillery batteries commanded by Brevet Maj. Gen. George Crook moved into Winchester. Crook was a popular and solid leader who had experienced significant action while commanding a cavalry division at Chickamauga and Antietam.[12] Lt. Col. Rutherford B. Hayes stated that Crook was "the best general we have ever served under."[13] Hayes, of course, had most recently served under Sigel and Hunter, thus his evaluation might be somewhat suspect. Duffie's Cavalry Division rode in and Crook's little army increased to almost ninety-five hundred blue-coats.[14]

Crook marched his infantry south on July 23 and deployed them north of Kernstown. That evening he took them back to camp near Winchester but returned early the following morning. On July 24, Crook aligned his divisions for an expected attack by gray-clad infantry. Each infantry division had two brigades, and he placed a division right of the Valley Pike, another left of the road and retained a third division in reserve.[15] At daybreak on July 24, Early moved his troops north from Fisher's Hill. The small corps of Maj. Gen. John Breckinridge, composed of his division and that of John Gordon, led as the divisions of Rodes and Ramseur followed. Early rode near the van of his 12,000 infantrymen and studied Crook's compact battle line. He decided to attack with Gordon's men while Breckinridge's Division swung east to turn the Federal left. Ramseur was moved forward to extend the Confederate left while Rodes was to circle further east around Breckinridge.[16] Quickly, the Federal left began to leak retreating blue-coats, so Crook sent his reserves to this position.[17] But from behind a ridge, Breckinridge launched Wharton's Division in a textbook attack on Crook's flank. Gordon then charged and the entire Union front collapsed.[18]

Early pursued hard to Winchester where he allowed his panting soldiers a rest. Rodes' Division on the far right never delivered its attack, for the Union force was defeated and retreated so rapidly that contact was never established. Crook was aware that another large force was on his right and withdrew before it could pose a threat to cut off his army.[19] Rodes continued to pursue the Federals to Stephenson's Depot, north of Winchester. His division marched twenty-seven miles, capturing hundreds of prisoners and engaging in a dozen small firefights.[20] Federal retreat continued through Bunker Hill to Martinsburg, then across the Potomac into Sharpsburg by June 26.[21] Union casualties were about sixteen hundred soldiers or about twenty percent of Crook's force.[22] Most of the Confederate prisoners captured from Ramseur at Stephenson's Depot were recovered, including Brigadier General Lilley.[23]

Early had turned the tables again in a "smart little battle" as he whipped Crook. Crook's infantry, slightly outnumbered, was inexperienced and no match for its Confederate counterparts, and Crook's cavalry advantage had not been exploited. Once the Union infantry was defeated, Duffie's riders performed yeoman work in limiting Southern pursuit.

Early had aggressively set out to crush Crook and probably should have. But he divided his army into too many parts and could not bring his entire force to bear on the enemy. Early seemed to fight one division at a time: Gordon at Monocacy, Rodes at Cool Springs, and now Breckinridge at Kernstown. In pursuit Early's cavalry again failed him badly, for once through Winchester the Union retreat became unraveled, and well-led cavalry could have destroyed Crook's army.

A new type of unique warfare was developing in which tactical maneuver became the premium method of military expression. For nearly two months following Kernstown no pitched battle occurred between Union and Confederate armies although both forces maneuvered constantly in an area around Winchester marked by Martinsburg, Sharpsburg, and Harper's Ferry to the north, Berryville to the east, and Strasburg in the south. Within this relatively small arena the forces confronted each other daily, skirmishing, and attacking with small cavalry units.

The armies marched almost every day, seldom camping in the same spot for more than one night. Jubal Early proved a capable, adept practitioner of this strategy. His ability to divide forces, deceive the enemy, and force enemy reaction to his initiatives was exceptional. So well did he execute that Federal estimates of his forces were constantly in error. Early, however, still had little faith in cavalry so he utilized infantry divisions to repel blue-clad cavalry incursions. The veteran gray-backs were far too tough for Union cavalry to contest, but the constant marching wore the energies of the soldiers badly. One stated:

> reconnaissances may be important and very interesting to generals and field officers who ride, but those of the line and fighting privates wish they were less frequent, or less tiresome this sultry weather.[24]

Warfare of this sort was constant and day to day, with a fluidity of marches, countermarches, cold camps, picket duty, and surprise attacks

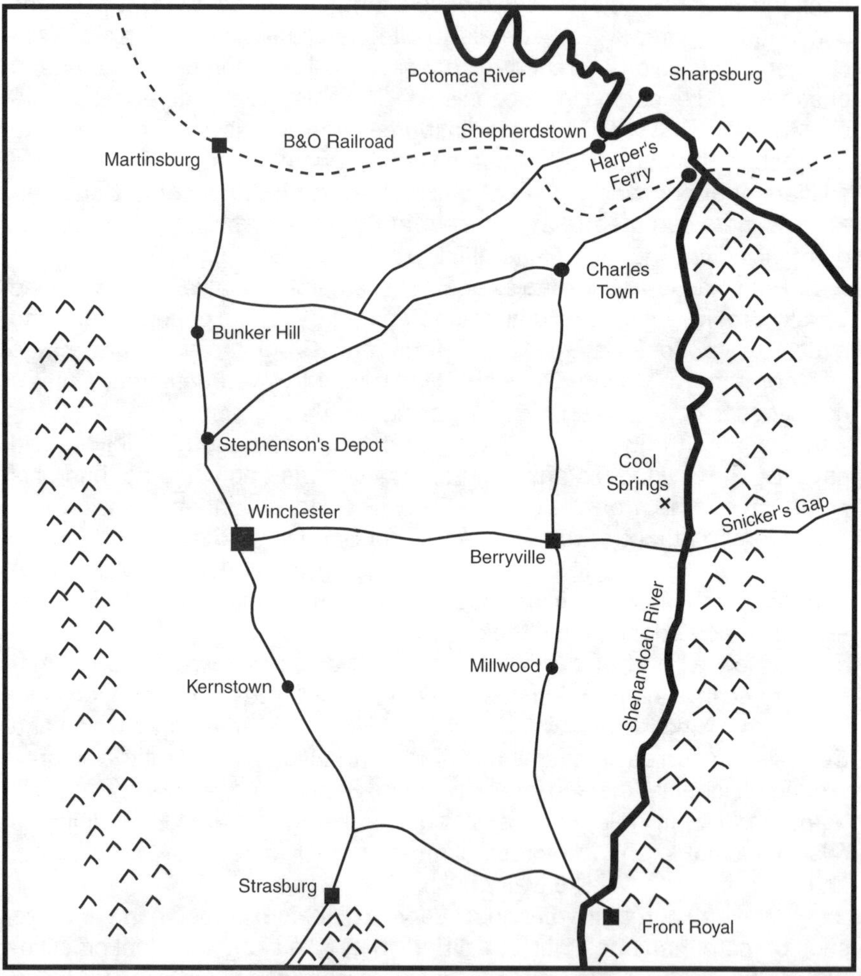

Area of Valley Combat, Summer 1864

Within this small geographic area, almost surrounded by mountains and rivers, General Early and General Sheridan sparred daily, conducting a furious contest for control of the lower valley.

that exhausted the participants. Robert Rodes, in writing to General Ewell, explained the difficulty of living under the constant pressures of combat. He apologized to Ewell and wrote further:

> I regret very much I have not yet been able to furnish you my report of operations up to the time you left us. I have not had the time and the courage at the same moment to undertake it; and in truth our life here is one of such constant motion, and constant separation from baggage...and constant expectations of a cavalry fight...even when in camp, that I am unable to concentrate my thoughts upon anything except my immediate military duty.[25]

For men as well as officers there was little normal life, little relaxation, not enough rest. Even letters to loved ones were a chore and cleanliness of person and clothing impossible. Thankfully, rations improved somewhat. The steady Confederate diet of hard bread and bacon crumpled fine and ground into a hash called "cush"[26] was supplemented by the late summer cherries, apples, and corn which were readily available in the valley area.

Rodes was now acting in command of a small corps composed of his troops and Ramseur's. On his initial foray he took two days demolishing the Baltimore and Ohio tracks. He then took his divisions across the Potomac and into Williamsport.[27] Next, Rodes demonstrated toward Hagerstown, driving Federal cavalry in retreat as he screened the river crossing at McCoy's Ferry for Brig. Gen. John McCausland's cavalry raiders.[28] McCausland, accompanied by Bradley Johnson's Brigade, was off on the infamous raid which culminated in the burning of Chambersburg, Pennsylvania. Rodes led his diversionary force back into Virginia and returned south to camp at Bunker Hill on July 31.[29]

Rodes used Bunker Hill as a base for several months. While seldom there for more than a day or two, his division pitched its tents at that location nine times in six weeks.[30] Veteran Confederates often commented that they had walked the Valley Pike so often that they knew not only every house, fence, spring, and shade tree, but also many of the local citizens, even their wives and children.[31] After three days at Bunker Hill, Rodes again led his men and Ramseur's north, crossing the river and camping at St. James College before again returning to Bunker Hill.[32]

In early August, Grant, disturbed by Crook's defeat at Kernstown, decided to change field commanders in the Valley. He assigned Maj. Gen. Phillip H. Sheridan, his chief of cavalry, to command a newly organized Army of the Shenandoah.[33] Grant also increased the forces available to his new commander when he canceled the return of the VI Corps to Petersburg lines and returned units of the XIX Corps to Sheridan. The Army of the Shenandoah thus contained seven infantry divisions.[34] Sheridan also received additional cavalry units, so critical in this war of maneuver. Sheridan's total force by September 1 totaled 43,000 officers and men.[35]

His first offensive action on August 10 was a rapid advance from Sharpsburg toward Winchester. Early retreated to protect the city, establishing a defensive line north and east of the town limits. But a strong Federal cavalry thrust threatened to cut the Valley Pike to his rear, so he fell back to Strasburg.[36] Retreating further to Fisher's Hill, Early began construction of a stout line of earthworks, and the two forces faced each other for several days. On July 16, Maj. Gen. Richard H. Anderson, temporary commander of the Confederate 1st Corps, marched over the Blue Ridge and into the Valley with Maj. Gen. Joseph Kershaw's 3,500-man Division and a battalion of artillery.[37] Lee realized Early's numerical deficiencies and attempted to assist his lieutenant as much as possible. Sheridan, convinced that the entire 1st Confederate Corps had arrived, fell back through Winchester to Halltown where he anchored both flanks on the Shenandoah River.[38] Soon Rodes' men were camped back at their Bunker Hill base. Early decided to use his temporary advantage by moving north on several roads, attempting to destroy a part of Sheridan's force. Rodes with Ramseur's assistance attacked the Federal VI Corps near Shepherdstown in a tough little fight which cost Wright's Federal force 260 casualties.[39] But Anderson's Division, marching on another road, was delayed by Federal cavalry, and when they failed to appear, Early was forced to abort his attack effort.[40] An angry Early rode with Rodes' small corps back to Bunker Hill.

Sheridan's major advantage was in his numerous, aggressive cavalry force which he well knew how to employ. Rodes' Division was called out on at least five occasions in the next few weeks to dispel blue-jackets which were driving Confederate cavalry or interrupting Southern supply columns.[41] Rodes was distraught over the severe wound received by Lieutenant Arrington, his aide. His thigh had been broken by a musket-ball, an injury which was to prove fatal.[42]

The first weeks of September saw an end to the drought in the form of heavy rains and thunderstorms. Marching was curtailed by the weather, to the elation of men and officers. When the weather broke, the Confederate infantry attempted to cut and thresh grain, which they would then grind into flour at local mills. Rodes commented to a dejected Ramseur that they must persevere, and stand tall in their duty, for elections were soon to be held in the North, and newspaper predictions were forecasting the election of a peace candidate. Rodes confidently predicted an armistice by the new year.[43]

On the evening before departure of Kershaw's Division to rejoin Lee, the band of the 4th North Carolina staged a concert.[44] This peaceful moment was long remembered by thousands of men. As Kershaw's Division of South Carolinians, accompanied by Cutshaw's Artillery, departed, Sheridan's advantage became enormous. Within a day Sheridan knew of Kershaw's departure. Miss Rebecca Wright, a Quaker school teacher and avid Union sympathizer, sent a message to the Union commander by a trusted Negro vegetable peddler.[45] The news was soon picked up in Northern newspapers, and at least one Union picket warned his Southern counterpart that "we don't want to kill you fellows so you better get away because we are coming."[46]

Despite inferior numbers, Early decided to send a column toward Martinsburg on September 17 to destroy newly repaired railway tracks.[47] He detailed two infantry divisions, those of Robert Rodes and John Gordon. Rodes argued vehemently with Early that the army should not be divided with Sheridan camped so near.[48] He accused Early of underestimating Sheridan, but Jubal refused to heed the alarm even when Gordon added his support to Rodes' argument.[49] Thus the two divisions marched north in full view of blue-coated lookouts.[50]

While Early was using infantry as cavalry to destroy railways, Sheridan eyed bigger game. He planned to move south toward Newtown, cutting the Valley Pike, but when he observed the Confederate commander split his forces, he decided to throw most of his army out the Berryville Pike upon Ramseur's isolated division. He would wreck Ramseur's force, then destroy the remaining Confederate divisions as they returned.[51] Sheridan sent Brig. Gen. James Wilson's Cavalry Division splashing over the fords of Opequon River followed by Wright's VI Corps and Emory's XIX Corps. Crook would follow with his VIII Corps as a reserve. The two attacking corps became entangled as they advanced through a small, narrow canyon outside Berryville and were late arriving on the field. This delay, to Sheridan's disgust, severely curtailed the early effectiveness of the Federal battle plan.[52]

The field upon which the third Battle of Winchester would be contested was largely a wooded plateau northeast of Winchester, bisected by the Berryville Pike, and bounded by Abrahams Creek on the south and Redbud Run on the north.[53] Both streams were tributaries of Obequon River which the Federals crossed to enter the battlefield. Upon hearing of the Union advance, Early hurriedly summoned the troops of Gordon and Rodes which were now camped near Bunker Hill.

Rodes hastily gathered his men around their battle flags, explained the serious nature of their march, and, following Gordon's troops, started south. He relentlessly drove his soldiers for he knew Ramseur's plight was grave. A private in Breckinridge's Division observed Rodes' infantry column passing south: "They were footsore and some almost crying with fatigue."[54] Mounted officers ranged the column, screaming at the men to push the pace. As the sweating soldiers approached Winchester an incident occurred which relieved the tension. They were overtaken by a carriage driven at a breakneck pace with Union cavalry only a short distance behind. Rodes recognized the passenger as Mrs. John Gordon, who despite Early's sneering comments, was never far from her husband's side. Smiling, Rodes tipped his hat and threw a skirmish line across the road to discourage the bluecoats as Mrs. Gordon sped by to a hearty cheer.[55]

Two of Sheridan's three corps deployed for battle. Brig. Gen. George Getty's 2nd Division aligned on the Union left with Brig. Gen. James B. Ricketts' 3rd Division alongside. In reserve was Brig. Gen. David A. Russell's 1st Division, all of Wright's VI Corps. Loosely attached to Ricketts' right was the XIX Corps Division of Brig. Gen. Cuvier Grover with Brig. Gen. William Dwight's Division closely following.[56] Five massive blue-clad divisions were thus prepared to step off upon the signal gun.

As the Southern units arrived on the plateau about 10 A.M. Gordon's men deployed on the far left and three of Rodes' Brigades were positioned between Gordon and Ramseur, all within cover of woods.[57] The tired gray-backs had barely won their race. Grover's two brigades advanced smartly on the Confederate left, gaining some advantage on Evans' Georgia Brigade of Gordon's Division despite sporadic Confederate artillery. Suddenly, the gunners of Lt. Col. C.M. Braxton and Col. T.H. Carter got their range with canister and case and it seemed as if the Federals hit a stone wall.[58] Gordon's men charged with a volley and a yell.[59] Despite General Emory's fury, Grover's entire division turned and ran for the rear, stopping only when Dwight's Division moved on line to curb the gray-backs. When the signal cannon boomed, Getty's and Ricketts' Divisions stepped out en masse as if on dress parade. But within a few hundred yards, Confederate artillery began to punch holes in their ranks. Gradually the two divisions lost contact in the rough terrain and a gap of several hundred yards ensued. Battle's Brigade of Rodes' Division arrived late and Rodes wisely held them for just such an opportunity. Swiftly he threw the Alabamians into the gap in a wild, full-out charge, soldiers sprinting at top speed and screaming. Ramseur's Division had been slowly driven backward and were almost at the point of collapse. As the stronger of Ramseur's troops formed another line and attempted to build adequate fire, Rodes' Old Alabama Brigade charged out of the woods almost beside their position. A private in Ramseur's Brigade recalled:

> we had been in line only a short time when muskets began to crack on our left. This cracking became a perfect roar as the cannon joined in and then the rebel yell. This was celestial music to our ears. Rodes had gotten up and was attacking Sheridan's flank. Soon we saw the enemy running back and those in our front began to run. I don't think I ever heard such a noise as was made when Rodes started in. It sounded as if every tree in the woods was falling down and a terrific thunder storm was raging in the woods. When our men heard all this noise and saw the Yankee's running, they got over their panic and started to return, back down the road.[60]

The two Union corps were split asunder and driven in panic. Only the prompt reaction of Brig. Gen. Emory Upton of Russell's Division in committing his brigade into the gap and taking horrible casualties prevented a complete rout of the VI and XIX Corps.[61] As his line moved forward Rodes spurred to

Third Battle of Winchester

Rodes' Division advanced to attack through these fields alternating with groves of trees. Rodes was struck down riding closely behind the line of battle.

Robert Carter

his left flank and conferred with John Gordon. Unable to locate Early, the two officers determined that their only recourse was to continue to attack the enemy, and cause as much confusion as possible.[62] Union numbers were so great that any other plan seemed to invite disaster. Rodes galloped back to his lines being joined by Brig. Gen. William R. Cox, who miraculously would survive this war despite a stunning total of eleven combat wounds.[63] Cox and Rodes proceeded through a strip of woods, emerging into a large open field in full view of masses of blue-coated soldiers.[64] Rodes, noting their uncertainty, stood in his stirrups yelling loudly, "Charge them, boys, charge them!"[65] as the field officers bawled, "Guide Center, Charge!" The brigades smoothly moved forward as an enemy battery opened. The gunners immediately found the range and almost every shell burst in the faces of the attackers. Rodes was riding a few paces behind the first line and his huge black horse, which he had ridden so long, became excited under the shell bursts, Rodes holding him with difficulty.[66] Sgt. Marcus Herring, assigned to sharpshooter duty, was making his way left to right as the sharpshooters peeled off to rejoin their regiments. He looked back to the formation to see General Rodes lean forward for an instant, then fall headlong from his horse.[67] As Rodes, struck with a shell fragment in the head, fell lifeless to the ground his splendid black mare panicked and ran to the rear.[68] Herring ran to catch her bridle and lead her behind a low hill where she was protected from bullets.[69] An aide arrived and took charge of the steed, the proud gift to a grateful officer from his friends in Lynchburg.

Rodes' men continued to drive the enemy, sometimes in hand-to-hand fighting, with scores of blue-coats lying down in ravines to be taken captive later. The excited Confederates rushed across open fields and into another timbered tract only to find their numbers diminished. Gradually they fell back, forming a new line in the fields. As the battle line reformed, Capt. Robert Park, a stellar member of that "damned chicken-thieving" 12th Alabama, experienced an unusual premonition which he described as:

> Maj. Peyton, A.A.G. to Maj. Gen. Rodes rode up, and an indescribable, unexplained something, I know not what carried me to his side, as he sat motionless upon his horse. I had heard nothing, not even a rumor, nor a whispered suggestion, yet something impelled me to ask in a low tone, "Major, has General Rodes been killed?", In an equally low, subdued tone that gallant officer answered, "Yes, but keep it to yourself, do not let the men know"....This dreadful news of Rodes' sudden death, at such a critical moment, distressed and grieved me beyond expression. There was no better officer in the entire army than he, very few as brave, skillful, and thoroughly trained. His men regarded him as second only to General Lee, excelled by none other.[70]

Rodes was struck at about 2 P.M. just as Confederate troops appeared to be sweeping forward to an impressive victory. The XIX Federal Corps was badly shaken and had left the field and Wright's VI Corps was barely hanging on despite the heroics of Upton and his men.[71] But Sheridan had more troops to utilize and he did not hesitate. Crook's two divisions were advanced into the area vacated by the XIX Corps; fresh Union batteries were dispatched to critical points and from north of Redbud a seemingly endless column of blue-coated cavalry advanced at the trot, sabers flashing in the sun. Confederate cavalry had been driven back on the infantry, completely defeated by their Union foes.[72] The Confederate line fell back, step by step, until almost in the environs of Winchester, fighting gamely until darkness fell. A Confederate veteran recalled that "in all the battles I had been in, I had never seen our army driven off the field before."[73]

Rodes' aides located a field ambulance in which the slain officer's remains were removed from the battlefield. Fighting through crowds of ambulances, medical wagons, and ordnance carriers, Captain Randolph of Rodes' staff, along with his driver, slowly maneuvered the ambulance down Market Street and eventually out onto the Valley Pike.[74] As the Confederates retreated south, the pike was soon packed with horses, men, and wagons, but Randolph and his driver maintained their pace. Early on September 20, the ambulance topped Hudd's Hill at New Market and moved safely behind Early's line.[75] Randolph dispatched a rider to carry the sad news ahead to Staunton to inform a pregnant Mrs. Virginia Rodes that she

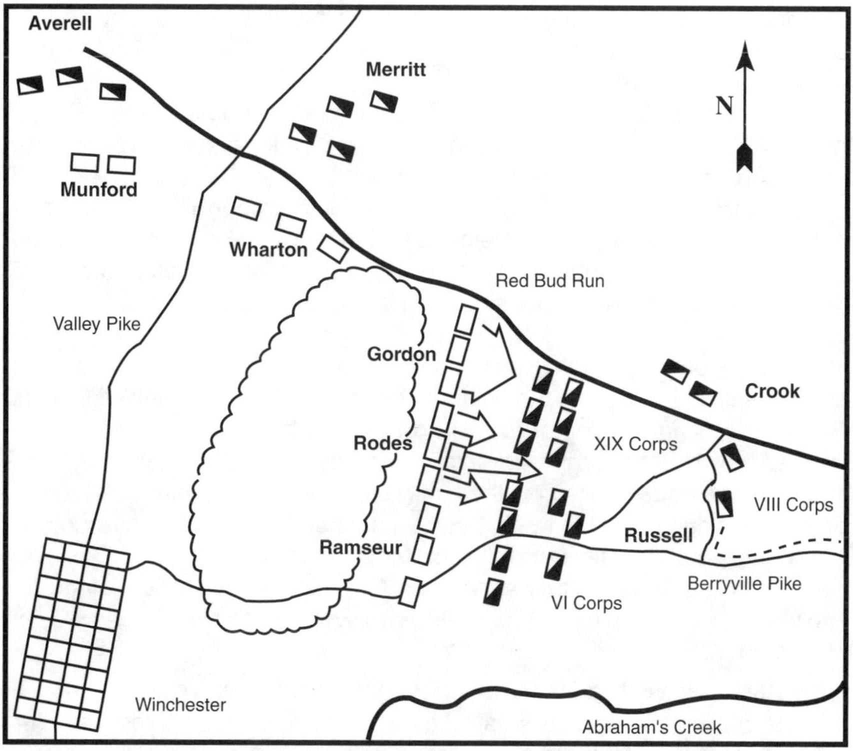

Third Battle of Winchester, September 19, 1864

About 3 P.M. the forward progress of Sheridan's VI and XIX Federal Corps toward Winchester was abruptly halted by Confederate counterattack. Gordon's Division assaulted the XIX Corps, and Rodes opportunistically threw Battle's Alabama Brigade into a gap between the two Federal corps. The XIX Corps and most of the VI Corps were driven in rout from the field. But Rodes was slain as he rode behind Battle's line, and Federal General Upton rallied Russell's Division of the VI Corps to plug the Confederate breakthrough. Soon Crook's reserve VIII Corps arrived and with capable assistance of Merritt's and Averell's Cavalry drove Early's army slowly but deliberately back through Winchester.

was now a widow. She was visiting with Robert's sister, Sallie Rodes Nelson, in the Staunton area, and the two young women made arrangements to entrain for Lynchburg on the next available carriage.[76] An exhausting train journey of almost seven hours followed, and late on the evening of September 21, Rodes' body, accompanied by his wife, his sister, and Captain Randolph, was met at the Lynchburg depot by friends and relatives. An ambulance and carriages awaited to convoy Robert Rodes on his last journey to Harrison Street.[77]

Swiftly, preparations were completed, and on Friday, September 23 at 9:30 A.M. a lengthy procession of military units, masonic representatives, and civic leaders formed on Main Street.[78] All businesses in the city were ordered closed and large crowds began to gather along the procession route. The various units stretched for four city blocks when assembled, and promptly swung into motion at 10 A.M. with the first notes of a dirge. Slowly the marchers progressed up the steep hill amid a wall of silent, black-dressed mourners. Halting at the Rodes residence on Harrison Street, the procession stood mutely as pallbearers bore the casket down the circular stairway to the hearse, the column now joined by the grieving widow and family. Following the roll of muffled drums the black-draped hearse proceeded slowly amid a turnout remembered as the largest in the city's history.[79] As the cortege reached the family plot, the hearse halted, and Robert Rodes was carried to his resting place as virtually the city's entire population witnessed. The Reverend Doctor James Ramsey of the 2nd Presbyterian Church read the burial service as Gen. Robert E. Rodes joined the growing list of martyrs of the Southern revolution.[80] Maj. Green Peyton commented:

> Robert Rodes had for some months prior to his death written much to his wife of his soul's salvation and had a hope that god had forgiven him for his long separation from the church. Amid papers and maps found on his person, were two earnest prayers which he had written on cards.[81]

While not yet a supplicant, Rodes was seeking his peace with God in which he believed, and under whose blessings he was interred. One knowledgeable observer recalled that Robert Rodes was laid to rest in the same fields he had played upon as a child.[82]

Following Reverend Ramsey's benediction an aged, grey-haired firing squad fired a ragged salute. While the number of significant Confederate officers slain in battle would continue to increase as the conflict thundered to its now inevitable conclusion, few officers of such rank were so universally admired, loved, and respected by the soldiers who stood in the ranks as Robert E. Rodes. The distinctions and affinities of class rank so prevalent in the Southern armies seemed to disappear in the affection of Rodes for his men. He was tough on them, stern, even overbearing at times, but was never condescending to those who followed his flag. He lived with them, he was of them, he protected their welfare and attempted to alleviate their needs. Yet Rodes had ordered them to battle and ultimately to death on many occasions. Now Robert Emmett Rodes made that same sacrifice.

Warfare in the valley arena continued furiously but with decreasing Southern success. General Early completed a remarkable evacuation from Winchester, again falling back to Fisher's Hill near Strasburg. His little army seemed to have been beaten badly by Sheridan but had actually inflicted more casualties on the enemy (5,018) than it suffered (4,000).[83]

Presbyterian Cemetery, Lynchburg

Grave of Maj. Gen. Robert E. Rodes.

Penny Swisher

Rodes' friend, Stephen Ramseur, was transferred to command his division on September 20. Phillip Sheridan was not idle for long. Realizing he now had every advantage, he pushed the issue. Assaulting Early at Fisher's Hill on September 22, he released his cavalry around Early's flanks and soon the gray-clad infantry gave way and ran. Rodes' Division for the first time raced pell-mell from a battlefield, joining the remainder of the Confederate army in falling back twenty-five miles to Woodstock.[84] Again Union cavalry swept unopposed up the Valley Pike to Staunton, and when this blue tide finally receded the Valley was devastated from Staunton to Winchester.[85] Smoke rose from every farm and village as a trail of devastation marked the trail of the Northern riders.

After reinforcement by Kershaw's Division, Early made an attempt to wrest control and initiative from Sheridan. On October 19, he surprised the Federal commander with an early morning attack out of the fog at Cedar Creek. But the fog and mist created confusion among the Confederates and after initial Southern success the blue-coats rallied. Confederate retreat became a mindless rout and the Southern army a rabble.[86] Stephen D. Ramseur was shot down as he attempted to stem the tide of running men and abandoned to the enemy.

Dejected, the little Valley Army retreated. Early had reached the absolute nadir of his military career. Always outnumbered, his little army had long been blessed with outstanding divisional leaders. Now Ramseur and Rodes were gone, Breckinridge transferred, and John Gordon, Early's last remaining bulwark, fell into a serious disagreement with the army commander.

Gordon was critical of Early's overconfidence prior to the battle of Winchester and became more outspoken over Early's halting the advance at Cedar Creek before the Federal VI Corps was defeated. Early's problems did not end with Gordon, for his proliferation for strong drink now became an issue of public concern as the *Richmond Enquirer* insisted he resign. Several soldiers attested to General Early's drinking on the battlefield at Fisher's Hill.[87] But other publications defended his efforts in the face of so numerous an enemy.[88] Many of the claims and aspirations thrown at Early were correct, but even his detractors were to admit that he bravely and stubbornly resisted Sheridan against odds that few would have contested. Cantankerous, devious, and opinionated Jubal Early surely was, but he gave his heart and soul to the cause of Southern independence and later became its most unreconstructed rebel.

Sadly, Sheridan's blue-coated cavalry soon moved at will over the roads of the sacred Shenandoah—a valley of lush golden fields of grain, interspaced with outcroppings of limestone, watched over by sentinel peaks of the blue mountain ranges on either flank. An upland valley populated by hillside farmers of Scot-Irish and German descent. Serious, stern, hardworking people, who worshipped weekly in their Presbyterian and German Reformed churches, owned few slaves, but supported the Confederacy avidly because they were Virginians, exempt from outside interference. A valley which had witnessed much of the war from the whirlwind brilliance of Stonewall to the avert bravery of a battalion of young cadets; the senseless, vindictive destruction of David Hunter to the bulldog, stubborn obstinacy of Jubal Early. Their homes and villages had long been defended by a line of gray heroes. Now the shadows of defeat loomed large, and the memories of those gray-clad men who died to keep that valley free would seem to have been sacrificed in vain. General officers were also numbered in those indomitable defenders, a forgotten list of "Generals in Gray": Turner Ashby, William "Grumble" Jones, Stephen D. Ramseur, and Robert Emmett Rodes.

EPILOGUE

Throughout the battle-filled Confederate career of Robert Emmett Rodes, he consistently demonstrated courage, energy, persistence, and aggressiveness in battle. Fellow soldiers, of various ranks, who observed his actions attested to his attributes and abilities as a military officer. Such a stalwart as John Brown Gordon, who like Rodes, saw his share of tough fights, stated that "Robert Rodes had few equals in either army."[1] Maj. Green Peyton, Rodes' close friend and aide, described him as "firmness tempered with kindness, courage too little tempered with prudence."[2] Cavalry commander and ex-classmate Tom Munford recalled: "I knew him well at V.M.I., no truer knight ever flashed a blade or responded to bugle notes,"[3] while Bryan Grimes, who led a brigade in his division, stated: "Gen. Rodes was one of the bravest and best officers of the Confederate Army."[4] Generals Lee, Jackson, Longstreet, D.H. Hill, A.P. Hill, Stuart, Ewell, and Early all commented with praise and pride on the bravery, skill, and battlefield performance of Robert Rodes. Of even more acclaim are the comments and letters of scores of officers and men who followed his lead.

Despite this list of accomplishments and accolades, in the war for Southern independence, Rodes is truly the South's forgotten "Warrior in Gray"—forgotten by his native state, Virginia, as well as his adopted one, Alabama. An old veteran recalled: "It is surprising to me that so little has been published about one so high in rank, so brilliant in service, or so glorious in death."[5] No monuments to his triumphs stand at Chancellorsville, South Mountain, or Spotsylvania Court House. No marker to his death rises on the field of 3rd Winchester. Why have his significant contributions and military achievements become lost or forgotten in the volumes of material on Confederate Military History?

The reasons are multiple, and surely his death in combat and the aforementioned hardships of his family were important factors. A panoply of excellent Southern divisional and brigade commanders, who lost their lives in combat, share his fate, largely underappreciated and often unknown. Another cause which may be unique to Rodes was the absence of Battle Reports after his report on the battle of Gettysburg. He was a central figure in the army's actions in the Wilderness, at Spotsylvania, South Anna, and Cold Harbor. He then accompanied Early to Lynchburg, on toward Washington, and participated in the Valley Army's engagements until his death on September 19, 1864. Although Rodes attempted to complete these accounts, the day-to-day activity and pressure of divisional leadership prevented his filing these reports. Thus, in order to follow his participation in 1864 clashes and events, we must delve into the diaries, battle reports, and letters of others who were present and in some cases read large numbers of reports and accounts in a search for the truth.

Finally, for reasons known only to themselves, none of Rodes' contemporaries, save one, attempted the task of penning his life and career. Maj. Green Peyton wrote a brief but noteworthy biographical sketch for the Virginia Military Institute Memorial Volume, an account which has been oft cited by newspapers and biographical dictionaries. Perhaps John Gordon or Jubal Early could have written in an informative manner of Rodes, who although not close to either, was well known by each. Regrettably, the writings of these officers focus on their own efforts, deeds, and arguments, ignoring contributions of others.

Rodes' fine martial bearing and unassuming, modest demeanor concealed well the ambitious aspects of his personality. His driving desire to succeed was infused in his being when as a young man he became responsible for his own prospects, without financial egress. In the midst of the great egos of military leaders of the Confederacy his own ego was decidedly more sublimated than most. Only in a few distinct instances can Rodes' ambitious nature be attested.

When at Chancellorsville, Rodes yielded control of the 2nd Corps to General Stuart "For the good of the service," he still carefully wrote a report that clarified his position in that "I yielded...not because I thought him entitled to it...nor because I was unwilling to assume the responsibility...but because I inferred that Gen. Jackson or Gen. A.P. Hill had so ordered."[6] Rodes was quite properly stating that his acquiescence was based on his understandings that it was desired by his senior officers and that he in no way shrank from the task. He was not pleased to learn that a major on Jackson's staff made that decision and not "Stonewall" himself.

On another occasion while writing to General Ewell, Rodes guardedly revealed his ambition. He apologized to the general for the unfinished battle reports and assured him of a rapid completion. Rodes added:

> I hope you will not send in yours (report) till mine is before you, for I depend on you alone to get my share of the glory of the actions of the Wilderness and the 12th of May, which have so far reflected glory on all concerned on our side except me.[7]

Reluctant to speak out for fame on his own behalf but disturbed with those who roared so brazenly of their deeds and accomplishments, Robert sought to have his superiors support his contributions and deeds.

It was said that Rodes benefitted by the quality of those subordinate officers who served his command. Surely such men as John Gordon, when a regimental commander, and brigadiers like Stephen Ramseur, Junius Daniel, George Doles, Bryan Grimes, and Cullen Battle, all who performed well and who rose to high rank, were an asset to any command. But a measure of successful leadership can be found in the development of one's subordinates. Rodes' record of constant praise and open recommendation of merited subordinates is unrivaled by any, save Lee. He never hesitated to share the glory earned by his division.

We can best assess Rodes' military success by looking at his two principal levels of command and presupposing a third. As a brigadier general Robert Rodes stood out among a phalanx of truly exceptional brigadiers from his initial action. The stirring charge of his Alabama Brigade at Seven Pines established Rodes' reputation amid a promising field of reckless, hard-driving young officers, who under Lee's tutelage, would rise by ability alone to make Lee's army a truly feared force. Rodes' actions denote a racehorse straining against the reins. The epitome of aggression, his whole demeanor changed when battle was joined. Yet he retained his units under stern control, managed them adroitly, and made cool, clear adjustments under fire.

From that sudden fame and recognition, Robert matured as a brigade commander. At South Mountain, in a critical role, he defied a reinforced Federal corps with his brigade of 1,200 men, demonstrating mastery of defensive tactics, as he stubbornly gave ground while maintaining an aggressive face to the enemy. By the return from Maryland, Rodes was ranked among the army's best; aggressive and hard-hitting in attack, stubborn in defense, skillful in maneuver, and following the best tradition of Lee's army, he led from the front.

As major general of a division Rodes' career began auspiciously at Chancellorsville, but suffered through some early difficulties. His actions in Jackson's flank attack were highly commended and earned his rapid promotion and appointment to division command. But in his next action at Gettysburg he experienced setbacks and drew criticism. Arriving on the field he was aggressive, impulsive, almost rash, just as he led his brigade at Seven Pines. But these traits, which gained such praise for a brigadier, were not as prized in the commander of a division, for the roles differed substantially.

Divisional command demanded coordination of four to five brigades and application of their composite fire power at the correct time and place. While leadership was demanded at both levels, divisional command required a marked increase in management skills. Robert Rodes was a naturally gifted leader but the ability to manage a division was not as innate. He was forced to learn those abilities which brought out the best in his brigade leaders and created a division stronger than the sum of its brigades. And learn those skills he did! No better assessment of his increased abilities can be attested than his command of the salient at Spotsylvania, May 12, 1864. He coolly and in a calculated manner inserted the reinforcing brigades, sent him by Lee, into a fluid battle line where their firepower was most needed, utilizing the abilities of officers and men. Never did he consider leading a charge to clear the salient as he might have pondered at Gettysburg. He calmly led, inspiring each soldier to his best effort, as he held the front together until Lee's reserve line was complete; then he skillfully withdrew the exhausted veterans. He had learned to "manage" a fight, and on that day on that field, he managed to save the army.

Col. Thomas H. Carter, in presenting a speech to the Lee Camp, Confederate Veterans, posed the question often echoed by a score of others. Why was a soldier with such qualities not offered corps command? Any answer would be conjecture, for the timing of such promotion was never right, as Early was always the senior major general in the corps. A more germane question might be, could Rodes have led a corps successfully?

Surely the qualities of his leadership, his widespread appreciation by the rank and file, and his characteristic of following a rising curve of performance might lead one to venture, yes. Possibly as good or better than Ewell, Early, or even A.P. Hill, or Anderson. But as good as Jackson or Longstreet? Probably not!

Still Rodes is a figure worthy of considerable military repute. His ambition was documented although veiled by quiet modesty. There is, however, no evidence that the tall, martial officer desired to be anything more than he was: ranked among the best divisional captains in a gray-clad army which attained mythical fame, the Army of Northern Virginia.

During the later stages of the war, Rodes was the steady, reliable performer in Jubal Early's brave little army that dared to shake the gates of the Federal capital. As divisions shrunk to the size of brigades, and brigades to that of regiments, Rodes' loyal soldiers fought well and marched well, day after day, in action after action. Newspaper accounts consistently cited, "Rodes bore the brunt of the action" or "Rodes' brigade led the advance," or even "Rodes conducted the retreat."[8] His name and his division became synonymous with dependability, reliability, and trust; terms that denote the characteristics of his service to the Confederacy.

Capt. P.J. White possibly summarized best when he wrote:

> If modesty and merit be the criterion of meed and death upon the field of battle the seal of heroic mold, then unquestionably the hero of Seven Pines, the Right Bower of Stonewall Jackson at

Chancellorsville, the hero of the Salient at Spotsylvania, the paladin of Winchester and a host of other hard-won fields has carved with his sword, the right to a place among his compeers, and beside his great commander.[9]

RODES'S BRIGADE AT SEVEN PINES

Down by the valley 'mid thunder and lightning,
Down by the valley 'mid jettings of light,
Down by the deep-crimsoned valley of Richmond,
The twenty-five hundred moved on to the fight
Onward, still onward, to the portals of glory,
to the sepulchered chambers, yet never dismayed,
Down by the deep-crimsoned valley of Richmond
Marched the bold soldiers of Rodes's Brigade.

See ye the fires and flashings still leaping,
Hear ye the pelting and beating of storm?
See ye the banners of proud Alabama
In front of her columns move steadily on?
Hear ye the music that gladdens each comrade
As it floats through the air 'mid the torrent of sounds?
Hear ye! booming down the red valley
Carter unbuckles his swarthy old hounds.

Twelfth Mississippi, I saw your brave columns
Rush through the channels of living and dead.
Twelfth Alabama, why weep your old war horse?
He died as he wished, in the gear at your head
Seven Pines, ye will tell on the pages of glory
How the blood of the south ebbed away 'neath the shade,
How the lads of Virginia fought in the red valley
And fell in the columns of Rodes's Brigade.

Fathers and mothers, ye weep for your jewels;
Sisters, ye weep for your brothers in vain;
Maidens, ye weep for your sunny-eyed lovers.
Weep, for they never will come back again!
Weep ye, but know what a halo of light
Encircles each chamber of death newly made;
And know ye that victory, the shrine of the mighty,
Stands forth on the banners of Rodes's Brigade.

Daughters of Southland, come, bring ye bright flowers
Weave ye a chaplet for the brow of the brave;
Bring ye some emblem of freedom and victory,
Bring ye some emblem of death and the grave,
Bring ye some motto befitting a hero,

Bring ye exotics that never will fade;
Come to the deep-crimsoned valley of Richmond
And crown the young chieftain who led his brigade.

Author: Unknown

General Robert E. Rodes

National Archives

NOTES

INTRODUCTION

1. Douglas S. Freeman, *The South to Posterity* (New York: Scribner's and Sons, 1951), p. 73.
2. Archives of Virginia Military Institute, Lexington, Va.
3. Hampden Osborne, Columbus, Miss., *Southern Historical Society Papers*, vol. 30, 1917, p. 227.
4. Douglas S. Freeman, *Lee's Lieutenants* (New York: Scribner, Inc., 1942), vol. 2, p. xxxviii; vol. 3, p. xliv.
5. Thomas Carter, Archives of Virginia Military Institute, Lexington, Va.
6. Douglas S. Freeman, *Lee's Lieutenants*, vol. 1, p. xx.

CHAPTER 1

1. James Power Smith, Rev., "Stonewall Jackson's Last Battle," *Battles and Leaders of the Civil War,* Clarence Buel and Robert Johnson, eds. (Secaucus, N.J.: Castle Press, 1897), pp. 207–8.
2. Douglas S. Freeman, *Lee's Lieutenants* (New York: Scribner, Inc., 1942), vol. 3, p. xliv.
3. Maude J. Larkin, "General Robert E. Rodes," *The Critic,* Literary Magazine, Lynchburg High School, Lynchburg, Va. , June 1907, p. 10.
4. Rose Faulkner Yancy, *Lynchburg and its Neighbors* (Richmond, Va.: J.W. Ferguson Co., 1935), p. 402.
5. Presbyterian Cemetery, Lynchburg, Va.
6. Will of David Rodes, Court House, Lynchburg, Va.
7. Yancy, p. 402.
8. W. Asbury Christian, *Lynchburg and its People* (Lynchburg, Va.: J.P. Bell Press, 1900), p. 85.
9. Rodes Family Genealogical Study, unpublished paper prepared by Frances Robertson, Archives, Jones Memorial Library, Lynchburg, Va.
10. Allen S. Chambers, *Lynchburg: An Architectural History* (Charlottesville, Va.: University of Virginia Press, 1981), p. 54.
11. Letter from Martha Ann Rodes to her Sister, Feb. 14, 1836, Archives of Handley Library, Winchester, Va.
12. Ibid.

13. Yancy, p. 61.
14. Dorothy T. Potter and Clifton W. Potter, *Lynchburg: The Most Interesting Spot* (Lynchburg, Va.: Progress Printing Corp., 1976), p. 51.
15. Phillip L. Scruggs, *The History of Lynchburg, Virginia, 1786–1946* (Lynchburg, Va.: J.P. Bell, 1972), p. 81.
16. Letter from Virginius Rodes to David Rodes, Aug. 14, 1841, Archives of Handley Library, Winchester, Va.
17. Ibid.
18. Letter from David Rodes to Col. Francis Smith, May 23, 1848, Archives of Virginia Military Institute, Lexington, Va.
19. Will of David Rodes, Court House, Lynchburg, Va.
20. Presbyterian Cemetery, Lynchburg, Va.
21. Will of David Rodes.
22. William Couper, *One Hundred Years at V.M.I.* (Richmond, Va.: Garrett and Massie, 1939), vol. 1, p. 5.
23. Ibid., p. 8.
24. Ibid.
25. *Washington Post*, March 31, 1957.
26. Ibid.
27. Couper, vol. 1, p. 35.
28. Ibid., p. 31.
29. Curriculum Guide 1848, Virginia Military Institute, Lexington, Va.
30. Couper, vol. 1, p. 68.
31. Class Standings 1846, Archives of Virginia Military Institute, Lexington, Va.
32. Letter from Col. Francis Smith to Gen. David Rodes, Feb. 11, 1847, Archives of Virginia Military Institute, Lexington, Va.
33. Class Standings 1847, Archives of Virginia Military Institute, Lexington, Va.
34. Letter from Col. Smith to David Rodes, May 23, 1848, Archives of Virginia Military Institute, Lexington, Va.
35. Class Standings 1848, Archives of Virginia Military Institute, Lexington, Va.
36. Thomas H. Carter, Remarks on the Presentation of a Portrait of Gen. Robert Rodes to Lee Camp, Sons of Confederate Veterans, Archives of Virginia Military Institute, Lexington, Va.
37. Letter of William Yancy, Feb. 28, 1848: Letter of Col. Smith, Feb. 22,1848, Archives of Handley Library, Winchester, Va.
38. Letter of Col. Smith, Feb. 22, 1848, Handley Library, Winchester, Va.
39. Letter from Gen. Rodes to Col. Smith, May 25, 1848, Archives of Virginia Military Institute, Lexington, Va.
40. Archives of Virginia Military Institute, Lexington, Va.
41. Couper, vol. 1, p. 184.
42. Ibid., p. 189.
43. Ibid., p. 233.
44. Ibid., p. 215.
45. Ibid., p. 221.
46. Ibid.
47. Letter from Robert E. Rodes to David Rodes, May 2, 1850, Archives of Handley Library, Winchester, Va.
48. Ibid.

49. Minutes of North River Navigation Company, July 6, 1850, Private Collection of T.G. Hobbs, Lynchburg, Va.
50. Ibid., Sept. 27, 1850.
51. Letter from Robert E. Rodes to Col. Francis Smith, Sept. 23, 1850, Archives of Virginia Military Institute, Lexington, Va.
52. Letter from Col. Smith to Robert E. Rodes, Sept. 24, 1850, Archives of Virginia Military Institute, Lexington, Va.
53. Couper, vol. 1, p. 249.
54. Jennings C. Wise, *The Military History of the Virginia Military Institute, 1839–1865* (Lynchburg, Va.: J.P. Bell Press, 1915), p. 67.
55. Couper, vol. 2, p. 249.
56. Minutes of North River Navigation Company, Nov. 29, 1850.
57. Letter from Robert E. Rodes to David Rodes, Jan. 3, 1851, Archives of Handley Library, Winchester, Va.
58. Ibid.
59. Green Peyton, "Robert E. Rodes," *Virginia Military Institute Memorial Volume*, Charles D. Walker, ed. (Philadelphia, Pa., 1875), p. 441.
60. Scruggs, p. 90.
61. Letter from Robert E. Rodes to David Rodes, Dec. 7, 1852, Archives of Handley Library, Winchester, Va.
62. Ibid., Nov. 17, 1851.
63. Ibid., Dec. 7, 1852.
64. Letter of Ms. Dimond, Archives of Virginia Military Institute, Lexington, Va.
65. Ibid.
66. Ibid.
67. Peyton, p. 441.
68. Ibid., p. 401.
69. Letter from Robert Rodes to Col. Smith, Aug. 5, 1856, Archives of Virginia Military Institute, Lexington, Va.
70. Ibid., Oct. 8, 1856.
71. Peyton, p. 401.
72. Letter from Col. Smith to Robert Rodes, Nov. 3, 1856, Archives of Virginia Military Institute, Lexington, Va.
73. Ibid.
74. Ibid., Dec. 9, 1856.
75. William Couper, *The New Market Cadets* (Charlottesville, Va.: Michie Co., 1933), p. 248.
76. Peyton, p. 401.
77. Letter from Robert Rodes to Col. Smith, June 7, 1859, Archives of Virginia Military Institute, Lexington, Va.
78. Letter from Col. Smith to Robert Rodes, June 20, 1859, Archives of Virginia Military Institute, Lexington, Va.
79. Letter from Robert Rodes to Col. Smith, Aug. 17, 1859, Archives of Virginia Military Institute, Lexington, Va.
80. Couper, vol. 1, pp. 350–51.
81. Ibid., p. 351.
82. Confederate Military History, Clement Evans, ed. (Atlanta, Ga.: Confederate Publishing Co., 1899), p. 73.
83. Letter from Robert Rodes to Col. Smith, Jan. 13, 1861, Archives of Virginia Military Institute, Lexington, Va.
84. Ibid.

CHAPTER 2

1. Bruce Levine, *Half Slave and Half Free: The Roots of Civil War* (New York: Hill and Wang Co., 1992), p. 160.
2. Robert V. Remini, *Andrew Jackson and the Course of American Freedom* (New York: Harper and Rowe, 1981), vol. 2, p. 137.
3. Ibid., p. 191.
4. Donald E. Reynolds, *Editors Make War: Southern Newspapers in the Secessionist Crisis* (Nashville, Tenn.: Vanderbilt University Press, 1970), p. 13.
5. Letter from Robert Rodes to Col. Smith, Jan. 13, 1861, Archives of Virginia Military Institute, Lexington, Va.
6. Ibid.
7. Ibid.
8. Ibid.
9. P.A. Cribbs, *Confederate Veteran,* vol. 21, p. 480.
10. Will of Robert E. Rodes, Apr. 13, 1861, Archives of Virginia Military Institute, Lexington, Va.
11. Walter L. Fleming, *Civil War and Reconstruction in Alabama* (New York: Columbia University Press, 1905), p. 221.
12. United States Archives, Washington, D.C.
13. Official Records of the Union and Confederate Armies (Washington, D.C.: U.S. War Department, 1880–1901), vol. 1, p. 444.
14. John E. Johns, *Florida During the Civil War* (Gainesville, Fla.: University of Florida Press, 1963), p. 26.
15. Vann C. Woodward, ed., *Mary Chesnut's Civil War* (New Haven, Conn.: Yale University Press, 1981), p. 6.
16. Ibid., p. 35.
17. Green Peyton, "Robert E. Rodes" *Virginia Military Institute Memorial Volume*, Charles Walker, ed., p. 441.
18. United States Archives.
19. J.W. Minnich, "Incidents of the Peninsular Campaign," *Confederate Veteran*, vol. 30, p. 55.
20. Susan Blackford, *Letters from Lee's Army* (New York: Scribner and Sons, 1947), p. 23.
21. Annette Tobert, *The Brothers' War* (New York: Time Books, 1988), p. 7. Letter from Thomas Lightfoot, 6th Alabama to His Mother, May 29, 1861.
22. United States Archives.
23. Blackford, p. 23.
24. Clement A. Evans, *Confederate Military History* (Atlanta, Ga.: Confederate Publishing Co., 1899), Alabama Volume, p. 86.
25. Official Records, vol. 2, p. 537.
26. James B. Fry, "McDowell's Advance to Bull Run," *Battles and Leaders* (Secaucus, N.J.: Castle Press, 1897), vol. 1, p. 177.
27. Ibid., p. 176.
28. Ibid., p. 179.
29. Christian G. Samito, "Robert Rodes: Warrior in Gray," *America's Civil War*, Jan. 1995, p. 48.
30. P.G.T. Beauregard, "The First Battle of Bull Run," *Battles and Leaders*, vol. 1, p. 201.
31. Campbell Brown, "General Ewell at Bull Run," *Battles and Leaders*, vol. 1, p. 260.
32. Ibid., p. 260.
33. Ibid.

34. Tobert, Maj. Eugene Blackford to His Father, July 22, 1861, p. 26.
35. Ibid.
36. Robert E. Park, *Sketches of the 12th Alabama Infantry* (Richmond, Va.: W. Ellis Jones, 1906), p. 6.
37. Jubal Anderson Early, *Jubal Early's Memoirs* (Baltimore, Md.: Nautical and Aviation Publishing Company of America, 1989), pp. 92–93.
38. Blackford, pp. 46–47.
39. Robert G. Hartje, *Van Dorn: The Life and Times of a Confederate General* (Nashville, Tenn.: Vanderbilt University Press, 1967), pp. 92–93.
40. Official Records, vol. 5, p. 1012.
41. Early, p. 50.
42. J. W. Reid, *History of the Fourth Regiment, South Carolina Volunteers* (Dayton, Ohio: Morningside Press, 1975), p. 57.
43. Unites States Archives.
44. *Battles and Leaders*, vol. 2, p. 201.
45. Samito, p. 49.
46. Stephen W. Sears, *To the Gates of Richmond: The Peninsular Campaign* (New York: Ticknor and Fields, 1992), p. 164.
47. Douglas S. Freeman, *R. E. Lee* (New York: Charles Scribner's Sons, 1946), vol. 2, p. 26.
48. Biographical Dictionary of the Confederacy, John Wakelyn, ed. (Westport, Conn.: Greenwood Press, 1977), p. 325.
49. Freeman, *R. E. Lee*, vol. 2, p. 28.
50. Early, p. 52.
51. Freeman, *R. E. Lee*, vol. 2, p. 24.
52. Ken Norman and C. E. Avery, "Notes on Pvt. Robert A. Ware, 6th Alabama," *Confederate Veteran*, vol. 1, 1997, p. 11.
53. Early, p. 56.
54. Ibid., p. 237.
55. Sears, p. 84.
56. Park, p. 27.
57. J.W. Minnich, "Incidents of the Peninsular Campaign," *Confederate Veteran*, vol. 30, p. 55.
58. Ibid.
59. Ibid.

CHAPTER 3

1. Joseph E. Johnston, "Manassas to Seven Pines," *Battles and Leaders*, Robert Johnson and Clarence Buel, eds. (Secaucus, N.J.: Castle Press, 1897), vol. 2, p. 208.
2. Official Records of the Union and Confederate Armies (Washington, D.C.: U.S. Government Printing Office, 1880–1901), vol. 11, pt. 3, p. 475.
3. *Richmond Examiner*, May 13, 1862, p. 1.
4. John M. Coski, "Drewry's Bluff," *The Confederate Veteran*, vol. 6, 1996, p. 18.
5. Russell J. Soley, "The Navy in the Peninsular Campaign," *Battles and Leaders*, vol. 2, p. 270.
6. Ibid., p. 269.
7. Coski, p. 21.
8. Soley, p. 270.
9. Jeffrey Wert, "The Battle of Seven Pines," *Civil War Times Illustrated*, pt. 1, Oct. 1988, pp. 24–25.

10. Stephen W. Sears, *To the Gates of Richmond: The Peninsular Campaign* (New York: Ticknor and Fields, 1992), p. 120.
11. Richard Wheeler, *Sword Over Richmond* (New York: Harper and Rowe, 1986), pp. 225–26.
12. Charles D. Wainwright, *A Diary of Battle*, Allen Nevins, ed. (New York: Hardcourt, Brace, and World, 1962), p. 75.
13. Wheeler, p. 226.
14. Douglas S. Freeman, *Lee's Lieutenants* (New York: Scribner's Inc., 1942), vol. 1, p. 224.
15. Johnston, *Battles and Leaders*, vol. 2, p. 211.
16. Porter Alexander, *Military Memoirs of a Confederate* (Dayton, Ohio: Morningside Press, 1990), p. 80.
17. William G. Piston, *Lee's Tarnished Lieutenant: James Longstreet and His Place in Southern History* (Athens, Ga.: University of Georgia Press, 1987), p. 33.
18. Hal Bridges, *Lee's Maverick General: Daniel Harvey Hill* (New York: McGraw-Hill Publishing, 1961), p. 39: Alexander, p. 80.
19. Report of Gen. R. E. Rodes, Battle of Seven Pines, June 7, 1862, Official Records, vol. 11, pt. 1, p. 971.
20. Ibid.
21. Gustavus Smith, "Two Days of Battle at Seven Pines," *Battles and Leaders,* vol. 2, p. 230.
22. Report of Robert Rodes, Official Records, vol. 11, pt. 1, p. 971.
23. Wert, pt. 2, p. 28.
24. Report of Col. C.C. Peques, 5th Alabama, Battle of Seven Pines, Official Records, vol. 11, pt. 1, p. 977.
25. William E. Dunn, "On the Peninsular: Civil War Letters of William E. Dunn," *Civil War Times Illustrated*, July 1985, p. 17.
26. Wert, pt. 2, p. 28.
27. Ibid.
28. Ibid., p. 24.
29. Report of Robert Rodes, Official Records, vol. 11, pt. 1, p. 973.
30. Wheeler, p. 232.
31. Official Records, vol. 11, pt. 1, pp. 971–73, 977–80.
32. Wheeler, p. 232.
33. Report of Robert Rodes, Official Records, vol. 11, pt. 1, p. 974.
34. Report of John Gordon, Official Records, vol. 11, pt. 1, p. 977.
35. Ralph L. Eckert, *John Brown Gordon: Soldier, Southerner, American* (Baton Rouge, La.: Louisiana State University Press, 1989), p. 27.
36. Letter from Robert Miller to his Cousin, June 25, 1862, *Virginia Magazine of History and Biography*, Forest Conner, ed., vol. 70, 1962, p. 85.
37. Letter from Richard Anderson to Daniel Harvey Hill, Oct. 26, 1867, Virginia State Library.
38. Report of Daniel H. Hill, Battle of Seven Pines, Official Records, vol. 11, pt. 1, p. 944.
39. Report of Micah Jenkins, Battle of Seven Pines, Official Records, vol. 11, pt. 1, pp. 947–49.
40. Report of Lt. Kirby, Battle of Seven Pines, Official Records, vol. 11, pt. 1, p. 796.
41. Alexander, p. 86.
42. Johnston, *Battles and Leaders*, vol. 2, p. 215.
43. Clifford Dowdy, "The Seven Days: The Emergence of Robert E. Lee" (New York: The Fairfax Press, 1978), pp. 126–27.
44. Sears, pp. 146–47.
45. Report of Daniel Harvey Hill, Official Records, vol. 11, pt. 1, p. 944.
46. Report of Robert Rodes, Official Records, vol. 11, pt. 1, p. 976.

47. Alexander, p. 83.
48. Sears, p. 148.
49. Heros Von Borcke, "The Prussian Remembers," Stuart Wright, ed., *Civil War Times Illustrated*, Feb. 1981, p. 42.
50. Robert E. Park, "Sketch of the 12th Alabama Infantry" (Richmond, Va.: Jones, 1906), p. 35.
51. John S. Tucker, "Diary of John S. Tucker: A Soldier From Alabama," Gary Wilson, ed., *Alabama Historical Quarterly*, vol. 43, Spring, 1981, p. 28.
52. Wert, pt. 2, p. 26.
53. Freeman, *Lee's Lieutenants,* vol. 1, p. 248.
54. Alexander, p. 77.
55. Freeman, *Lee's Lieutenants,* vol. 1, p. 238.
56. *Richmond Examiner*, May 22, 1861.
57. Joseph C. Elliott, *Lt. Gen. Richard Heron Anderson: Lee's Noble Soldier* (Dayton, Ohio: Morningside Press, 1985), pp. 9, 47.
58. James K. Swisher, *Prince of Edisto* (Berryville, Va.: Rockbridge Press, 1996), p. 54.
59. Report of Daniel H. Hill, Official Records, vol. 11, pt. 1, pp. 943–45.
60. Report of James Longstreet, Official Records, vol. 11, pt. 1, p. 279.
61. *Richmond Whig*, July 4, 1862.
62. Wert, p. 22.
63. Thomas L. Connelly, *The Marble Man: Robert E. Lee and His Image in American Society* (Baton Rouge, La.: Louisiana State University Press, 1978), p. 5.
64. James I. Robertson, *General A.P. Hill: The Story of a Confederate Warrior* (New York: Random House, 1987), p. 63.
65. *Richmond Examiner*, June 4, 1862, p. 2.
66. Connelly, p. 198.
67. Stephen W. Sears, *George B. McClellan: The Young Napoleon* (New York: Ticknor and Fields, 1988), p. 80.
68. Freeman, *R. E. Lee*, vol. 2, p. 89.
69. *Lee's Confidential Dispatches to Jefferson Davis*, Douglas Freeman, ed. (New York: Grady, McWhiney, Putnam, and Sons, 1957), pp. 10–12.
70. *Richmond Dispatch*, July 9, 1862.
71. Official Records, vol. 11, pt. 2, p. 499.
72. *Lynchburg Virginian*, Mar. 27, 1862.
73. Letter from Robert Rodes to Superintendent Smith, July 17, 1862, Archives of Virginia Military Institute, Lexington, Va.
74. Green Peyton, "Robert E. Rodes," *Virginia Military Institute Memorial Volume*, Charles Walker, ed. (Philadelphia, Pa.: 1875), p. 443.
75. Freeman, *R. E. Lee*, vol. 2, p. 118.
76. Sears, *McClellan*, p. 189.
77. Alexander, p. 77.
78. Sears, *McClellan*, p. 209.
79. Lawrence R. Laboda, *From Selma to Appomattox: The History of the Jeff Davis Artillery* (New York: Oxford University Press, 1994), p. 35.
80. Ibid., p. 37.
81. John Purifoy, *History of the Jeff Davis Artillery* (Montgomery, Ala.: Alabama Department of Archives and History, July 27, 1901, Unpublished), p. 25.
82. Freeman, *Lee's Lieutenants,* vol. 2, pp. 526–27.

83. Eckert, p. 28.
84. Freeman, *Lee's Lieutenants,* vol. 2, p. 533.
85. Official Records, vol. 11, pt. 2, pp. 625–26.
86. Park, p. 38.
87. Ibid.
88. Daniel H. Hill, "Lee's Attack North of the Chickahominy," *Battles and Leaders*, vol. 2, p. 359.
89. Alexander, p. 132.
90. Peyton, p. 443.
91. Official Records, vol. 11, pt. 2, p. 569.
92. Piston, pp. 74–75.
93. Freeman, *R. E. Lee*, vol. 2, p. 159.
94. Alexander, p. 133.
95. Official Records, vol. 11, pt. 2, p. 789.
96. Armistead L. Long, *Memoirs of Robert E. Lee* (Secaucus, N.J.: Blue and Gray Press, 1983), p. 175.
97. Sears, *McClellan*, p. 297.
98. Battles and Leaders, vol. 2, p. 381.
99. Letter from Thomas Coffey to his Mother, *Confederate Veteran*, Mar. 1918, p. 107.
100. Sears, *McClellan*, p. 222.
101. Alexander, p. 174.
102. Sears, *McClellan*, p. 345.
103. Constance Cary Harrison, "Richmond Scenes in 62," *Battles and Leaders*, vol. 2., p. 446.
104. William E. Dunn, "Letters of William Dunn," *Civil War Times Illustrated*, July 8, 1985, p. 17.
105. Letter from J.W. Reid to His Wife, June 29, 1862, *History of the Fourth Regiment: South Carolina Volunteers* (Dayton, Ohio: Morningside Press, 1975), p. 54.

CHAPTER 4

1. George L. Kilmer, "The Army of the Potomac at Harrison's Landing," *Battles and Leaders of the Civil War*, Clarence Buel and Robert Johnson, eds. (Secaucus, N.J.: Castle Press, 1897), vol. 2, p. 428.
2. *New York Tribune*, July 3, 1862.
3. *Chicago Tribune*, July 14, 1862.
4. Official Records of The Union and Confederate Armies (Washington, D.C.: United States War Department, 1880–1901), vol. 12, pt. 1, p. 476.
5. Ibid., pt. 3, pp. 936–37.
6. Ibid.
7. Ibid., p. 90.
8. Horace Montgomery, *Howell Cobb's Confederate Career* (Tuscaloosa, Ala.: Privately Published, 1959), p. 68.
9. Ralph L. Eckert, *John Brown Gordon: Soldier, Southerner, American* (Baton Rouge, La.: Louisiana State University Press, 1989), p. 30.
10. John M. Priest, *Before Antietam: The Battle for South Mountain* (New York: Oxford Press, 1992), p. 9.
11. Freeman, Douglas S., *Lee's Lieutenants* (New York: Scribner, Inc., 1942), vol. 2, p. 153.
12. Official Records, vol. 19, pt. 1, p. 814.
13. Alexander Hunter, "A High Private's Account of Sharpsburg," *Southern Historical Society Papers*, vol. 10, 1882, p. 510.

14. Otis D. Smith, "Reminiscences," Thach Papers, Southern Historical Collection, University of North Carolina, Chapel Hill, N.C., p. 6.
15. Priest, p. 34.
16. Green Peyton, "Robert E. Rodes," *Virginia Military Institute Memorial Volume*, Charles Walker, ed. (Philadelphia, Pa.: 1875), p. 443.
17. Report of John H. Steiner, M.D., Sanitary Commission Inspector (New York: Anson Randolph, 1862), p. 22.
18. Daniel Harvey Hill, "The Battle of South Mountain or Boonsboro," *Battles and Leaders*, vol. 2, p. 574.
19. Douglas S. Freeman, *R. E. Lee* (New York: Charles Scribner's Sons, 1946), vol. 2, p. 353.
20. Stephen W. Sears, *Landscape Turned Red: The Battle of Antietam* (New York: Ticknor and Fields, 1983), p. 82.
21. Mark Grimsley, "On the Edge of Disaster: Lee and McClellan at South Mountain," *Civil War Times Illustrated,* Nov. 1986, vol. 24, p. 20.
22. Freeman, *R. E. Lee,* vol. 2, p. 361.
23. Freeman, *Lee's Lieutenants,* vol. 2, p. 160.
24. Steiner, p. 24.
25. Ibid., p. 27.
26. Freeman, *R. E. Lee,* vol. 2, p. 365.
27. Walter H. Taylor, *Four Years with General Lee* (New York: Bonanza Books, 1962), p. 67.
28. Silas Colgrove, "The Finding of Lee's Lost Order," *Battles and Leaders*, vol. 2, p. 603.
29. George D. Grattan, "The Battle of Boonsboro Gap or South Mountain," *Southern Historical Society Papers*, vol. 39, 1914, p. 31; Official Records, vol. 19, pt. 1, p. 603.
30. Hal Bridges, *Lee's Maverick General: Daniel Harvey Hill* (New York: McGraw-Hill Publishers, 1961), pp. 96–97.
31. Hill, *Battles and Leaders*, vol. 2, p. 560.
32. Grattan, p. 34.
33. Ibid., p. 36.
34. Opposing Forces in the Maryland Campaign, *Battles and Leaders,* vol. 2, p. 601.
35. Priest, p. 131.
36. Grattan, p. 35.
37. Lawrence R. Laboda, *From Selma to Appomattox: The History of the Jeff Davis Artillery* (New York: Oxford University Press, 1994), p. 48.
38. Hill, *Battles and Leaders*, vol. 2, p. 570.
39. Report of Col. D.K. McRae, 5th North Carolina, Official Records, vol. 19, pt. 1, pp. 1041–43.
40. Ibid., pp. 563–64.
41. Ibid., vol. 10, pt. 1, p. 1041.
42. Jacob D. Cox, "Forcing Fox's Gap and Turner's Gap," *Battles and Leaders*, vol. 2, pp. 586–87.
43. Priest, p. 150.
44. Laboda, p. 49.
45. Priest, p. 175.
46. Robert E. Park, *Sketch of the 12th Alabama Infantry* (Richmond, Va.: Jones, 1906), p. 88.
47. Report of Robert Rodes, Official Records, vol. 19, pt. 1, p. 1034.
48. Official Records, vol. 19, pt. 1, pp. 908–9.
49. Grimsley, p. 23.
50. Hill, *Battles and Leaders*, p. 569.

51. Grattan, p. 39.
52. Official Records, vol. 19, pt. 1, pp. 459–60.
53. Priest, p. 215.
54. Guide to the Battlefield of Antietam, Jay Luvaas and Harold Nelson, eds., (Lawrence, Kans.: University of Kansas Press, 1996), p. 286.
55. Official Records, vol. 19, pt. 1, pp. 267–68.
56. Freeman, *Lee's Lieutenants,* vol. 2, p. 182.
57. Official Records, vol. 19, pt.1, p. 1034.
58. Priest, p. 227.
59. Park, p. 88.
60. Josiah R. Sypher, *History of the Pennsylvania Reserve Corps* (Lancaster, Pa: Barr and Co., 1865), p. 368.
61. Grimsley, p. 44.
62. Ibid., p. 45.
63. Priest, p. 232.
64. Park, p. 88.
65. Hill, *Battles and Leaders*, vol. 2, p. 572.
66. Park, p. 88.
67. Report of Robert Rodes, Official Records, vol. 19, pt. 1, p. 1035.
68. Priest, p. 239.
69. Ibid., p. 244.
70. Sypher, p. 87.
71. Official Records, vol. 19, pt. 1, p. 1035.
72. Ibid., p. 1036.
73. Ibid.
74. Harold R. Woodward, *The Confederacy's Forgotten Son: James L. Kemper* (Berryville, Va.: Rockbridge Press, 1994) p. 68.
75. Official Records, vol. 19, pt. 1, pp. 242–46.
76. Ibid., pp. 894–95.
77. Priest, p. 265.
78. Ibid., p. 268.
79. Official Records, vol. 19, pt. 1, pp. 249–50.
80. Report of Alfred Colquitt, Official Records, vol. 19, pt. 1, pp. 249–50.
81. Grattan, p. 33.
82. Report of Daniel Hill, Official Records, vol. 19, pt.1, p. 1021.
83. Ibid.
84. Eckert, p. 32.
85. Report of Robert Rodes, Official Records, vol. 19, pt. 1, p. 1035.
86. Sears, *Landscape Turned Red,* p. 159.
87. Report of Robert Rodes, Official Records, vol. 19, pt. 1, p. 1036.
88. Sears, *Landscape Turned Red*, p. 162.
89. Hunter Alexander, "A High Privates Account of Sharpsburg," *Southern Historical Society Papers*, vol. 11, 1883, p. 10.
90. Ibid., p. 10
91. Report of Robert Rodes, Official Records, vol. 19, pt. 1, p. 1036.
92. Official Records, vol. 19, pt. 1, p. 82.
93. Ibid., p. 160.

94. Bruce Catton, *The Army of the Potomac: Mr. Lincoln's Army* (Garden City, N.Y.: Doubleday Inc., 1962), p. 322.
95. Joseph T. Glatthaar, "Forged in Battle: The Civil War Alliance of Black Soldiers and White Officers" (New York: Free Press, 1990), p. 9.
96. Sears, *Landscape Turned Red*, p. 162.
97. Hal Bridges, "Lee's Maverick General: Daniel Harvey Hill" (New York: McGraw-Hill Publishers, 1961), p. 116.
98. Ibid.
99. Report of Robert Rodes, Official Records, vol. 19, pt. 1, p. 1036.
100. Catton, p. 259.
101. Freeman, *Lee's Lieutenants*, vol. 2, p. 206.
102. Catton, p. 274.
103. Ibid., p. 277.
104. John C. Walker, "Sharpsburg," *Battles and Leaders*, vol. 2, p. 677.
105. Sears, *Landscape Turned Red*, p. 213.
106. Report of Robert Rodes, Official Records, vol. 19, pt. 1, p. 1037.
107. Bridges, p. 120.
108. Catton, p. 284.
109. Jacob D. Cox, "The Battle of Antietam," *Battles and Leaders*, vol. 2, p. 645.
110. Charles C. Coffin, "Antietam Scenes," *Battles and Leaders*, vol. 2, p. 684.
111. Official Records, vol. 19, pt.1, p. 337.
112. Catton, p. 292.
113. Report of Gen. French, Official Records, vol. 19, pt. 1, p. 324.
114. Guide to Antietam, p. 197.
115. Report of Robert Rodes, Official Records, vol. 29, pt. 1, p. 1037.
116. Eckert, p. 36.
117. Catton, p. 295.
118. Report of Alfred Colquitt, Official Records, vol. 19, pt. 1, p. 1053.
119. Robert H. Miller, "Letters to His Family," *Virginia Magazine of History and Biography*, vol. 70, 1962, p. 87.
120. Freeman, *R.E. Lee,* vol. 2, p. 393.
121. Official Records, vol. 19, pt. 1, pp. 1036–38.
122. Report of Daniel H. Hill, Official Records, vol. 19, pt. 1, p. 1024.
123. Official Records, vol. 19, pt. 1. p. 848.
124. Laboda, p. 56.
125. Report of Capt. Boyce, Official Records, vol. 19, pt. 1, p. 943.
126. Official Records, vol. 19, pt. 1, p. 291.
127. Report of Gen. French, Official Records, vol. 19, pt.1, p. 327.
128. Freeman, *Lee's Lieutenants,* vol. 2, p. 212.
129. Eckert, p. 36.
130. Ibid., p. 37.
131. Report of Robert Rodes, Official Records, vol. 19, pt. 1, pp. 1038–39.
132. Opposing Forces in the Maryland Campaign, *Battles and Leaders*, vol. 2, p. 602.
133. Ibid.
134. Cox, p. 649.
135. Guide to Antietam, pp. 226–27.
136. Cox, p. 653.

137. David L. Thompson, "With Burnside at Antietam," *Battles and Leaders*, vol. 2, pp. 660–61.
138. Catton, p. 304.
139. Walter Clark, ed., *History of Several Regiments and Battalions from North Carolina in the Great War of 1864–1865* (Raleigh, N.C.: State Department of Archives and History, 1901), p. 437.
140. Freeman, *R.E. Lee,* vol. 2, p. 404.
141. Official Records, vol. 19, pt. 1, p. 1026.
142. James Longstreet, "The Invasion of Maryland," *Battles and Leaders*, vol. 2, p. 672.
143. Mary B. Mitchell, "A Woman's Recollections of Antietam," *Battles and Leaders*, vol. 2, p. 691.
144. Calvin Leach Diary, Sept. 18, 1862, Southern Historical Collection, University of North Carolina, Chapel Hill, N.C.
145. Official Records, vol. 19, pt. 1, p. 972.

CHAPTER 5

1. Peter W. Houck, *A Prototype of a Confederate Hospital Center in Lynchburg, Virginia* (Lynchburg, Va.: Warwick Publishing, 1986), p. 21.
2. Lawrence R. Laboda, *From Selma to Appomattox: The History of the Jeff Davis Artillery* (New York: Oxford University Press, 1994), pp. 64–65.
3. Official Records of the Union and Confederate Armies (Washington, D.C.: Government Printing Office, 1880–1901), vol. 19, pt. 2, pp. 656–57.
4. Laboda, p. 181.
5. Henry W. Thomas, "History of the Doles-Cook Brigade (Dayton, Ohio: Morningside Press, 1988), p. 70.
6. Gary W. Gallagher, *Stephen Dodson Ramseur: Lee's Gallant General* (Chapel Hill, N.C.: University of North Carolina Press, 1985), p. 48.
7. Ralph L. Eckert, *John Brown Gordon: Soldier, Southerner, American* (Baton Rouge, La: Louisiana State University Press, 1989), p. 38.
8. Hal Bridges, *Lee's Maverick General: Daniel Harvey Hill* (New York: McGraw-Hill, 1961), p. 151.
9. Ibid., p. 152.
10. Ibid.
11. Jay Luvaas and Harold Nelson, eds., *The United States Army Guide to the Battles of Chancellorsville and Fredericksburg* (Carlisle, Pa.: South Mountain Press, 1988), p. viii.
12. Official Records, vol. 19, pt. 2, p. 569.
13. Luvaas and Nelson, *United States Army Guide to the Battles of Chancellorsville and Fredericksburg*, p. vii.
14. James Longstreet, "The Battle of Fredericksburg," *Battles and Leaders of the Civil War* (Secaucus, N.J.: Castle Press, 1897), vol. 3, p. 70.
15. Official Records, vol. 19, pt. 2. pp. 553–54.
16. Ibid., p. 353.
17. Bridges, p. 154.
18. Bryan Grimes, *Extract of Letters of Maj. Gen. Bryan Grimes to His Wife*, Pulaski Cowper, ed. (Raleigh, N.C.: Broughton, Edwards, and Co. , 1883), p. 23.
19. Ibid., p. 49.
20. Laboda, p. 66.
21. Ibid., p. 67.
22. John Purifoy, "History of the Jeff Davis Artillery," unpublished account filed in Alabama Department of Archives and History, Montgomery, Ala., 1901, p. 38.

23. Letter from William R. Slaughter, 2nd Lt., 6th Alabama Inf., to his Mother and Sisters, Dec. 13, 1862, "The Brothers' War" (New York: Time Books, 1988), p. 118.
24. Purifoy, p. 38.
25. Report of Gen. Thomas Jackson, Official Records, vol. 21, pt. 1, pp. 630–32.
26. Laboda, p. 73.
27. Slaughter, p. 119.
28. Douglas S. Freeman, *Lee's Lieutenants* (New York: Scribner, Inc., 1942), vol. 2, pp. 370–71.
29. Slaughter, p. 120.
30. Report of Gen. Thomas Jackson, Official Records, vol. 21, pt. 1, p. 634.
31. Luvaas and Nelson, *United States Army Guide to the Battles of Chancellorsville and Federicksburg*, p. 33.
32. Ibid.
33. Longstreet, *Battles and Leaders*, vol. 3, p. 81.
34. Bruce Catton, *The Army of the Potomac: Mr. Lincoln's Army* (Garden City, N.Y.: Doubleday Inc., 1962), p. 186.
35. William F. Fox, *Regimental Losses in the Civil War* (New York: Albany Press, 1889), p. 164.
36. John Brown Gordon, *Reminiscences of the Civil War* (New York: Scribner's, 1903), p. 231.
37. Howard was in error. Rodes was still a brigadier at this point, soon to be promoted.
38. McHenry Howard, *Recollections of a Maryland Confederate Soldier and Staff Officer* (Dayton, Ohio: Morningside Press, 1975), p. 191.
39. Gallagher, p. 52.
40. Mary Anna Jackson, *Memoirs of Stonewall Jackson* (Louisville, Ky.: Prentice Press, 1895), p. 397.
41. Burke Davis, *They Called Him Stonewall* (New York: Rinehart and Co., 1954), p. 395.
42. Letter from Thomas Coffee to his Mother and Sisters, Jan. 24, 1863, *Confederate Veteran*, vol. 26, p. 157.
43. Robert E. Park, *Sketch of the 12th Alabama Infantry* (Richmond, Va.: Jones, 1906), p. 16.
44. Official Records, vol. 19, pt. 1. p. 1025.
45. Letter from Eugene Blackford to his Father, Jan. 1, 1863, Leigh Collection, University of North Carolina, Chapel Hill, N.C.
46. Park, p. 42.
47. Mary B. Chesnut, *Mary Chesnut's Civil War Diary* (New Haven, Conn.: Yale Press, 1981), p. 233.

CHAPTER 6

1. Rush Hawkins, "Why Burnside Did Not Renew The Attack at Fredericksburg," *Battles and Leaders of the Civil War*, Robert Johnson and Clarence Buel, eds. (Secaucus, N.J.: Castle Press, 1897), p. 127.
2. Darius N. Couch, "The Chancellorsville Campaign" *Battles and Leaders*, vol. 3, p. 154.
3. Warren W. Hassler, Jr., *Commanders of the Army of the Potomac* (Baton Rouge, La.: Louisiana State University Press, 1962), p. 130.
4. Ernest B. Furgurson, *Chancellorsville 1863: The Souls of the Brave* (New York: Vintage Books, 1993), p. 24.
5. Noah Brooks, *Mr. Lincoln's Washington* (New York: Thomas Yoseloff, 1967), p. 56.
6. Furgurson, p. 88.
7. Couch, *Battles and Leaders*, vol. 3, p. 156.

8. Alfred Pleasonton, "The Successes and Failures of Chancellorsville," *Battles and Leaders*, vol. 3, p. 172.
9. Al Hemingway, "Day One at Chancellorsville," *America's Civil War*, Mar. 1996, p. 44.
10. Couch, *Battles and Leaders*, vol. 3, p. 157.
11. Hemingway, p. 47.
12. Ralph Happell, "The Chancellors of Chancellorsville," *Virginia Magazine of History and Biography*, vol. 71, July 1963, p. 260.
13. Samuel P. Bates, "Hooker's Comments on Chancellorsville," *Battles and Leaders*, vol. 3, pp. 217–18.
14. James Power Smith, "Stonewall Jackson's Last Battle," *Battles and Leaders*, vol. 3, p. 203.
15. Burke Davis, *They Called Him Stonewall* (New York: Rinehart and Co., 1954), p. 401.
16. Gary W. Gallagher, *Stephen Dodson Ramseur: Lee's Gallant General* (Chapel Hill, N.C.: University of North Carolina Press, 1985), p. 52.
17. Frank E. Vandiver, *Mighty Stonewall* (New York: McGraw-Hill Co., 1957), p. 455.
18. Gallagher, p. 53.
19. Louis Mandarin, "North Carolina Troops, 1861–1865," Weymouth Jordan, ed. (Raleigh, N.C.: North Carolina Division of Archives and Libraries, 1981), vol. 8, p. 315.
20. Gallagher, p. 51.
21. Report of Robert Rodes, Battle of Chancellorsville, *Southern Historical Society Papers*, Richmond, Va., Oct. 1876, vol. 2, no. 4, p. 162.
22. Official Records of the Union and Confederate Armies (Washington, D.C.: Government Printing Office, 1880–1901), vol. 25, pt. 2, pp. 756–57.
23. Davis, p. 31.
24. Douglas S. Freeman, *Lee's Lieutenants* (New York: Scribner's Inc., 1941), vol. 2, p. 528.
25. Mandarin, North Carolina Troops, vol. 3, p. 316.
26. Official Records, vol. 19, pt. 2, p. 677.
27. J. L. Schaub, "General Robert E. Rodes," *Confederate Veteran*, vol. 16, p. 269.
28. Report of Robert Rodes, Battle of Chancellorsville, p. 162.
29. Report of Lafayette McLaws, Official Records, vol. 25, pt. 1, p. 925.
30. Hemingway, p. 49.
31. Report of Gen. A.R. Wright, Official Records, vol. 25, pt. 1, pp. 865–66.
32. Official Records, vol. 25, pt. 1, pp. 796–97.
33. Gallagher, pp. 55–57.
34. Report of Robert Rodes, Battle of Chancellorsville, p. 162.
35. Vandiver, p. 452.
36. Freeman, *Lee's Lieutenants,* vol. 2, p. 538.
37. Porter Alexander, *Military Memoirs of a Confederate* (Dayton, Ohio: Morningside Press, 1990), p. 328.
38. United States Army Guide to the Battles of Chancellorsville and Fredericksburg, Jay Luvaas and Harold Nelson, eds.(Carlisle Pa.: South Mountain Press, 1988), p. 172.
39. Vandiver, p. 463.
40. Mark Grimsley, "Master General: His Mode of War," *Civil War Times Illustrated*, Nov. 1985, p. 32.
41. Walter H. Taylor, *Four Years with General Lee* (New York: Bonanza Books, 1962), p. 84.
42. Freeman, *Lee's Lieutenants,* vol. 2, p. 539; Vandiver, p. 464.
43. Ibid., p. 541.
44. Official Records, vol. 25, pt. 2, p. 940.
45. Freeman, p. 546.

46. Taylor, p. 84.
47. Furgurson, p. 130.
48. Happell, p. 272.
49. Couch, *Battles and Leaders*, vol. 3, p. 170.
50. Luvaas and Nelson, *United States Army Gude to the Battle of Chancellorsville and Fredericksburg*, p. 177.
51. Alexander, p. 330.
52. General Order #26, 2nd Corps, CSA, Official Records, vol. 25, pt. 2, pp. 719–20.
53. Report of Robert Rodes, *Southern Historical Society Papers*, p. 162.
54. Report of Col. Emory Best, 23rd Georgia, Luvaas and Nelson, p. 180.
55. Report of Gen. Daniel Sickles, Official Records, vol. 25, pt. 1, p. 386.
56. Robert C. Cheeks, "Fire and Fury at Catharine's Furnace," *America's Civil War*, May 1995, p. 33.
57. Report of Col. Hiram Berdan, Luvaas and Nelson, p. 184.
58. Cheeks, pp. 36–37.
59. Ibid., p. 37.
60. Official Records, vol. 25, pt. 1, pp. 979–80.
61. Report of Robert Rodes, *Southern Historical Society Papers*, p. 163.
62. Cheeks, p. 37.
63. Official Records, vol. 25, pt. 1, p. 502.
64. John R. Collins, "When Stonewall Jackson Turned Our Right," *Battles and Leaders*, vol. 3, p. 183.
65. John Purifoy, "Jackson's Last Battle," *Confederate Veteran*, vol. 28, Mar. 1920, p. 94.
66. Gallagher, p. 58.
67. Marcellus Moorman, *Southern Historical Society Papers*, vol. 30, 1902, p. 111.
68. Vandiver, p. 472.
69. Gallagher, p. 58.
70. Report of Robert Rodes, *Southern Historical Society Papers*, p. 163.
71. Freeman, *Lee's Lieutenants,* vol. 2, pp. 555–56.
72. Smith, p. 208.
73. Oliver O. Howard, "The XIth Corps at Chancellorsville," *Battles and Leaders*, vol. 25, pt. 1, p. 631.
74. General Order #9, May 10, 1863, Official Records, vol. 25, pt. 1, p. 631.
75. Alfred Pleasonton, *Battles and Leaders*, vol. 3, p. 181.
76. Alexander, p. 333.
77. Howard, p. 197.
78. Purifoy, p. 95.
79. Henry W. Thomas, *History of the Doles-Cook Brigade* (Dayton, Ohio: Morningside Press, 1988), p. 72.
80. Report of Robert Rodes, *Southern Historical Society Papers*, p. 164.
81. Report of Carl Schurz, Official Records, vol. 25, pt. 1, p. 654.
82. Rose F. Yancy, *Lynchburg and Its Neighbors* (Richmond, Va.: J.W. Ferguson Inc., 1935), p. 102.
83. Lawrence R. Laboda, *From Selma to Appomattox: The History of the Jeff Davis Artillery* (New York: Oxford University Press, 1994), p. 112.
84. Report of Dodson Ramseur, Official Records, vol. 25, pt. 1, p. 995.
85. Report of Robert Rodes, *Southern Historical Society Papers*, p. 165.

86. Report of Capt. M.F. Bonham, 3rd Alabama, Official Records, vol. 25, pt. 1, p. 956.
87. Gallagher, p. 59.
88. Moorman, p. 112.
89. Official Records, vol. 25, pt. 1, pp. 941–42.
90. Laboda, p. 112; Southern Historical Society Papers, p. 163.
91. John Purifoy, *History of the Jeff Davis Artillery* (Montgomery, Ala.: Unpublished July 21, 1901), p. 94.
92. Alexander, p. 340.
93. Ibid.
94. Report of James Lane, Official Records, vol. 25, pt. 1, p. 916.
95. Edward J. Carpender, "The Charge of the Eighth Pennsylvania Cavalry," *Battles and Leaders*, vol. 3, p. 187.
96. Moorman, p. 114.
97. Smith, pp. 209–12.
98. Report of Robert Rodes, *Southern Historical Society Papers*, p. 166.
99. Report of Hobard Ward, Official Records, vol. 25, pt. 1, pp. 429–30.
100. Report of James Lane, Official Records, vol. 25, pt. 1, pp. 916–17.
101. Gallagher, p. 59.
102. Freeman, *Lee's Lieutenants,* vol. 2, p. 571, fn. 27.
103. Alexander, p. 342.
104. Report of Robert Rodes, *Southern Historical Society Papers*, p. 166.
105. Report of Gen. J.E.B. Stuart, Official Records, vol. 25, pt. 1, p. 886.
106. Report of Edward O'Neal, Official Records, vol. 25, pt. 1, p. 887.
107. John Bigelow, Jr., *The Campaign of Chancellorsville* (New Haven, Conn.: Yale Press, 1910), p. 24.
108. Alexander, p. 342.
109. Report of James Lane, Official Records, vol. 25, pt. 1, pp. 917–18.
110. Report of Harry Heth, Official Records, vol. 25, pt.1. p. 891.
111. Alexander, p. 346.
112. Report of Daniel Sickles, Official Records, vol. 25, pt. 1, p. 390.
113. Micajah Martin, "A Soldier's Letter," *Virginia Magazine of History and Biography*, vol. 37, 1929, pp. 22–24.
114. Alexander, p. 346.
115. Report of J.E.B. Stuart, Official Records, vol. 25, pt. 1, p. 888.
116. Freeman, *Lee's Lieutenants,* vol. 2, p. 592.
117. Report of Ambrose P. Hill, Official Records, vol. 25, pt. 1, p. 886.
118. Ibid., pp. 1006–7.
119. Freeman, *Lee's Lieutenants,* vol. 2, p. 590.
120. Official Records, vol. 25, pt. 1, p. 905.
121. Report of Robert Rodes, *Southern Historical Society Papers*, p. 166.
122. Ibid.
123. Freeman, *Lee's Lieutenants,* vol. 2, p. 591.
124. Report of Edward O'Neal, Official Records, vol. 25, pt. 1, p. 952.
125. Report of Robert Rodes, *Southern Historical Society Papers*, p. 168.
126. Report of Alfred Iverson, Official Records, vol. 25, pt. 1, pp. 986–87.
127. Report of Robert Rodes, *Southern Historical Society Papers*, p. 168.
128. Ibid., p. 171.

129. Report of Dodson Ramseur, Official Records, vol. 25, pt. 1, p. 996.
130. Ibid.
131. Gallagher, p. 62.
132. Official Records, vol. 25, pt. 1, pp. 944, 996.
133. Bryan Grimes, "Extract of Letters of Maj. Gen. Bryan Grimes to his Wife while in Active Service with the Army of Northern Virginia," Pulaski Cowper, ed. (Raleigh, N.C.: Broughton, Edwards and Co., 1883), pp. 33–34.
134. Luvaas and Nelson, *United States Army Guide to the Battles of Chancellorsville and Fredericksburg*, p. 279.
135. Report of J.E.B. Stuart, Official Records, vol. 25, pt. 1, p. 888.
136. Report of R.E. Colston, Official Records, vol. 25, pt. 1, p. 1007.
137. Official Records, vol. 25, pt. 1, p. 945.
138. Ibid.
139. Report of Robert Rodes, *Southern Historical Society Papers*, p. 170.
140. Laboda, p. 114.
141. Ibid.
142. Report of John Gibbon, Official Records, vol. 25, pt. 1, p. 350.
143. Davis, p. 35.
144. Report of Jubal Early, Official Records, vol. 25, pt. 1, p. 1001.
145. Freeman, *Lee's Lieutenants,* vol. 2, p. 618.
146. Phillip Bolte, "Lonely Command," *Magazine of the Civil War Society*, vol. 61, Apr. 1997, p. 44.
147. Report of Cadmus Wilcox, Official Records, vol. 25, pt. 1, p. 857.
148. Bolte, p. 47.
149. Hunnington Jackson, "Sedgwick at Fredericksburg and Salem Heights," *Battles and Leaders*, vol. 3, p. 230.
150. Report of William Brooks, Official Records, vol. 25, pt. 1, p. 230.
151. Bolte, p. 47.
152. Alexander, p. 353.
153. Report of William Brooks, Official Records, vol. 25, pt. 1, p. 568.
154. Jackson, *Battles and Leaders*, vol. 3, p. 231.
155. Alexander, p. 353.
156. Report of Cadmus Wilcox, Official Records, vol. 25, pt. 1, p. 860.
157. Bolte, p. 46.
158. Alexander, p. 356.
159. Jackson, *Battles and Leaders*, vol. 3, p. 231.
160. Alexander, p. 356.
161. Report of Robert Rodes, *Southern Historical Society Papers*, p. 170.
162. Alexander, p. 358.
163. Report of Robert Rodes, *Southern Historical Society Papers*, p. 170.
164. Freeman, *Lee's Lieutenants,* vol. 3, p. 2.
165. Luvaas and Nelson, *United States Army Guide to the Battles of Chancellorsville and Fredericksburg*, p. xxi.
166. Report of Ambrose P. Hill, Official Records, vol. 25, pt. 1, p. 886.
167. James I. Robertson, "Stonewall Jackson: The Man, The Soldier, The Legend" (New York: MacMillan Publishing, 1997), p. 743.
168. Report of Robert E. Lee, Official Records, vol. 25, pt. 1, p. 803.
169. Freeman, *Lee's Lieutenants,* vol. 2, p. 653.

170. Bigelow, p. 475.
171. Furgurson, pp. 364–65.
172. Ibid.
173. Official Records, vol. 25, pt. 2, p. 813.
174. Ibid., p. 814.
175. James E. Green, "As They Saw General Lee," *Civil War Times Illustrated,* Edward H. Smith, ed., Oct. 1986, p. 21.

CHAPTER 7

1. Gary Eggleston, *History of the Confederate War* (New York: Negro University Press, 1910), vol. 2, p. 118.
2. Edwin B. Coddington, *The Gettysburg Campaign: A Study in Command* (New York: Scribner's and Sons, 1984), p. 34.
3. Douglas S. Freeman, *R.E. Lee* (New York: Charles Scribner's Sons, 1946), vol. 3, p. 11.
4. Burke Davis, *They Called Him Stonewall* (New York: Rinehart and Co., 1954), pp. 449–50.
5. Official Records of the Union and Confederate Armies (Washington, D.C.: Government Printing Office, 1880–1901), vol. 37, pt. 1, p. 947.
6. Clifford Dowdy, *Death of a Nation* (New York: Alfred A. Knopf Co., 1958), p. 31.
7. Coddington, p. 12.
8. Freeman, *R.E. Lee,* vol. 3, p. 11.
9. Wilbur S. Nye, *Here Come the Rebels* (Dayton, Ohio: Morningside Press, 1988), p. 39.
10. Freeman, *R.E. Lee,* vol. 3, p. 11.
11. Ibid., p. 12.
12. Coddington, p. 13.
13. Dowdy, p. 37.
14. Coddington, p. 592.
15. Robert Park, "Sketch of the 12th Alabama Infantry" (Richmond, Va.: Jones, 1906), p. 51.
16. Official Records, vol. 27, pt. 1, p. 347.
17. Report of Robert Rodes, Gettysburg, *Southern Historical Society Papers,* vol. 13, p. 137.
18. Letter from R. E. Lee to his wife, June 9. 1863.
19. Douglas S. Freeman, *Lee's Lieutenants* (New York: Scribner's Inc., 1942), vol. 3, p. 10.
20. Freeman, *R.E. Lee,* vol. 3, p. 31.
21. Coddington, p. 59.
22. Report of Robert Rodes, Gettysburg, p. 138.
23. Nye, p. 73.
24. Report of Robert Rodes, Gettysburg, p. 138.
25. Coddington, p. 90.
26. Report of Robert Rodes, Gettysburg, p. 138.
27. Nye, p. 87.
28. Report of Robert Rodes, Gettysburg, p. 138.
29. John Purifoy, "With Jackson in the Valley," *Confederate Veteran,* vol. 30, p. 384.
30. Gary W. Gallagher, *Stephen Dodson Ramseur: Lee's Gallant General* (Chapel Hill, N.C.: University of North Carolina Press, 1985), p. 69.
31. Lawrence R. Laboda, *From Selma to Appomattox: The History of the Jeff Davis Artillery* (New York: Oxford University Press, 1994), p. 127.
32. Coddington, p. 114.
33. Report of Robert Rodes, Gettysburg, p. 142.
34. Nye, p. 91.

35. Official Records, vol. 27, pt. 2, p. 54.
36. Coddington, p. 91.
37. Ibid., p. 100.
38. Ibid., p. 101.
39. Ibid., p. 122.
40. Antietam Campaign.
41. Dowdy, p. 81.
42. Gallagher, p. 69.
43. Dowdy, p. 43.
44. Freeman, *Lee's Lieutenants,* vol. 3, p. 27.
45. Report of Robert Rodes, Gettysburg, p. 143.
46. Park, p. 56.
47. Coddington, p. 143.
48. Freeman, *Lee's Lieutenants,* vol. 3, p. 31.
49. Report of Robert Rodes, Gettysburg, p. 142.
50. Ibid., p. 143.
51. Nye, p. 239.
52. Coddington, p. 154.
53. Nye, p. 251.
54. Freeman, *Lee's Lieutenants,* vol. 3, p. 57.
55. Ibid., p. 30.
56. Henry W. Thomas, *History of the Doles-Cook Brigade* (Dayton, Ohio: Morningside Press, 1988), p. 10.
57. Nye, p. 305.
58. Park, p. 57.
59. Coddington, p. 171.
60. Ibid., p. 171.

CHAPTER 8

1. Edwin B. Coddington, *The Gettysburg Campaign: A Study in Command* (New York: Scribner's and Sons, 1984), p. 177.
2. Glen Tucker, *High Tide at Gettysburg* (New York: Bobbs-Merrill, 1958), p. 63.
3. Wilbur S. Nye, *Here Come the Rebels* (Dayton, Ohio: Morningside Press, 1988), p. 310.
4. Gerald A. Patterson, "The Death of Iverson's Brigade," *Gettysburg Magazine*, July 1990, no. 5, p. 14.
5. Ibid.
6. Jedediah Hotchkiss, *Make Me a Map of the Valley: The Civil War Journal of Stonewall Jackson's Topographer* (Dallas, Tex.: Southern Methodist University Press, 1973), June 28, 1863.
7. Official Records of the Union and Confederate Armies (Washington, D.C.: Government Printing Office, 1880–1901), vol. 27, pt. 2, p. 316.
8. Edwin C. Fishel, *The Secret War for the Union* (New York: Houghton Mifflin Co., 1960), p. 486.
9. Coddington, p. 183.
10. Official Records, vol. 27, pt. 2, p. 316.
11. Nye, p. 344.
12. James L. Morrison, Jr., ed. *The Memoirs of Henry Heth* (Westport, Conn.: Greenwood Press, 1974), p. 174.
13. Fishel, p. 499.

14. Warren W. Hassler, *Crisis at the Crossroads: The First Day at Gettysburg* (Tuscaloosa, Ala.: University of Alabama Press, 1970), p. 10.
15. Nye, p. 344.
16. Coddington, p. 181.
17. Ibid., p. 189.
18. Ibid., p. 196.
19. Porter Alexander, *Military Memoirs of a Confederate* (Dayton, Ohio: Morningside Press, 1990), p. 379.
20. Coddington, p. 206.
21. Ibid., p. 196.
22. Hassler, p. 11.
23. Report of Robert Rodes, Battle of Gettysburg, *Southern Historical Society Papers*, p. 145.
24. Rodes' Division was well supplied with Union army knapsacks secured from the fleeing XI Federal Corps at Chancellorsville.
25. Henry W. Thomas, *History of the Doles-Cook Brigade* (Dayton, Ohio: Morningside Press, 1988), p. 363.
26. Nye, p. 357.
27. Sarah Mott, *Personal Experiences of a House that Stood on the Road* (Carlisle, Pa.: South Mountain Press, 1941), pp. 8–9.
28. John Purifoy, "History of the Jeff Davis Artillery" (Montgomery, Ala.: Alabama Department of Archives and History, 1901), p. 48.
29. Hassler, p. 34.
30. Porter Alexander, *Fighting for the Confederacy: The Personal Recollections of Gen. Edward Porter Alexander,* Gary Gallagher, ed. (Chapel Hill, N.C.: University of North Carolina Press, 1989), p. 229.
31. John Purifoy, "With Ewell and Rodes in Pennsylvania" *Confederate Veteran*, vol. 30, p. 462.
32. Report of Robert Rodes, Gettysburg, p. 145.
33. Nye, p. 363.
34. Hassler, p. 24.
35. Alexander, *Military Memoirs*, p. 382.
36. Clifford Dowdy, *Death of a Nation* (New York: Alfred A. Knopf Co., 1958), p. 93.
37. Ibid., p. 93.
38. Hassler, p. 38.
39. Coddington, p. 307.
40. Ibid., p. 275.
41. Hassler, p. 32.
42. Ibid., p. 53.
43. Dowdy, p. 96.
44. Ibid., p. 97.
45. Lance J. Herdegen and William Beaudot, *In the Bloody Railroad Cut at Gettysburg* (Dayton, Ohio: Morningside Press, 1990), p. 196.
46. Hassler, p. 49.
47. James I. Robertson, *General A.P. Hill: The Story of a Confederate Warrior* (New York: Random House, 1987), p. 209.
48. Dowdy, p. 98.
49. Griffin D. Massey, "Rodes on Oak Hill: A Study of Rodes' division on the 1st Day at Gettysburg," *Gettysburg Magazine*, Jan. 1991, #4, p. 34.

50. Official Records, vol. 27, pt. 2, p. 552.
51. Ibid.
52. Griffin, p. 36.
53. Dowdy, p. 132.
54. Griffin, p. 43.
55. Report of Robert Rodes, Gettysburg, p. 147.
56. Griffin, p. 38.
57. Gary Lash, "General Henry Baxter's Brigade at Gettysburg," *Gettysburg Magazine*, Jan. 1994, #10, p. 18.
58. Patterson, p. 13.
59. Griffin, p. 38.
60. Report of Cullen Battle, "Battle of Gettysburg," *Southern Historical Society Papers*, vol. 13, p. 177.
61. Official Records, vol. 27, pt. 2, pp. 592, 601.
62. Report of Robert Rodes, Gettysburg, p. 147.
63. Griffin, p. 40.
64. Lash, p. 18.
65. Walter Clark, ed., *History of Several Regiments from North Carolina in the Great War of 1864–65* (Raleigh, N.C.: North Carolina Department of Archives and History, 1901), vol. 1, p. 236.
66. Patterson, p. 18.
67. Official Records, vol. 27, pt. 2, p. 553.
68. Griffin, p. 45.
69. Clark, vol. 2, pp. 325–26.
70. Report of Robert Rodes, Gettysburg, p. 148.
71. Lawrence R. Laboda, *From Selma to Appomattox: The History of the Jeff Davis Artillery* (New York: Oxford University Press, 1994), p. 136.
72. Douglas S. Freeman, *Lee's Lieutenants* (New York: Scribner and Sons, 1942), vol. 3, p. 87n.
73. Thomas, p. 44.
74. Dowdy, p. 136.
75. Coddington, p. 290.
76. Gary W. Gallagher, *Stephen Dodson Ramseur: Lee's Gallant General* (Chapel Hill, N.C.: University of North Carolina Press, 1985), p. 72.
77. Griffin, p. 47.
78. Freeman, *Lee's Lieutenants,* vol. 3, p. 87.
79. Clark, vol. 3, p. 514.
80. Hassler, p. 105.
81. Griffin, p. 45.
82. Herdegen, p. 224.
83. Ibid., p. 227.
84. Harry W. Pfanz, *Gettysburg: Culp's Hill and Cemetery Hill* (Chapel Hill, N.C.: University of North Carolina Press, 1993), p. 62.
85. Report of Robert Rodes, Gettysburg, p. 149.
86. Hassler, p. 127.
87. Gallagher, p. 73.
88. John B. Gordon, *Reminiscences of the Civil War* (New York: Scribner's, 1903), p. 157.
89. Report of Robert Rodes, Gettysburg, p. 149.

90. Coddington, p. 319.
91. Ibid., p. 363.
92. Ibid., p. 364.
93. Ibid., p. 365.
94. Alexander, *Fighting for the Confederacy*, pp. 232–33.
95. Dowdy, p. 161.
96. Pfanz, p. 79.
97. Official Records, vol. 27, pt. 2, p. 553.
98. Clark, vol. 1, p. 635.
99. Official Records, vol. 27, pt. 2, pp. 771–72.
100. William Blackford, *War Years with Jeb Stuart* (New York: Scribner and Sons, 1945), pp. 231–32.
101. Pfanz, p. 128.
102. Official Records, vol. 27, pt. 2, p. 555.
103. Pfanz, pp. 120–21.
104. Ibid., p. 127.
105. William G. Piston, *Lee's Tarnished Lieutenant: James Longstreet and His Place in Southern History* (Athens, Ga.: University of Georgia Press, 1987), p. 49.
106. Alexander, *Fighting for the Confederacy*, p. 411.
107. Piston, p. 50.
108. Coddington, p. 374.
109. Freeman, *Lee's Lieutenants,* vol. 3, p. 116.
110. Dowdy, p. 237.
111. Alexander, *Military Memoirs*, p. 411.
112. Report of Robert Rodes, Gettysburg, p. 151.
113. Freeman, *Lee's Lieutenants,* vol. 3, p. 132.
114. Pfanz, p. 278.
115. Freeman, *Lee's Lieutenants,* vol. 3, p. 132.
116. Coddington, p. 435.
117. Pfanz, p. 253.
118. Dowdy, p. 236.
119. Pfanz, p. 275.
120. Official Records, vol. 27, pt. 1, p. 706.
121. Coddington, p. 439.
122. Dowdy, p. 238.
123. Report of Robert Rodes, Gettysburg, p. 151.
124. Freeman, *Lee's Lieutenants,* vol. 3, p. 141.
125. Dowdy, p. 260.
126. Ibid., p. 260.
127. Ibid., p. 262.
128. Coddington, p. 471.
129. Jesse H. Jones and George S. Greene, "The Breastworks at Culp's Hill," *Battles and Leaders*, vol. 3, pp. 316–17.
130. Freeman, *R.E. Lee,* vol. 3, pp. 118–19.
131. Report of Robert Rodes, Gettysburg, p. 151.
132. Freeman, *Lee's Lieutenants,* vol. 3, p. 140.
133. Alexander, *Military Memoirs*, p. 435.

134. Report of Robert Rodes, Gettysburg, p. 152.
135. Dowdy, p. 344.
136. Alexander, *Fighting for the Confederacy*, p. 275.
137. Casualties for Rodes' Division totaled 36% for the campaign.
138. Alexander, *Military Memoirs*, p. 393.
139. Report of Robert Rodes, Gettysburg, p. 153.
140. Robert E. Park, "Diary," *Southern Historical Society Papers*, vol. 2, 1876, p. 173.
141. Dowdy, p. 346.
142. Coddington, p. 346.
143. Ibid., p. 538.
144. John Purifoy, "The Retreat From Gettysburg," *Confederate Veteran,* vol. 33, Sept. 1925, p. 339.
145. Ibid.
146. Report of Robert Rodes, Gettysburg, p. 153.
147. Laboda, p. 154.
148. Coddington, p. 564.
149. Alexander, *Military Memoirs*, p. 440.
150. Laboda, p. 158.
151. Thomas, p. 11.
152. Report of Robert Rodes, Gettysburg, pp. 153–54.

CHAPTER 9

1. John W. Daniel, "Memoir of the Battle of Gettysburg," Virginia Historical Society, Richmond, Va., Unpublished, p. 17.
2. Henry W. Thomas, *History of the Doles-Cook Brigade* (Dayton, Ohio: Morningside Press, 1988), p. 11.
3. Report of Robert Rodes, "Battle of Gettysburg," *Southern Historical Society Papers*, vol. 2, p. 155.
4. Ibid.
5. Thomas, p. 12.
6. Report of Robert Rodes, Gettysburg, p. 157.
7. Ibid.
8. Ibid., p. 158.
9. Ibid., p. 155.
10. Official Records of the Union and Confederate Armies (Washington, D.C.: Government Printing Office, 1880–1901), vol. 51, pt. 2, p. 844.
11. Opposing Forces, Beginning of Grant's Campaign Against Richmond, *Battles and Leaders*, Robert Johnson and Clarence Buel, eds. (Secaucus, N.J.: Castle Press, 1897), vol. 4, p. 179.
12. Ezra J. Warner, *Generals in Gray* (Baton Rouge, La.: Louisiana State University Press, 1959), p. 147.
13. Douglas S. Freeman, ed., *Lee's Confidential Dispatches to Jefferson Davis, 1862–1865* (New York: Grady McWhiney, Putnam and Sons, 1957), #49, p. 94.
14. Douglas S. Freeman, *Lee's Lieutenants* (New York: Scribner's Inc., 1942), vol. 3, p. 199.
15. Douglas S. Freeman, *R.E. Lee* (New York: Charles Scibner's Sons, 1946), vol. 3, p. 199.
16. Ibid., p. 222.
17. Freeman, *Confidential Dispatches*, p. 225.
18. Warner, p. 226.

19. Robert E. Park, *Sketch of the 12th Alabama Infantry* (Richmond, Va.: Jones, 1906), p. 57.
20. Warner, p. 20.
21. Jeffrey Wert, "Robert E. Rodes: So High in Rank, So Brilliant in Service, So Glorious in Death," *Civil War Times Illustrated*, 1970, p. 44.
22. Application for Membership, Daughters of the American Revolution, Mrs. Louise Rodes Schoch, Archives of Virginia Military Institute, Lexington, Va.
23. Park, p. 56.
24. Ibid., p. 100.
25. Ibid., p. 59.
26. Freeman, *Lee's Lieutenants,* vol. 3, p. 239.
27. Official Records, vol. 29, pt. 1, pp. 405–6.
28. Robert C. Neal, "Bury Those Poor Men," *America's Civil War*, Nov. 1990, p. 37.
29. Freeman, *Lee's Lieutenants,* vol. 3, p. 245.
30. James I. Robertson, *General A.P. Hill: The Story of a Confederate Warrior* (New York: Random House, 1987), p. 235.
31. Martin T. McMahon, "From Gettysburg to The Coming of Grant," *Battles and Leaders*, vol. 4, p. 84.
32. Robertson, p. 236.
33. Freeman, *Lee's Lieutenants,* vol. 3, p. 245.
34. Freeman, *R. E. Lee,* vol. 3, p. 183.
35. Neal, p. 40.
36. Freeman, *Lee's Lieutenants,* p. 247.
37. Park, p. 61.
38. Asbury Christian, *Lynchburg and Its People* (Lynchburg, Va.: J.P. Bell, 1900), p. 213.
39. Charles C. Osborne, *Jubal: The Life and Times of Gen. Jubal A. Early* (Baton Rouge, La.: Louisiana State University Press, 1992), p. 205.
40. Official Records, vol. 29, pt. 1, pp. 632–33.
41. Gary W. Gallagher, *Stephen Dodson Ramseur: Lee's Gallant General* (Chapel Hill, N.C.: University of North Carolina Press, 1985), p. 86.
42. Osborne, p. 207.
43. McMahon. pp. 90–91.
44. Park, p. 64.
45. Osborne, p. 212.
46. Official Records, vol. 29, pt. 1, p. 836.
47. Park, p. 65.
48. McMahon, vol. 4, p. 92.
49. Ibid., pp. 90–91.
50. Park, p. 59.
51. Green Peyton, "Robert E. Rodes," Virginia Military Institute Memorial Volume, Charles Walker, ed. (Philadelphia, Pa.:1875), p. 450.
52. Park, p. 69.
53. Peyton, p. 450.
54. Glen Tucker, "Zeb Vance: Champion of Personal Freedom" (Indianapolis, Ind.: Broehill, 1965), pp. 338–40.
55. Peyton, p. 451.
56. Letter from Thomas Coffee to His Mother, Jan. 15, 1864, *Confederate Veteran*, vol. 36, p. 353.
57. Speech of Col. Thomas Carter, Virginia Military Institute Archives, Lexington, Va.

CHAPTER 10

1. U.S. Grant, "Preparing for the Campaign of 64," *Battles and Leaders of the American Civil War* (Secaucus, N.J.: Castle Press, 1897), vol. 4, p. 97.
2. Ibid., p. 98.
3. Reid Mitchell, *Civil War Soldiers: Their Expectations and Their Experiences* (New York: Viking Penquin, 1988), p. 45.
4. Grant, p. 104.
5. Ibid., p. 108.
6. Porter Alexander, *Military Memoirs of a Confederate* (Dayton, Ohio: Morningside Press, 1990), p. 495.
7. Ibid., p. 495.
8. Ibid., p. 496.
9. Gordon C. Rhea, *The Battle of the Wilderness* (Baton Rouge, La.: Louisiana State University, 1994), p. 42.
10. William G. Piston, *Lee's Tarnished Lieutenant: James Longstreet and his Place in Southern History* (Athens, Ga.: University of Georgia Press, 1987), p. 87.
11. Official Records of the Union and Confederate Armies (Washington, D.C.: Government Printing Office, 1880–1901), vol. 36, pt. 1, p. 18.
12. Glen Tucker, *Hancock the Superb* (Dayton, Ohio: Morningside Press, 1980), p. 180.
13. Rhea, p. 32.
14. Douglas S. Freeman, *Lee's Lieutenants* (New York: Scribner's Inc., 1942), vol. 3, p. 345.
15. Rhea, p. 32.
16. Ibid., p. 85.
17. Ibid., p. 23.
18. Official Records, vol. 51, pt. 2, p. 890.
19. Official Records, vol. 36, pt. 1, p. 614.
20. Ezra J. Warner, *Generals in Gray* (Baton Rouge, La.: Louisiana State University Press, 1959), p. 20.
21. Rhea, p. 145.
22. Louis H. Mandarin, *North Carolina Troops: 1861–1865* (Raleigh, N.C.: North Carolina Department of Archives and History, 1971), vol. 5, p. 27.
23. Official Records, vol. 51, pt. 2, p. 890.
24. Ibid., p. 230.
25. Mandarin, p. 28.
26. Richard Wheeler, *On Fields of Fury* (New York: Harper and Rowe, 1991), p. 96.
27. George Q. Peyton, "A Civil War Record: 1864–1865," Unpublished Diary, Jones Memorial Library, Lynchburg, Va., p. 23.
28. Jennings C. Wise, "The Long Arm of Lee: A History of the Artillery of the Army of Northern Virginia" (Lynchburg, Va.: J.P. Bell Co., 1915), p. 767.
29. Porter Alexander, *Fighting for the Confederacy*, Gary Gallagher, ed. (Chapel Hill, N.C.: University of North Carolina Press, 1989), p. 357.
30. Alexander Webb, "Through The Wilderness," *Battles and Leaders*, vol. 4, p. 156.
31. Gary W. Gallagher, *Stephen Dodson Ramseur: Lee's Gallant General* (Chapel Hill, N.C.: University of North Carolina Press, 1985), p. 101.
32. Ibid.,
33. Official Records, vol. 36, pt. 1, p. 1081.
34. Alexander, *Military Memoirs*, p. 508.
35. Alexander, *Fighting for the Confederacy*, p. 365.

36. Rhea, p. 16.
37. Alexander, *Military Memoirs*, p. 508.
38. E.M. Law, "From the Wilderness to Cold Harbor," *Battles and Leaders*, vol. 4, p. 122.
39. George Peyton, p. 23.

CHAPTER 11

1. William D. Matter, *If it Takes All Summer: The Battle of Spotsylvania* (Chapel Hill, N.C.: University of North Carolina Press, 1988), p. 5.
2. Richard Wheeler, *On Fields of Fury* (New York: Harper and Rowe, 1991), p. 188.
3. Douglas S. Freeman, *Lee's Lieutenants* (New York: Scribner's Inc., 1942), vol. 3, p. 380.
4. Ibid.,
5. Douglas S. Freeman, *R.E. Lee* (New York: Charles Scribner and Sons, 1946), vol. 3, p. 305.
6. Official Records of the Union and Confederate Armies (Washington, D.C.: Government Printing Office, 1880–1901), vol. 36, pt. 1, p. 1071.
7. Ibid.
8. George Q. Peyton, "A Civil War Record," Unpublished Diary, Jones Memorial Library, Lynchburg, Va., pp. 23–24.
9. Matter, p. 86.
10. Ibid., p. 90.
11. Ibid., pp. 88–89.
12. Freeman, *Lee's Lieutenants,* vol. 3, p. 387.
13. Ibid.
14. George Peyton, p. 24.
15. Gary W. Gallagher, *Stephen Dodson Ramseur: Lee's Gallant General* (Chapel Hill, N.C.: University of North Carolina Press, 1985), p. 105.
16. Official Records, vol. 36, pt. 1, p. 1084.
17. Freeman, *Lee's Lieutenants,* vol. 3, p. 386.
18. Ibid., p. 394.
19. Matter, p. 106.
20. Official Records, vol. 36, pt. 1, p. 1079.
21. Freeman, *Lee's Lieutenants,* vol. 3, p. 446.
22. Presbyterian Cemetery, Lynchburg, Va.
23. Matter, p. 102.
24. Martin T. McMahon, "The Death of General John Sedgwick," *Battles and Leaders of the Civil War* (Secaucus, N.J.: Castle Press, 1897), vol.4, p. 175.
25. Henry W. Thomas, *History of the Doles-Cook Brigade* (Dayton, Ohio: Morningside Press, 1988), p. 76.
26. Matter, p. 149.
27. Official Records, vol. 36, pt. 1, p. 297.
28. Ibid., p. 712.
29. Freeman, *Lee's Lieutenants,* vol. 3, p. 396.
30. Official Records, vol. 36, pt. 1, p. 667.
31. Matter, p. 159.
32. Ibid.
33. Official Records, vol. 36, pt. 1, pp. 490–91.
34. Thomas, p. 48.
35. Official Records, vol. 36, pt. 1, p. 668.

36. Ibid., pp. 668, 1089.
37. Ibid., p. 1089.
38. Ibid.
39. Ibid., p. 695.
40. Matter, p. 160.
41. Official Records, vol. 36, pt. 1, p. 1072.
42. Hampden Osborne, *Confederate Veteran*, vol. 30, 1917, p. 227.
43. Matter, p. 172.
44. Ibid., p. 175.
45. Official Records, vol. 36, pt. 1, pp. 1044, 1086.
46. Porter Alexander, *Military Memoirs of a Confederate* (Dayton, Ohio: Morningside Press, 1990), p. 518.
47. Freeman, *Lee's Lieutenants,* vol. 3, p. 399.
48. Matter, p. 183.
49. Ibid., p. 189.
50. Ibid.
51. Freeman, *Lee's Lieutenants,* vol. 3, pp. 401–2.
52. Alexander, *Military Memoirs*, p. 520.
53. Freeman, *Lee's Lieutenants,* vol. 3, p. 402.
54. Ibid., p. 403.
55. Matter, p. 199.
56. Alexander, *Military Memoirs*, p. 521.
57. Matter, p. 200.
58. Gallagher, p. 108.
59. Alexander, *Military Memoirs*, p. 522.
60. Official Records, vol. 36, pt. 1, p. 1092.
61. Ibid., p. 1094.
62. Freeman, *Lee's Lieutenants,* vol. 3, p. 408.
63. Matter, p. 346.
64. *Southern Historical Society Papers*, vol. 14, p. 513.
65. P. J. White, "General Robert Rodes," *Confederate Veteran*, vol. 35, p. 101.
66. Green Peyton, "Robert E. Rodes," Virginia Military Institute Memorial Volume, Charles Walker, ed., p. 453.
67. Robert Stiles, *Four Years Under Marse Robert* (New York: Neale, 1903), p. 261.
68. Freeman, *Lee's Lieutenants,* vol. 3, p. 417.
69. Matter, p. 212.
70. Norton G. Calloway, "Hand-to-Hand Fighting at Spotsylvania," *Battles and Leaders*, vol. 4, p. 173.
71. Matter, p. 249.
72. Thomas Hyde, *Follow the Greek Cross* (New York: Houghton Mifflin, 1894), p. 200.
73. Robert McAllister, "McAllister's Brigade at the Bloody Angle," *Battles and Leaders*, vol. 4, p. 175.
74. Freeman, *R.E. Lee,* vol. 3, p. 325.
75. Green Peyton, p. 453.
76. Matter, p. 271.
77. Ezra J. Warner, *Generals in Gray* (Baton Rouge, La.: Louisiana State University Press, 1959), p. 66.

78. Ibid., p. 484.
79. Matter, p. 305.
80. Official Records, vol. 36, pt. 2, pp. 867–68.
81. Ibid., pt. 1, pp. 1087–88.
82. Ibid., p. 1090.
83. Matter, p. 311.
84. Ibid., p. 317.
85. Official Records, vol. 36, pt. 1, p. 1073.
86. Ibid., pp. 1082–83.
87. Matter, p. 325.
88. Ibid., p. 326.
89. C.S. Venable, "Wilderness to Petersburg," *Southern Historical Society Papers*, vol. 14, pp. 532–33.
90. Freeman, *Lee's Lieutenants,* vol. 3, p. 448.

CHAPTER 12

1. Walter H. Taylor, *Four Years with General Lee* (New York: Bonanza Books, 1962), p. 132.
2. Official Records of the Union and Confederate Armies (Washington, D.C.: Government Printing Office, 1880–1901), vol. 36, pt. 1, p. 1058.
3. Taylor, p. 136.
4. Porter Alexander, *Military Memoirs of a Confederate* (Dayton, Ohio: Morningside Press, 1990), p. 530.
5. Douglas S. Freeman, *Lee's Lieutenants* (New York: Scribner's Inc., 1942), vol. 3, p. 497.
6. Ibid., p. 531.
7. E.M. Law, "From the Wilderness to Cold Harbor," *Battles and Leaders*, (Secaucus, N.J.: Castle Press, 1897), vol. 4, p. 136.
8. Official Records, vol. 36, pt. 1, pp. 127–28.
9. Ibid., p. 209.
10. C.S. Venable, "The Campaign from the Wilderness to Petersburg," *Southern Historical Society Papers*, vol. 14, p. 534.
11. Alexander, p. 531.
12. Official Records, vol. 36, pt. 1, p. 211.
13. Venable, p. 534.
14. Official Records, vol. 36, pt. 1, p. 206.
15. Alexander, p. 534.
16. Official Records, vol. 36, pt. 3, p. 253.
17. Freeman, *R.E. Lee,* vol. 3, p. 369.
18. Gary W. Gallagher, *Stephen Dodson Ramseur: Lee's Gallant General* (Chapel Hill, N.C.: University of North Carolina Press, 1985), pp. 115–16.
19. Official Records, vol. 36, pt. 3, p. 854.
20. C.B. Christian, "The Battle of Bethesda Church," *Southern Historical Society Papers*, vol. 37, p. 238.
21. Gallagher, p. 115.
22. Freeman, *Lee's Lieutenants,* vol. 3, p. 502.
23. Christian, p. 238.
24. Ibid.
25. Ibid., p. 239.
26. Ibid., p. 240.

27. Ibid., p. 239.
28. George Q. Peyton, "A Civil War Record: 1864–1865," Unpublished Diary, Jones Memorial Library, Lynchburg, Va., p. 38.
29. Gallagher, p. 116.
30. Freeman, *R.E. Lee,* vol. 4, p. 504.
31. Ibid., p. 998.
32. Freeman, *R.E. Lee,* vol. 4, p. 504.
33. Official Records, vol. 36, pt. 1, p. 999.
34. Brian C. Pohanka, "Not War, But Murder," *America's Civil War*, Jan. 1989, p. 36.
35. Ibid.
36. Alexander, p. 538.
37. Henry W. Thomas, *The History of the Doles-Cook Brigade* (Dayton, Ohio: Morningside Press, 1988), p. 77.
38. Thomas, p. 47.
39. Pohanka, p. 37.
40. McMahon, pp. 215–16.
41. Pohanka, p. 37.
42. Freeman, *R.E. Lee,* vol. 4, p. 508.
43. Glen Tucker, *Hancock the Superb* (Dayton, Ohio: Morningside Press, 1980), p. 220.
44. Ibid.
45. Pohanka, p. 38.
46. Ibid., p. 38.
47. Freeman, *R.E. Lee,* vol. 3, p. 390.
48. Pohanka, p. 40.
49. Freeman, *R.E. Lee,* vol. 3, p. 392.
50. McMahon, p. 219.
51. Freeman, *R.E. Lee,* vol. 3, p. 508.
52. George C. Eggleston, "Notes on Cold Harbor," *Battles and Leaders*, vol. 4, pp. 230–31.
53. Tucker, p. 232.
54. Eggleston, p. 231.
55. Green Peyton, "Robert E. Rodes," *Virginia Memorial Institute Memorial Volume*, Charles Walker, ed., 1885, p. 451.
56. Taylor, p. 178.

CHAPTER 13

1. W.W. Old, "Diary: The Operations of Lt. Gen. Jubal A. Early in the Valley of Virginia and Maryland, June 13, 1864 to Aug. 12, 1864. Unpublished, p. 1.
2. Charles C. Osborne, *Jubal: The Life and Times of Gen. Jubal A. Early* (Baton Rouge, La.: Louisiana State University Press, 1992), p. 245.
3. Robert E. Park, *Sketch of the 12th Alabama Infantry* (Richmond, Va.: Jones, 1906), p. 71.
4. Jedediah Hotchkiss, *Make Me a Map of the Valley: the Civil War Journal of Stonewall Jackson's Topographer*, Archie McDonald, ed. (Dallas, Tex.: Southern Methodist University Press, 1973), p. 211.
5. Old, p. 1.
6. I.G. Bradwell, "Cold Harbor, Lynchburg, and the Valley Campaign of 1864," *Confederate Veteran*, vol. 28, 1920, p. 139.
7. Official Record of the Union and Confederate Armies (Washington, D.C.: U.S. Government Printing Office, 1880–1901), pt. 1, pp. 762–63.

8. Hotchkiss, p. 211.
9. Osborne, p. 252.
10. Howard Coleman, "The Lion of Virginia: The Story of Jubal Anderson Early," *Lynchburg: The Magazine of Central Virginia*, Apr./May 1981, pt. 2, vol. 13, p. 18.
11. William Allen, "Papers," Southern Historical Collection, University of North Carolina, Chapel Hill, N.C.
12. Charles M. Blackford, "The Battle of Lynchburg," *Southern Historical Society Papers*, vol. 30, 1902, p. 287.
13. Gary Walker, *Yankee Soldiers in Virginia's Valleys: Hunter's Raid* (Roanoke, Va.: A and W Enterprises, 1989), p. 271.
14. Rose F. Yancy, *Lynchburg and Its Neighbors* (Richmond, Va.: J.W. Ferguson Inc., 1935), pp. 81–82.
15. Hotchkiss, p. 211.
16. Coleman, pt. 2, p. 20.
17. Hotchkiss, p. 211.
18. Milton W. Humphreys, *A History of the Lynchburg Campaign* (Charlottesville, Va.: Michie Publishing, 1924), p. 62.
19. William C. Davis, *The Battle of New Market* (Garden City, N.J.: Doubleday Co., 1975), p. 169.
20. Marshall M. Brice, *Conquest of a Valley* (Charlottesville, Va.: University of Virginia Press, 1965), p. 14.
21. Frank E. Vandiver, *Jubal's Raid: Early's Attack on Washington in 1864* (New York: McGraw-Hill Co., 1960), p. 6.
22. Brice, p. 77.
23. Report of David Hunter, Official Records, vol. 37, pt. 1, p. 95.
24. Ibid.
25. Vandiver, p. 7.
26. Charles Blackford, p. 280.
27. Henry A. DuPont, *The Campaign of 1864 in the Shenandoah Valley and the Expedition to Lynchburg* (New York: National Americana Society, 1925), p. 68.
28. Brice, p. 115.
29. DuPont, p. 79.
30. Humphreys, p. 55.
31. Charles Blackford, p. 284.
32. Osborne, p. 254.
33. Charles Blackford, p. 289.
34. Vandiver, p. 37.
35. Jubal Anderson Early, *Jubal Early's Memoirs* (Baltimore, Md.: Nautical and Aviation Publishing, 1912), p. 374.
36. Ibid.
37. Brice, p. 119.
38. Walker, p. 289.
39. Official Records, vol. 37, pt. 1, p. 121.
40. Charles Blackford, p. 290.
41. Walker, p. 296.
42. Charles Blackford, p. 290.
43. Report of George Crook, Official Records, vol. 37, pt. 1, p. 121.
44. DuPont, p. 79.
45. Pond, p. 37.

46. Charles Blackford, p. 310.
47. Susan Blackford, *Letters from Lee's Army* (New York: Scribner and Sons, 1947), p. 256.
48. Official Records, vol. 37, pt. 1, p. 144.
49. Ibid.
50. Vandiver, p. 51.
51. Bryan Grimes, "Extract of Letters of Maj. Gen. Bryan Grimes to his Wife," Pulaski Cowper, ed. (Raleigh, N.C.: Broughton, Edwards, and Co., 1883), p. 55.
52. DuPont, p. 76.
53. Hotchkiss, p. 212.
54. Old, p. 2.
55. Walker, p. 357.
56. Old, p. 2.
57. DuPont, p. 89.
58. Vandiver, p. 61.
59. Walker, p. 360.
60. Humphreys, p. 57.
61. DuPont, p. 86.
62. Old, p. 2.
63. Grimes, p. 56.
64. Walker, p. 386.
65. Official Records, vol. 37, pt. 1, p. 149.
66. DuPont, p. 88.
67. Hotchkiss, p. 222.
68. DuPont, p. 90.
69. B.F. Cooling, *Jubal Early's Raid on Washington in 1864* (Baltimore, Md.: Nautical and Aviation Publishing Co., 1989), p. 13.
70. Osborne, pp. 258–59.

CHAPTER 14

1. Jedediah Hotchkiss, *Make Me a Map of the Valley: The Civil War Journal of Stonewall Jackson's Topographer,* Archie McDonald, ed. (Dallas, Tex.: Southern Methodist University Press, 1973), p. 213.
2. Howard Coleman, "The Lion of Virginia: The Story of Jubal Anderson Early," *Lynchburg: The Magazine of Central Virginia*, vol. 13, June/July 1981, pp. 17–23.
3. B.F. Cooling, *Jubal Early's Raid on Washington in 1864* (Baltimore, Md.: Nautical and Aviation Publishing Co., 1989), p. 16.
4. I.G. Bradwell, "Early's March to Washington, 1864," *Confederate Veteran*, vol. 27, 1920, p. 176.
5. Jubal A. Early, "Early's March to Washington in 1864," *Battles and Leaders of the Civil War* (Secaucus, N.J.: Castle Press, 1897), vol. 4, p. 493.
6. Jubal A. Early, "Jubal Early's Memoirs," Frank Vandiver, ed. (Baltimore, Md.: Nautical and Aviation Publishing, 1989), p. 382.
7. Frank E. Vandiver, *Jubal's Raid: Early's Attack on Washington in 1864* (New York: McGraw-Hill, 1960), p. 68.
8. Ibid., p. 67.
9. Charles C. Osborne, *Jubal: The Life and Times of Gen. Jubal A. Early, C.S.A.* (Baton Rouge, La.: Louisiana State University Press, 1992), p. 264.
10. Vandiver, p. 66.

11. John B. Gordon, *Reminiscences of the Civil War* (New York: Scribner's, 1903), pp. 317–18.
12. Robert E. Park, *Sketch of the 12th Alabama Infantry* (Richmond, Va.: Jones, 1906), p. 72.
13. Early, *Battles and Leaders*, vol. 4, p. 463.
14. W.W. Old, "Diary: The Operations of Lt. Gen. Jubal A. Early in the Valley of Virginia and Maryland: June 13, 1864–August 12, 1864," Unpublished, Jones Memorial Library, Lynchburg, Va., p. 2.
15. Henry W. Thomas, *History of the Doles-Cook Brigade* (Dayton, Ohio: Morningside Press, 1988), pp. 200–206.
16. Hotchkiss, p. 214.
17. Old, p. 2.
18. Official Records, vol. 37, pt. 1, p. 174.
19. I.G. Bradwell, "Sheridan and Trevilian's Station," *Confederate Veteran*, vol. 38, p. 453.
20. Park, p. 74.
21. Cooling, p. 27.
22. Vandiver, p. 81.
23. Old, p. 2.
24. Osborne, p. 267.
25. Eric J. Wittenburg, "Roadblock en Route to Washington," *America's Civil War*, Nov. 1993, p. 53.
26. Osborne, p. 267.
27. Hotchkiss, p. 214.
28. Old, p. 3.
29. George Q. Peyton, "A Civil War Record: 1864–1865," Unpublished Diary, Jones Memorial Library, Lynchburg, Va., p. 54.
30. Wittenburg, p. 53.
31. Ibid.
32. Cooling, p. 58.
33. Bradwell, "Early's March," p. 176.
34. Vandiver, p. 105.
35. Ibid., p. 109.
36. Osborne, p. 273.
37. Official Records, vol. 37, pt. 1, p. 350.
38. Ibid., p. 351.
39. Osborne, p. 275.
40. Ibid.
41. Vandiver, p. 118.
42. Coleman, vol. 3, p. 18.
43. Official Records, vol. 37, pt. 2, p. 594.
44. Gary W. Gallagher, *Stephen Dodson Ramseur: Lee's Gallant General* (Chapel Hill, N.C.: University of North Carolina Press, 1985), p. 127.
45. Official Records, vol. 37, pt. 2, p. 594.
46. Old, p. 4.
47. Vandiver, p. 153.
48. Park, p. 76.
49. Ibid., p. 243.
50. Douglas S. Freeman, *Lee's Lieutenants* (New York: Scribner's Inc., 1942), vol. 3, p. 566.

51. Osborne, p. 284.
52. Vandiver, p. 162.
53. Ibid., p. 170.
54. Official Records, vol. 37, pt. 1, p. 277.
55. George Peyton, p. 57.
56. Park, p. 77.
57. Peter J. Meaney, *The Civil War Engagement at Cool Springs* (Berryville, Va.: Privately Published, 1980), p. 8.
58. Ibid., p. 55.
59. Official Records, vol. 37, pt. 1, p. 320.
60. Pond, p. 82.
61. Park, p. 77.
62. Ibid., p. 78.
63. Jeffrey Wert, "The Snicker's Gap War," *Civil War Times Illustrated*, July 1978, p. 38.
64. Meaney, p. 22.
65. Official Records, vol. 37, pt. 1, p. 320.
66. Wert, p. 38.
67. Official Records, vol. 37, pt. 1, p. 321.
68. Meaney, p. 15.
69. Report of George Crook, Official Records, vol. 37, pt. 1, p. 286.
70. Ibid., pp. 290–91.
71. Ibid., p. 291.
72. Meaney, pp. 19–20.
73. Wert, p. 39.
74. Meaney, p. 25.
75. Official Records, vol. 37, pt. 1, p. 281.
76. Ibid., vol. 43, pt. 1, p. 1022.
77. Meaney, p. 26.
78. Pond, p. 83.
79. Meaney, p. 28.
80. Wert, p. 39.
81. Meaney, p. 40.
82. Ibid., p. 39.
83. Official Records, vol. 43, pt. 1, p. 603.
84. Park, p. 79.
85. Wert, p. 39.
86. Meaney, p. 47.
87. Official Records, vol. 37, pt. 1, p. 292.
88. Meaney, p. 42.
89. Park, p. 79.

CHAPTER 15

1. Gary W. Gallagher, *Stephen Dodson Ramseur: Lee's Gallant General* (Chapel Hill, N.C.:University of North Carolina Press, 1985), p. 130.
2. Official Records of the Union and Confederate Armies (Washington, D.C.: U.S. Government Printing Office, 1880–1901), vol. 37, pt. 1, p. 326.
3. Ibid., p. 353.

4. Gallagher, p. 131.
5. Ibid.
6. Official Records, vol. 37, pt. 1, p. 353.
7. W.W. Old, "The Operations of Lt. Gen. Jubal A. Early in the Valley of Virginia and Maryland: June 13, 1864–Aug. 12, 1864," Unpublished Diary, Jones Memorial Library, Lynchburg, Va., p. 5.
8. Jedediah Hotchkiss, *Make Me a Map of the Valley: The Civil War Journal of Stonewall Jackson's Topographer,* Archie McDonald, ed. (Dallas, Tex.: Southern Methodist University Press, 1973), p. 215.
9. Gallagher, p. 133.
10. George Q. Peyton, "A Civil War Record; 1864–1865," Unpublished Diary, Jones Memorial Library, Lynchburg, Va., p. 60.
11. Letter from Robert Rodes to Richard Ewell, Official Records, vol. 37, pt. 1, p. 353.
12. Patricia L. Faust, ed. "Historical Times Illustrated Encyclopedia of the Civil War" (New York: Harper and Rowe, 1986), p. 193.
13. Jeffrey Wert, "The Second Battle of Kernstown, 1864: The Old Killing Ground," *Civil War Times Illustrated*, Oct. 1984, p. 43.
14. Ibid.
15. Ibid., pp. 43–44.
16. Official Records, vol. 37, pt. 1, p. 347.
17. Ibid., p. 293.
18. Ibid., p. 311.
19. Report of George Crook, Official Records, vol. 37, pt. 1, p. 286.
20. George F. Pond, *The Shenandoah Valley in 1864* (New York: Scribner and Sons, 1883), p. 97.
21. Ibid., p. 98.
22. Official Records, vol. 37, pt. 1, p. 290.
23. *Richmond Examiner*, Aug. 1, 1864.
24. Robert E. Park, *Sketch of the 12th Alabama Infantry* (Richmond, Va.: Jones, 1906), p. 85.
25. Official Records, vol. 37, pt. 1, p. 354.
26. George Peyton, p. 35.
27. Hotchkiss, p. 221.
28. Charles C. Osborne, *Jubal: The Life and Times of Lt. Gen. Jubal A. Early, C.S.A.* (Baton Rouge, La.: Louisiana State University Press, 1992), p. 302.
29. Old, p. 5.
30. Green Peyton, "Robert E. Rodes," *Virginia Military Institute Memorial Volume*, Charles Walker, ed., p. 455.
31. Park, p. 85.
32. Old, p. 6.
33. Wert, p. 47.
34. Ibid.
35. Opposing Forces in the Valley Campaign, *Battles and Leaders* (Secaucus, N.J.: Castle Press, 1897), vol. 4, p. 531.
36. Wesley Merritt, "Sheridan in the Shenandoah," *Battles and Leaders*, vol. 4, pp. 501–2.
37. Osborne, p. 323.
38. Ibid., p. 324.
39. Merritt, p. 504.
40. Pond, p. 135.
41. Hotchkiss, pp. 222–23.

42. Green Peyton, p. 456.
43. Gallagher, p. 136.
44. Bryan Grimes, "Extract of Letters of Maj. Gen. Bryan Grimes to his Wife," Pulaski Cowper, ed. (Raleigh, N.C.: Broughton, Edwards and Co., 1883), p. 65.
45. Albert Hemingway, "Whirling Through Winchester," *America's Civil War*, May 1991, p. 40.
46. "An Incident at the Battle of Winchester or Opequon" Unknown Author, *Southern Historical Society Papers,* vol. 9, p. 232.
47. Henry A. DuPont, *The Campaign of 1864 in the Shenandoah Valley and the Expedition to Lynchburg* (New York: National Americana Society, 1925), p. 108.
48. Pond, p. 154.
49. John B. Gordon, *Reminiscences of the Civil War* (New York: Scribner's, 1903), p. 318.
50. I.G. Bradwell, "Sheridan and Trevilian's Station," *Confederate Veteran*, vol. 38, p. 453.
51. DuPont, pp. 107–8.
52. Merritt, p. 506.
53. Ibid.
54. I.E. Baker, "Diary and Recollections," Unpublished, Winchester-Frederick County Historical Society, p. 107.
55. Gordon, p. 320.
56. Hemingway, p. 42.
57. Jubal A. Early, "Winchester, Fisher's Hill and Cedar Creek," *Battles and Leaders*, vol. 4, p. 523.
58. Ibid.
59. Hemingway, p. 42.
60. George Peyton, p. 80.
61. DuPont, p. 114.
62. Gordon, p. 321.
63. Faust, p. 188.
64. *Richmond Times Dispatch*, P.J. White, Feb. 16, 1929.
65. Marcus Herring, "General Rodes at Winchester," *Confederate Veteran*, vol. 27, p. 184.
66. J.L. Schaub, "Gen. Robert E. Rodes," *Confederate Veteran*, vol. 16, p. 269.
67. Herring, p. 184.
68. Schaub, p. 269.
69. Herring, p. 184.
70. Park, p. 91.
71. DuPont, p. 112.
72. Merritt, p. 509.
73. Schaub, p. 269.
74. James M. Garnett, "Diary of Capt. James Garnett: Ordnance Officer, Rodes' Division, 2nd Corps" Aug. 5, 1864 to Nov. 30, 1864, *Southern Historical Society Papers*, vol. 27, 1899, p. 6.
75. Hotchkiss, p. 223.
76. *Lynchburg Virginian*, Sept. 22, 1864.
77. Ibid.
78. *Lynchburg Virginian*, Sept. 24, 1864.
79. Asbury Christian, *Lynchburg and Its People* (Lynchburg, Va.: J.P. Bell Publisher, 1900), pp. 228–29.
80. *Lynchburg Virginian*, Sept. 24, 1864.

81. Green Peyton, p. 471.
82. Henry C. Sommerville, "Diary: 1862–1865" Unpublished, Virginia State Library, Richmond, Va., p. 78.
83. Early, *Battles and Leaders,* vol. 4, p. 524n.
84. Osborne, p. 345.
85. Merritt, p. 513.
86. Garnett, p. 13.
87. George Peyton, p. 86.
88. *Lynchburg Virginian*, Oct. 24, 1864.

EPILOGUE

1. John B. Gordon, *Reminiscences of the Civil War* (New York: Scribner's, 1903), pp. 321–22.
2. Green Peyton, "Robert E. Rodes," *Virginia Military Institute Memorial Volume*, Charles Walker, ed., p. 457.
3. Thomas Munford, *Southern Historical Society Papers*, vol. 12, p. 448.
4. Bryan Grimes, *Extract of Letters of Maj. Gen. Bryan Grimes to His Wife*, Pulaski Cowper, ed. (Raleigh, N.C.: Broughton, Edwards, and Co., 1883), p. 22.
5. J. L. Schaub, "General Robert E. Rodes," *Confederate Veteran*, vol. 16, p. 269.
6. Report of Robert E. Rodes, *Southern Historical Society Papers*, vol. 2, p. 166.
7. Official Records of the Union and Confederate Armies (Washington, D.C.: Government Printing Office, 1880–1901), vol. 27, pt. 1, p. 354.
8. Robert E. Park, *Sketch of the 12th Alabama Infantry* (Richmond, Va.: Jones, 1906), p. 83.
9. P.J. White, "Gen. Robert E. Rodes," *Confederate Veteran*, vol. 35, p. 100.

BIBLIOGRAPHY

BOOKS

Alexander, Porter. *Fighting For the Confederacy: The Personal Recollections of Gen. Porter Alexander*. Gary Gallagher, ed., Chapel Hill, N.C.: University of North Carolina Press, 1989.

———. *Military Memoirs of a Confederate*. Dayton, Ohio: Morningside Press, 1990.

Battles and Leaders of the Civil War. Robert Johnson and Clarence Clough Buel, eds. Secaucus, N.J.: Castle Press, 1897, 4 vols.

Bigelow, John, Jr. *The Campaign of Chancellorsville*. New Haven, Conn.: Yale Press, 1910.

Biographical Dictionary of the Confederacy. Jon L. Wakelyn, ed. Westport, Conn.: Greenwood Press, 1977.

Blackford, Susan. *Letters from Lee's Army*. New York: Scribner and Sons, 1947.

Blackford, William. *War Years with Jeb Stuart*. New York: Scribner and Sons, 1945.

Brice, Marshall M. *Conquest of a Valley*. Charlottesville, Va.: University of Virginia Press, 1965.

Bridges, Hal. *Lee's Maverick General: Daniel Harvey Hill*. New York: McGraw-Hill Publishers, 1961.

Brooks, Noah. *Mr. Lincoln's Washington*. New York, Thomas Yoseloff, Inc., 1967.

Catton, Bruce. *The Army of the Potomac: Mr. Lincoln's Army*. Garden City, N.Y.: Doubleday, Inc., 1962.

Chamberlayne, John Hampton. *Letters and Papers of an Artillery Officer: 1861–1865.* C.G. Chamberlayne, ed. Richmond, Va.: Dietz Press, 1932.

Chambers, S. Allen. *Lynchburg: An Architectural History.* Charlottesville, Va.: University of Virginia Press, 1981.

Chesnut, Mary B. *Mary B. Chesnut's Civil War Diary*. New Haven, Conn.: Yale Press, 1981.

Christian, Asbury W. *Lynchburg and Its People*. Lynchburg, Va.: J.P. Bell Press, 1900.

Coddington, Edwin B. *The Gettysburg Campaign: A Study in Command.* New York: Charles Scribner's and Sons, 1984.

Confederate Veteran Magazine. Nashville, Tenn.: 40 vols., 1893–1932.

Connelly, Thomas L. *The Marble Man, Robert E. Lee and His Image in American Society*. Baton Rouge, La.: Louisiana State University Press, 1978.

Cooling, B.F. *Jubal Early's Raid on Washington in 1864*. Baltimore, Md.: Nautical and Aviation Publishing Co., 1989.

Couper, William. *History of the Shenandoah Valley*. New York, vol. 2, 1952.

———. *The New Market Cadets*. Charlottesville, Va.: Michie Co., 1933.

———. *One Hundred Years at V.M.I.* Richmond, Va.: Garrett and Massie Co., 4 vols., 1939.

Clark, Walter, ed. *History of Several Regiments and Battalions from North Carolina in the Great War of 1864–1865*. Raleigh, N.C.: North Carolina Department of Archives and History, 1901.

Davis, Burke. *They Called Him Stonewall.* New York: Rinehart and Co., 1954.

Davis, William C. *The Battle of New Market.* Garden City, N.J.: Doubleday and Co., 1975.

Dowdy, Clifford. *Death of a Nation*, New York: Alfred A. Knopf Co., 1958.

———. *The Seven Days: The Emergence of Robert E. Lee*, New York: The Fairfax Press, 1978.

Dowdy, Clifford, and Louis Manarin. *The Wartime Papers of Robert E. Lee.* New York: Bramhall House, 1961.

Dunlop, W.L. *Lee's Sharpshooters or The Forefront of Battle*. Dayton, Ohio: Morningside Press, 1988.

DuPont, Henry A. *The Campaign of 1864 in the Shenandoah Valley and the Expedition to Lynchburg*. New York: National Americana Society, 1925.

Early, Jubal Anderson. *Jubal Early's Memoirs*. Baltimore, Md.: Nautical and Aviation Publishing Co. of America, 1989.

Eckert, Ralph Lowell. *John Brown Gordon: Soldier, Southerner, American.* Baton Rouge, La.: Louisiana State University Press, 1989.

Eggleston, Gary. *History of the Confederate War.* New York: Negro University Press, 1910. Vols. 1 and 2.

Elliott, Joseph Cantley. *Lieutenant General Richard Heron Anderson: Lee's Noble Soldier.* Dayton, Ohio: Morningside Press, 1985.

Evans, Clement A., *Confederate Military History.* Atlanta, Ga.: Confederate Publishing Co., 1899, 8 vols.

Faust, Patricia L. *Historical Times Illustrated Encyclopedia of the Civil War.* New York: Harper and Rowe, 1986.

Fishel, Edwin C. *The Secret War for The Union.* New York: Houghton Mifflin, 1960.

Fleming, Walter L. *Civil War and Reconstruction in Alabama.* New York: Columbia University Press, 1905.

Fox, William F. *Regimental Losses in the Civil War.* Albany, New York: 1889.

Frassanito, William A. *Grant and Lee: Virginia Campaigns, 1864–1865.* New York: Charles Scribner and Sons, 1983.

Freeman, Douglas S., ed. *Lee's Confidential Dispatches to Jefferson Davis, 1862–1865.* New York, Grady McWhiney, Putnam and Sons, 1957.

———. *Lee's Lieutenants.* New York: Scribner's Inc., vols. 1, 2, 3, 1942.

———. *R.E. Lee.* New York: Charles Scribner's Sons, vols. 1, 2, 3, 4, 1946.

———. *The South to Posterity.* New York: Charles Scribner's and Sons, 1951.

Fugurson, Ernest B. *Chancellorsville 1863: The Souls of the Brave.* New York: Vintage Books, 1993.

Gallagher, Gary W. *Stephen Dodson Ramseur: Lee's Gallant General.* Chapel Hill, N.C.: University of North Carolina Press, 1985.

Glatthaar, Joseph T. *Forged in Battle: The Civil War Alliance of Black Soldiers and White Officers.* New York: Free Press, 1990.

Gordon, John B. *Reminiscences of the Civil War.* New York, Scribner's, 1903.

Grimes, Bryan. *Extract of Letters of Major General Bryan Grimes to His Wife, Written While in Active Service in the Army of Northern Virginia together with Some Personal Recollections of the War.* Pulaski Cowper, ed., Raleigh, N.C.: Broughton, Edwards, and Co., 1883.

Hartje, Robert G. *Van Dorn: The Life and Times of a Confederate General.* Nashville, Tenn.: Vanderbilt University Press, 1967.

Hassler, Warren W., Jr. *Commanders of the Army of the Potomac.* Baton Rouge, La.: Louisiana State University Press, 1962.

———. *Crisis at the Crossroads: The First Day at Gettysburg.* Tuscaloosa, Ala.: University of Alabama Press, 1970.

Herdegen, Lance J., and William Beaudot. *In the Bloody Railway Cut at Gettysburg*. Dayton, Ohio: Morningside Press, 1990.

Hotchkiss, Jedediah. *Make Me a Map of the Valley: The Civil War Journal of Stonewall Jackson's Topographer*. Archie McDonald, ed., Dallas. Tex.: Southern Methodist University Press, 1973.

Houck, Peter W. *A Prototype of a Confederate Hospital Center in Lynchburg, Virginia*. Lynchburg, Va.: Warwick Publishing, 1986.

Howard, McHenry. *Recollections of a Maryland Confederate Soldier and Staff Officer*. Dayton, Ohio: Morningside Press, 1975.

Humphreys, Milton W. *A History of the Lynchburg Campaign*. Charlottesville, Va.: Michie Publishing Co., 1924.

Hyde, Thomas. *Following the Greek Cross: Memories of the 6th Army Corps*. New York: Houghton Mifflin, 1894.

Izlar, William V. *History of the Edisto Rifles*. Camden, S.C.: Kohn Press, 1908.

Jackson, Mary Anna. *Memoirs of Stonewall Jackson*. Louisville, Ky.: Prentice Press, 1895.

Johns, John E. *Florida During the Civil War*. Gainesville, Fla.: University of Florida Press, 1963.

Jones, Terry L. *Lee's Tigers: The Louisiana Infantry in the Army of Northern Virginia*. Baton Rouge, La.: Louisiana State University Press, 1987.

Laboda, Lawrence R. *From Selma to Appomattox: The History of the Jeff Davis Artillery*. New York: Oxford University Press, 1994.

Levine, Bruce. *Half Slave and Half Free: The Roots of Civil War*. New York: Hill and Wang, 1992.

Long, Armistead L. *Memoirs of Robert E. Lee*. Secaucus, N.J.: Blue and Gray Press, 1983.

Matter, William D. *If it Takes All Summer, The Battle of Spotsylvania*. Chapel Hill, N.C.: University of North Carolina Press, 1988.

Meaney, Peter J. *The Civil War Engagement at Cool Springs*. Berryville, Va.: Private Publisher, 1980.

Mitchell, Reid. *Civil War Soldiers: Their Expectations and Their Experiences*. New York: Viking-Penguin, 1988.

Montgomery, Horace. *Howell Cobb's Confederate Career*. Tuscaloosa, Ala.: 1959.

Morgan, William H. *Personal Recollections of the War of 1861–1865*. Lynchburg, Va.: J.P. Bell, 1911.

Morrison, James L., Jr., ed. *Memoirs of Henry Heth*. Westport, Conn.: Greenwood Press, 1974.

Mott, Sarah. *Personal Experiences of a House That Stood on the Road*. Carlisle, Pa.: South Mountain Press, 1941.

Murfin, James V. *The Gleam of Bayonets*. Baton Rouge, La.: Louisiana State University Press, 1965.

Nye, Wilbur S. *Here Come the Rebels*. Dayton, Ohio: Morningside Press, 1988.

Official Records of the Union and Confederate Armies. Washington, D.C.: United States War Department, Government Printing Office, 1880–1901.

Osborne, Charles C. *Jubal: The Life and Times of Gen. Jubal A. Early, CSA: Defender of the Lost Cause*. Baton Rouge, La.: Louisiana State University Press, 1992.

Park, Robert Emory. *Sketch of the 12th Alabama Infantry*. Richmond, Va.: Jones, 1906.

Pfanz, Harry W. *Gettysburg: Culp's Hill and Cemetery Hill*. Chapel Hill, N.C.: University of North Carolina Press, 1993.

Piston, William Garrett. *Lee's Tarnished Lieutenant: James Longstreet and His Place in Southern History*. Athens, Ga.: University of Georgia Press, 1987.

Pond, George F. *The Shenandoah Valley in 1864*. New York: Scribner and Sons, 1883.

Potter, Dorothy T., and Clifton W. Potter. *Lynchburg: The Most Interesting Spot*, Lynchburg, Va.: Progress Printing, 1976.

Priest, John M. *Before Antietam: The Battle for South Mountain*. New York: Oxford University Press, 1992.

Reid, J.W. *History of the Fourth Regiment, South Carolina Volunteers*. Dayton, Ohio: Morningside Press, 1975.

Remini, Robert V., *Andrew Jackson and the Course of American Freedom*. New York: Harper and Rowe, vol. 2, 1988.

Reynolds, Donald E. *Editors Make War: Southern Newspapers in the Secession Crisis*. Nashville, Tenn.: Vanderbilt University Press, 1970.

Rhea, Gordon C. *The Battle of the Wilderness, May 5–6, 1864*. Baton Rouge, La.: Louisiana State University Press, 1994.

———. *The Battle for Spotsylvania Court House and the Road to Yellow Tavern*. Baton Rouge, La.: Louisiana State University Press, 1997.

Robertson, James I., *General A.P. Hill: The Story of a Confederate Warrior*, New York: Random House, 1987.

———. *Stonewall Jackson, The Man, The Soldier, The Legend*. New York: MacMillan Publishing, 1997.

Royster, Charles. *The Destructive War*. New York, Vintage Books, 1993.

Scott, Robert Garth. *Into the Wilderness with the Army of the Potomac*. Bloomington, Ind.: Indiana University Press, 1985.

Scruggs, Phillip Lightfoot. *The History of Lynchburg, Va. 1786–1946.* Lynchburg, Va.: J.P. Bell, Inc., 1972.

Sears, Stephen W. *To the Gates of Richmond: The Peninsular Campaign.* New York: Ticknor and Fields, 1992.

———. *George B. McClellan, The Young Napoleon.* New York: Ticknor and Fields, 1988.

———. *Landscape Turned Red: The Battle of Antietam.* New York: Ticknor and Fields, 1983.

Sorrell, G. Moxley. *Recollections of a Confederate Staff Officer.* Jackson, Tenn.: McCowat-Mercer Co., 1958.

Southern Historical Society Papers. Richmond, Va. 39 vols., 1876–1919.

Stiles, Robert. *Four Years Under Marse Robert.* New York: Neale, 1903.

Swisher, James K. *Prince of Edisto: Brigadier General Micah Jenkins, CSA.* Berryville, Va.: Rockbridge Press, 1996.

Sypher, Josiah R. *History of the Pennsylvania Reserve Corps.* Lancaster, Pa.: Barr and Co., 1865.

Taylor, Walter H. *Four Years With General Lee.* New York: Bonanza Books, 1962.

Thomas, Henry W. *History of the Doles-Cook Brigade.* Dayton, Ohio: Morningside Press, 1988.

Tobert, Annette. *The Brothers' War.* New York: Time Books, 1988.

Tousey, Thomas. *The Military History of Carlisle Barracks.* Richmond, Va.: 1939.

Tucker, Glen. *Chickamauga: Bloody Battle in the West.* Dayton, Ohio: Moringside Press, 1976.

———. *Hancock the Superb.* Dayton, Ohio: Morningside Press, 1980.

———. *High Tide at Gettysburg.* Indianapolis, Ind.: Bobbs-Merrill, 1958.

———. *Zebulon Vance: Champion of Personal Freedom.* Indianapolis, Ind.: Broehill, 1965.

United States Army Guide to the Battles of Chancellorsville and Fredericksburg. Jay Luvaas and Harold Nelson, eds. Carlisle, Pa.: South Mountain Press, 1988.

United States Army Guide to the Battle of Antietam. Jay Luvaas and Harold Nelson, eds. Lawrence, Kans.: University of Kansas Press, 1996.

United States Army Guide to the Battle of Gettysburg. Jay Luvaas and Harold Nelson, eds. Carlisle, Pa.: South Mountain Press, 1987.

Vandiver, Frank E. *Jubal's Raid: Early's Attack on Washington in 1864.* New York: McGraw-Hill Co., 1960.

———. *Mighty Stonewall.* New York: McGraw-Hill Co., 1957.

Von Borcke, Heros. *Memoirs of the Confederate War for Independence.* Dayton, Ohio: Morningside Press, vol. 1, 1985.

Walker, Charles D., ed. *Virginia Military Institute Memorial Volume.* Philadelphia, Pa.: 1875.

Walker, Gary. *Yankee Soldiers in Virginia's Valley: Hunter's Raid.* Roanoke, Va.: A and W Enterprises, 1989.

Wainwright, Charles D. *A Diary of Battle.* Allen Nevins, ed. New York: Hardcourt, Brace and World, 1962.

Ward, James. *The 12th Ohio Volunteers,* Ripley, Ohio: O.C. Smith, 1864.

Warner, Ezra J. *Generals in Gray,* Baton Rouge, La.: Louisiana State University Press, 1959.

Wheeler, Richard. *On Fields of Fury.* New York: Harper and Rowe, Inc., 1991.

———. *Sword Over Richmond.* New York: Harper and Rowe, Inc., 1986.

Wise, Jennings C. *The Long Arm of Lee: History of the Artillery of the Army of Northern Virginia.* Lynchburg, Va.: J.P. Bell, Inc., 1915.

———. *The Military History of the Virginia Military Institute 1839–1865.* Lynchburg, Va.: J.P. Bell, Inc., 1915.

Woodward, C. Vann, ed. *Mary Chesnut's Civil War,* New Haven, Conn.: Yale University Press, 1981.

Woodward, Harold R. *The Confederacy's Forgotten Son: James L. Kemper.* Berryville, Va.: Rockbridge Press, 1994.

Yancy, Rose Faulkner. *Lynchburg and Its Neighbors.* Richmond, Va.: J.W. Ferguson, Inc., 1935.

UNPUBLISHED MATERIALS

Anderson, Richard H. Letter to D.H. Hill, Oct. 26, 1867. Virginia State Library, Richmond, Va.

Allen, William. Papers. Southern Historical Collection, University of North Carolina, Chapel Hill, N.C.

Baker, I.E. Diary and Recollections. Winchester-Frederick County Historical Society, Winchester, Va.

Beardsworth, Susan R. "Life of Lynchburg's Confederate Generals," W.P.A. Article. Jan. 17, 1938, Jones Memorial Library, Lynchburg, Va.

Brown, Campell G. "Military Reminiscences of Major Campbell Brown." Tennessee State Library Archives.

Carter, Thomas. Speech Upon Presentation of Portrait of Robert E. Rodes to Lee Camp, Confederate Veterans. Archives of Virginia Military Institute, Lexington, Va.

Class Standings, Virginia Military Institute. 1846. 1847. 1848. Lexington, Va.

Curriculum. Virginia Military Institute. 1848, Lexington, Va.

Daniel, John Warwick, Papers. Daniel Collection. University of Virginia, Charlottesville, Va.

Daniel, John W. "Memoir of the Battle of Gettysburg." Virginia Historical Society, Richmond, Va.

Daughters of the American Revolution Application. Louise Rodes Schoch. Archives of Virginia Military Institute, Lexington, Va.

General Orders #42. #43. Virginia Military Institute, Lexington, Va.

Larkin, Maude J. "General Robert E. Rodes," *The Critic,* Magazine, Lynchburg High School, June 1907, pp. 10–13, Jones Memorial Library, Lynchburg, Va.

Leach, Calvin. "Diary." Southern Historical Collection. University of North Carolina, Chapel Hill, N.C.

North River Navigation Company. Minutes of the Board. July 8, 1850–Feb. 7, 1851. Private Collection of T. Gibson Hobbs. Lynchburg, Va.

Old, W.W. "Diary: The Operations of Lt. Gen. Jubal A. Early in the Valley of Virginia and Maryland, June 13, 1864 to Aug. 12, 1864." Jones Memorial Library, Lynchburg, Va.

Peyton, George Quintas. "A Civil War Record: 1864–1865." 1929, Jones Memorial Library, Lynchburg, Va.

Purifoy, John. "History of the Jeff Davis Artillery." Alabama Department of History and Archives, Montgomery, Ala., July 21, 1901.

Rodes, David. Letters. Archives of Handley Library, Winchester, Va.

———. Archives of Virginia Military Institute, Lexington, Va.

Rodes, Martha. Letters. Archives of Handley Library, Winchester, Va.

Rodes, Robert E. Letters. Archives of Handley Library, Winchester, Va.

———. Letters. Archives of Virginia Military Institute, Lexington, Va.

———. Military Record. National Archives and Records, Administration, Washington, D.C.

Rodes, Virginia. Letters. Archives of Virginia Military Institute, Lexington, Va.

Rodes, Virginius. Letters. Archives of Handley Library, Winchester, Va.

Rodes, Family. Study by Frances Robertson. Jones Memorial Library, Lynchburg, Va.

Sommerville, Henry C. Diary. 1862–1865, Virginia State Library, Richmond, Va.

Smith, Francis. Letters. Archives of Virginia Military Institute, Lexington, Va.

Smith, Otis D. "Reminiscences." Thach Papers. Southern Historical Collection, University of North Carolina, Chapel Hill, N.C.

ARTICLES

Abbott, Asa T. "Lincoln At Fort Stevens." *Civil War Times Illustrated*, July 1978, vol. 17, p. 33.

Allen, William. "The First Maryland Campaign." *Southern Historical Society Papers*, vol. 14, 1886, pp. 102–18.

Bates, P. Samuel. "Hooker's Comments on Chancellorsville." *Battles and Leaders*, vol. 3, pp. 215–23.

Battle, Cullen. "Report of 3rd Alabama, Battle of Gettysburg." *Southern Historical Society Papers*, vol. 13, pp. 177–78.

Beauregard, P.G.T. "The First Battle of Bull Run." *Battles and Leaders*, vol. 1, pp. 196–227.

Blackford, Charles M. "The Battle of Lynchburg." *Southern Historical Society Papers*, vol. 30, 1902, pp. 279–332.

Blackford, Eugene. "Report of Sharpshooters, Battle of Gettysburg." *Southern Historical Society Papers*, vol. 13, pp. 178–79.

Bolte, Phillip. "Lonely Command." *Magazine of the Civil War Society*, vol. 61, April 1997, pp. 42–47.

Bradwell, I.G. "Cold Harbor, Lynchburg, and the Valley Campaign of 1864." *Confederate Veteran*, vol. 28, 1920, pp. 138–39.

———. "First Valley Campaign of General Early." *Confederate Veteran*, vol. 19, pp. 230–31.

———. "Early's Demonstration Against Washington." *Confederate Veteran*, vol. 22, 1914, pp. 438–39.

———. "Early's March to Washington, 1864." *Confederate Veteran*, vol. 28, 1920, pp. 176–77.

———. "Sheridan and Trevilian's Station." *Confederate Veteran*, vol. 38, pp. 452–55.

Broadwater, Robert D. "The Battle of Folck's Mill and the Fourth Confederate Invasion of Maryland." *Confederate Veteran*, vol. 4, 1996, pp. 30–38.

Brown, Campbell. "General Ewell at Bull Run." *Battles and Leaders*, vol. 1, pp. 259–61.

Calendar of Events. *Battles and Leaders*, p. 1.

Carpender, J. Edward. "The Charge of the 8th Pennsylvania Cavalry." *Battles and Leaders*, vol. 3, p. 187.

Carrington, James M. "First Day at Gettysburg." *Southern Historical Society Papers*, vol. 37, 1909, pp. 326–27.

Cheeks, Robert C. "Fire and Fury at Catharine's Furnace." *America's Civil War*, May 1995, pp. 30–37.

Christian, C.B. "Battle of Bethesda Church." *Southern Historical Society Papers*, vol. 37, 1909, pp. 236–42.

Coffey, Thomas. "Letter From Fredericksburg, 9/24/1863." *Confederate Veteran*, vol. 26, p. 157.

———. "Letter to Mother, 1/15/1864." *Confederate Veteran*, vol. 26, p. 353.

Coffin, Charles C. "Antietam Scenes." *Battles and Leaders*, vol. 2, pp. 682–85.

Coleman, Howard. "The Lion of Virginia: The Story of Jubal Anderson Early." *Lynchburg: The Magazine of Central Virginia*, vol. 13, parts, 1, 2, 3, 4. March, April, July, September 1981.

Collins, John R. "When Stonewall Jackson Turned Our Right." *Battles and Leaders*, vol. 3, pp. 183–85.

Colgrove, Silas. "The Finding of Lee's Lost Order." *Battles and Leaders*, vol. 2, p. 603.

Conway, Dr. William. "Talks with General Early." *Southern Historical Society Papers*, vol. 30, 1902, pp. 250–55.

Coski, John M. "Drewry's Bluff." *Confederate Veteran*, vol. 6, 1996, pp. 16–26.

Couch, Darius N. "The Chancellorsville Campaign." *Battles and Leaders*, vol. 3, pp. 154–71.

Cox, Jacob D. "Forcing Fox's Gap and Turner's Gap." *Battles and Leaders*, vol. 2, pp. 583–91.

———. "The Battle of Antietam." *Battles and Leaders*, vol. 2, pp. 630–60.

Daniel, John Warwick. "General Jubal A. Early," *Southern Historical Society Papers*, vol. 22, 1894, pp. 281–340.

Davis, Danny. "Return to Fredericksburg." *America's Civil War*, September 1992, pp. 30–37.

Dunn, William E. "On the Peninsular: Civil War Letters of William E. Dunn," *Civil War Times Illustrated*, July 1985, p. 17.

Early, Jubal A. "Early's March to Washington in 1864." *Battles and Leaders*, vol. 4, pp. 492–98.

———. "The Attack on Washington in 1864." *Southern Historical Society Papers*, vol. 9, 1881, pp. 297–312.

———. "Winchester, Fisher's Hill, and Cedar Creek." *Battles and Leaders*, vol. 4, pp. 522–29.

Eggleston, George Cary. "Notes on Cold Harbor." *Battles and Leaders*, vol. 4, pp. 230–32.

Firey, Frank. "On the Battlefield of South Mountain." *Confederate Veteran*, vol. 23, 1915, pp. 70–78.

Fry, James B. "McDowell's Advance to Bull Run." *Battles and Leaders*, vol. 1, pp. 167–93.

Galloway, G. Norton. "Hand to Hand Fighting at Spotsylvania." *Battles and Leaders*, vol. 4, pp. 170–74.

Garnett, James M. "Diary of Capt. James Garnett: Ordnance Officer, Rodes Division, 2nd Corps Aug. 5, 1864 to Nov. 30, 1864." *Southern Historical Society Papers*, vol. 28, 1899, pp. 1–16.

Grant, Ulysses S. "Preparing for the Campaign of 64." *Battles and Leaders*, vol. 4, pp. 97–117.

Grattan, George D. "The Battle of Boonsboro Gap or South Mountain." *Southern Historical Society Papers*, vol. 39, 1914, pp. 31–44.

Green, James E. "As They Saw General Lee." *Civil War Times Illustrated*, Edward Smith, ed. October 1986, p. 21.

Grimsley, Mark. "Master General: His Mode of War." *Civil War Times Illustrated*, November 1985, pp. 28–33.

———. "On the Edge of Disaster: Lee and McClelland at South Mountain." *Civil War Times Illustrated*, November 1986, pp. 18–23, 44–50.

Happell, Ralph. "The Chancellors of Chancellorsville." *Va. Magazine of History and Biography*, vol. 71, 1963, pp. 259–77.

Harrison, Constance Cary. "Richmond Scenes in 62." *Battles and Leaders*, vol. 2, pp. 439–48.

Harvie, E.J. "Fox's Gap." *Confederate Veteran*, vol. 4, 1896, p. 27.

———. "General Joseph E. Johnston." *Confederate Veteran*, vol. 18, 1910, p. 521.

Hawkins, Rush. "Why Burnside Did Not Renew the Attack at Fredericksburg." *Battles and Leaders*, vol. 3, pp. 127–28.

Hemingway, Al. "Day One at Chancellorsville." *America's Civil War*, March 1996, pp. 42–49, 82.

———. "Whirling Through Winchester." *America's Civil War*, May 1991, pp. 38–44.

Herring, Marcus. "General Rodes at Winchester." *Confederate Veteran*, vol. 27, pp. 184–85.

Hill, Daniel Harvey. "An Address at the Virginia Reunion, Army of Northern Virginia, 1885." *Southern Historical Society Papers*, vol. 13, 1885, pp. 267–81.

———. "Lee's Attack North of the Chickahominy." *Battles and Leaders*, vol. 2, p. 347–62.

———. "The Battle of South Mountain or Boonsboro." *Battles and Leaders*, vol. 2, pp. 559–81.

Howard, Oliver O. "The XIth Corps at Chancellorsville." *Battles and Leaders*, vol. 3, pp. 189–202.

Hunter, Alexander. "A High Private's Account of Sharpsburg." *Southern Historical Society Papers*, vol. 10, 1882, part 1, pp. 503–12.

———. "A High Private's Account of Sharpsburg." *Southern Historical Society Papers*, vol. 11, 1883, part 2, pp. 10–21.

Jackson, Hunnington. "Sedgwick at Fredericksburg and Salem Heights." *Battles and Leaders*, vol. 3, pp. 224–32.

Johnson, Bradley T. "Stonewall Jackson's Intentions at Harper's Ferry." *Battles and Leaders*, vol. 2, pp. 615–18.

Johnston, Joseph E. "Manassas to Seven Pines." *Battles and Leaders*, vol. 2, pp. 202–18.

Jones, Jesse H., and George S. Greene. "The Breastworks at Culp's Hill." *Battles and Leaders*, vol. 3, pp. 316–17.

Kilmer, George L. "The Army of the Potomac at Harrison's Landing." *Battles and Leaders*, vol. 2, pp. 428–29.

Lash, Gary, "General Henry Baxter's Brigade at Gettysburg, July 1." *Gettysburg Magazine*, #10, January 1994, pp. 6–18.

Law, E.M. "From the Wilderness to Cold Harbor." *Battles and Leaders*, vol. 4, pp. 118–44.

Longstreet, James. "Battle of Fredericksburg." *Battles and Leaders*, vol 3, pp. 70–85.

———. "Lee's Invasion of Pennsylvania." *Battles and Leaders*, vol. 3, pp. 244–51.

———. "The Invasion of Maryland." *Battles and Leaders*, vol. 2, pp. 663–74.

Martin, Micajah D. "Chancellorsville, A Soldier's Letter." *Virginia Magazine of History and Biography*, vol. 37, 1929, pp. 22–24.

Martin, Samuel. "Did Baldy Ewell Lose Gettysburg?" *America's Civil War*, July 1997, pp. 34–40.

Massey, Griffin D. "Rodes on Oak Hill: A Study of Rodes' Division on the 1st Day at Gettysburg." *Gettysburg Magazine*, #4, January 1991, pp. 33–48.

McAllister, Robert. "McAllister's Brigade at the Bloody Angle." *Battles and Leaders*, vol. 4, pp. 177–78.

McMahon, Martin T. "From Gettysburg to the Coming of Grant." *Battles and Leaders*, vol 4, pp. 81–94.

———. "Cold Harbor." *Battles and Leaders*, vol. 4., pp. 213–20.

———. "The Death of General John Sedgwick." *Battles and Leaders*, vol. 4, p. 175.

Merritt, Wesley. "Sheridan in the Shenandoah." *Battles and Leaders*, vol. 4, pp. 500–521.

Miller, Robert H. "Letters To His Family, 1861–1862." *Va. Magazine of History and Biography*, vol. 70, 1962, pp. 62–89.

Minnich, J.W. " Incidents of the Peninsular Campaign." *Confederate Veteran*, vol. 30, p. 55.

Mitchell, Mary B. "A Woman's Recollections of Antietam." *Battles and Leaders*, vol. 2, 686–95.

Moorman, Marcellus, "Letters." *Southern Historical Society Papers*, vol. 30, 1902, pp. 110–16.

Neal, Robert C. "Bury Those Poor Men." *America's Civil War*, November 1990, pp. 34–40.

Norman, Ken, and C.E. Avery. "Notes on Pvt. Robert A. Ware, 6th Alabama." *Confederate Veteran*, vol. 1, 1997, pp. 31–37.

Opposing Armies at Bull Run. *Battles and Leaders*, vol. 1, p. 194.

Opposing Armies in Maryland Campaign. *Battles and Leaders*, vol. 2, p. 601.

Opposing Armies at Williamsburg. *Battles and Leaders*, vol. 2, p. 200.

Osborne, Hampden. *Southern Historical Society Papers*, vol. 30, 1917, p. 227.

Patterson, Gerald A. "The Death of Iverson's Brigade." *Gettysburg Magazine*, #2, July 1990, pp. 13–18.

Peyton, Green. "Robert E. Rodes." *VMI Memorial Volume*, Charles Walker, ed., pp. 440–57.

Pleasonton, Alfred. "The Successes and Failures of Chancellorsville." *Battles and Leaders*, vol. 3, pp. 172–82.

Pohanka, Brian C. "Not War, But Murder." *America's Civil War*, January 1989.

Purifoy, John. " The Battle of Gettysburg." *Confederate Veteran*, vol. 31, 1923, pp. 22–25.

———. "Concerning the Battle of Gettysburg." *Confederate Veteran*, vol. 19, 1911, p. 77.

———. "The Horror of War." *Confederate Veteran*, vol. 33, 1925, pp. 224–25, 237.

———. "Jackson's Last Battle." *Confederate Veteran*, vol. 28, 1920, pp. 193–96.

———. "The Retreat From Gettysburg." *Confederate Veteran*, vol. 33, 1925, pp. 338–40.

———. "With Jackson in the Valley." *Confederate Veteran*, vol. 30, 1922, pp. 383–85.

———. "With Ewell and Rodes in Pennsylvania," *Confederate Veteran*, vol. 30, p. 462.

Rodes, Robert. "Report of Battle of Gettysburg." *Southern Historical Society Papers*, vol. 13, pp. 135–58.

———. "Report of the Battle of Chancellorsville." *Southern Historical Society Papers*, vol. 2, 1876, pp. 161–72.

Samito, Christian G. "Robert Rodes: Warrior in Gray." *America's Civil War*, January 1995, pp. 46–88.

Schaub, J.L. "General Robert E. Rodes." *Confederate Veteran*, vol. 16, pp. 269–70.

Skoch, George F. "A Test of Rebel Rails." *Civil War Times Illustrated*, December 1986, pp. 12–18.

Slaughter, William R. "Letter to Mother and Sisters." *The Brothers' War*, Dec. 13, 1862, 2nd Lt., 6th Alabama.

Smith, Gustavus. "Two Days of Battle at Seven Pines." *Battles and Leaders*, vol. 2, pp. 220–63.

Smith, James Power. "Stonewall Jackson's Last Battle." *Battles and Leaders*, vol. 3, pp. 203–14.

Smith, William Farrar. "The XVIII Corps at Cold Harbor." *Battles and Leaders*, vol. 4, pp. 221–29.

Soley, J. Russell. "The Navy in the Peninsular Campaign." *Battles and Leaders*, vol. 2, pp. 264–70.

Steiner, Dr. John. "Report." *U.S. Sanitary Commission*, New York, Anson Randolph, pp. 22–31.

Sutherland, Daniel. "Stars in Their Courses." *America's Civil War*, November 1991, p. 42.

Swisher, James K. "Virginia Military Institute: Father of Confederate Officers." *Confederate Veteran*, vol. 2, 1997, pp. 10–14.

Thompson, David L. "With Burnside at Antietam." *Battles and Leaders*, vol. 2, pp. 660–62.

Thompson, James. "A Georgia Boy With Stonewall Jackson." *Virginia Magazine of History and Biography*, vol. 70, 1962, pp. 36–41.

Tucker, John S. "Diary of John S. Tucker: A Soldier From Alabama." *Alabama Historical Quarterly*, Gary Wilson, ed., vol. 43, 1981.

Venable, C.S. "Wilderness to Petersburg." *Southern Historical Society Papers*, vol. 14, pp. 522–37.

Von Borcke, Heros. "The Prussian Remembers." *Civil War Times Illustrated*, Stuart Wright, ed. part 1, February 1981, pp. 40–43.

Walker, John. "Jackson's Capture of Harper's Ferry." *Battles and Leaders*, vol. 2, pp. 604–11.

———. "Sharpsburg." *Battles and Leaders*, vol. 2, pp. 675–82.

Webb, Alexander. "Through the Wilderness." *Battles and Leaders*, vol. 4, pp. 152–69.

Wert, Jeffrey. "The Battle of Seven Pines." *Civil War Times Illustrated*, part 1, October 1988, pp. 20–28.

———. "The Battle of Seven Pines." *Civil War Times Illustrated*, part 2, November 1988, pp. 21–25, 28, 29, 46, 50.

———. "The Second Battle of Kernstown, 1864: The Old Killing Ground." *Civil War Times Illustrated*, October 1984, pp. 40–47.

———. "The Snicker's Gap War." *Civil War Times Illustrated*, July 1978, pp. 31–40.

———. "Robert E. Rodes: So High in Rank, So Brilliant in Service, So Glorious in Death." *Civil War Times Illustrated*, 1970, pp. 4–9, 41–45.

White, P.J. "General Robert E. Rodes." *Confederate Veteran*, vol. 35, pp. 100–101.

Winschel, Terrence. "Heavy Was Their Loss: Joe Davis's Brigade at Gettysburg." *Gettysburg, Magazine*, #2, 1990, pp. 5–14.

Wittenburg, Eric J. "Roadblock en Route to Washington." *America's Civil War*, November 1993, pp. 50–56, 80, 82.

NEWSPAPERS

Chicago Tribune
July 14, 1862

Lynchburg Daily Virginian
July 2, 1855
Sept. 21, 1864
Sept. 22, 1864
Sept. 24, 1864
Sept. 30, 1864
Oct. 28, 1864

Lynchburg News and Advance
June 19, 1907
Apr. 13, 1924
July 7, 1941
Jan. 29, 1961

Lynchburg Virginian
May 25, 1846
Oct. 16, 1857
Mar. 27, 1862
May 16, 1864
Sept. 9, 1864
Jan. 18, 1879
June 13, 1879
June 14, 1879

New York Tribune
July 3, 1862

Richmond Dispatch
July 9, 1862

Richmond Examiner
May 22, 1861
May 13, 1862
June 4, 1862
Aug. 1, 1864

Richmond Times Dispatch
Feb. 16, 1929

Richmond Whig
July 4, 1862

Washington Post
Mar. 31, 1957

INDEX

First names are listed where known.

A

Abrahams Creek, 221
Alabama Units
  Jeff Davis Artillery, 45, 53, 54, 70, 142
  Cavalry
    51st, 24
  Infantry
    3rd, 43, 47, 57, 59–61, 99, 128–32, 146, 158
    4th, 30
    5th, 18–20, 22, 24, 33, 35, 38, 39, 45, 57, 59–61, 63, 127–30, 132, 205
    6th, 19, 20, 24, 33, 35, 38, 45, 50, 57, 59–62, 68–70, 128–30, 168
    12th, 22–24, 33, 35, 38, 45, 56, 60, 81, 82, 99, 118, 128–30, 148, 224
    26th, 43, 45, 57, 59–62, 128–30, 146
    61st, 146
Alexander, Porter, Brig. Gen., CSA, xiii, 42, 102, 105, 139, 175, 176, 186
Aldrich's Tavern, 88, 90
Allen, William, Col., CSA, 194
Alsops, 167
Amherst County, Va., 188
Amherst Heights, Va., 195
Anderson, George B., Brig. Gen., CSA, 33, 40, 56, 64, 70, 72, 75
Anderson, George T., Col., CSA, 56, 67
Anderson, Richard H., Lt. Gen., CSA, 32, 36, 40, 46, 92, 167, 168, 170, 220, 232
Andersonville Prison, 156
Antietam, Battle of, 62, 63, 66, 72, 203, 216
Appomattox, Va., 122
Archer, James, Brig. Gen., CSA, 97, 98, 100, 124, 125
Army of the James, USA, 156
Army of Northern Virginia, CSA, xiv, 2, 39, 40, 47, 106, 109, 118, 120, 139, 140, 163, 176, 182, 190, 232
  1st Corps, 76, 78, 109, 121, 142, 148, 158, 163, 167, 170, 171, 185, 186, 189, 220
  2nd Corps, 1, 75, 76, 89, 96, 97, 100, 109, 111, 114, 121, 135, 142, 147, 149–51, 154, 159, 167, 169–71, 179, 186, 187, 194, 200, 201, 230
  3rd Corps, 124, 136, 142, 147, 149, 158, 162, 165, 167, 170, 171, 185, 186
Army of the Potomac, USA, 76, 80, 106, 108, 120, 121, 139, 152, 155, 156, 189, 190
  I Corps, 57, 61, 64, 65, 76, 124, 125, 127, 128
  II Corps, 31, 32, 66, 102, 109, 115, 142, 149, 152, 157, 158, 162, 166, 175–77, 183, 185, 186, 193
  III Corps, 29, 35, 47, 92, 95–97, 121, 132, 133, 151, 152
  IV Corps, 29, 33, 37
  V Corps, 44, 86, 151, 152, 157, 161, 166, 167, 186
  VI Corps, 31, 76, 78, 86, 88, 105, 142, 151, 152, 157, 158, 160, 162, 167, 169, 170, 186, 189, 206, 207, 210, 213, 219–22, 224, 225, 228
  VIII Corps, 203, 221, 225
  IX Corps, 54, 56, 72, 76, 155, 163, 164, 166, 175, 186, 188
  X Corps, 188
  XI Corps, 2, 86, 89, 93–95, 124, 125, 127, 128, 131, 132
  XII Corps, 52, 65, 86–88, 96, 139
  XVIII Corps, 188, 189
  XIX Corps, 206, 207, 219, 221, 222, 224, 225

Army of the Shenandoah, USA, 219
Army of Tennessee, CSA, 148
Army of West Virginia, USA, 207
Arrington, Lieutenant, CSA, 220
Ashby, Turner, Brig. Gen., CSA, 228
Auburn College, Ala., 22
Auburn, Va., 149
Averell, William, Maj. Gen., USA, 195–97, 199, 200, 215, 225

B

Bagby, John, Capt., CSA, 35
Bailey, Guilford, Col., USA, 34
Balcony Falls, 10, 195
Baltimore Ave., 135
Baltimore, Md., 51, 121, 203, 204
Baltimore and Ohio RR, 115, 219
Baltimore Pike, 203
Banks' Ford, 103, 105
Banks, Nathaniel B., Maj. Gen., USA, 156
Bank of Monroe, Mich., 207
Barclay, William, Col., CSA, 62
Barksdale, William, Brig. Gen., CSA, 102
Batteries, CSA
  Cutshaw's, 175, 176, 220
  Dance's, 183
  Griffin's, 183
  Jones', 183
  Lambkin's, 191
  Lewis', 103
  Nelson's, 187
  Page's, 126, 175, 176
  Smith's, 183
Battle, Cullen A., Brig. Gen., CSA, xiii, 60–62, 128, 131, 146, 148, 158, 190, 202, 203, 231
Baxter, Henry, Brig. Gen., USA, 128, 130, 132
Beaver Dam Creek, Va., 44
Beauregard, P.G.T., Gen., CSA, 19–22
Bell, John, 17
Berdan, Hiram, Col., USA, 92
Berryville Pike, 221
Berryville, Va., 111, 114, 207, 217, 221
Best, Emory, Col., CSA, 90, 92
Best Farm, Md., 50, 51
Bethesda Church, 44, 187, 216
Big Lick, Va., 199
Big Otter River, 196, 198
Birney, John, Lt., CSA, 70
Black Warrior River, 17
Blackburn's Ford, 21
Blackford, Eugene, Maj., CSA
  adjutant, 1
  Chancellorsville, 82, 93, 94
  Cold Harbor, 189
  Company Commander 5th Alabama, 19, 20, 22
  Gettysburg, 125, 131, 135
  Manassas Gap, 145
  Lynchburg, 198
Blackford, Mrs. Susan, 197
Blackford, William, Col., CSA, 20
Blair House, Md., 206
"Bloody Angle," 179, 181
"Bloody Lane," 67, 70, 71
Blue Ridge Mountains, 111, 121, 207
Bondurant, J.W., Capt., CSA, 53–55
Bonham, Milledge L., Brig. Gen., CSA, 24
"Bonnie Blue Flag," 112, 117, 172
Boonsboro, Md., 52, 53, 56
Botelers Ford, 73
Botetourt Springs, Va., 199
Boyce, Richard, Capt., CSA, 70
Bragg, Braxton, Gen., CSA, 63, 148
Brandy Station, Va., 111
Braswell, I.G., xiii
Braxton, Carter M., Lt. Col., CSA, 222
Breckinridge, John C., Maj. Gen., CSA, 17, 185, 195, 196, 203, 206, 216, 217, 228
Brigades, CSA
  Anderson's, 36, 45, 62, 66, 69
  Battle's, 111, 148, 158, 160, 161, 168, 172, 173, 183, 193, 202, 211, 222, 225
  Benning's, 72
  Bratton's, 171
  Colquitt's, 46, 62, 64, 65, 90, 92, 93, 98, 99, 106, 110
  Cooke's, 202, 203, 211
  Cox's, 203, 211
  Daniel's, 106, 110, 118, 127–29, 131, 135, 138, 140, 142, 158–61, 168, 174, 180, 183
  Doles', 100, 101, 117, 125–27, 132, 133, 135, 140, 142, 148, 158–60, 168, 171, 174, 183, 188, 211
  Early's, 21, 23, 25, 26, 66, 67
  Evans', 21, 178, 180, 222
  Ewell's, 21, 23
  Featherston's, 25, 33, 40
  Garland's, 35, 36, 44, 45, 53–55, 62, 64
  Gordon's, 103, 132, 158–61, 163
  Grimes', 183, 184, 203, 211, 229
  Hampton's, 21
  Harris', 179, 180
  Hoffman's, 178, 180
  Hoke's, 103, 138, 185
  Iron, 124, 125, 133
  Iverson's, 93, 98, 99, 110, 118, 125, 127, 128, 130, 131, 135, 140, 144
  Jackson's, 21
  Johnston's, 153, 158, 178, 180
  Jones', 21, 98, 99, 137, 158–61
  Kemper's, 32, 36, 58, 61
  Lewis', 215, 216
  Lilley's, 215
  Longstreet's, 21
  McGowan's, 96–99, 179, 180
  Nicholls', 137
  O'Neal's, 93, 94, 101, 127–29, 135

Patton's, 209
Pegram's, 188
Pender's, 99
Rains', 25, 33, 35, 43
Ramseur's
attached to Rodes' Division, 76
battles of
Chancellorsville, 87, 88, 90, 93–95, 98, 99–101
Gettysburg, 127, 131–33, 135, 140
Mine Run, 151, 153, 154
Spotsylvania, 168, 178, 179, 183
Wilderness, 158, 163, 165
capture of the Potomac Fords, 112
marching north, 118
Ripley's, 46, 56, 64, 65
Rodes', 19, 24–27, 30, 32, 33, 35–37, 44, 45, 47, 48, 50–52, 56, 62, 64–71, 74–76, 78, 80
Seven Pines, poem, 233–34
Smith's, 103, 133
Stafford's, 158, 160, 162, 202
Steuart's, 158, 160, 176
Taylor's, 195
Terry's, 204
Walker's, 138, 158, 162
Wilcox's, 47, 103, 104
Witcher's, 172
Brigades, USA
Ayres', 160, 161
Bartlett's, 158, 160, 161
Baxter's, 127–31, 135
Berry's, 35
Bidwell's, 206
Cutler's, 127, 128, 160, 161
Eustis', 168
Frost's, 208, 211
Hays', 138, 162, 202
Neill's, 160, 162, 168, 171, 178, 183
Paul's, 131, 132
Sweitzer's, 160, 161
Tyler's, 204
Wells', 208
Bristoe Station, Va., 149
Broad Run Creek, 149.
Brock Road, 92, 93, 167–69, 171
Brooks, William, Brig. Gen., USA, 103
Buchanan, James, 16
Buchanan, Va., 198
Buena Vista, Va., 12
Buford's Gap, Va., 198, 199
Buford, John, Maj. Gen., USA, 124, 125
Bull Run, 20–24
Bunker Hill, Va., 74, 75, 217, 219–21
Burnside, Ambrose E., Maj. Gen., USA, 72, 76, 78–80, 84, 163, 164, 175, 188
Buschbeck, Adolphus, Col., USA, 95
Bushwhackers, 116, 122
Butler, Benjamin F., Maj. Gen., USA, 156, 188

C

Caledonia Iron Works, 116
Caldwell, John C., Brig. Gen., USA, 70
Calhoun, John C., 16
Camp Chase Prison, 156
Carlisle Barracks, 118, 119, 130
Carlisle, Pa., 114, 116–18, 121, 122, 182
Carlisle Road, 124
Carter, Thomas H., Col., CSA
commands artillery battalion, 110
eulogizes Rodes, xiii, 232
Gettysburg, 125, 126, 131, 140, 142
Mine Run, 144, 145, 153
Seven Pines, 33, 35, 41
Spotsylvania, 170, 176, 183
Winchester, 222
Carter, W.P., Capt., CSA, 41
Cary, Mr., 5
Casey, Silas, Brig. Gen., USA, 31, 33, 34, 36
"Casey's Redoubt," 33, 37
Cashtown, Pa., 121, 123, 140
Castleman's Ferry, 207–10, 213
Catharine's Furnace, 88, 90, 91
Catlett's Station, 150
Cedar Creek, Battle of, 227, 228
Cemetery Hill, 124, 133–36, 138
Cemetery Ridge, 124
Centreville, Va., 21, 22
Chambersburg, Pa., 116, 117, 120, 121, 219
Chambersburg Pike, 116, 124
Chancellorsville, Battle of
Confederate attack of May 3, 97–100
fight at Salem Church, 103, 104
Hooker's opening move, 85–87
Jackson's flank march, 90–93
Jackson wounded, 96
Lee counters Hooker, 87–90
Rodes gives command to Stuart, 96, 97
Rodes leads Jackson's flank assault, 94, 95
Rodes praised and promoted, 106
Chancellor House, 88, 90, 93, 100, 101
Chancellor's, 1, 100
Chantilly, Va., 50
Charge d'affaires, 13
Charles City Road, 30, 32
Charlestown Pike, 202
Charlottesville, Va., 147, 150, 153, 194
Chattanooga, Tenn., 19, 148, 156
Chester Gap, 111
Chickahominy River, 27, 28, 30, 43, 44, 47
Chickamauga, Battle of, 148, 216
Chimborazo Hill, 39
Christian Associations, 148
Christian, C.B., Col., CSA, 188
Christie, Daniel H., Col., CSA, 99, 144
Church Street, 5
Church Hill, 37
Citadel, The, 41
Clay, Clement C., 24

Clark Mountain, 157
Cobb, Howell, Maj. Gen., CSA, 50
Cold Harbor, Battle of, 44, 185, 188, 191, 193, 196, 230
Colquitt, Alfred H., Brig. Gen., CSA, 53, 54, 56, 58, 62, 66, 75, 94, 95
Colston, Raleigh E., Brig. Gen., CSA, 87, 88, 95, 96, 98–101, 109
Columbiad, 29
Confederate Commissary Department, 26
Confederate Engineer Corps, 29
Confederate Navy, 29
Connecticut Units
 Infantry
  18th, 210, 211
Conscription Act, 74
Constitutional Union Party, 17
Cook, Joel, 37
Cooke, John R., Brig. Gen., CSA, 149, 150
Cool Springs, Battle of, Va., 209, 210, 212, 217
Cool Springs Farm, Va., 209
Cool Springs House, 210
Corbin Family, 80
Couch, Darius N., Maj. Gen., USA, 31, 33, 37
Countess, John, Pvt., CSA, 131
Cox, Jacob D., Maj. Gen., USA, 54–56
Cox, William R., Brig. Gen., CSA, 211, 223
Craddock, John, xiii
Crampton's Gap, 203
Crook, George, Brig. Gen., USA, 195, 197, 207–9, 213, 215–17, 219, 221, 224, 225
Cross Keys, Battlefield, 203
Crozet, Claudius, 6
Crutchfield, Stapleton, Col., CSA, 95
CSS *Virginia,* 29
Culpeper Court House, 110, 114
Culpeper, Va., 76, 112, 149
Culp's Hill, 124, 134–39
Cumberland College, Pa., 12
Cumberland Valley, 114, 116
"Cush," 219
Cutshaw, W.E., Col., CSA, 175

D

Dahlgren Raid, 153
Dahlgren Road, 57–61
Dallas County, Ark., 19
Daniel, John W., Maj., CSA, 133, 144
Daniel, Junius, Brig. Gen., CSA, 106, 130, 132, 138, 144, 151, 165, 167, 178, 182, 183, 190, 231
Darkesville, Va., 145
Davidson College, N.C., 25
Davis, Jefferson, 18, 23, 25, 28, 29, 63, 89, 109, 146, 148
Davis, Joseph R., Brig. Gen., CSA, 124, 125, 131
Dawes, Rufus R., Maj., USA, 125
"Dead March," 172
Democratic Party, xiii, 16, 17, 146
Devil's Den, 126, 136
de Wolfe, Winthrop, 13
Dickerson's Mill, 185
Dickinson College, Pa., 118
Dimond, Mr., 13
Dimond, Rose, 13
Dispatch #191, 52, 53
Divisions, CSA
 Anderson's, 85, 87, 90, 92, 97–100, 105, 145
 Breckinridge's, 1, 197, 202, 204, 221
 Colston's, 85, 93, 97–99, 101
 Early's, 25, 78, 87, 105, 109, 113, 116, 121, 132, 133, 146, 154, 158, 162, 178, 185
 Ewell's, 64, 75
 Field's, 189
 Gordon's, 153, 168, 170, 172, 173, 180, 182, 183, 193, 194, 202, 204, 207, 216, 221, 222, 225
 Heth's, 98, 124, 140, 149, 162
 Hill's, A.P., 44, 65, 75, 78, 87, 93, 97, 101
 Hill's, D.H., 34, 44, 47, 49, 50, 52, 64, 71, 73, 75–78, 81, 82, 91, 109
 Hoke's, 189
 Huger's, 44
 Jackson's, 65
 Johnson's, 109, 113, 116, 121, 134, 135, 151, 158, 161, 168, 170, 171, 175–77, 180, 182, 202
 Jones', 56, 72, 73
 Kershaw's, 168, 189, 220, 227
 Longstreet's, 24, 44, 52, 61
 McLaws', 50, 67, 85, 87, 105
 Mahone's, 43, 87, 179
 Pender's, 131, 135, 136, 141
 Pickett's, 136, 185, 189
 Ramseur's, 193, 194, 198, 201, 204, 206, 216, 220, 221
 Rodes' Division
  battles of
   Chancellorsville, 87, 90, 94–97, 100
   Cold Harbor, 192–94
   Cool Springs, 210–13
   Gettysburg, 125, 134, 135, 138, 139, 142
   Kernstown, 215–17
   Lynchburg, 197–99
   Mine Run, 144, 145, 149, 151, 153
   Monocacy, 201, 203, 205
   South Anna, 186–89
   Spotsylvania, 167, 169, 171, 182, 183
   Washington, 207, 208
   Wilderness, 158, 159
   Winchester III, 220–24
  Berryville, 106–12
  Carlisle Barracks, 119, 121, 122
  commanded by Ramseur, 227
  moving north, 114–16
 Taliaferro's, 78

Wharton's, 209, 217
Whiting's, 30, 34
Divisions, USA
Barlow's, 175, 178
Birney's, 175, 183
Brooks', 103, 104
Brown's, 160
Crawford's, 168
Crook's, 197, 199
Dwight's, 222
French's, 67
Getty's, 162, 222
Gibbon's, 102, 175
Griffin's, 158
Mott's, 171–73, 175
Newton's, 102–4
Ricketts', 59, 183, 203, 204, 213, 222
Russell's, 151, 171, 178, 222, 225
Sullivan's, 197
"Dixie," 172
Doles, George, Brig. Gen., CSA
asset to Rodes, 231
assigned to brigade command, 75
Carlisle, Pa., 122
Chancellorsville, 93, 94, 98, 99
Gettysburg, 131, 138, 140
in reorganization of division, 110
Mine Run, 144
slain at Cold Harbor, 190
Spotsylvania, 170, 172, 173, 175
Wilderness, 165
Doubleday, Abner, Maj. Gen., USA, 65, 124
Douglas, H. Kyd, Maj., CSA, 203
Douglas, Stephen, 17
Dowdall's Tavern, 95
Downsville, Md., 142
Drewry's Bluff, 29, 49
Duffie, Alfred N., Maj. Gen., USA, 196–99, 207, 208, 216, 217
Dunker Church, 64, 65
Dunn, William C., 48
DuPont, Henry A., Lt. Col., USA, 198
Duryea, Abram, Brig. Gen., USA, 59
Duval, Hiram, Col., USA, 215

E

Early, Jubal A., Lt. Gen., CSA
assessment, xiv, 232
battles of
Cedar Creek, 225
Chancellorsville, 86–88, 100, 102, 103
Fredericksburg, 75
Gettysburg, 125, 126, 134–36
Kernstown, 214–18
Lynchburg to Washington, 192–207
Manassas I, 24, 25
Mine Run, 150, 151, 153
South Anna, 187–89
Spotsylvania, 182
Wilderness, 163, 165, 167
Williamsburg, 33
Winchester III, 220, 221, 223–25
dinner with Jackson, 80
marching north, 122, 123
valley campaign, 227–30
winter camp, 81
Early, Robert, Capt., CSA, 160
East Tennessee Valley, 148
Echols, John, Brig. Gen., CSA, 202
Eggleston, Gary, Sgt., CSA, 191
Elmira Prison, N.Y., 156
Ely, William, Col., USA, 211
Ely's Ford, 93, 157
Emancipation Proclamation, 64
Enfield Rifle, 39, 214
England, 63
Ewell, Richard S., Lt. Gen., CSA
assessment, xiii, 229–31
battles of
Gettysburg, 123, 133, 134, 136, 138, 140, 145
Manassas I, 20, 22, 24
Mine Run, 150, 151
South Anna, 187
Spotsylvania, 168, 179, 182–84
Wilderness, 158, 162, 163, 165, 167, 168
Carlisle, Pa., 122
moving north, 111, 113, 114, 116–18
promoted to corps command, 109
support of Rodes, 216, 219

F

Fairfax Court House, Va., 23
Fairfield, Pa., 142
Fair Oaks Station, Va., 32, 34, 37, 39
Falling Waters, 142, 143
Farmville, Va., 12
Farris Crossroads, 20
Fayetteville, Pa., 121
Featherston, William S., Brig. Gen., CSA, 25, 40
Fifth Street Hill, 194, 195, 197
Fisher's Hill, 216, 220, 227, 228
Fleetwood Hill, 111
Floyd, John, 3
Forest Road, 197, 198
Forrest, Nathan B., Lt. Gen., CSA, 3, 24
Forsberg, August, Col., CSA, 209
Forsyth, Charles, Lt. Col., CSA, 43
Fort Gaines, Ala., 15, 18
Fort Morgan, Ala., 15, 18
Fort Pickens, Fla., 19
Fort Stevens, D.C., 204
Fort Sumter, S.C., 19
Fortress Monroe, Va., 25
Fox's Gap, 54–56, 203
Fowler, Henry, Cpl., CSA, 81, 82
France, 63

Frayser's Farm, Battle of, 47
Frederick, Md., 50–52, 203
Fredericksburg, Va., 74, 76–78, 80–82, 85, 86, 100–103, 146, 156–58
Fredericksburg Camps, 80, 81, 86
Freeman, Douglas S., xi, xiii, 2, 184
French, William H., Maj. Gen., USA, 66
Front Royal, Va., 145, 202
Frosttown Road, 56, 57
Fulk, J.H., Col., CSA, 98
Furlough and Bounty Act, 24
Furnace Road, 88, 90

G

Gaines Mill, Battle of, 46, 51, 62, 109
Gallagher, Thomas F., Col., USA, 57
Gardner's Crossroads, 193
Garland, Samuel, Brig. Gen., CSA, 30, 33–35, 37, 39–41, 46, 54, 56, 72, 75, 145
Garnett, Richard B., Brig. Gen., CSA, 58, 61
Garrett, T.S., Col., CSA, 98
Gayle, Bristor, Col., CSA, 59, 60, 62, 72
Gaylord, Va., 208
Geary, John W., Maj. Gen., USA, 137
General Order #72, 116
Georgia Units
 Infantry
  4th, 75, 117, 144, 170–72
  12th, 171, 188, 202
  21st, 122, 132
  23rd, 62, 90
  44th, 171, 172
Germanna Ford, 157
German Reformed Church, 228
Gettysburg, Pa., 114, 123, 124, 126, 127, 129, 130, 132, 133, 135, 137–41, 145–47, 149, 165, 168, 182, 231
Gibbon, John, Maj. Gen., USA, 58, 61, 182
Gilham, William, Maj., VMI, 10, 11
Glendale, Va., 47
Godwin, Archibald, Brig. Gen., CSA, 151
Gordon, John B., Maj. Gen., CSA
 assessment of Rodes, xiii, 228–31
 battles of
  Antietam, 69, 70, 72
  Gettysburg, 133, 138, 146
  Kernstown, 216, 217
  Lynchburg, 193, 198–200
  Monocacy, 202, 205, 206
  Seven Days, 45, 47, 49, 50
  Seven Pines, 33, 35, 36, 39
  South Anna, 187
  South Mountain, 56, 59, 60, 62
  Spotsylvania, 176, 178, 179, 184
  Wilderness, 163, 165, 167
  Winchester III, 221, 223
Gordon, Mrs. John, 221
Gordonsville, Va., 76
Grace, Charles, Sgt., CSA, 170
Grace Church, 81–83, 106
Grace Street, 39
Grant, Ulysses S., Gen., USA
 Cold Harbor, 189–93
 South Anna, 186–88
 Spotsylvania, 166–68, 171, 175, 177, 181, 184, 185
 strategy, 154–57, 195
 Wilderness, 162–65
Greencastle, Pa., 116, 117
Green County, Ala., 19
Green, James, Lt., CSA, 107
Greenwich, Va., 149
Grimes, Bryan, Maj. Gen., CSA, 75, 76, 100, 184, 198, 231
Grimsley, Andrew, Col., CSA, 66
Guiney Station, Va., 110

H

Hagerstown, Md., 52, 115, 140, 142, 145, 219
Hagerstown Road, 65
Halifax, N.C., 182
Halleck, Henry, Gen., USA, 113, 155
Halltown, Va., 202, 220
Halsey, Donald P., Capt., CSA, 129, 144
Hampden-Sydney College, Va., 6
Hampton Roads, Va., 156
Hampton, Wade, Lt. Gen., CSA, 52, 110, 141, 194
Hancock, Winfield, Maj. Gen., USA, 25, 157, 162, 163, 175–77, 179, 182, 186, 190
Hanging Rock, Va., 199
Hanover Court House, Va., 158, 186
Hanover Junction, Va., 49, 153
Hanover Town, Va., 187
Harper's Ferry, Va., 51, 52, 62, 63, 65, 73, 112–15, 202, 207, 217
Harrisburg, Pa., 116, 120–22
Harrisburg Road, 124
Harris Farm, 183
Harrison, Henry T., 120
Harrison's Landing, Va., 46, 47, 49
Harrison Street, 3, 198, 226
Hatch, John P., Brig. Gen., USA, 58, 59, 61
Hayes, Rutherford B., Col., USA, 54, 216
Hayman, Samuel, Col., USA, 96
Hays, Harry T., Maj. Gen., CSA, 113, 150, 151, 152, 196
Hazel Grove, Va., 97, 98, 101, 102
Hedgesville, Va., 144
Heidlersburg, Pa., 122
Heidlersburg Road, 125
Heintzelman, Samuel P., Brig. Gen., USA, 29
Henry House Hill, 21, 22
Herring, Marcus, Sgt., CSA, xiii, 223
Herr's Ridge, 124
Heth, Harry, Maj. Gen., CSA, 96, 97, 101, 120, 125, 135

Hill, Ambrose P., Lt. Gen., CSA
Antietam, 73
Bristoe Station, 149, 150
Chancellorsville, 85, 88, 95, 96, 230
Cold Harbor, 189
compliments Rodes, 106, 229
Gaines Mill, 44, 45
Gettysburg, 123, 125, 131
Glendale, 47
in command of a division, 43
in the reorganization of army, 75
promoted to corps command, 109
South Anna, 186
Wilderness, 158, 163, 167
Hill, Daniel H., Lt. Gen., CSA
Antietam, 65, 66, 71
comments on Rodes, xii, 38, 40, 62, 229
Frederick, Md., 52, 53
Fredericksburg, 77, 78
in division command, 42
in reorganization of army, 75, 76
leaves A.N.V., 82
marching to the Potomac, 50, 51
Seven Days', 44–46
Seven Pines, 30, 33, 36, 37, 40
South Mountain, 54–56
Williamsburg, 25–27
Hobson, E.L., Maj., CSA, 60, 62
Hood, John, Lt. Gen., CSA, 64, 65, 136, 141
Hooker, Joseph, Maj. Gen., USA, 43, 64, 65, 84–86, 88–91, 97, 100–102, 104, 105, 108, 113, 120, 121
"Home Sweet Home," 174
Howard, McHenry, 80
Howard, Oliver O., Maj. Gen., USA., 85, 86, 89, 93, 124, 127
Howard, Reuben, 7
Hudd's Hill, 224
Huger, Benjamin, Maj. Gen., CSA, 28–32, 36, 39, 43
Hunter, David, Maj. Gen., USA, 193–96, 198–201, 207, 216, 228

I

Imboden, John D., Maj. Gen., CSA, 141, 196, 197
Island Ford, 207, 208, 210
Ivy Creek, 197
Ives, Joseph, Col., CSA, 42
Iverson, Alfred, Brig. Gen., CSA, 75, 101, 127–29, 134, 141, 145

J

Jackson, Andrew, 16
Jackson, Mrs. Anna, 81
Jackson, Thomas J., Lt. Gen., CSA
assessment of Rodes, xiii, 228–30
battles of
Antietam, 62–65
Chancellorsville, 1, 2, 85–93, 95, 96, 98, 103, 105, 106, 108, 109
Fredericksburg, 75–80
Manassas I, 21, 22, 25
Capture of Harper's Ferry, 51, 52
dinner party, 82
distinctive leadership, 165
his grave honored, 201
instructor, VMI, 12
loss felt by Lee, 112
missed at Gettysburg, 121, 122
right bower of, 232
promotion for Iverson, 145
valley campaign, 203
James River, 4, 6, 25, 28, 46, 47, 85, 156, 192, 193
James River and Kanawha Canal, 5, 10, 195
Jefferson, Thomas, 3, 16
Jeffersontown, Va., 148
Jenkins, Alfred, Brig. Gen., CSA, 111, 112, 116, 117
Jenkins, Micah, Brig. Gen., CSA, 22, 34, 36, 37, 40, 41, 47
Jericho Mills, Va., 186
Johnson, Bradley, Brig. Gen., CSA, 219
Johnson, Edward, Maj. Gen., CSA
arrives at Gettysburg, 133
Gettysburg, 135–38
Mine Run, 151–52
preferred for Hill's Division, 82, 83, 87
Spotsylvania, 170, 172, 176, 177, 180, 182
Wilderness, 158, 161, 162, 164
Winchester, 114
Johnson's Island Prison, 156
Johnston, Joseph E., Gen., CSA, 21, 23, 25, 28–31, 37, 39, 41, 42, 137
Johnston, Robert D., Brig. Gen., CSA, 145, 178, 180
Johnston's Farm, 187, 215
Jones Farm, 164
Jones, John R., Brig. Gen., CSA, 65, 160
Jones, R.T., Col., CSA, 33, 35
Jones, William, Brig. Gen., CSA, 195, 228
Jug Bridge, 203

K

Kearny, Philip, Maj. Gen., USA, 35, 47
Keedysville, Md., 62
Kelly's Ford, Va., 86, 87, 150
Kemper, James L., Maj. Gen., CSA, 47
Kernstown, Va., 202, 216, 217, 219
Kershaw, Joseph B., Maj. Gen., CSA, 25, 178
Keswick Depot, Va., 194
Keyes, Erasmus D., Brig. Gen., USA, 29
Kilpatrick, Judson, Maj. Gen., USA, 142, 153
Kirby, Edmund, Lt., USA, 37
Kirkland, William, Brig. Gen., CSA, 149, 150
Kimball, Nathan, Brig. Gen., USA, 67
King William Artillery, CSA, 33

Knipe, Joseph, Brig. Gen., USA, 116
Know-Nothing Party, 17
Knoxville, Tenn., 148

L

Lacy, Rev., 119
Lager Beer, 119
Lafayette, Marquis de, 3
LaGrange College, Ga., 146
Lane, James H., Brig. Gen., CSA, 95, 96
Lane, John, Capt., CSA, 53, 54, 56, 57, 59, 61
Langhorne, Maurice, 5
Langston's Crossroads, Va., 23
Latimer, Joseph W., Maj., CSA, 136
Law, E. McIvor, Brig. Gen., CSA, 32, 37, 78, 171, 190
Lawton, Alexander, Brig. Gen., CSA, 64
Lee, Fitzhugh, Maj. Gen., CSA, 21, 22, 88, 93, 110, 142
Lee, Robert E., Gen., CSA
  battles of
    Antietam, 62–64, 70, 72–75
    Chancellorsville, 85–90, 100, 102–11
    Cold Harbor, 192, 193
    Fredericksburg, 77–79
    Gettysburg, 125, 130, 133, 134, 136, 138, 140–42
    Mine Run, 145–52
    Seven Days, 47–49
    South Anna, 185–90
    South Mountain, 51–53
    Spotsylvania, 165–67, 171, 174, 175, 179, 180, 183, 231
    Wilderness, 156, 157, 163
  invasion, 113–17
  military advisor, President Davis, 25, 28, 32
  Pennsylvania camps, 120–23
  praises Rodes, 229
  reinforces Early, 220
  reorganizes Army of Northern Va., 102–11
  Rodes ranked with, 224
  takes command, 41–44
Lee, W. F. H., Maj. Gen., CSA, 110
Leesburg, Va., 50, 76, 207
Leon, Private, CSA, 162
Letcher, John, 195
Lexington, Va., 6, 9, 10, 195, 200, 201
Libby Prison, Richmond, Va., 156
Liberty, Va., 196, 198
Lightfoot, James, Lt. Col., CSA, 70, 72
Lilley, Robert D., Brig. Gen., CSA, 215–17
Lincoln, Abraham, 17, 18, 49, 53, 64, 76, 84, 155, 191, 204, 206
Lincoln, Mrs. Abraham, 84
Little Otter River, 196
Little River, 186
"Listen to the Mockingbird," 114
Locust Grove, Va. 151, 152, 158
Lomax, Tennett, Col., CSA, 19
Long, Armistead, Brig. Gen., CSA, 175, 193, 201
Long Lane, 138
"Long Roll," 84
Longstreet, James , Lt. Gen., CSA
  assessment of Grant, 154
  assessment of Rodes, 229, 232
  battles of
    Antietam, 64, 67, 70, 75
    Fredericksburg, 76, 78, 79
    Gettysburg, 134, 136, 138, 140
    Manassas I, 25
    Seven Days, 43–45, 47
    Seven Pines, 30–32, 36, 39, 40
    Wilderness, 154, 156, 158, 163–65
  Harrison the Spy, 120
  Maryland, 51, 60
  movement west, 148
  reorganization of army, 109
  winter quarters, 81, 85
Louisa Court House, Va., 193
Louisiana Military Academy, 14
Louisiana Units
  Infantry
    6th, 20, 22
Luray Valley, 145
Lyle, Mike, 7
Lynch, John, 4
Lynchburg, Va., 4, 5, 10, 12, 19, 43, 56, 74, 193, 194–96, 199, 224, 226, 230

M

McAllister, Robert, Col., USA, 171
McCausland, John, Brig. Gen., CSA, 196–99, 204, 219
McClellan, George B., Maj. Gen., USA
  Antietam, 63, 64, 72
  anxious to face Lee, 42
  Harrison's Landing, 49
  masses army at Fortress Monroe, 25
  moves on Richmond, 28, 29
  replaced as Union commander, 76
  Seven Days', 44, 46–48
  Seven Pines, 35
  South Mountain, 52
McCoy's Ferry, 219
McDowell, Irvin, Maj. Gen., USA, 21
McGuire, Hunter, M.D., 80
McLaws, Lafayette, Maj. Gen., CSA, 49, 88, 103, 104
McLean's Ford, 21, 22
McPherson's Ridge, 124, 133
McRae, D. K., Col., CSA, 54, 64–66, 72
McReynolds, Andrew, Col., USA, 111
Madison Court House, Va., 145
Magilton, Albert, Col., USA, 57
Magruder, John, Maj. Gen., CSA, 25, 43
Main Street, 116, 226

Maine Units
Infantry
6th, 151
16th, 131, 132
Malvern Hill, Battle of, 47, 51, 75, 140
Manassas, Battle of 1st, 2, 23
Manassas Gap, 145
Manassas Junction, Va., 19, 20
Maness, Dick, 147
Mansfield, Joseph K., Maj. Gen., USA, 65
Market Street, 224
Martinsburg, Va., 112, 114, 202, 215, 217, 220
Marye's Heights, 79, 102, 103
Maryland Heights, Md., 202
"Maryland My Maryland," 50, 51
Mason-Dixon Line, 115
Massachusetts Units
Heavy Artillery
1st, 183
Infantry
7th, 102
13th, 132
34th, 208
Massie, James, Lt., VMI, 10
Meade, George, Maj. Gen., USA
assigned to command Army of the Potomac, 120, 121
Chancellorsville, 85, 86
Cold Harbor, 190
Gettysburg, 142
Mine Run, 148, 149, 151, 152
South Mountain, 57–61
Spotsylvania, 166, 168, 171, 175, 183
Wilderness, 155
Meagher, Thomas F., Brig. Gen., USA, 69, 70
Mechanicsville, Va., 44, 193
Mechanicsville Road, 187
Meredith, Solomon, Maj. Gen., USA, 124
Mexico, 41, 84
Michigan Units
Infantry
3rd, 35
Middle Street, 135
Middleton, Va., 53, 216
Middleton Road, 125
Middletown, Pa., 123
Miles, Nelson A., Lt. Col., USA, 71
Military Road, 87
Miller, Mr., 66
Miller, M.B., Capt., CSA, 71
Miller, Robert, 36
Milledgeville, Ga., 171
Millwood Road, 111
Milroy, Robert, Maj. Gen., USA, 111, 113
Mine Run, 152
Minnich, J. W., 26, 27
Mississippi Units
Infantry
2nd, 125
12th, 24, 33, 35, 38, 43
18th, 102
43rd, 125
Mississippi River, 144
Mobile, Ala., 156
Moore, Albert B., 15, 18, 19
Monocacy Junction, Md., 203, 217
Monocacy River, 203–5
Montgomery, Ala., 17–19
Morgan, John Tyler, Brig. Gen., CSA, xiii, 24, 146
Morris Bridge, 186
Morris, Dwight, Col., USA, 67
Morrison, Joseph, Lt., CSA, 86
Morton's Ford, 148
Moss Neck, Va., 80
Mott, John, 122
Mott, Sarah, 122
Mountain House, 53, 54, 56
Mount Carmel Church, 185
Mount Jackson, Va., 202
Mount Vernon, Ala., 15, 18
Mud Tavern, 185
Mullens, James, Pvt., CSA, 122
Mummasburg Road, 124
Munford, Thomas T., Brig. Gen., CSA, 90, 92, 93, 229
Munson's Hill, 23
Myer, Corporal, CSA, 60

N

Napoleon Bonaparte, 30
Nashville, Tenn., 155
National Highway, 51–54, 56–58, 61
Natural and Experimental Philosophy, Professor of, 11
"Nearer My God to Thee," 172
Nelson, Mrs. Sallie Rodes, 226
New Hampshire Units
Infantry
12th, 190
New Market, Va., 195, 224
New Orleans, La., 13, 102, 156
New York Units
Artillery
1st, 33
Infantry
43rd, 206
44th, 30
45th, 128–30
55th, 34
61st, 71
90th, 130
94th, 132
104th, 132
107th, 132
121st, 104
146th, 160

Newtown, Va., 215, 221
Nicholls, Francis T., Brig. Gen., CSA, 195
Nine Mile Road, 30, 32, 37
Ninth Street Bridge, 195
Norfolk, Va., 9, 10, 28, 29, 85
North Anna River, 185–87
North Carolina Military Institute, 25
North Carolina Units
  Infantry
    2nd, 130–32, 150
    2nd Batt., 132, 138
    4th, 40, 75, 100, 132, 220
    5th, 54, 129, 130
    6th, 37
    7th, 95, 96
    12th, 54, 129–31
    13th, 54
    14th, 112, 132, 182
    18th, 95, 96
    20th, 45, 54, 129, 130
    23rd, 54, 99, 129, 130, 144
    28th, 95
    30th, 132, 151
    32nd, 119, 130, 132
    38th, 95, 96
    43rd, 130–32
    45th, 130, 132, 178
    49th, 75
    53rd, 106, 130–32, 162, 211
Northeast and Southwest Alabama RR, 13
North Garden, Va., 194
North Missouri RR, 14
North River, 10
North River Navigation Co., 10, 12

O

Oak Hill, 125–28, 139
Oak Ridge, 124, 127, 129, 131
Occoquon River, 23
Ohio Units
  Infantry
    23rd, 54
    30th, 54
    32nd, 52
    60th, 52
    116th, 197, 210, 213
Old Church Road, 44
Old Point Comfort, Va., 25
O'Neal, Edward, Brig. Gen., CSA
  an unforgiving enemy, xiii
  Chancellorsville, 98, 99
  colonel, 26th Alabama, 43
  commands Alabama Brigade, 110
  Fredericksburg, 82
  Gettysburg, 128–30, 132, 134, 138, 140
  reassigned, 145, 146
  South Mountain, 60, 72
Opequon Creek, 202, 221
Orange and Alexandria RR, 149, 194
Orange Court House, Va., 152, 158
Orange Depot, 146
Orange Plank Road, 87, 90, 93, 157, 158, 162–64, 167
Orange Turnpike, 93, 157, 158, 161, 164, 166
Osborne, Hampden, xii, 174
Otey, C.C., Capt., CSA, 33, 35
Otey, Kirkwood, 5
Owens, William, Col., USA, 211
Ox Ford, 186

P

Pamunkey River, 187
Park, Robert, Capt., CSA, xiii, 45, 59, 60, 62, 82, 118, 148, 213, 224
Paris, Va., 77
Payne's Farm, 151, 152
Paxton, E.F., Brig. Gen., CSA, 98
Peach Orchard, 136
Peaks of Otter, 198
Peck, Major, USA, 11
Pegram, William, Col., CSA, 124
Pender, W. Dorsey, Maj. Gen., CSA, 32, 97, 101, 138
Pendleton, Alexander, Lt. Col., CSA, 79, 96
Pendleton, William, Brig. Gen., CSA, 175
Penn, Davidson, Col., CSA, 150, 151
Pennsylvania Units
  Infantry
    11th, 130
    49th, 172
    51st, 72
    61st, 36
    83rd, 130
    88th, 130
    90th, 128–30
    96th, 171
    143rd, 131, 132
    149th, 131, 132
  Reserves
    1st, 59
    2nd, 59
    4th, 60
    7th, 60
    8th, 59
    9th, 59
    11th, 59
    12th, 59
    13th, 59
Pensacola, Fla., 18, 19, 26
Peques, C.G., Col., CSA, 33
Perry, Madison S., 18
Petersburg, Pa., 122
Petersburg, Va., 9, 12
Pettigrew, Johnson, Brig. Gen., CSA, 139
Peyton, Green, Col., CSA, xiii, 33, 62, 87, 172, 181, 224, 226, 229, 230
Phelan, James, 146
Philadelphia, Pa., 121

Philadelphia *Press*, 122
Pickens County, Ala., 19
Pickens, Samuel, Col., CSA, 60, 211
Pickett, George, Maj. Gen., CSA, 139
Piedmont, Va., 195
Pleasant Valley, Md., 56, 203
Pleasonton, George, Maj. Gen., USA, 110, 111
Poague, William T., Col., CSA, 149, 162
Pope, John, Maj. Gen., USA, 49
Po River, 171
Porter, Fitz-John, Maj. Gen., USA, 44, 46
Port Fires, 142
Port Republic, Va., 202
Port Royal, Va., 77
Posey, Carnot, Brig. Gen., CSA, 87
Potomac Ford, 63, 114
Potomac River, 50, 51, 63, 76, 112, 114, 115, 141, 142, 144, 203, 207, 217, 219
Powhite Swamp, 44
Presbyterian Church, 195, 226, 228
Pryor, Roger A., Brig. Gen., CSA, 70
Purcellsville, Va., 207
Purifoy, John, xiii

Q

Quaker Cemetery, 196
Quaker Meeting House, 196

R

Radical Republicans, 116
Rains, Gabriel, Brig. Gen., CSA, 33–35, 38
Ramseur, Nellie, 86
Ramseur, Stephen D., Maj. Gen., CSA
 appointed brigadier general, 75
 assessment, 228, 231
 battles of
  Chancellorsville, 86, 99
  Cold Harbor, 187, 188, 190, 192, 193
  Getttysburg, 131, 133, 138
  Kernstown, 215–17
  Lynchburg, 199, 200
  Monocacy, 203, 204
  Spotsylvania, 163, 167, 174, 180, 184
  Wilderness, 144
  Winchester III, 219, 220
 Berryville, 110
Ramsey, Rev. James, 226
Randolph, M.L., Capt., CSA, 224, 226
Rapidan River, 148, 151, 152, 155–57, 167
Rappahannock RR Bridge, 150, 151
Rappahannock River, 86–88, 102, 105, 108, 110, 148, 150
Ratchford, J. W., 76
Redbud Run, 221, 224
"Red Spread," 117
Reid, Jessie, 48
Reno, Jessie, Maj. Gen., USA, 56
Republican Party, 16, 17
Reynolds, John, Maj. Gen., USA, 46, 124
Rhode Island Units
 1st R.I. Heavy Artillery, 210, 213
Rice, James, Brig. Gen., USA, 160, 161
Richardson, Israel, Maj. Gen., USA, 68, 71
Ricketts, James B., Brig. Gen., USA, 59, 168, 203
Richmond, Va., 9, 10, 17, 19, 25, 26, 28, 37, 44, 46, 49, 76, 80, 83, 85, 87, 146, 153, 156, 216
Richmond *Examiner*, 42, 216
Richmond *Inquirer*, 228
Ridge Road, 54–56
Ripley, Roswall, Brig. Gen., CSA, 56, 62, 66, 72, 75
Roane, William B., 3
Robertson, Beverly, Brig. Gen., CSA, 120
Rockbridge Alum Springs, Va., 9
Rockett's Landing, 29
Rodes, Allen, 5
Rodes, Ann Blackwell, 3
Rodes, Ann Maria, 3, 5
Rodes, David, 3–5, 7, 8, 12, 43
Rodes, Fanny, 43
Rodes, Matthew, 3
Rodes, Robert Emmett, Maj. Gen., CSA
 assessment of, 40, 41, 106, 139, 160, 230, 231
 battles of
  Antietam, 64–67, 69–73
  Chancellorsville, 1, 2, 85–88, 90–102, 105, 106
  Cool Springs, 207, 209–11, 215
  Cold Harbor, 189, 190, 192
  Fredericksburg, 76
  Gettysburg, 125–29, 131–37, 139–43
  Kernstown, 216, 217
  Lynchburg, 193, 197–200
  Manassas I, 21, 22, 32
  Mine Run, 144, 146–50, 152–54
  Monocacy, 203, 205
  Seven Days, 44–46
  Seven Pines, 30–40
  South Anna, 186–88
  South Mountain, 56–62
  Spotsylvania, 166–74, 176, 178–82, 184
  Washington, 201–7
  Wilderness, 158–65
  Winchester, 73, 219–25, 228
 Berryville, 111–13, 116, 117
 as cadet, VMI, 7, 8
 Carlisle Barracks, 119, 122
 childhood, 3–5
 defending Ramseur, 154, 216
 dinner with Jackson, 80
 dinner party, 81, 82
 difficulty with Grimes, 76
 as engineer, canal, 10, 11
 engineer, RR, 13, 14

Fort Morgan, 11
friendship with Ramseur, 153
funeral of, 226
instructor, VMI, 9–12
Iverson's failure, 145
Lynchburg, 3, 4
marriage of, 14
as militia officer, 17, 18
O'Neal's censure, 146
Pensacola, 26
promotion to brig. gen., 24
promotion to maj. gen., 106
tribute to, 229, 230
Rodes, Robert Emmett, II, 147, 153, 198
Rodes, Sallie Harrison, 3, 13
Rodes, Virginia W., xii, 18, 43, 81, 147, 150, 153, 198, 224
Rodes, Virginius, 3, 5, 7, 13
Rogers, John, Comdr., USN, 29
Rohrersville, Va., 54
Roulette Farm, 67
Round Top, Little, 124, 136
Round Top, 124, 136
Ruffin, Thomas, Lt. Col., CSA, 54
Russell, David, Brig. Gen., USA, 162, 171

S

St. James College, Md., 219
Salem, Va., 198, 199
Salem Church, 103, 104
Salem Pike, 195, 197, 198
Salient, The, 232
Sanfort, Mr., 12
Sangster's Crossroads, Va., 20
Santa Rosa Island, Fla., 19
Scammon, Eliakim P., Brig. Gen., USA, 54
Saunders Field, 159–62
Schaub, J.L., xiii
Schimmelfennig, Alexander, Brig. Gen., USA, 127
School of Roads and Bridges, 15
Schurz, Carl, Brig. Gen., USA, 94
Seddon, James A., Sec. of War, 120
Sedgwick, John, Maj. Gen., USA
Antietam, 66
Chancellorsville, 85–88, 100, 102–5
Cold Harbor, 152
Mine Run, 142
Spotsylvania, 168, 170
Wilderness, 158, 160, 162, 163
Seminary Ridge, 124, 139
Semmes, Paul J., Brig. Gen., CSA, 87, 103, 104
Seven Days, Battle of, 47
Seven Pines, Battle of, 2, 30, 31, 33, 37, 39, 41, 43, 51, 63, 146, 231
Seventh Street, 204
Seymour, Truman, Brig. Gen., USA, 57, 59, 160, 161, 163
Shadwell, Va., 194
Shady Grove Church, 167
Shady Grove Church Road, 167, 169
Shaler, Alexander, Col., USA, 102, 163
Sharpsburg, Md., 62–65, 75, 146, 203, 217, 220
Sharpsburg Road, 54, 56, 71
Sharpshooters, 80, 125, 152, 191, 197, 223
Shenandoah River, 76, 111, 207, 210, 211, 220
Shenandoah Valley, 6, 111, 156, 193, 221, 228
Shepherdstown, Va., 202, 220
Sheridan, Philip H., Maj. Gen., USA, 194, 218–22, 224, 225, 227, 228
Sherman, William, Lt. Gen., USA, 155, 156
Shiloh, Tenn., 203
Sickles, Daniel, Maj. Gen., USA, 86, 92
Sigel, Franz, Maj. Gen., USA, 156, 194, 202, 203, 216
Silver Spring, Md., 204, 206
Slocom, Henry, Maj. Gen., USA, 85–88
Smith, B.H., 171
Smith, Francis H., Col., VMI, xii, 6–9, 11, 14, 15, 43
Smith, Gustavus, Maj. Gen., CSA, 37
Smith, James P., Maj., CSA, 1
Smith, Kirby, Gen., CSA, 24, 63
Smith, Thomas, 209
Smith, William F., Maj. Gen., USA, 78, 188–90
Snicker's Gap, Va., 207, 208, 215
Sorrell, Moxley, Brig. Gen., CSA, xiii
South Anna River, 185, 186, 193, 230
South Carolina Units
Infantry
4th, 48
6th, 36
Palmetto Sharpshooters, 36
South Mountain, Battle of
Early advances in 1864, 203
Fox's Gap action, 54–56
Garland slain, 40, 145
losses in Rodes' Brigade, 63, 72
Lost Dispatch, 52
Rodes' achievements, 231
serves as screen for Lee's Army, 116, 122
Turner's Gap Battle, 58–62
Southside RR, 12
Spotsylvania, Battle of, 211, 230, 232
Spotsylvania Court House, Va., 166–70, 174, 176, 177, 180, 185
Stafford Heights, Va., 77, 80, 84
Stage Road, 102
"Star Spangled Banner," 174
Staunton, Va., 74, 195, 200, 201, 224, 226, 227
Steiner, Dr. Lewis, 51, 52
Stephenson's Depot, Va., 113, 217
Steuart, George H., Brig. Gen., CSA, 137, 138

Stevens, Thaddeus, 116
Steward, Alexander, 11, 12
Stiles, Robert, Maj., CSA, xiii
Stone, Roy, Brig. Gen., USA, 161
Stonema, George, Brig. Gen., USA, 85
Strasburg, Va., 202, 216, 217, 220, 227
Stuart, James Ewell Brown, Maj. Gen., CSA
  cavalry command, 38
  Chancellorsville, 88
  commands II Corps, 96–101, 231
  Frederick, Md., 53
  Gettysburg Campaign, 118, 120, 142
  Mine Run, 148, 149, 153
  review and battle at Brandy Station, 110, 111
  slain at Yellow Tavern, 174
Summerville Ford, 148
Summit Point, 112, 113
Sumner, Edwin, Maj. Gen., USA, 32, 60, 67, 69
Sumter County, Ala., 19
Sunken Road, 68, 69, 75
Susquehanna River, 121
Sweeney, James W., Maj., CSA, 111
Sykes, George, Maj. Gen., USA, 87, 88

T

Tabernacle Church, 87
Tactics, Professor of, 9
Taliaferro, William, Brig. Gen., CSA, 75
Talley Farm, 94
Taylor, Walter, Col., CSA, 22, 23
Telegraph Road, 87, 103, 185
Terrill, Colonel, CSA, 188
Terry, William, Brig. Gen., CSA, 202
Texas Pacific RR, 13
Thoburn, Joseph, Col., USA, 208–12
Thorton's Gap, 145
Trevilian's Station, 193
Trimble, Isaac, Maj. Gen., CSA, 87
Tucker, John, xiii, 39
Turner's Gap, 51–58
Tuscaloosa, Ala., 14, 15, 17, 18, 43

U

Union Mills Ford, 21–23
United States Artillery, 3, 7
United States Capitol, 23, 206
Unites States Dragoons, 118
United States Navy, 29
Unites States Sharpshooters
  1st US, 92
  2nd US, 92
University of Alabama, 14
University of Virginia, Charlottesville, Va., 10, 19, 194
Upton, Emory, Maj. Gen., USA, 104, 160, 161, 171–75, 189, 222, 224, 225
USS *Aroostook,* 29
USS *Galena,* 29
USS *Monitor,* 29
USS *Naugatuck,* 29
USS *Port Royal,* 29

V

Valley Pike, 195, 201, 216, 219–21, 224, 227
Vance, Zebulon, 153
Van Dorn, Earl, Maj. Gen., CSA, 23, 24
Vaughn, John, Brig. Gen., CSA, 215, 216
Venable, Charles, Col., CSA, 184, 191
Vera Cruz, Mexico, 13
Vicksburg, Miss., 144, 156
Virginia Capital, 28, 29
Virginia Units
  Heavy Artillery
    4th, 33, 35, 38, 43
  Cavalry
    2nd, 90
    12th, 148
  Infantry
    13th, 188
    49th, 188
Virginia Military Institute, Lexington, Va., xii, 2, 5, 6, 8, 10, 14, 17, 33, 41, 93, 150, 195, 201, 229
Virginia Military Institute Memorial Volume, 230
Voill, Theodore, Adj., USA, 189
Von Borcke, Heros, Maj., CSA, 38
Von Gilsa, Leopold, Col., USA, 94

W

Wallace, Lew, Maj. Gen., USA, 203–5
Walnut Hollow Road, 116
Ward, Hobart, Brig. Gen., USA, 96
Warren, Gouverneur, Maj. Gen., USA, 149, 150 152, 157, 158, 162, 163, 168, 186
Warrenton, Va., 76
Warrenton Pike, 21, 148
Warrenton Springs, 148
Warrick River, 25
Warrior Guards, 15, 17, 18
Washington, D.C., 19, 51, 113, 121, 183, 201, 203–6, 213, 230
Washington Artillery, CSA, 102, 103
Washington College, Va., 12, 25
Washington Pike, 204
Weber, Max, Brig. Gen., USA, 67, 202
Webster, Captain, CSA, 46
Wellford, Charles, 88
Western North Carolina RR, 14
West Fort, 113
West Point, USMA, N.Y., 3, 6, 25, 41, 84, 103, 195
West Virginia Units
  Infantry
    4th, 211
    12th, 210, 211, 213
Wharton, Gabriel, Brig. Gen., CSA, 209–11

Wheat Field, 136
Wheeler, Joseph, Lt. Gen., CSA, 145
Whig Party, 17
Wisconsin Units
  Infantry
    6th, 125
    7th, 125
White Oak Swamp, 32
White House Landing, 28, 38, 46
White, P. J., Capt., CSA, 232, 233
White's Ford, 50, 51, 207
White Sulfur Springs, Va., 199
Whiting, Chase, Maj. Gen., CSA, 31, 32, 37, 39
Whiting, H.A., Maj., CSA, 41, 50, 99
Whitworth Rifle, 170, 197
Widow Tapp Farm, 162
Wilcox, Cadmus, Brig. Gen., CSA, 103, 104, 162
Wilderness, Battle of, 156, 157, 159, 161, 164, 165, 191, 230
Willcox, Orlando, Maj. Gen., USA, 54
Williamsburg Road, 25, 32, 33, 35, 43
Williamsburg Stage Road, 30, 38
Williamsburg, Va., 26
Williamson, Thomas H., Maj., VMI, 10, 11
Williamsport, Md., 112, 114, 140, 142, 219
Williamsport Road, 142
Willis, Edward, Col., CSA, 186
Wilson, James, Maj. Gen., USA, 221
Winchester, Va.
  camps of army in 1862, 74, 76
  camps in 1863, 145
  center of Early's 1864 maneuvers, 215–17, 220, 221
  Confederate army retreats, 224, 225, 227
  Federal garrison captured in 1862, 111–114
  Rodes' remains borne through the streets, 224
Winchester, Third Battle of, 221, 223, 225, 229
Winn, D.R.E., Lt. Col., CSA, 144
Woodruff, David, 14
Woodruff, Eliza , 14
Woodruff, Virginia H., 14
Woodstock, Va., 227
Wright, Ambrose, Brig. Gen., CSA, 44, 87, 145
Wright, Horatio, Maj. Gen., USA, 142, 160, 171, 190, 207–9, 213, 215, 220, 221
Wright, Rebecca, 220

Y

Yancey, William L., 24
Yancy, Henry D., Lt., CSA, 170
Yancy, Joel, 3
Yancy, Martha A., 3
Yancy, Peggy B., 3
Yancy, William, 8
"Yankee Doodle," 172
York, Pa., 121
York Pike, 122
York River, 25
York RR, 28, 38
Yorktown, Va., 25, 26
York, Zebulon, Brig. Gen., CSA, 202, 204
Young, Samuel, Lt. Col., USA, 210, 211

Z

Zouaves, Brooklyn, 22